# Introductory
# Double Entry Accounting
# Practice Workbook

**1000 Questions
with Solutions**

**L Castelluzzo**

## Preface

This book provides the reader with an opportunity to practice the double entry system of accounting. It contains 1000 practice questions. The solutions are provided for each question, along with an explanation, so that the student will be able to pinpoint exactly where any errors may have been made.

These questions pertain to fictitious companies with revenues from services and sales. They include sales revenue, sales returns, various expenses, capital purchases, depreciation, dividend payouts, unearned revenue, and prepaid expenses. There are also practice questions for business loans, which include the posting of interest expense as well as the principal portion of the loan repayment.

This book does not teach the theory, but instead, it is intended to allow students to practice what they have learned in their introductory accounting or introductory bookkeeping course.

## Types of Accounts

Debits are represented by "DR" and credits are represented by "CR".

Asset accounts represent money or any other items that the company owns or something which will provide the company with a future benefit. When assets are increased, they are debited. When assets are decreased, they are credited.

Liability accounts represent money or any other amounts that the company does not own. When liabilities are increased, they are credited. When liabilities are decreased, they are debited.

Revenue accounts represent amounts that the company has earned from their regular operations. When revenues are increased, they are credited. When revenues are decreased, they are debited.

Expense accounts represent amounts that the company has spent through the course of their regular operations. When expenses are increased, they are debited. When expenses are decreased, they are credited.

Contra accounts represent a reduction to an account, which is tracked separately. Examples of contra accounts are sales returns, allowance for doubtful accounts, and accumulated depreciation on the property plant & equipment accounts. Debits and credits to contra accounts are posted in a reverse manner, when compared to the account to which they apply.

The following is a guide for how these entries are posted.

Sell services:
DR  Accounts Receivable
  CR  Sales

Buy inventory:
DR  Inventory
  CR  Accounts Payable

Sell inventory:
DR  Accounts Receivable
  CR  Sales Revenue
DR  Cost of Goods Sold
  CR  Inventory

Sales are returned:
DR  Sales Returns
  CR  Accounts Receivable
DR  Inventory
  CR  Cost of Goods Sold

Pay rent:
DR  Rent Expense
  CR  Accounts Payable

Pay employees:
DR  Wages Expense
  CR  Accounts Payable

Cash is received from accounts receivable for sales:
DR  Cash
  CR  Accounts Receivable

Cash is paid to settle amounts owing in accounts payable for purchases:
DR  Accounts Payable
  CR  Cash

When it is estimated that an amount might not be collectible:
DR  Bad Debt Expense
  CR  Allowance for Doubtful Accounts

When it is confirmed that an amount will not be collectible:
DR  Allowance for Doubtful Accounts
  CR  Accounts Receivable

Buy equipment that will be used by the business for more than one year:
DR  Equipment
  CR  Accounts Payable

Depreciate equipment for the portion of the useful life that has passed:
DR  Depreciation Expense
  CR  Accumulated Depreciation

Buy a building :
DR  Building
  CR  Cash

Depreciate building for the portion of the useful life that has passed:
DR  Depreciation Expense
  CR  Accumulated Depreciation

Receive a loan that is to be repaid over the course of more than one year:
DR  Cash
  CR  Note Payable

Payment is made to repay a long-term loan
DR  Interest Expense
DR  Note Payable
   CR  Cash

Pay upfront for expenses that will be incurred in the future:
DR  Prepaid Expense
   CR  Accounts Payable
\* NOTE: Prepaid Expense is an asset account because it represents a future benefit whereby the company will receive goods/services in the future.

Amortize a prepaid expense as it is incurred:
DR  Expense
   CR  Prepaid Expense

Receive upfront payment goods/services that will be provided in the future:
DR  Cash
   CR  Unearned Revenue

Provide the goods/services that had been paid for upfront beforehand:
DR  Unearned Revenue\*
   CR  Revenue
\* NOTE: Unearned Revenue is a liability account because it represents an obligation to provide goods/services in the future.

Pay a dividend to a shareholder:
DR  Retained Earnings
   CR  Cash

## QUESTIONS:

1    David & Johnson sells various legal services. This January, David & Johnson has made an advance payment to cover the next 12 months of utility bills, which have a monthly cost of $2400.

2    Paytech Ltd sells various payroll transaction processing services. This January, Paytech Ltd has made an advance payment to cover the next 12 months of utility bills, which have a monthly cost of $1200.

3    Club Disco is a company which offers their customers a wide selection of dance venue rentals for large family gatherings. Club Disco has just received a cash payment for the full amount that this customer owed to the company for all of their purchases to date. The outstanding balance which has now been paid was $75000.

4    Mr. Mop provides their customers with household cleaners. Mr. Mop has just received a cash payment for the full amount that this customer owed to the company for all of their purchases to date. The outstanding balance which has now been paid was $35000.

5    A to Z Event Guru Ltd sells various start-to-finish event planning services for large gatherings. This January, A to Z Event Guru Ltd has made an advance payment to cover the next 12 months of utility bills, which have a monthly cost of $2400.

6    Mr. Mop is a market leader that is well-known for their brand of household cleaners. This month, Mr. Mop has estimated that 10% of the accounts receivable might not end up being collectable, based on past experience. The accounts receivable will need to be adjusted from its current balance of $21000.

7    David & Johnson is an organization which specializes in providing their customers with legal services. David & Johnson has just provided 2300 large orders which had been paid for in advance last year. Each order was in the amount of $1900.

8    Hogtown Records is a company which offers their customers a wide selection of audio services for local musicians to record their music albums. Hogtown Records has just received a cash payment for the full amount that this customer owed to the company for all of their purchases to date. The outstanding balance which has now been paid was $33000.

9    Mr. Mop is a corporation which sells household cleaners. Today Mr. Mop sold 31800 tons of cleaning solution which had a 30% mark-up. They had originally been bought from their suppliers for a unit cost of $2350.

10    Pharma Drug Company Ltd. is a privately-held corporation which focuses on their niche of premium medications. This month, Pharma Drug Company Ltd. has estimated that 20% of the accounts receivable might not end up being collectable, based on past experience. The accounts receivable will need to be adjusted from its current balance of $73000.

11    Kola-Nut Ltd is a corporation which sells soft drinks. This month, Kola-Nut Ltd must amortize 1 month worth of utility bills which they had prepaid at the beginning of the year. The amount that they had paid upfront for the year was $18000.

12    Paytech Ltd sells various payroll transaction processing services. Today Paytech Ltd signed up for a loan with a 5% interest rate, and so the bank immediately transferred cash to the company in the amount of $89000.

13    Hogtown Records sells various audio services for local musicians to record their music albums. This month, Hogtown Records must amortize 1 month worth of utility bills which they had prepaid at the beginning of the year. The amount that they had paid upfront for the year was $28800.

14    Jameson & Jameson is a company which offers their customers a wide selection of soap products. This month, Jameson & Jameson paid for 1 month of rent for their company's office space. Each month, the rent owing was $18000.

15    Sprike Inc is a market leader that is well-known for their brand of athletic apparel. This December, Sprike Inc recognized 1 year of depreciation on a building which had a total useful life of 25 years, and which had originally been bought for $752000.

16    Jameson & Jameson provides their customers with soap products. Today Jameson & Jameson sold 38300 truckloads of bars of soap which had a 30% mark-up. They had originally been bought from their suppliers for a unit cost of $1910.

17    McGerald's sells several different types of fast food meals. This December, McGerald's has paid each of the company's 1300 owners an annual dividend in the amount of $18000.

18    Air America is a company which offers their customers a wide selection of global flights. This January, Air America has made an advance payment to cover the next 12 months of utility bills, which have a monthly cost of $2500.

19    Payday Now is a market leader that is well-known for their brand of short-term loan arrangements. Today Payday Now signed up for a loan with a 5% interest rate, and so the bank immediately transferred cash to the company in the amount of $115000.

20    Club Disco sells various dance venue rentals for large family gatherings. This December, Club Disco recognized 1 year of depreciation on a building which had a total useful life of 25 years, and which had originally been bought for $42000.

21    Pharma Drug Company Ltd. is a company which offers their customers a wide selection of medications. This week, Pharma Drug Company Ltd. purchased 3820 batches of pills which were placed into the warehouse, and which had a per-unit cost of $2200.

22    McGerald's provides their customers with fast food meals. Today McGerald's signed up for a loan with a 5% interest rate, and so the bank immediately transferred cash to the company in the amount of $100000.

23    Air America is a privately-held corporation which focuses on their niche of premium global flights. Today, Air America has paid cash to their supplier to fully pay off their account payable balance, which was $70000.

24    Grand Convention Ltd is a company which offers their customers a wide selection of banquet hall rentals for corporate meetings. Today Grand Convention Ltd signed up for a loan with a 5% interest rate, and so the bank immediately transferred cash to the company in the amount of $57000.

25    Kola-Nut Ltd is a privately-held corporation which focuses on their niche of premium soft drinks. This December, Kola-Nut Ltd recognized 1 year of depreciation on a building which had a total useful life of 25 years, and which had originally been bought for $525000.

26    Pharma Drug Company Ltd. is a corporation which sells medications. This week, Pharma Drug Company Ltd. purchased 2260 batches of pills which were placed into the warehouse, and which had a per-unit cost of $2800.

27    Jameson & Jameson is an organization which specializes in providing their customers with soap products. This December, Jameson & Jameson recognized 1 year of depreciation on equipment which had a total useful life of 10 years, and which had originally cost $90000.

28    Pharma Drug Company Ltd. sells several different types of medications. This month, Pharma Drug Company Ltd. paid for 1 month of rent for the warehouse room, which has a monthly cost of $2600.

29    Toyonda is a corporation which sells cars. Today, Toyonda has paid cash to their supplier to fully pay off their account payable balance, which was $82000.

30    Mount Tessory Academy is a privately-held corporation which focuses on their niche of premium private school education. Mount Tessory Academy has just provided 1200 large orders which had been paid for in advance last year. Each order was in the amount of $2100.

31 Payday Now is a market leader that is well-known for their brand of short-term loan arrangements. This month, Payday Now paid for 1 month of rent for their company's office space. Each month, the rent owing was $26000.

32 A to Z Event Guru Ltd is a market leader that is well-known for their brand of start-to-finish event planning services for large gatherings. This January, A to Z Event Guru Ltd has made an advance payment to cover the next 12 months of utility bills, which have a monthly cost of $1700.

33 Kola-Nut Ltd is a market leader that is well-known for their brand of soft drinks. This month, Kola-Nut Ltd accepted 7700 batches of soda bottles which were returned by customers. These products had been marked up by 35% and they had originally been bought at a per-unit cost of $1200.

34 Pharma Drug Company Ltd. sells several different types of medications. Today Pharma Drug Company Ltd. sold 44600 batches of pills which had a 30% mark-up. They had originally been bought from their suppliers for a unit cost of $2070.

35 Cirque du Lune is an organization which specializes in providing their customers with circus performances. This December, Cirque du Lune recognized 1 year of depreciation on equipment which had a total useful life of 10 years, and which had originally cost $200000.

36 Toyonda is a company which offers their customers a wide selection of cars. Today, Toyonda has paid cash to their supplier to fully pay off their account payable balance, which was $29000.

37 Kola-Nut Ltd provides their customers with soft drinks. This week, Kola-Nut Ltd purchased 4080 batches of soda bottles which were placed into the warehouse, and which had a per-unit cost of $2400.

38 NY Fitness is an organization which specializes in providing their customers with gym memberships for professional sports teams. Today, NY Fitness received payment upfront for 1100 large orders which will not be provided until early next year. Each order was in the amount of $1500.

39 LA Met Theatre Company is an organization which specializes in providing their customers with live theatrical performances. This month, LA Met Theatre Company has estimated that 20% of the accounts receivable might not end up being collectable, based on past experience. The accounts receivable will need to be adjusted from its current balance of $53000.

40 Pharma Drug Company Ltd. offers their customers a wide range of medications. This month, Pharma Drug Company Ltd. paid 1 monthly loan repayment towards their long-term note payable. The interest portion was 60% of the payment. The total amount paid in cash was $14000.

41    David & Johnson is a market leader that is well-known for their brand of legal services. David & Johnson has just purchased a building using cash, which has an expected useful life of 30 years, and which had a total cost of $1013000.

42    Jameson & Jameson is an organization which specializes in providing their customers with soap products. This month, Jameson & Jameson paid for 1 month of rent for the warehouse room, which has a monthly cost of $2200.

43    NY Fitness is an organization which specializes in providing their customers with gym memberships for professional sports teams. This year, NY Fitness has provided 1300 team memberships each of which earned revenues of $2370.

44    NY Fitness offers their customers a wide range of gym memberships for professional sports teams. NY Fitness has just received a cash payment for the full amount that this customer owed to the company for all of their purchases to date. The outstanding balance which has now been paid was $69000.

45    Mr. Mop provides their customers with household cleaners. Today, Mr. Mop received an upfront payment for 1390 tons of cleaning solution which will be provided to the customer 6 months from now. The payment for each was $2600.

46    Jameson & Jameson is a market leader that is well-known for their brand of soap products. This month, Jameson & Jameson paid for 1 month of rent for the warehouse room, which has a monthly cost of $1000.

47    A to Z Event Guru Ltd sells several different types of start-to-finish event planning services for large gatherings. This month, A to Z Event Guru Ltd must amortize 1 month worth of utility bills which they had prepaid at the beginning of the year. The amount that they had paid upfront for the year was $21600.

48    Sprike Inc is a corporation which sells athletic apparel. This month, Sprike Inc accepted 6100 batches of athletic t-shirts which were returned by customers. These products had been marked up by 35% and they had originally been bought at a per-unit cost of $2400.

49    Fairway Malls is a company which offers their customers a wide selection of retail spaces in their shopping centers. This year, Fairway Malls has provided 2200 monthly retail space rentals each of which earned revenues of $2440.

50    AC&C Ltd. is a privately-held corporation which focuses on their niche of premium cell phone plans. AC&C Ltd. has just received a cash payment for the full amount that this customer owed to the company for all of their purchases to date. The outstanding balance which has now been paid was $59000.

51      Payday Now is a privately-held corporation which focuses on their niche of premium short-term loan arrangements. Today, Payday Now has paid cash to their supplier to fully pay off their account payable balance, which was $26000.

52      Grand Convention Ltd is a corporation which sells banquet hall rentals for corporate meetings. Today, Grand Convention Ltd has paid cash to their supplier to fully pay off their account payable balance, which was $64000.

53      Mr. Mop is a privately-held corporation which focuses on their niche of premium household cleaners. This month, Mr. Mop paid for 1 month of rent for the warehouse room, which has a monthly cost of $1600.

54      Sprike Inc provides their customers with athletic apparel. This month, Sprike Inc paid for 1 month of rent for the warehouse room, which has a monthly cost of $2600.

55      McGerald's offers their customers a wide range of fast food meals. This year, McGerald's has provided 1700 burger combos each of which earned revenues of $2060.

56      Comedy 253 provides their customers with live performances of stand-up comedy. This month, Comedy 253 paid 1 monthly loan repayment towards their long-term note payable. The interest portion was 60% of the payment. The total amount paid in cash was $23000.

57      Paytech Ltd sells several different types of payroll transaction processing services. Today, Paytech Ltd received payment upfront for 1700 large orders which will not be provided until early next year. Each order was in the amount of $2200.

58      Pharma Drug Company Ltd. is a privately-held corporation which focuses on their niche of premium medications. This month, Pharma Drug Company Ltd. paid for 1 month of rent for their company's office space. Each month, the rent owing was $20000.

59      Paytech Ltd is a company which offers their customers a wide selection of payroll transaction processing services. This month, Paytech Ltd has estimated that 30% of the accounts receivable might not end up being collectable, based on past experience. The accounts receivable will need to be adjusted from its current balance of $44000.

60      Club Disco is a company which offers their customers a wide selection of dance venue rentals for large family gatherings. Today, Club Disco received payment upfront for 2000 large orders which will not be provided until early next year. Each order was in the amount of $1900.

61    Mount Tessory Academy is a corporation which sells private school education. This December, Mount Tessory Academy has paid each of the company's 2100 owners an annual dividend in the amount of $23000.

62    Payday Now sells various short-term loan arrangements. This month, Payday Now paid for 1 month of rent for their company's office space. Each month, the rent owing was $13000.

63    Payday Now is an organization which specializes in providing their customers with short-term loan arrangements. This year, Payday Now has provided 1100 payday loans each of which earned revenues of $1900.

64    Fairway Malls offers their customers a wide range of retail spaces in their shopping centers. This month, Fairway Malls paid 1 monthly loan repayment towards their long-term note payable. The interest portion was 60% of the payment. The total amount paid in cash was $25000.

65    Kola-Nut Ltd is a market leader that is well-known for their brand of soft drinks. Today Kola-Nut Ltd sold 5900 batches of soda bottles which had a 30% mark-up. They had originally been bought from their suppliers for a unit cost of $2910.

66    Grand Convention Ltd sells several different types of banquet hall rentals for corporate meetings. This month, Grand Convention Ltd paid for 1 month of rent for their company's office space. Each month, the rent owing was $16000.

67    Pharma Drug Company Ltd. offers their customers a wide range of medications. Pharma Drug Company Ltd. has just purchased a building using cash, which has an expected useful life of 30 years, and which had a total cost of $802000.

68    Payday Now is a privately-held corporation which focuses on their niche of premium short-term loan arrangements. Today Payday Now signed up for a loan with a 5% interest rate, and so the bank immediately transferred cash to the company in the amount of $34000.

69    David & Johnson is a market leader that is well-known for their brand of legal services. This month, David & Johnson paid 1 monthly loan repayment towards their long-term note payable. The interest portion was 60% of the payment. The total amount paid in cash was $9000.

70    NY Fitness sells several different types of gym memberships for professional sports teams. This January, NY Fitness has made an advance payment to cover the next 12 months of utility bills, which have a monthly cost of $1600.

71    Jameson & Jameson is a privately-held corporation which focuses on their niche of premium soap products. This month, Jameson & Jameson paid for 1 month of rent for the warehouse room, which has a monthly cost of $1900.

72 Mount Tessory Academy sells various private school education subscriptions. Mount Tessory Academy has just received a cash payment for the full amount that this customer owed to the company for all of their purchases to date. The outstanding balance which has now been paid was $34000.

73 Jameson & Jameson is a privately-held corporation which focuses on their niche of premium soap products. This month, Jameson & Jameson paid for 1 month of rent for their company's office space. Each month, the rent owing was $20000.

74 Mr. Mop is a market leader that is well-known for their brand of household cleaners. This month, Mr. Mop accepted 6500 tons of cleaning solution which were returned by customers. These products had been marked up by 35% and they had originally been bought at a per-unit cost of $1500.

75 Grand Convention Ltd sells several different types of banquet hall rentals for corporate meetings. This December, Grand Convention Ltd recognized 1 year of depreciation on equipment which had a total useful life of 10 years, and which had originally cost $130000.

76 Club Disco is a company which offers their customers a wide selection of dance venue rentals for large family gatherings. This year, Club Disco has provided 1100 evening rentals each of which earned revenues of $1050.

77 Hogtown Records is a market leader that is well-known for their brand of audio services for local musicians to record their music albums. Hogtown Records has just purchased a building using cash, which has an expected useful life of 30 years, and which had a total cost of $193000.

78 Payday Now sells various short-term loan arrangements. This month, Payday Now paid for 1 month of rent for their company's office space. Each month, the rent owing was $26000.

79 Sprike Inc is a privately-held corporation which focuses on their niche of premium athletic apparel. Today, Sprike Inc received an upfront payment for 4800 batches of athletic t-shirts which will be provided to the customer 6 months from now. The payment for each was $2100.

80 David & Johnson offers their customers a wide range of legal services. Today David & Johnson signed up for a loan with a 5% interest rate, and so the bank immediately transferred cash to the company in the amount of $117000.

81 Payday Now is a company which offers their customers a wide selection of short-term loan arrangements. Today Payday Now signed up for a loan with a 5% interest rate, and so the bank immediately transferred cash to the company in the amount of $41000.

82 Mr. Mop is a privately-held corporation which focuses on their niche of premium household cleaners. Today Mr. Mop sold 19800 tons of cleaning solution which had a 30% mark-up. They had originally been bought from their suppliers for a unit cost of $2840.

83 Kola-Nut Ltd is a company which offers their customers a wide selection of soft drinks. Kola-Nut Ltd has just purchased a building using cash, which has an expected useful life of 30 years, and which had a total cost of $792000.

84 Mr. Mop sells several different types of household cleaners. This week, Mr. Mop purchased 3010 tons of cleaning solution which were placed into the warehouse, and which had a per-unit cost of $1800.

85 Mount Tessory Academy is a company which offers their customers a wide selection of private school education. Mount Tessory Academy has just provided 1100 large orders which had been paid for in advance last year. Each order was in the amount of $1200.

86 McGerald's provides their customers with fast food meals. This month, McGerald's must amortize 1 month worth of utility bills which they had prepaid at the beginning of the year. The amount that they had paid upfront for the year was $12000.

87 Kola-Nut Ltd is an organization which specializes in providing their customers with soft drinks. This month, Kola-Nut Ltd paid 1 monthly loan repayment towards their long-term note payable. The interest portion was 60% of the payment. The total amount paid in cash was $24000.

88 Jameson & Jameson is a privately-held corporation which focuses on their niche of premium soap products. Today, Jameson & Jameson bought equipment which has a 5 year useful life, and which had a cost of $11000.

89 Club Disco is an organization which specializes in providing their customers with dance venue rentals for large family gatherings. This month, Club Disco must amortize 1 month worth of utility bills which they had prepaid at the beginning of the year. The amount that they had paid upfront for the year was $22800.

90 Grand Convention Ltd is a company which offers their customers a wide selection of banquet hall rentals for corporate meetings. This December, Grand Convention Ltd recognized 1 year of depreciation on equipment which had a total useful life of 10 years, and which had originally cost $170000.

91 A to Z Event Guru Ltd is a privately-held corporation which focuses on their niche of premium start-to-finish event planning services for large gatherings. A to Z Event Guru Ltd has just purchased a building using cash, which has an expected useful life of 30 years, and which had a total cost of $398000.

92    Cirque du Lune sells several different types of circus performances. This month, Cirque du Lune paid 1 monthly loan repayment towards their long-term note payable. The interest portion was 60% of the payment. The total amount paid in cash was $21000.

93    Payday Now is a corporation which sells short-term loan arrangements. This month, Payday Now paid for 1 month of rent for their company's office space. Each month, the rent owing was $9000.

94    Club Disco is a company which offers their customers a wide selection of dance venue rentals for large family gatherings. This month, Club Disco has estimated that 10% of the accounts receivable might not end up being collectable, based on past experience. The accounts receivable will need to be adjusted from its current balance of $23000.

95    Mr. Mop sells several different types of household cleaners. Today Mr. Mop sold 9600 tons of cleaning solution which had a 30% mark-up. They had originally been bought from their suppliers for a unit cost of $2950.

96    Toyonda sells various cars. This month, Toyonda must amortize 1 month worth of utility bills which they had prepaid at the beginning of the year. The amount that they had paid upfront for the year was $37200.

97    Kola-Nut Ltd is a corporation which sells soft drinks. Kola-Nut Ltd has just purchased a building using cash, which has an expected useful life of 30 years, and which had a total cost of $768000.

98    Pharma Drug Company Ltd. offers their customers a wide range of medications. This week, Pharma Drug Company Ltd. purchased 1340 batches of pills which were placed into the warehouse, and which had a per-unit cost of $1000.

99    Paytech Ltd is a privately-held corporation which focuses on their niche of premium payroll transaction processing services. Paytech Ltd has just received a cash payment for the full amount that this customer owed to the company for all of their purchases to date. The outstanding balance which has now been paid was $75000.

100    Sprike Inc offers their customers a wide range of athletic apparel. Sprike Inc has just received a cash payment for the full amount that this customer owed to the company for all of their purchases to date. The outstanding balance which has now been paid was $53000.

101    David & Johnson is a privately-held corporation which focuses on their niche of premium legal services. David & Johnson has just purchased a building using cash, which has an expected useful life of 30 years, and which had a total cost of $153000.

102    Club Disco offers their customers a wide range of dance venue rentals for large family gatherings. Club Disco has just provided 1200 large orders which had been paid for in advance last year. Each order was in the amount of $1400.

103    A to Z Event Guru Ltd offers their customers a wide range of start-to-finish event planning services for large gatherings. A to Z Event Guru Ltd has just provided 2300 large orders which had been paid for in advance last year. Each order was in the amount of $1500.

104    David & Johnson sells several different types of legal services. David & Johnson has just purchased a building using cash, which has an expected useful life of 30 years, and which had a total cost of $844000.

105    AC&C Ltd. is a corporation which sells cell phone plans. This December, AC&C Ltd. has paid each of the company's 1700 owners an annual dividend in the amount of $16000.

106    McGerald's is a privately-held corporation which focuses on their niche of premium fast food meals. This week, McGerald's paid each of the 2020 staff members their bi-weekly wages, which per person had a cost of $2200.

107    Payday Now is a privately-held corporation which focuses on their niche of premium short-term loan arrangements. Today Payday Now signed up for a loan with a 5% interest rate, and so the bank immediately transferred cash to the company in the amount of $102000.

108    Cirque du Lune is a market leader that is well-known for their brand of circus performances. This January, Cirque du Lune has made an advance payment to cover the next 12 months of utility bills, which have a monthly cost of $1000.

109    Sprike Inc is a corporation which sells athletic apparel. This month, Sprike Inc paid for 1 month of rent for the warehouse room, which has a monthly cost of $2400.

110    Fairway Malls sells various retail spaces in their shopping centers. This month, Fairway Malls must amortize 1 month worth of utility bills which they had prepaid at the beginning of the year. The amount that they had paid upfront for the year was $33600.

111    Club Disco is a privately-held corporation which focuses on their niche of premium dance venue rentals for large family gatherings. Club Disco has just received a cash payment for the full amount that this customer owed to the company for all of their purchases to date. The outstanding balance which has now been paid was $64000.

112 Sprike Inc is a market leader that is well-known for their brand of athletic apparel. Today, Sprike Inc received an upfront payment for 5850 batches of athletic t-shirts which will be provided to the customer 6 months from now. The payment for each was $2500.

113 Air America is a company which offers their customers a wide selection of global flights. Air America has just provided 2200 large orders which had been paid for in advance last year. Each order was in the amount of $2200.

114 Kola-Nut Ltd is an organization which specializes in providing their customers with soft drinks. This week, Kola-Nut Ltd purchased 4400 batches of soda bottles which were placed into the warehouse, and which had a per-unit cost of $2200.

115 Mr. Mop is a privately-held corporation which focuses on their niche of premium household cleaners. Today Mr. Mop signed up for a loan with a 5% interest rate, and so the bank immediately transferred cash to the company in the amount of $69000.

116 Cirque du Lune is a privately-held corporation which focuses on their niche of premium circus performances. This January, Cirque du Lune has made an advance payment to cover the next 12 months of utility bills, which have a monthly cost of $1100.

117 AC&C Ltd. is a company which offers their customers a wide selection of cell phone plans. Today, AC&C Ltd. has paid cash to their supplier to fully pay off their account payable balance, which was $19000.

118 Payday Now sells various short-term loan arrangements. This year, Payday Now has provided 1100 payday loans each of which earned revenues of $1370.

119 LA Met Theatre Company is an organization which specializes in providing their customers with live theatrical performances. Today, LA Met Theatre Company bought equipment which has a 5 year useful life, and which had a cost of $11000.

120 Kola-Nut Ltd is a corporation which sells soft drinks. This December, Kola-Nut Ltd has paid each of the company's 1300 owners an annual dividend in the amount of $20000.

121 Pharma Drug Company Ltd. offers their customers a wide range of medications. This December, Pharma Drug Company Ltd. recognized 1 year of depreciation on a building which had a total useful life of 25 years, and which had originally been bought for $927000.

122     LA Met Theatre Company sells various live theatrical performances. Today LA Met Theatre Company signed up for a loan with a 5% interest rate, and so the bank immediately transferred cash to the company in the amount of $75000.

123     Grand Convention Ltd provides their customers with banquet hall rentals for corporate meetings. Today, Grand Convention Ltd received payment upfront for 1600 large orders which will not be provided until early next year. Each order was in the amount of $2000.

124     Hogtown Records sells various audio services for local musicians to record their music albums. This month, Hogtown Records paid 1 monthly loan repayment towards their long-term note payable. The interest portion was 60% of the payment. The total amount paid in cash was $24000.

125     Jameson & Jameson is a corporation which sells soap products. Today, Jameson & Jameson received an upfront payment for 3350 truckloads of bars of soap which will be provided to the customer 6 months from now. The payment for each was $1900.

126     Air America is a company which offers their customers a wide selection of global flights. Today, Air America bought equipment which has a 5 year useful life, and which had a cost of $10000.

127     Comedy 253 provides their customers with live performances of stand-up comedy. This month, Comedy 253 has estimated that 5% of the accounts receivable might not end up being collectable, based on past experience. The accounts receivable will need to be adjusted from its current balance of $25000.

128     Club Disco is an organization which specializes in providing their customers with dance venue rentals for large family gatherings. Today, Club Disco has paid cash to their supplier to fully pay off their account payable balance, which was $37000.

129     Air America provides their customers with global flights. Today Air America signed up for a loan with a 5% interest rate, and so the bank immediately transferred cash to the company in the amount of $61000.

130     McGerald's sells various fast food meals. This December, McGerald's recognized 1 year of depreciation on equipment which had a total useful life of 10 years, and which had originally cost $220000.

131     A to Z Event Guru Ltd is a company which offers their customers a wide selection of start-to-finish event planning services for large gatherings. This December, A to Z Event Guru Ltd recognized 1 year of depreciation on equipment which had a total useful life of 10 years, and which had originally cost $230000.

132    Payday Now is a privately-held corporation which focuses on their niche of premium short-term loan arrangements. This December, Payday Now recognized 1 year of depreciation on a building which had a total useful life of 25 years, and which had originally been bought for $707000.

133    Mount Tessory Academy is a company which offers their customers a wide selection of private school education. Mount Tessory Academy has just purchased a building using cash, which has an expected useful life of 30 years, and which had a total cost of $541000.

134    Grand Convention Ltd sells various banquet hall rentals for corporate meetings. Grand Convention Ltd has just received a cash payment for the full amount that this customer owed to the company for all of their purchases to date. The outstanding balance which has now been paid was $74000.

135    Pharma Drug Company Ltd. is an organization which specializes in providing their customers with medications. Today, Pharma Drug Company Ltd. has paid cash to their supplier to fully pay off their account payable balance, which was $49000.

136    Club Disco is an organization which specializes in providing their customers with dance venue rentals for large family gatherings. Today, Club Disco has paid cash to their supplier to fully pay off their account payable balance, which was $60000.

137    Mount Tessory Academy is a company which offers their customers a wide selection of private school education. Mount Tessory Academy has just received a cash payment for the full amount that this customer owed to the company for all of their purchases to date. The outstanding balance which has now been paid was $71000.

138    NBG Media Corporation is a company which offers their customers a wide selection of broadcasting services for advertising agencies. This January, NBG Media Corporation has made an advance payment to cover the next 12 months of utility bills, which have a monthly cost of $1900.

139    David & Johnson sells various legal services. Today, David & Johnson received payment upfront for 1300 large orders which will not be provided until early next year. Each order was in the amount of $2000.

140    Kola-Nut Ltd offers their customers a wide range of soft drinks. This week, Kola-Nut Ltd purchased 3260 batches of soda bottles which were placed into the warehouse, and which had a per-unit cost of $2700.

141    Kola-Nut Ltd offers their customers a wide range of soft drinks. Today Kola-Nut Ltd sold 9600 batches of soda bottles which had a 30% mark-up. They had originally been bought from their suppliers for a unit cost of $1290.

142    Kola-Nut Ltd is an organization which specializes in providing their customers with soft drinks. This month, Kola-Nut Ltd has estimated that 15% of the accounts receivable might not end up being collectable, based on past experience. The accounts receivable will need to be adjusted from its current balance of $55000.

143    Jameson & Jameson provides their customers with soap products. This month, Jameson & Jameson paid 1 monthly loan repayment towards their long-term note payable. The interest portion was 60% of the payment. The total amount paid in cash was $20000.

144    Sprike Inc is a privately-held corporation which focuses on their niche of premium athletic apparel. Today, Sprike Inc bought equipment which has a 5 year useful life, and which had a cost of $24000.

145    Mr. Mop is a privately-held corporation which focuses on their niche of premium household cleaners. This month, Mr. Mop paid for 1 month of rent for the warehouse room, which has a monthly cost of $2100.

146    AC&C Ltd. is a company which offers their customers a wide selection of cell phone plans. This year, AC&C Ltd. has provided 2300 monthly cell phone service each of which earned revenues of $1880.

147    Jameson & Jameson sells various soap products. This month, Jameson & Jameson paid for 1 month of rent for the warehouse room, which has a monthly cost of $1200.

148    Hogtown Records is a company which offers their customers a wide selection of audio services for local musicians to record their music albums. Today, Hogtown Records bought equipment which has a 5 year useful life, and which had a cost of $19000.

149    Pharma Drug Company Ltd. is a market leader that is well-known for their brand of medications. This month, Pharma Drug Company Ltd. paid for 1 month of rent for the warehouse room, which has a monthly cost of $1600.

150    Club Disco provides their customers with dance venue rentals for large family gatherings. This December, Club Disco has paid each of the company's 2200 owners an annual dividend in the amount of $11000.

151    LA Met Theatre Company is a privately-held corporation which focuses on their niche of premium live theatrical performances. This year, LA Met Theatre Company has provided 1400 shows each of which earned revenues of $1030.

152 Club Disco is a corporation which sells dance venue rentals for large family gatherings. This December, Club Disco has paid each of the company's 1800 owners an annual dividend in the amount of $17000.

153 Pharma Drug Company Ltd. is a privately-held corporation which focuses on their niche of premium medications. Today Pharma Drug Company Ltd. sold 5900 batches of pills which had a 30% mark-up. They had originally been bought from their suppliers for a unit cost of $1230.

154 Club Disco is a corporation which sells dance venue rentals for large family gatherings. Club Disco has just purchased a building using cash, which has an expected useful life of 30 years, and which had a total cost of $385000.

155 Pharma Drug Company Ltd. is a privately-held corporation which focuses on their niche of premium medications. This month, Pharma Drug Company Ltd. accepted 4400 batches of pills which were returned by customers. These products had been marked up by 35% and they had originally been bought at a per-unit cost of $1400.

156 Kola-Nut Ltd sells various soft drinks. This month, Kola-Nut Ltd accepted 18900 batches of soda bottles which were returned by customers. These products had been marked up by 35% and they had originally been bought at a per-unit cost of $1500.

157 Jameson & Jameson is a corporation which sells soap products. This month, Jameson & Jameson accepted 10300 truckloads of bars of soap which were returned by customers. These products had been marked up by 35% and they had originally been bought at a per-unit cost of $1500.

158 Kola-Nut Ltd is a privately-held corporation which focuses on their niche of premium soft drinks. Today, Kola-Nut Ltd received an upfront payment for 2700 batches of soda bottles which will be provided to the customer 6 months from now. The payment for each was $2200.

159 Kola-Nut Ltd is a market leader that is well-known for their brand of soft drinks. This week, Kola-Nut Ltd purchased 3620 batches of soda bottles which were placed into the warehouse, and which had a per-unit cost of $1500.

160 Jameson & Jameson offers their customers a wide range of soap products. This month, Jameson & Jameson paid for 1 month of rent for the warehouse room, which has a monthly cost of $1000.

161 LA Met Theatre Company is an organization which specializes in providing their customers with live theatrical performances. This year, LA Met Theatre Company has provided 1700 shows each of which earned revenues of $1780.

162    Paytech Ltd is a company which offers their customers a wide selection of payroll transaction processing services. Today, Paytech Ltd has paid cash to their supplier to fully pay off their account payable balance, which was $82000.

163    Sprike Inc is a privately-held corporation which focuses on their niche of premium athletic apparel. This month, Sprike Inc accepted 1300 batches of athletic t-shirts which were returned by customers. These products had been marked up by 35% and they had originally been bought at a per-unit cost of $1200.

164    Pharma Drug Company Ltd. sells various medications. This month, Pharma Drug Company Ltd. paid for 1 month of rent for the warehouse room, which has a monthly cost of $2500.

165    Jameson & Jameson is a company which offers their customers a wide selection of soap products. Today, Jameson & Jameson received an upfront payment for 1420 truckloads of bars of soap which will be provided to the customer 6 months from now. The payment for each was $2300.

166    Air America is a privately-held corporation which focuses on their niche of premium global flights. Air America has just purchased a building using cash, which has an expected useful life of 30 years, and which had a total cost of $512000.

167    Cirque du Lune is an organization which specializes in providing their customers with circus performances. This month, Cirque du Lune paid 1 monthly loan repayment towards their long-term note payable. The interest portion was 60% of the payment. The total amount paid in cash was $25000.

168    Hogtown Records offers their customers a wide range of audio services for local musicians to record their music albums. This December, Hogtown Records has paid each of the company's 2100 owners an annual dividend in the amount of $26000.

169    Kola-Nut Ltd sells several different types of soft drinks. This December, Kola-Nut Ltd recognized 1 year of depreciation on equipment which had a total useful life of 10 years, and which had originally cost $180000.

170    Hogtown Records provides their customers with audio services for local musicians to record their music albums. This December, Hogtown Records recognized 1 year of depreciation on a building which had a total useful life of 25 years, and which had originally been bought for $434000.

171    Kola-Nut Ltd is a corporation which sells soft drinks. This month, Kola-Nut Ltd paid for 1 month of rent for the warehouse room, which has a monthly cost of $2400.

172     Cirque du Lune sells various circus performances. This year, Cirque du Lune has provided 1700 shows each of which earned revenues of $2470.

173     Comedy 253 is a market leader that is well-known for their brand of live performances of stand-up comedy. This December, Comedy 253 recognized 1 year of depreciation on equipment which had a total useful life of 10 years, and which had originally cost $150000.

174     Club Disco is a privately-held corporation which focuses on their niche of premium dance venue rentals for large family gatherings. This December, Club Disco recognized 1 year of depreciation on a building which had a total useful life of 25 years, and which had originally been bought for $249000.

175     Jameson & Jameson sells several different types of soap products. This month, Jameson & Jameson paid for 1 month of rent for the warehouse room, which has a monthly cost of $1800.

176     Grand Convention Ltd sells various banquet hall rentals for corporate meetings. This month, Grand Convention Ltd must amortize 1 month worth of utility bills which they had prepaid at the beginning of the year. The amount that they had paid upfront for the year was $30000.

177     Hogtown Records is a privately-held corporation which focuses on their niche of premium audio services for local musicians to record their music albums. This month, Hogtown Records paid for 1 month of rent for their company's office space. Each month, the rent owing was $20000.

178     Jameson & Jameson is a market leader that is well-known for their brand of soap products. Today Jameson & Jameson sold 10400 truckloads of bars of soap which had a 30% mark-up. They had originally been bought from their suppliers for a unit cost of $2370.

179     Paytech Ltd sells various payroll transaction processing services. Today, Paytech Ltd bought equipment which has a 5 year useful life, and which had a cost of $11000.

180     A to Z Event Guru Ltd provides their customers with start-to-finish event planning services for large gatherings. A to Z Event Guru Ltd has just purchased a building using cash, which has an expected useful life of 30 years, and which had a total cost of $726000.

181     AC&C Ltd. sells various cell phone plans. This week, AC&C Ltd. paid each of the 2910 staff members their bi-weekly wages, which per person had a cost of $1500.

182   Paytech Ltd sells various payroll transaction processing services. Today, Paytech Ltd received payment upfront for 2400 large orders which will not be provided until early next year. Each order was in the amount of $1100.

183   Hogtown Records provides their customers with audio services for local musicians to record their music albums. This December, Hogtown Records has paid each of the company's 1200 owners an annual dividend in the amount of $23000.

184   Jameson & Jameson is a privately-held corporation which focuses on their niche of premium soap products. Today Jameson & Jameson sold 9400 truckloads of bars of soap which had a 30% mark-up. They had originally been bought from their suppliers for a unit cost of $2490.

185   Pharma Drug Company Ltd. is an organization which specializes in providing their customers with medications. Today Pharma Drug Company Ltd. sold 48600 batches of pills which had a 30% mark-up. They had originally been bought from their suppliers for a unit cost of $1020.

186   Hogtown Records provides their customers with audio services for local musicians to record their music albums. This December, Hogtown Records has paid each of the company's 1100 owners an annual dividend in the amount of $21000.

187   Paytech Ltd is a market leader that is well-known for their brand of payroll transaction processing services. Today, Paytech Ltd has paid cash to their supplier to fully pay off their account payable balance, which was $54000.

188   Mr. Mop offers their customers a wide range of household cleaners. This January, Mr. Mop has made an advance payment to cover the next 12 months of utility bills, which have a monthly cost of $1900.

189   A to Z Event Guru Ltd is an organization which specializes in providing their customers with start-to-finish event planning services for large gatherings. A to Z Event Guru Ltd has just purchased a building using cash, which has an expected useful life of 30 years, and which had a total cost of $579000.

190   NY Fitness is a privately-held corporation which focuses on their niche of premium gym memberships for professional sports teams. This December, NY Fitness has paid each of the company's 1600 owners an annual dividend in the amount of $9000.

191   Mr. Mop is a market leader that is well-known for their brand of household cleaners. Today Mr. Mop signed up for a loan with a 5% interest rate, and so the bank immediately transferred cash to the company in the amount of $27000.

192     Grand Convention Ltd is a corporation which sells banquet hall rentals for corporate meetings. Grand Convention Ltd has just received a cash payment for the full amount that this customer owed to the company for all of their purchases to date. The outstanding balance which has now been paid was $92000.

193     Mount Tessory Academy is a privately-held corporation which focuses on their niche of premium private school education. Mount Tessory Academy has just received a cash payment for the full amount that this customer owed to the company for all of their purchases to date. The outstanding balance which has now been paid was $33000.

194     Comedy 253 offers their customers a wide range of live performances of stand-up comedy. This year, Comedy 253 has provided 2100 shows each of which earned revenues of $1220.

195     Jameson & Jameson offers their customers a wide range of soap products. This month, Jameson & Jameson accepted 29700 truckloads of bars of soap which were returned by customers. These products had been marked up by 35% and they had originally been bought at a per-unit cost of $1800.

196     McGerald's is an organization which specializes in providing their customers with fast food meals. This January, McGerald's has made an advance payment to cover the next 12 months of utility bills, which have a monthly cost of $1300.

197     Sprike Inc sells several different types of athletic apparel. This month, Sprike Inc accepted 7300 batches of athletic t-shirts which were returned by customers. These products had been marked up by 35% and they had originally been bought at a per-unit cost of $2800.

198     Sprike Inc provides their customers with athletic apparel. This month, Sprike Inc must amortize 1 month worth of utility bills which they had prepaid at the beginning of the year. The amount that they had paid upfront for the year was $30000.

199     AC&C Ltd. sells several different types of cell phone plans. This month, AC&C Ltd. paid for 1 month of rent for their company's office space. Each month, the rent owing was $12000.

200     Air America is a corporation which sells global flights. This December, Air America recognized 1 year of depreciation on a building which had a total useful life of 25 years, and which had originally been bought for $754000.

201     David & Johnson sells several different types of legal services. Today, David & Johnson received payment upfront for 1000 large orders which will not be provided until early next year. Each order was in the amount of $2700.

202 NBG Media Corporation sells various broadcasting services for advertising agencies. This January, NBG Media Corporation has made an advance payment to cover the next 12 months of utility bills, which have a monthly cost of $2700.

203 Sprike Inc is a corporation which sells athletic apparel. Today, Sprike Inc received an upfront payment for 2290 batches of athletic t-shirts which will be provided to the customer 6 months from now. The payment for each was $1800.

204 Fairway Malls is a market leader that is well-known for their brand of retail spaces in their shopping centers. This December, Fairway Malls recognized 1 year of depreciation on a building which had a total useful life of 25 years, and which had originally been bought for $35000.

205 Toyonda is a market leader that is well-known for their brand of cars. Today Toyonda signed up for a loan with a 5% interest rate, and so the bank immediately transferred cash to the company in the amount of $49000.

206 David & Johnson offers their customers a wide range of legal services. David & Johnson has just provided 2200 large orders which had been paid for in advance last year. Each order was in the amount of $2300.

207 NBG Media Corporation offers their customers a wide range of broadcasting services for advertising agencies. Today NBG Media Corporation signed up for a loan with a 5% interest rate, and so the bank immediately transferred cash to the company in the amount of $92000.

208 Pharma Drug Company Ltd. sells several different types of medications. Today, Pharma Drug Company Ltd. has paid cash to their supplier to fully pay off their account payable balance, which was $46000.

209 Hogtown Records is a corporation which sells audio services for local musicians to record their music albums. This week, Hogtown Records paid each of the 3710 staff members their bi-weekly wages, which per person had a cost of $1300.

210 Hogtown Records provides their customers with audio services for local musicians to record their music albums. Today, Hogtown Records has paid cash to their supplier to fully pay off their account payable balance, which was $41000.

211 Club Disco sells various dance venue rentals for large family gatherings. Today, Club Disco received payment upfront for 2400 large orders which will not be provided until early next year. Each order was in the amount of $1300.

212 AC&C Ltd. is a corporation which sells cell phone plans. This December, AC&C Ltd. recognized 1 year of depreciation on equipment which had a total useful life of 10 years, and which had originally cost $140000.

213    Mr. Mop sells several different types of household cleaners. This January, Mr. Mop has made an advance payment to cover the next 12 months of utility bills, which have a monthly cost of $1500.

214    Club Disco is an organization which specializes in providing their customers with dance venue rentals for large family gatherings. This year, Club Disco has provided 2400 evening rentals each of which earned revenues of $2100.

215    Mount Tessory Academy is a corporation which sells private school education. This month, Mount Tessory Academy paid 1 monthly loan repayment towards their long-term note payable. The interest portion was 60% of the payment. The total amount paid in cash was $24000.

216    AC&C Ltd. is a corporation which sells cell phone plans. This month, AC&C Ltd. has estimated that 15% of the accounts receivable might not end up being collectable, based on past experience. The accounts receivable will need to be adjusted from its current balance of $43000.

217    Mr. Mop is a market leader that is well-known for their brand of household cleaners. This month, Mr. Mop paid for 1 month of rent for the warehouse room, which has a monthly cost of $2700.

218    Pharma Drug Company Ltd. provides their customers with medications. This week, Pharma Drug Company Ltd. purchased 4550 batches of pills which were placed into the warehouse, and which had a per-unit cost of $2800.

219    Sprike Inc sells several different types of athletic apparel. Sprike Inc has just purchased a building using cash, which has an expected useful life of 30 years, and which had a total cost of $818000.

220    Jameson & Jameson provides their customers with soap products. Today Jameson & Jameson signed up for a loan with a 5% interest rate, and so the bank immediately transferred cash to the company in the amount of $85000.

221    Jameson & Jameson provides their customers with soap products. This month, Jameson & Jameson paid 1 monthly loan repayment towards their long-term note payable. The interest portion was 60% of the payment. The total amount paid in cash was $17000.

222    Pharma Drug Company Ltd. provides their customers with medications. Today Pharma Drug Company Ltd. sold 38600 batches of pills which had a 30% mark-up. They had originally been bought from their suppliers for a unit cost of $1910.

223    Fairway Malls sells several different types of retail spaces in their shopping centers. This month, Fairway Malls paid for 1 month of rent for their company's office space. Each month, the rent owing was $21000.

224     LA Met Theatre Company is a privately-held corporation which focuses on their niche of premium live theatrical performances. This year, LA Met Theatre Company has provided 1100 shows each of which earned revenues of $2930.

225     Cirque du Lune sells several different types of circus performances. This December, Cirque du Lune has paid each of the company's 1900 owners an annual dividend in the amount of $24000.

226     Paytech Ltd is a privately-held corporation which focuses on their niche of premium payroll transaction processing services. This month, Paytech Ltd paid 1 monthly loan repayment towards their long-term note payable. The interest portion was 60% of the payment. The total amount paid in cash was $20000.

227     Toyonda offers their customers a wide range of cars. Today, Toyonda has paid cash to their supplier to fully pay off their account payable balance, which was $41000.

228     Mr. Mop provides their customers with household cleaners. This month, Mr. Mop paid for 1 month of rent for the warehouse room, which has a monthly cost of $2700.

229     Jameson & Jameson is a company which offers their customers a wide selection of soap products. This week, Jameson & Jameson purchased 2700 truckloads of bars of soap which were placed into the warehouse, and which had a per-unit cost of $2600.

230     Air America offers their customers a wide range of global flights. Today, Air America has paid cash to their supplier to fully pay off their account payable balance, which was $11000.

231     Sprike Inc is an organization which specializes in providing their customers with athletic apparel. Today Sprike Inc sold 3400 batches of athletic t-shirts which had a 30% mark-up. They had originally been bought from their suppliers for a unit cost of $1880.

232     Comedy 253 is a corporation which sells live performances of stand-up comedy. This month, Comedy 253 paid 1 monthly loan repayment towards their long-term note payable. The interest portion was 60% of the payment. The total amount paid in cash was $12000.

233     Payday Now is an organization which specializes in providing their customers with short-term loan arrangements. Today Payday Now signed up for a loan with a 5% interest rate, and so the bank immediately transferred cash to the company in the amount of $33000.

234   David & Johnson is an organization which specializes in providing their customers with legal services.  This January, David & Johnson has made an advance payment to cover the next 12 months of utility bills, which have a monthly cost of $1800.

235   Mount Tessory Academy provides their customers with private school education. This month, Mount Tessory Academy must amortize 1 month worth of utility bills which they had prepaid at the beginning of the year. The amount that they had paid upfront for the year was $45600.

236   Jameson & Jameson sells various soap products.  This month, Jameson & Jameson paid for 1 month of rent for the warehouse room, which has a monthly cost of $2000.

237   Paytech Ltd is a company which offers their customers a wide selection of payroll transaction processing services.  This month, Paytech Ltd has estimated that 10% of the accounts receivable might not end up being collectable, based on past experience. The accounts receivable will need to be adjusted from its current balance of $95000.

238   Sprike Inc is a market leader that is well-known for their brand of athletic apparel. Sprike Inc has just purchased a building using cash, which has an expected useful life of 30 years, and which had a total cost of $864000.

239   Mr. Mop offers their customers a wide range of household cleaners.  This month, Mr. Mop accepted 2900 tons of cleaning solution which were returned by customers. These products had been marked up by 35% and they had originally been bought at a per-unit cost of $2800.

240   A to Z Event Guru Ltd sells various start-to-finish event planning services for large gatherings.  This month, A to Z Event Guru Ltd has estimated that 10% of the accounts receivable might not end up being collectable, based on past experience. The accounts receivable will need to be adjusted from its current balance of $45000.

241   Cirque du Lune is a company which offers their customers a wide selection of circus performances.  This December, Cirque du Lune recognized 1 year of depreciation on equipment which had a total useful life of 10 years, and which had originally cost $80000.

242   Hogtown Records is an organization which specializes in providing their customers with audio services for local musicians to record their music albums. This December, Hogtown Records recognized 1 year of depreciation on equipment which had a total useful life of 10 years, and which had originally cost $200000.

243     NY Fitness is a market leader that is well-known for their brand of gym memberships for professional sports teams. This year, NY Fitness has provided 1200 team memberships each of which earned revenues of $1760.

244     Pharma Drug Company Ltd. is an organization which specializes in providing their customers with medications. This week, Pharma Drug Company Ltd. paid each of the 3620 staff members their bi-weekly wages, which per person had a cost of $1800.

245     Grand Convention Ltd offers their customers a wide range of banquet hall rentals for corporate meetings. Today Grand Convention Ltd signed up for a loan with a 5% interest rate, and so the bank immediately transferred cash to the company in the amount of $65000.

246     Fairway Malls is a company which offers their customers a wide selection of retail spaces in their shopping centers. This December, Fairway Malls recognized 1 year of depreciation on equipment which had a total useful life of 10 years, and which had originally cost $120000.

247     LA Met Theatre Company is a company which offers their customers a wide selection of live theatrical performances. Today, LA Met Theatre Company received payment upfront for 1600 large orders which will not be provided until early next year. Each order was in the amount of $2700.

248     Kola-Nut Ltd is a company which offers their customers a wide selection of soft drinks. This month, Kola-Nut Ltd paid for 1 month of rent for the warehouse room, which has a monthly cost of $2600.

249     David & Johnson is a market leader that is well-known for their brand of legal services. This December, David & Johnson recognized 1 year of depreciation on a building which had a total useful life of 25 years, and which had originally been bought for $308000.

250     McGerald's sells several different types of fast food meals. Today McGerald's signed up for a loan with a 5% interest rate, and so the bank immediately transferred cash to the company in the amount of $89000.

251     Club Disco is a market leader that is well-known for their brand of dance venue rentals for large family gatherings. This December, Club Disco recognized 1 year of depreciation on a building which had a total useful life of 25 years, and which had originally been bought for $326000.

252     Fairway Malls offers their customers a wide range of retail spaces in their shopping centers. This month, Fairway Malls paid 1 monthly loan repayment towards their long-term note payable. The interest portion was 60% of the payment. The total amount paid in cash was $9000.

253 Sprike Inc is a company which offers their customers a wide selection of athletic apparel. Sprike Inc has just purchased a building using cash, which has an expected useful life of 30 years, and which had a total cost of $177000.

254 NBG Media Corporation sells several different types of broadcasting services for advertising agencies. Today, NBG Media Corporation bought equipment which has a 5 year useful life, and which had a cost of $10000.

255 Mr. Mop provides their customers with household cleaners. This December, Mr. Mop recognized 1 year of depreciation on a building which had a total useful life of 25 years, and which had originally been bought for $891000.

256 Grand Convention Ltd is an organization which specializes in providing their customers with banquet hall rentals for corporate meetings. This December, Grand Convention Ltd recognized 1 year of depreciation on equipment which had a total useful life of 10 years, and which had originally cost $210000.

257 Club Disco sells several different types of dance venue rentals for large family gatherings. Club Disco has just provided 1700 large orders which had been paid for in advance last year. Each order was in the amount of $1500.

258 Air America sells several different types of global flights. Today, Air America bought equipment which has a 5 year useful life, and which had a cost of $16000.

259 Hogtown Records sells several different types of audio services for local musicians to record their music albums. This month, Hogtown Records must amortize 1 month worth of utility bills which they had prepaid at the beginning of the year. The amount that they had paid upfront for the year was $18000.

260 Toyonda is a market leader that is well-known for their brand of cars. This January, Toyonda has made an advance payment to cover the next 12 months of utility bills, which have a monthly cost of $1300.

261 LA Met Theatre Company is an organization which specializes in providing their customers with live theatrical performances. This year, LA Met Theatre Company has provided 1100 shows each of which earned revenues of $1080.

262 Toyonda sells several different types of cars. This December, Toyonda recognized 1 year of depreciation on a building which had a total useful life of 25 years, and which had originally been bought for $464000.

263 A to Z Event Guru Ltd is a privately-held corporation which focuses on their niche of premium start-to-finish event planning services for large gatherings. This year, A to Z Event Guru Ltd has provided 1600 events each of which earned revenues of $2390.

264     Cirque du Lune is a corporation which sells circus performances. Today Cirque du Lune signed up for a loan with a 5% interest rate, and so the bank immediately transferred cash to the company in the amount of $84000.

265     Jameson & Jameson is a company which offers their customers a wide selection of soap products. This December, Jameson & Jameson recognized 1 year of depreciation on a building which had a total useful life of 25 years, and which had originally been bought for $459000.

266     Pharma Drug Company Ltd. sells several different types of medications. Today Pharma Drug Company Ltd. sold 44300 batches of pills which had a 30% mark-up. They had originally been bought from their suppliers for a unit cost of $2170.

267     Kola-Nut Ltd sells various soft drinks. This week, Kola-Nut Ltd purchased 2220 batches of soda bottles which were placed into the warehouse, and which had a per-unit cost of $1000.

268     Toyonda provides their customers with cars. This month, Toyonda paid 1 monthly loan repayment towards their long-term note payable. The interest portion was 60% of the payment. The total amount paid in cash was $23000.

269     Air America sells various global flights. This December, Air America recognized 1 year of depreciation on a building which had a total useful life of 25 years, and which had originally been bought for $461000.

270     Paytech Ltd sells several different types of payroll transaction processing services. This December, Paytech Ltd has paid each of the company's 1100 owners an annual dividend in the amount of $19000.

271     Fairway Malls provides their customers with retail spaces in their shopping centers. This month, Fairway Malls paid for 1 month of rent for their company's office space. Each month, the rent owing was $16000.

272     Hogtown Records sells various audio services for local musicians to record their music albums. This December, Hogtown Records recognized 1 year of depreciation on equipment which had a total useful life of 10 years, and which had originally cost $230000.

273     Pharma Drug Company Ltd. is an organization which specializes in providing their customers with medications. Today Pharma Drug Company Ltd. sold 52700 batches of pills which had a 30% mark-up. They had originally been bought from their suppliers for a unit cost of $2630.

274     A to Z Event Guru Ltd offers their customers a wide range of start-to-finish event planning services. A to Z Event Guru Ltd has just provided 1600 large orders which had been paid for in advance last year. Each order was in the amount of $2700.

275    Kola-Nut Ltd sells several different types of soft drinks. This month, Kola-Nut Ltd paid for 1 month of rent for the warehouse room, which has a monthly cost of $1400.

276    Sprike Inc sells several different types of athletic apparel. This month, Sprike Inc has estimated that 15% of the accounts receivable might not end up being collectable, based on past experience. The accounts receivable will need to be adjusted from its current balance of $25000.

277    AC&C Ltd. sells several different types of cell phone plans. This December, AC&C Ltd. recognized 1 year of depreciation on a building which had a total useful life of 25 years, and which had originally been bought for $615000.

278    Air America provides their customers with global flights. This year, Air America has provided 1400 flights each of which earned revenues of $2920.

279    Sprike Inc is a corporation which sells athletic apparel. This month, Sprike Inc has estimated that 5% of the accounts receivable might not end up being collectable, based on past experience. The accounts receivable will need to be adjusted from its current balance of $50000.

280    Mr. Mop offers their customers a wide range of household cleaners. This month, Mr. Mop accepted 25900 tons of cleaning solution which were returned by customers. These products had been marked up by 35% and they had originally been bought at a per-unit cost of $1500.

281    Sprike Inc is a corporation which sells athletic apparel. Today, Sprike Inc received an upfront payment for 3060 batches of athletic t-shirts which will be provided to the customer 6 months from now. The payment for each was $1500.

282    Pharma Drug Company Ltd. offers their customers a wide range of medications. Today, Pharma Drug Company Ltd. received an upfront payment for 1950 batches of pills which will be provided to the customer 6 months from now. The payment for each was $2000.

283    Jameson & Jameson is an organization which specializes in providing their customers with soap products. This month, Jameson & Jameson accepted 10800 truckloads of bars of soap which were returned by customers. These products had been marked up by 35% and they had originally been bought at a per-unit cost of $2700.

284    Jameson & Jameson offers their customers a wide range of soap products. Today Jameson & Jameson sold 35400 truckloads of bars of soap which had a 30% mark-up. They had originally been bought from their suppliers for a unit cost of $1330.

285 Fairway Malls is a privately-held corporation which focuses on their niche of premium retail spaces in their shopping centers. Fairway Malls has just purchased a building using cash, which has an expected useful life of 30 years, and which had a total cost of $23000.

286 Mr. Mop is a privately-held corporation which focuses on their niche of premium household cleaners. Today, Mr. Mop bought equipment which has a 5 year useful life, and which had a cost of $20000.

287 Payday Now sells several different types of short-term loan arrangements. This month, Payday Now must amortize 1 month worth of utility bills which they had prepaid at the beginning of the year. The amount that they had paid upfront for the year was $22800.

288 Payday Now is a market leader that is well-known for their brand of short-term loan arrangements. This December, Payday Now has paid each of the company's 2300 owners an annual dividend in the amount of $20000.

289 Fairway Malls is an organization which specializes in providing their customers with retail spaces in their shopping centers. Fairway Malls has just purchased a building using cash, which has an expected useful life of 30 years, and which had a total cost of $323000.

290 AC&C Ltd. sells several different types of cell phone plans. Today, AC&C Ltd. received payment upfront for 1600 large orders which will not be provided until early next year. Each order was in the amount of $2600.

291 Jameson & Jameson sells various soap products. This month, Jameson & Jameson paid for 1 month of rent for the warehouse room, which has a monthly cost of $2700.

292 Payday Now is a market leader that is well-known for their brand of short-term loan arrangements. This month, Payday Now paid for 1 month of rent for their company's office space. Each month, the rent owing was $18000.

293 Hogtown Records is a market leader that is well-known for their brand of audio services for local musicians to record their music albums. Today, Hogtown Records bought equipment which has a 5 year useful life, and which had a cost of $17000.

294 Sprike Inc sells several different types of athletic apparel. This month, Sprike Inc paid for 1 month of rent for the warehouse room, which has a monthly cost of $2300.

295 Pharma Drug Company Ltd. is a market leader that is well-known for their brand of medications. This month, Pharma Drug Company Ltd. paid for 1 month of rent for the warehouse room, which has a monthly cost of $2800.

296    Toyonda offers their customers a wide range of cars. This week, Toyonda paid each of the 1290 staff members their bi-weekly wages, which per person had a cost of $1300.

297    Club Disco is a company which offers their customers a wide selection of dance venue rentals for large family gatherings. This month, Club Disco paid for 1 month of rent for their company's office space. Each month, the rent owing was $22000.

298    NY Fitness is a privately-held corporation which focuses on their niche of premium gym memberships for professional sports teams. NY Fitness has just purchased a building using cash, which has an expected useful life of 30 years, and which had a total cost of $373000.

299    Payday Now is an organization which specializes in providing their customers with short-term loan arrangements. This week, Payday Now paid each of the 1070 staff members their bi-weekly wages, which per person had a cost of $2700.

300    Sprike Inc offers their customers a wide range of athletic apparel. This week, Sprike Inc purchased 4480 batches of athletic t-shirts which were placed into the warehouse, and which had a per-unit cost of $2300.

301    Kola-Nut Ltd is a market leader that is well-known for their brand of soft drinks. Today Kola-Nut Ltd sold 35900 batches of soda bottles which had a 30% mark-up. They had originally been bought from their suppliers for a unit cost of $2770.

302    Sprike Inc is an organization which specializes in providing their customers with athletic apparel. Today, Sprike Inc received an upfront payment for 4580 batches of athletic t-shirts which will be provided to the customer 6 months from now. The payment for each was $2400.

303    David & Johnson offers their customers a wide range of legal services. This month, David & Johnson has estimated that 5% of the accounts receivable might not end up being collectable, based on past experience. The accounts receivable will need to be adjusted from its current balance of $34000.

304    McGerald's sells various fast food meals. McGerald's has just purchased a building using cash, which has an expected useful life of 30 years, and which had a total cost of $360000.

305    Air America is a corporation which sells global flights. This December, Air America recognized 1 year of depreciation on equipment which had a total useful life of 10 years, and which had originally cost $80000.

306     NBG Media Corporation is an organization which specializes in providing their customers with broadcasting services for advertising agencies. Today, NBG Media Corporation has paid cash to their supplier to fully pay off their account payable balance, which was $30000.

307     McGerald's is a market leader that is well-known for their brand of fast food meals. This December, McGerald's has paid each of the company's 1800 owners an annual dividend in the amount of $15000.

308     Fairway Malls sells various retail spaces in their shopping centers. This month, Fairway Malls paid for 1 month of rent for their company's office space. Each month, the rent owing was $22000.

309     Kola-Nut Ltd sells several different types of soft drinks. Today Kola-Nut Ltd sold 39100 batches of soda bottles which had a 30% mark-up. They had originally been bought from their suppliers for a unit cost of $1220.

310     NY Fitness is a privately-held corporation which focuses on their niche of premium gym memberships for professional sports teams. This week, NY Fitness paid each of the 2760 staff members their bi-weekly wages, which per person had a cost of $1400.

311     AC&C Ltd. sells various cell phone plans. This December, AC&C Ltd. recognized 1 year of depreciation on a building which had a total useful life of 25 years, and which had originally been bought for $801000.

312     Grand Convention Ltd sells various banquet hall rentals for corporate meetings. This December, Grand Convention Ltd recognized 1 year of depreciation on equipment which had a total useful life of 10 years, and which had originally cost $100000.

313     Comedy 253 is a privately-held corporation which focuses on their niche of premium live performances of stand-up comedy. This December, Comedy 253 recognized 1 year of depreciation on equipment which had a total useful life of 10 years, and which had originally cost $200000.

314     Paytech Ltd is a corporation which sells payroll transaction processing services. This month, Paytech Ltd must amortize 1 month worth of utility bills which they had prepaid at the beginning of the year. The amount that they had paid upfront for the year was $42000.

315     Kola-Nut Ltd sells several different types of soft drinks. This month, Kola-Nut Ltd paid 1 monthly loan repayment towards their long-term note payable. The interest portion was 60% of the payment. The total amount paid in cash was $12000.

316 Jameson & Jameson sells various soap products. Today Jameson & Jameson signed up for a loan with a 5% interest rate, and so the bank immediately transferred cash to the company in the amount of $96000.

317 Mr. Mop is a privately-held corporation which focuses on their niche of premium household cleaners. This month, Mr. Mop paid for 1 month of rent for the warehouse room, which has a monthly cost of $1100.

318 Fairway Malls is a market leader that is well-known for their brand of retail spaces in their shopping centers. This December, Fairway Malls recognized 1 year of depreciation on equipment which had a total useful life of 10 years, and which had originally cost $190000.

319 Kola-Nut Ltd is an organization which specializes in providing their customers with soft drinks. Today, Kola-Nut Ltd has paid cash to their supplier to fully pay off their account payable balance, which was $26000.

320 Sprike Inc offers their customers a wide range of athletic apparel. This December, Sprike Inc recognized 1 year of depreciation on a building which had a total useful life of 25 years, and which had originally been bought for $61000.

321 Mr. Mop provides their customers with household cleaners. Today, Mr. Mop received an upfront payment for 5090 tons of cleaning solution which will be provided to the customer 6 months from now. The payment for each was $2000.

322 Pharma Drug Company Ltd. is a market leader that is well-known for their brand of medications. This week, Pharma Drug Company Ltd. purchased 5510 batches of pills which were placed into the warehouse, and which had a per-unit cost of $1300.

323 A to Z Event Guru Ltd is a company which offers their customers a wide selection of start-to-finish event planning services for large gatherings. This year, A to Z Event Guru Ltd has provided 1000 events each of which earned revenues of $1910.

324 Sprike Inc is a corporation which sells athletic apparel. Today, Sprike Inc bought equipment which has a 5 year useful life, and which had a cost of $8000.

325 Mount Tessory Academy offers their customers a wide range of private school education. This December, Mount Tessory Academy has paid each of the company's 1600 owners an annual dividend in the amount of $16000.

326 Comedy 253 is a company which offers their customers a wide selection of live performances of stand-up comedy. This year, Comedy 253 has provided 2200 shows each of which earned revenues of $1080.

327 Toyonda is a corporation which sells cars. This December, Toyonda recognized 1 year of depreciation on equipment which had a total useful life of 10 years, and which had originally cost $150000.

328 Grand Convention Ltd sells several different types of banquet hall rentals for corporate meetings. Today, Grand Convention Ltd bought equipment which has a 5 year useful life, and which had a cost of $24000.

329 NY Fitness is a privately-held corporation which focuses on their niche of premium gym memberships for professional sports teams. This January, NY Fitness has made an advance payment to cover the next 12 months of utility bills, which have a monthly cost of $2000.

330 Mr. Mop offers their customers a wide range of household cleaners. Today, Mr. Mop received an upfront payment for 1420 tons of cleaning solution which will be provided to the customer 6 months from now. The payment for each was $1600.

331 Jameson & Jameson is a company which offers their customers a wide selection of soap products. This month, Jameson & Jameson accepted 27900 truckloads of bars of soap which were returned by customers. These products had been marked up by 35% and they had originally been bought at a per-unit cost of $2300.

332 Kola-Nut Ltd is a market leader that is well-known for their brand of soft drinks. This month, Kola-Nut Ltd accepted 29400 batches of soda bottles which were returned by customers. These products had been marked up by 35% and they had originally been bought at a per-unit cost of $1300.

333 Pharma Drug Company Ltd. is an organization which specializes in providing their customers with medications. This month, Pharma Drug Company Ltd. paid for 1 month of rent for the warehouse room, which has a monthly cost of $1000.

334 NY Fitness sells various gym memberships for professional sports teams. Today, NY Fitness received payment upfront for 1800 large orders which will not be provided until early next year. Each order was in the amount of $2500.

335 NBG Media Corporation is a company which offers their customers a wide selection of broadcasting services for advertising agencies. This week, NBG Media Corporation paid each of the 1230 staff members their bi-weekly wages, which per person had a cost of $2100.

336 A to Z Event Guru Ltd is an organization which specializes in providing their customers with start-to-finish event planning services for large gatherings. Today, A to Z Event Guru Ltd has paid cash to their supplier to fully pay off their account payable balance, which was $69000.

337    Pharma Drug Company Ltd. provides their customers with medications. Pharma Drug Company Ltd. has just received a cash payment for the full amount that this customer owed to the company for all of their purchases to date. The outstanding balance which has now been paid was $92000.

338    A to Z Event Guru Ltd is a privately-held corporation which focuses on their niche of premium start-to-finish event planning services for large gatherings. A to Z Event Guru Ltd has just provided 1500 large orders which had been paid for in advance last year. Each order was in the amount of $1800.

339    A to Z Event Guru Ltd is a company which offers their customers a wide selection of start-to-finish event planning services for large gatherings. Today, A to Z Event Guru Ltd received payment upfront for 1800 large orders which will not be provided until early next year. Each order was in the amount of $1600.

340    Mr. Mop is a company which offers their customers a wide selection of household cleaners. Today, Mr. Mop has paid cash to their supplier to fully pay off their account payable balance, which was $13000.

341    Mount Tessory Academy is a corporation which sells private school education. This December, Mount Tessory Academy recognized 1 year of depreciation on equipment which had a total useful life of 10 years, and which had originally cost $110000.

342    Kola-Nut Ltd sells several different types of soft drinks. This week, Kola-Nut Ltd purchased 1490 batches of soda bottles which were placed into the warehouse, and which had a per-unit cost of $1200.

343    Hogtown Records is an organization which specializes in providing their customers with audio services for local musicians to record their music albums. This year, Hogtown Records has provided 1400 albums each of which earned revenues of $2260.

344    Sprike Inc is a corporation which sells athletic apparel. This month, Sprike Inc accepted 20600 batches of athletic t-shirts which were returned by customers. These products had been marked up by 35% and they had originally been bought at a per-unit cost of $2200.

345    Cirque du Lune is a privately-held corporation which focuses on their niche of premium circus performances. This December, Cirque du Lune has paid each of the company's 2400 owners an annual dividend in the amount of $25000.

346    David & Johnson is a company which offers their customers a wide selection of legal services. Today, David & Johnson bought equipment which has a 5 year useful life, and which had a cost of $14000.

347    Pharma Drug Company Ltd. is a privately-held corporation which focuses on their niche of premium medications. This month, Pharma Drug Company Ltd. must amortize 1 month worth of utility bills which they had prepaid at the beginning of the year. The amount that they had paid upfront for the year was $13200.

348    Mr. Mop is an organization which specializes in providing their customers with household cleaners. This month, Mr. Mop accepted 23300 tons of cleaning solution which were returned by customers. These products had been marked up by 35% and they had originally been bought at a per-unit cost of $1300.

349    Mount Tessory Academy offers their customers a wide range of private school education. This year, Mount Tessory Academy has provided 1400 annual tuition memberships each of which earned revenues of $2420.

350    Pharma Drug Company Ltd. sells several different types of medications. Today, Pharma Drug Company Ltd. received an upfront payment for 3730 batches of pills which will be provided to the customer 6 months from now. The payment for each was $2600.

351    Kola-Nut Ltd sells various soft drinks. This month, Kola-Nut Ltd accepted 20200 batches of soda bottles which were returned by customers. These products had been marked up by 35% and they had originally been bought at a per-unit cost of $1000.

352    Payday Now is an organization which specializes in providing their customers with short-term loan arrangements. Today Payday Now signed up for a loan with a 5% interest rate, and so the bank immediately transferred cash to the company in the amount of $44000.

353    Mr. Mop is a corporation which sells household cleaners. This week, Mr. Mop purchased 3760 tons of cleaning solution which were placed into the warehouse, and which had a per-unit cost of $1200.

354    NY Fitness is a privately-held corporation which focuses on their niche of premium gym memberships for professional sports teams. This December, NY Fitness has paid each of the company's 2100 owners an annual dividend in the amount of $21000.

355    Jameson & Jameson is an organization which specializes in providing their customers with soap products. Today Jameson & Jameson sold 45300 truckloads of bars of soap which had a 30% mark-up. They had originally been bought from their suppliers for a unit cost of $1480.

356    Pharma Drug Company Ltd. is an organization which specializes in providing their customers with medications. This week, Pharma Drug Company Ltd. purchased 2020 batches of pills which were placed into the warehouse, and which had a per-unit cost of $1500.

357 Mount Tessory Academy offers their customers a wide range of private school education. Today Mount Tessory Academy signed up for a loan with a 5% interest rate, and so the bank immediately transferred cash to the company in the amount of $112000.

358 Fairway Malls is a company which offers their customers a wide selection of retail spaces in their shopping centers. This December, Fairway Malls recognized 1 year of depreciation on a building which had a total useful life of 25 years, and which had originally been bought for $81000.

359 Cirque du Lune is a privately-held corporation which focuses on their niche of premium circus performances. This December, Cirque du Lune recognized 1 year of depreciation on a building which had a total useful life of 25 years, and which had originally been bought for $211000.

360 Kola-Nut Ltd is a company which offers their customers a wide selection of soft drinks. Today Kola-Nut Ltd sold 15400 batches of soda bottles which had a 30% mark-up. They had originally been bought from their suppliers for a unit cost of $2950.

361 Kola-Nut Ltd offers their customers a wide range of soft drinks. This December, Kola-Nut Ltd has paid each of the company's 1300 owners an annual dividend in the amount of $26000.

362 Comedy 253 is an organization which specializes in providing their customers with live performances of stand-up comedy. This month, Comedy 253 has estimated that 10% of the accounts receivable might not end up being collectable, based on past experience. The accounts receivable will need to be adjusted from its current balance of $45000.

363 Kola-Nut Ltd is a corporation which sells soft drinks. Today Kola-Nut Ltd sold 5800 batches of soda bottles which had a 30% mark-up. They had originally been bought from their suppliers for a unit cost of $1430.

364 Pharma Drug Company Ltd. provides their customers with medications. This month, Pharma Drug Company Ltd. accepted 20400 batches of pills which were returned by customers. These products had been marked up by 35% and they had originally been bought at a per-unit cost of $2000.

365 Payday Now offers their customers a wide range of short-term loan arrangements. Today, Payday Now received payment upfront for 2100 large orders which will not be provided until early next year. Each order was in the amount of $2400.

366 Mount Tessory Academy offers their customers a wide range of private school education. Today, Mount Tessory Academy received payment upfront for 1600 large orders which will not be provided until early next year. Each order was in the amount of $1900.

367 Cirque du Lune offers their customers a wide range of circus performances. This month, Cirque du Lune has estimated that 5% of the accounts receivable might not end up being collectable, based on past experience. The accounts receivable will need to be adjusted from its current balance of $20000.

368 Kola-Nut Ltd is a market leader that is well-known for their brand of soft drinks. Today Kola-Nut Ltd signed up for a loan with a 5% interest rate, and so the bank immediately transferred cash to the company in the amount of $86000.

369 Mr. Mop offers their customers a wide range of household cleaners. Today, Mr. Mop bought equipment which has a 5 year useful life, and which had a cost of $20000.

370 David & Johnson sells several different types of legal services. This month, David & Johnson must amortize 1 month worth of utility bills which they had prepaid at the beginning of the year. The amount that they had paid upfront for the year was $19200.

371 Paytech Ltd is a corporation which sells payroll transaction processing services. This year, Paytech Ltd has provided 2000 batches of transactions for the current period each of which earned revenues of $2860.

372 NBG Media Corporation is an organization which specializes in providing their customers with broadcasting services for advertising agencies. NBG Media Corporation has just received a cash payment for the full amount that this customer owed to the company for all of their purchases to date. The outstanding balance which has now been paid was $69000.

373 Sprike Inc is a market leader that is well-known for their brand of athletic apparel. This month, Sprike Inc accepted 4700 batches of athletic t-shirts which were returned by customers. These products had been marked up by 35% and they had originally been bought at a per-unit cost of $1300.

374 Mount Tessory Academy is a company which offers their customers a wide selection of private school education. This December, Mount Tessory Academy recognized 1 year of depreciation on a building which had a total useful life of 25 years, and which had originally been bought for $168000.

375 Comedy 253 is an organization which specializes in providing their customers with live performances of stand-up comedy. Today, Comedy 253 received payment upfront for 2100 large orders which will not be provided until early next year. Each order was in the amount of $1100.

376     Paytech Ltd offers their customers a wide range of payroll transaction processing services. Today, Paytech Ltd received payment upfront for 1900 large orders which will not be provided until early next year. Each order was in the amount of $1400.

377     Sprike Inc sells several different types of athletic apparel. Today Sprike Inc sold 11200 batches of athletic t-shirts which had a 30% mark-up. They had originally been bought from their suppliers for a unit cost of $2050.

378     Pharma Drug Company Ltd. sells several different types of medications. This week, Pharma Drug Company Ltd. paid each of the 3760 staff members their bi-weekly wages, which per person had a cost of $2400.

379     Hogtown Records is an organization which specializes in providing their customers with audio services for local musicians to record their music albums. This January, Hogtown Records has made an advance payment to cover the next 12 months of utility bills, which have a monthly cost of $1200.

380     McGerald's provides their customers with fast food meals. This year, McGerald's has provided 1100 burger combos each of which earned revenues of $1790.

381     Cirque du Lune is a market leader that is well-known for their brand of circus performances. This December, Cirque du Lune has paid each of the company's 2000 owners an annual dividend in the amount of $18000.

382     Kola-Nut Ltd is a market leader that is well-known for their brand of soft drinks. This month, Kola-Nut Ltd paid for 1 month of rent for the warehouse room, which has a monthly cost of $1300.

383     Kola-Nut Ltd is a privately-held corporation which focuses on their niche of premium soft drinks. Kola-Nut Ltd has just received a cash payment for the full amount that this customer owed to the company for all of their purchases to date. The outstanding balance which has now been paid was $87000.

384     McGerald's offers their customers a wide range of fast food meals. This year, McGerald's has provided 1500 burger combos each of which earned revenues of $1660.

385     LA Met Theatre Company is an organization which specializes in providing their customers with live theatrical performances. This January, LA Met Theatre Company has made an advance payment to cover the next 12 months of utility bills, which have a monthly cost of $1800.

386     Mr. Mop is a corporation which sells household cleaners. Today, Mr. Mop received an upfront payment for 5160 tons of cleaning solution which will be provided to the customer 6 months from now. The payment for each was $1100.

387 Sprike Inc is an organization which specializes in providing their customers with athletic apparel. This month, Sprike Inc paid for 1 month of rent for the warehouse room, which has a monthly cost of $1500.

388 Jameson & Jameson is an organization which specializes in providing their customers with soap products. This week, Jameson & Jameson paid each of the 1800 staff members their bi-weekly wages, which per person had a cost of $1500.

389 Kola-Nut Ltd sells various soft drinks. This month, Kola-Nut Ltd paid for 1 month of rent for their company's office space. Each month, the rent owing was $11000.

390 Sprike Inc sells various athletic apparel. Today Sprike Inc sold 50500 batches of athletic t-shirts which had a 30% mark-up. They had originally been bought from their suppliers for a unit cost of $2370.

391 Pharma Drug Company Ltd. is a corporation which sells medications. This December, Pharma Drug Company Ltd. recognized 1 year of depreciation on equipment which had a total useful life of 10 years, and which had originally cost $140000.

392 Kola-Nut Ltd is a corporation which sells soft drinks. This month, Kola-Nut Ltd accepted 20100 batches of soda bottles which were returned by customers. These products had been marked up by 35% and they had originally been bought at a per-unit cost of $2200.

393 Sprike Inc sells various athletic apparel. Today Sprike Inc signed up for a loan with a 5% interest rate, and so the bank immediately transferred cash to the company in the amount of $82000.

394 Air America sells several different types of global flights. Today Air America signed up for a loan with a 5% interest rate, and so the bank immediately transferred cash to the company in the amount of $112000.

395 A to Z Event Guru Ltd is a company which offers their customers a wide selection of start-to-finish event planning services for large gatherings. A to Z Event Guru Ltd has just provided 2400 large orders which had been paid for in advance last year. Each order was in the amount of $2600.

396 Paytech Ltd is a privately-held corporation which focuses on their niche of premium payroll transaction processing services. Paytech Ltd has just provided 2100 large orders which had been paid for in advance last year. Each order was in the amount of $2000.

397    Mount Tessory Academy offers their customers a wide range of private school education. Mount Tessory Academy has just received a cash payment for the full amount that this customer owed to the company for all of their purchases to date. The outstanding balance which has now been paid was $57000.

398    Kola-Nut Ltd offers their customers a wide range of soft drinks. This month, Kola-Nut Ltd paid for 1 month of rent for the warehouse room, which has a monthly cost of $1900.

399    Mr. Mop is a privately-held corporation which focuses on their niche of premium household cleaners. Today Mr. Mop sold 6600 tons of cleaning solution which had a 30% mark-up. They had originally been bought from their suppliers for a unit cost of $1060.

400    Cirque du Lune offers their customers a wide range of circus performances. This December, Cirque du Lune recognized 1 year of depreciation on a building which had a total useful life of 25 years, and which had originally been bought for $69000.

401    Cirque du Lune is a company which offers their customers a wide selection of circus performances. Today, Cirque du Lune bought equipment which has a 5 year useful life, and which had a cost of $22000.

402    NBG Media Corporation is a corporation which sells broadcasting services for advertising agencies. This December, NBG Media Corporation has paid each of the company's 1900 owners an annual dividend in the amount of $26000.

403    Payday Now is a market leader that is well-known for their brand of short-term loan arrangements. Payday Now has just received a cash payment for the full amount that this customer owed to the company for all of their purchases to date. The outstanding balance which has now been paid was $69000.

404    Sprike Inc is a company which offers their customers a wide selection of athletic apparel. Today Sprike Inc sold 16200 batches of athletic t-shirts which had a 30% mark-up. They had originally been bought from their suppliers for a unit cost of $2780.

405    Paytech Ltd offers their customers a wide range of payroll transaction processing services. Today, Paytech Ltd received payment upfront for 1100 large orders which will not be provided until early next year. Each order was in the amount of $1500.

406    Cirque du Lune sells several different types of circus performances. Today Cirque du Lune signed up for a loan with a 5% interest rate, and so the bank immediately transferred cash to the company in the amount of $84000.

407   LA Met Theatre Company is an organization which specializes in providing their customers with live theatrical performances. Today, LA Met Theatre Company has paid cash to their supplier to fully pay off their account payable balance, which was $47000.

408   Club Disco is a privately-held corporation which focuses on their niche of premium dance venue rentals for large family gatherings. This year, Club Disco has provided 1900 evening rentals each of which earned revenues of $2670.

409   Club Disco sells various dance venue rentals for large family gatherings. This December, Club Disco recognized 1 year of depreciation on a building which had a total useful life of 25 years, and which had originally been bought for $854000.

410   Cirque du Lune sells several different types of circus performances. This year, Cirque du Lune has provided 1700 shows each of which earned revenues of $1590.

411   Mr. Mop provides their customers with household cleaners. Mr. Mop has just purchased a building using cash, which has an expected useful life of 30 years, and which had a total cost of $805000.

412   NBG Media Corporation offers their customers a wide range of broadcasting services for advertising agencies. This month, NBG Media Corporation paid for 1 month of rent for their company's office space. Each month, the rent owing was $19000.

413   Paytech Ltd is an organization which specializes in providing their customers with payroll transaction processing services. This December, Paytech Ltd recognized 1 year of depreciation on equipment which had a total useful life of 10 years, and which had originally cost $110000.

414   Payday Now is a privately-held corporation which focuses on their niche of premium short-term loan arrangements. This month, Payday Now paid 1 monthly loan repayment towards their long-term note payable. The interest portion was 60% of the payment. The total amount paid in cash was $17000.

415   NBG Media Corporation sells several different types of broadcasting services for advertising agencies. NBG Media Corporation has just purchased a building using cash, which has an expected useful life of 30 years, and which had a total cost of $383000.

416   Mr. Mop sells several different types of household cleaners. Mr. Mop has just received a cash payment for the full amount that this customer owed to the company for all of their purchases to date. The outstanding balance which has now been paid was $15000.

417     Pharma Drug Company Ltd. sells several different types of medications. This December, Pharma Drug Company Ltd. has paid each of the company's 1900 owners an annual dividend in the amount of $12000.

418     Cirque du Lune sells various circus performances. This year, Cirque du Lune has provided 1800 shows each of which earned revenues of $1500.

419     NY Fitness is a company which offers their customers a wide selection of gym memberships for professional sports teams. Today, NY Fitness bought equipment which has a 5 year useful life, and which had a cost of $11000.

420     LA Met Theatre Company is a privately-held corporation which focuses on their niche of premium live theatrical performances. LA Met Theatre Company has just provided 2200 large orders which had been paid for in advance last year. Each order was in the amount of $2800.

421     Paytech Ltd is a privately-held corporation which focuses on their niche of premium payroll transaction processing services. This December, Paytech Ltd has paid each of the company's 1900 owners an annual dividend in the amount of $23000.

422     McGerald's is a company which offers their customers a wide selection of fast food meals. This December, McGerald's recognized 1 year of depreciation on equipment which had a total useful life of 10 years, and which had originally cost $110000.

423     LA Met Theatre Company is a market leader that is well-known for their brand of live theatrical performances. LA Met Theatre Company has just received a cash payment for the full amount that this customer owed to the company for all of their purchases to date. The outstanding balance which has now been paid was $39000.

424     Jameson & Jameson is a corporation which sells soap products. This week, Jameson & Jameson purchased 2070 truckloads of bars of soap which were placed into the warehouse, and which had a per-unit cost of $2700.

425     Paytech Ltd sells various payroll transaction processing services. This year, Paytech Ltd has provided 2200 batches of transactions for the current period each of which earned revenues of $2240.

426     Sprike Inc is a privately-held corporation which focuses on their niche of premium athletic apparel. This month, Sprike Inc paid 1 monthly loan repayment towards their long-term note payable. The interest portion was 60% of the payment. The total amount paid in cash was $15000.

427 Comedy 253 sells several different types of live performances of stand-up comedy. This December, Comedy 253 recognized 1 year of depreciation on a building which had a total useful life of 25 years, and which had originally been bought for $376000.

428 Toyonda is an organization which specializes in providing their customers with cars. This December, Toyonda recognized 1 year of depreciation on a building which had a total useful life of 25 years, and which had originally been bought for $220000.

429 Comedy 253 sells various live performances of stand-up comedy. Today, Comedy 253 received payment upfront for 2200 large orders which will not be provided until early next year. Each order was in the amount of $2300.

430 Toyonda sells various cars. This January, Toyonda has made an advance payment to cover the next 12 months of utility bills, which have a monthly cost of $2000.

431 Grand Convention Ltd is an organization which specializes in providing their customers with banquet hall rentals for corporate meetings. Grand Convention Ltd has just provided 2400 large orders which had been paid for in advance last year. Each order was in the amount of $2200.

432 Club Disco sells various dance venue rentals for large family gatherings. Today, Club Disco bought equipment which has a 5 year useful life, and which had a cost of $17000.

433 A to Z Event Guru Ltd is a company which offers their customers a wide selection of start-to-finish event planning services for large gatherings. This January, A to Z Event Guru Ltd has made an advance payment to cover the next 12 months of utility bills, which have a monthly cost of $1000.

434 David & Johnson is a corporation which sells legal services. This year, David & Johnson has provided 2000 billable hours each of which earned revenues of $2100.

435 Sprike Inc sells several different types of athletic apparel. This month, Sprike Inc paid 1 monthly loan repayment towards their long-term note payable. The interest portion was 60% of the payment. The total amount paid in cash was $24000.

436 Fairway Malls offers their customers a wide range of retail spaces in their shopping centers. Fairway Malls has just received a cash payment for the full amount that this customer owed to the company for all of their purchases to date. The outstanding balance which has now been paid was $75000.

437   Pharma Drug Company Ltd. is a privately-held corporation which focuses on their niche of premium medications. Today Pharma Drug Company Ltd. sold 32900 batches of pills which had a 30% mark-up. They had originally been bought from their suppliers for a unit cost of $1460.

438   Kola-Nut Ltd is a company which offers their customers a wide selection of soft drinks. This month, Kola-Nut Ltd must amortize 1 month worth of utility bills which they had prepaid at the beginning of the year. The amount that they had paid upfront for the year was $43200.

439   Pharma Drug Company Ltd. offers their customers a wide range of medications. This month, Pharma Drug Company Ltd. accepted 5900 batches of pills which were returned by customers. These products had been marked up by 35% and they had originally been bought at a per-unit cost of $1400.

440   Kola-Nut Ltd is a company which offers their customers a wide selection of soft drinks. Today, Kola-Nut Ltd received an upfront payment for 4020 batches of soda bottles which will be provided to the customer 6 months from now. The payment for each was $1500.

441   LA Met Theatre Company is a privately-held corporation which focuses on their niche of premium live theatrical performances. LA Met Theatre Company has just purchased a building using cash, which has an expected useful life of 30 years, and which had a total cost of $392000.

442   Mount Tessory Academy sells several different types of private school education. This month, Mount Tessory Academy has estimated that 20% of the accounts receivable might not end up being collectable, based on past experience. The accounts receivable will need to be adjusted from its current balance of $86000.

443   NY Fitness provides their customers with gym memberships for professional sports teams. This January, NY Fitness has made an advance payment to cover the next 12 months of utility bills, which have a monthly cost of $2800.

444   Hogtown Records is a privately-held corporation which focuses on their niche of premium audio services for local musicians to record their music albums. Today, Hogtown Records bought equipment which has a 5 year useful life, and which had a cost of $17000.

445   Grand Convention Ltd provides their customers with banquet hall rentals for corporate meetings. Today, Grand Convention Ltd received payment upfront for 2300 large orders which will not be provided until early next year. Each order was in the amount of $1800.

446   AC&C Ltd. is an organization which specializes in providing their customers with cell phone plans. This week, AC&C Ltd. paid each of the 1770 staff members their bi-weekly wages, which per person had a cost of $2200.

447     Hogtown Records sells various audio services for local musicians to record their music albums. Today Hogtown Records signed up for a loan with a 5% interest rate, and so the bank immediately transferred cash to the company in the amount of $93000.

448     Paytech Ltd is a privately-held corporation which focuses on their niche of premium payroll transaction processing services. Paytech Ltd has just provided 1900 large orders which had been paid for in advance last year. Each order was in the amount of $1000.

449     Grand Convention Ltd provides their customers with banquet hall rentals for corporate meetings. This December, Grand Convention Ltd has paid each of the company's 2100 owners an annual dividend in the amount of $21000.

450     Pharma Drug Company Ltd. sells various medications. Today Pharma Drug Company Ltd. sold 40100 batches of pills which had a 30% mark-up. They had originally been bought from their suppliers for a unit cost of $1680.

451     Jameson & Jameson is a market leader that is well-known for their brand of soap products. Today Jameson & Jameson sold 48700 truckloads of bars of soap which had a 30% mark-up. They had originally been bought from their suppliers for a unit cost of $2870.

452     Club Disco is a market leader that is well-known for their brand of dance venue rentals for large family gatherings. This week, Club Disco paid each of the 1240 staff members their bi-weekly wages, which per person had a cost of $1900.

453     Hogtown Records is a privately-held corporation which focuses on their niche of premium audio services for local musicians to record their music albums. Hogtown Records has just provided 1500 large orders which had been paid for in advance last year. Each order was in the amount of $1600.

454     Pharma Drug Company Ltd. is a company which offers their customers a wide selection of medications. This December, Pharma Drug Company Ltd. recognized 1 year of depreciation on equipment which had a total useful life of 10 years, and which had originally cost $130000.

455     Club Disco is a market leader that is well-known for their brand of dance venue rentals for large family gatherings. Today, Club Disco bought equipment which has a 5 year useful life, and which had a cost of $23000.

456     NBG Media Corporation sells several different types of broadcasting services for advertising agencies. This week, NBG Media Corporation paid each of the 3820 staff members their bi-weekly wages, which per person had a cost of $1700.

457     Air America is a company which offers their customers a wide selection of global flights. Air America has just purchased a building using cash, which has an expected useful life of 30 years, and which had a total cost of $944000.

458     Mount Tessory Academy sells various private school education subscriptions. Mount Tessory Academy has just provided 1700 large orders which had been paid for in advance last year. Each order was in the amount of $1100.

459     Kola-Nut Ltd is a corporation which sells soft drinks. This December, Kola-Nut Ltd recognized 1 year of depreciation on a building which had a total useful life of 25 years, and which had originally been bought for $742000.

460     Fairway Malls is a company which offers their customers a wide selection of retail spaces in their shopping centers. Today, Fairway Malls bought equipment which has a 5 year useful life, and which had a cost of $13000.

461     Fairway Malls is a privately-held corporation which focuses on their niche of premium retail spaces in their shopping centers. This month, Fairway Malls paid 1 monthly loan repayment towards their long-term note payable. The interest portion was 60% of the payment. The total amount paid in cash was $20000.

462     Hogtown Records provides their customers with audio services for local musicians to record their music albums. Today, Hogtown Records has paid cash to their supplier to fully pay off their account payable balance, which was $19000.

463     Sprike Inc is a company which offers their customers a wide selection of athletic apparel. This December, Sprike Inc recognized 1 year of depreciation on a building which had a total useful life of 25 years, and which had originally been bought for $728000.

464     Mount Tessory Academy is a corporation which sells private school education. Mount Tessory Academy has just received a cash payment for the full amount that this customer owed to the company for all of their purchases to date. The outstanding balance which has now been paid was $55000.

465     Jameson & Jameson is a company which offers their customers a wide selection of soap products. This month, Jameson & Jameson accepted 21500 truckloads of bars of soap which were returned by customers. These products had been marked up by 35% and they had originally been bought at a per-unit cost of $1600.

466     NY Fitness is a market leader that is well-known for their brand of gym memberships for professional sports teams. This year, NY Fitness has provided 1500 team memberships each of which earned revenues of $2170.

467     Air America is a corporation which sells global flights. This year, Air America has provided 1000 flights each of which earned revenues of $2380.

468    Kola-Nut Ltd is an organization which specializes in providing their customers with soft drinks. This week, Kola-Nut Ltd purchased 5840 batches of soda bottles which were placed into the warehouse, and which had a per-unit cost of $2200.

469    Hogtown Records is an organization which specializes in providing their customers with audio services for local musicians to record their music albums. This December, Hogtown Records has paid each of the company's 1700 owners an annual dividend in the amount of $15000.

470    A to Z Event Guru Ltd is a market leader that is well-known for their brand of start-to-finish event planning services for large gatherings. This month, A to Z Event Guru Ltd paid for 1 month of rent for their company's office space. Each month, the rent owing was $17000.

471    Jameson & Jameson sells several different types of soap products. Jameson & Jameson has just purchased a building using cash, which has an expected useful life of 30 years, and which had a total cost of $141000.

472    Sprike Inc is a privately-held corporation which focuses on their niche of premium athletic apparel. This month, Sprike Inc paid for 1 month of rent for the warehouse room, which has a monthly cost of $1800.

473    Grand Convention Ltd is a corporation which sells banquet hall rentals for corporate meetings. This December, Grand Convention Ltd has paid each of the company's 1900 owners an annual dividend in the amount of $23000.

474    Jameson & Jameson is an organization which specializes in providing their customers with soap products. Today Jameson & Jameson sold 48800 truckloads of bars of soap which had a 30% mark-up. They had originally been bought from their suppliers for a unit cost of $2150.

475    Air America sells various global flights. Today Air America signed up for a loan with a 5% interest rate, and so the bank immediately transferred cash to the company in the amount of $65000.

476    Sprike Inc is an organization which specializes in providing their customers with athletic apparel. This December, Sprike Inc has paid each of the company's 1100 owners an annual dividend in the amount of $9000.

477    McGerald's is a corporation which sells fast food meals. This month, McGerald's has estimated that 10% of the accounts receivable might not end up being collectable, based on past experience. The accounts receivable will need to be adjusted from its current balance of $22000.

478    Hogtown Records is a corporation which sells audio services for local musicians to record their music albums. Today, Hogtown Records bought equipment which has a 5 year useful life, and which had a cost of $14000.

479    Jameson & Jameson is a company which offers their customers a wide selection of soap products. This month, Jameson & Jameson has estimated that 25% of the accounts receivable might not end up being collectable, based on past experience. The accounts receivable will need to be adjusted from its current balance of $22000.

480    Kola-Nut Ltd sells several different types of soft drinks. This month, Kola-Nut Ltd paid 1 monthly loan repayment towards their long-term note payable. The interest portion was 60% of the payment. The total amount paid in cash was $17000.

481    McGerald's sells various fast food meals. Today, McGerald's received payment upfront for 2300 large orders which will not be provided until early next year. Each order was in the amount of $1500.

482    Jameson & Jameson is a corporation which sells soap products. Today Jameson & Jameson sold 44900 truckloads of bars of soap which had a 30% mark-up. They had originally been bought from their suppliers for a unit cost of $2230.

483    Jameson & Jameson sells various soap products. Today Jameson & Jameson sold 28400 truckloads of bars of soap which had a 30% mark-up. They had originally been bought from their suppliers for a unit cost of $2480.

484    Jameson & Jameson sells various soap products. This month, Jameson & Jameson paid 1 monthly loan repayment towards their long-term note payable. The interest portion was 60% of the payment. The total amount paid in cash was $24000.

485    Mr. Mop is an organization which specializes in providing their customers with household cleaners. This week, Mr. Mop purchased 4300 tons of cleaning solution which were placed into the warehouse, and which had a per-unit cost of $1500.

486    Jameson & Jameson offers their customers a wide range of soap products. This month, Jameson & Jameson paid for 1 month of rent for the warehouse room, which has a monthly cost of $2600.

487    Paytech Ltd is a corporation which sells payroll transaction processing services. This January, Paytech Ltd has made an advance payment to cover the next 12 months of utility bills, which have a monthly cost of $1800.

488    Cirque du Lune provides their customers with circus performances. This January, Cirque du Lune has made an advance payment to cover the next 12 months of utility bills, which have a monthly cost of $2700.

489    Mount Tessory Academy sells several different types of private school education. Mount Tessory Academy has just received a cash payment for the full amount that this customer owed to the company for all of their purchases to date. The outstanding balance which has now been paid was $40000.

490    Sprike Inc is a market leader that is well-known for their brand of athletic apparel. Today Sprike Inc sold 27300 batches of athletic t-shirts which had a 30% mark-up. They had originally been bought from their suppliers for a unit cost of $1020.

491    Comedy 253 sells several different types of live performances of stand-up comedy. This December, Comedy 253 has paid each of the company's 1100 owners an annual dividend in the amount of $14000.

492    Kola-Nut Ltd sells several different types of soft drinks. This December, Kola-Nut Ltd recognized 1 year of depreciation on equipment which had a total useful life of 10 years, and which had originally cost $190000.

493    Comedy 253 sells various live performances of stand-up comedy. This December, Comedy 253 recognized 1 year of depreciation on equipment which had a total useful life of 10 years, and which had originally cost $110000.

494    Jameson & Jameson is a corporation which sells soap products. This week, Jameson & Jameson paid each of the 1420 staff members their bi-weekly wages, which per person had a cost of $2500.

495    Paytech Ltd is an organization which specializes in providing their customers with payroll transaction processing services. This December, Paytech Ltd has paid each of the company's 1400 owners an annual dividend in the amount of $12000.

496    NBG Media Corporation is a market leader that is well-known for their brand of broadcasting services for advertising agencies. Today, NBG Media Corporation has paid cash to their supplier to fully pay off their account payable balance, which was $33000.

497    Toyonda offers their customers a wide range of cars. This December, Toyonda has paid each of the company's 1600 owners an annual dividend in the amount of $17000.

498    Grand Convention Ltd is a corporation which sells banquet hall rentals for corporate meetings. This January, Grand Convention Ltd has made an advance payment to cover the next 12 months of utility bills, which have a monthly cost of $2800.

499     Grand Convention Ltd is a market leader that is well-known for their brand of banquet hall rentals for corporate meetings. Today, Grand Convention Ltd bought equipment which has a 5 year useful life, and which had a cost of $18000.

500     Kola-Nut Ltd provides their customers with soft drinks. Today Kola-Nut Ltd sold 37200 batches of soda bottles which had a 30% mark-up. They had originally been bought from their suppliers for a unit cost of $1370.

501     Hogtown Records is a company which offers their customers a wide selection of audio services for local musicians to record their music albums. This month, Hogtown Records paid 1 monthly loan repayment towards their long-term note payable. The interest portion was 60% of the payment. The total amount paid in cash was $24000.

502     Jameson & Jameson is a market leader that is well-known for their brand of soap products. Today Jameson & Jameson sold 44800 truckloads of bars of soap which had a 30% mark-up. They had originally been bought from their suppliers for a unit cost of $1440.

503     Mr. Mop is a company which offers their customers a wide selection of household cleaners. This month, Mr. Mop has estimated that 15% of the accounts receivable might not end up being collectable, based on past experience. The accounts receivable will need to be adjusted from its current balance of $79000.

504     Hogtown Records is a company which offers their customers a wide selection of audio services for local musicians to record their music albums. This December, Hogtown Records has paid each of the company's 2400 owners an annual dividend in the amount of $15000.

505     Pharma Drug Company Ltd. is a market leader that is well-known for their brand of medications. Today Pharma Drug Company Ltd. sold 23800 batches of pills which had a 30% mark-up. They had originally been bought from their suppliers for a unit cost of $2410.

506     AC&C Ltd. provides their customers with cell phone plans. This year, AC&C Ltd. has provided 1300 monthly cell phone service each of which earned revenues of $1260.

507     Paytech Ltd is an organization which specializes in providing their customers with payroll transaction processing services. This month, Paytech Ltd paid 1 monthly loan repayment towards their long-term note payable. The interest portion was 60% of the payment. The total amount paid in cash was $18000.

508     David & Johnson provides their customers with legal services. Today, David & Johnson has paid cash to their supplier to fully pay off their account payable balance, which was $76000.

509    Kola-Nut Ltd offers their customers a wide range of soft drinks. Today, Kola-Nut Ltd received an upfront payment for 2140 batches of soda bottles which will be provided to the customer 6 months from now. The payment for each was $2400.

510    Mr. Mop is a privately-held corporation which focuses on their niche of premium household cleaners. Today, Mr. Mop received an upfront payment for 4690 tons of cleaning solution which will be provided to the customer 6 months from now. The payment for each was $2000.

511    Toyonda is a market leader that is well-known for their brand of cars. This December, Toyonda recognized 1 year of depreciation on a building which had a total useful life of 25 years, and which had originally been bought for $522000.

512    NY Fitness is a corporation which sells gym memberships for professional sports teams. This month, NY Fitness has estimated that 5% of the accounts receivable might not end up being collectable, based on past experience. The accounts receivable will need to be adjusted from its current balance of $42000.

513    NY Fitness offers their customers a wide range of gym memberships for professional sports teams. This January, NY Fitness has made an advance payment to cover the next 12 months of utility bills, which have a monthly cost of $2000.

514    Sprike Inc provides their customers with athletic apparel. Sprike Inc has just received a cash payment for the full amount that this customer owed to the company for all of their purchases to date. The outstanding balance which has now been paid was $70000.

515    NBG Media Corporation is a company which offers their customers a wide selection of broadcasting services for advertising agencies. This month, NBG Media Corporation must amortize 1 month worth of utility bills which they had prepaid at the beginning of the year. The amount that they had paid upfront for the year was $18000.

516    David & Johnson is a company which offers their customers a wide selection of legal services. This month, David & Johnson must amortize 1 month worth of utility bills which they had prepaid at the beginning of the year. The amount that they had paid upfront for the year was $21600.

517    Pharma Drug Company Ltd. is a corporation which sells medications. Today Pharma Drug Company Ltd. sold 15200 batches of pills which had a 30% mark-up. They had originally been bought from their suppliers for a unit cost of $1450.

518    Cirque du Lune is a market leader that is well-known for their brand of circus performances. Today, Cirque du Lune bought equipment which has a 5 year useful life, and which had a cost of $11000.

519    Club Disco is an organization which specializes in providing their customers with dance venue rentals for large family gatherings. This January, Club Disco has made an advance payment to cover the next 12 months of utility bills, which have a monthly cost of $2300.

520    Cirque du Lune provides their customers with circus performances. This month, Cirque du Lune has estimated that 30% of the accounts receivable might not end up being collectable, based on past experience. The accounts receivable will need to be adjusted from its current balance of $66000.

521    LA Met Theatre Company is a market leader that is well-known for their brand of live theatrical performances. This December, LA Met Theatre Company recognized 1 year of depreciation on a building which had a total useful life of 25 years, and which had originally been bought for $910000.

522    AC&C Ltd. provides their customers with cell phone plans. This month, AC&C Ltd. paid for 1 month of rent for their company's office space. Each month, the rent owing was $15000.

523    Comedy 253 sells various live performances of stand-up comedy. Today, Comedy 253 received payment upfront for 1700 large orders which will not be provided until early next year. Each order was in the amount of $1900.

524    Kola-Nut Ltd offers their customers a wide range of soft drinks. This week, Kola-Nut Ltd purchased 5240 batches of soda bottles which were placed into the warehouse, and which had a per-unit cost of $1000.

525    Club Disco is an organization which specializes in providing their customers with dance venue rentals for large family gatherings. This month, Club Disco has estimated that 25% of the accounts receivable might not end up being collectable, based on past experience. The accounts receivable will need to be adjusted from its current balance of $81000.

526    Hogtown Records is a privately-held corporation which focuses on their niche of premium audio services for local musicians to record their music albums. This December, Hogtown Records has paid each of the company's 1800 owners an annual dividend in the amount of $13000.

527    Hogtown Records provides their customers with audio services for local musicians to record their music albums. This year, Hogtown Records has provided 1300 albums each of which earned revenues of $1750.

528    David & Johnson is a company which offers their customers a wide selection of legal services. Today David & Johnson signed up for a loan with a 5% interest rate, and so the bank immediately transferred cash to the company in the amount of $116000.

529    NBG Media Corporation is a market leader that is well-known for their brand of broadcasting services for advertising agencies.  Today, NBG Media Corporation bought equipment which has a 5 year useful life, and which had a cost of $9000.

530    David & Johnson is a market leader that is well-known for their brand of legal services.  David & Johnson has just received a cash payment for the full amount that this customer owed to the company for all of their purchases to date. The outstanding balance which has now been paid was $16000.

531    Pharma Drug Company Ltd. sells various medications.  This month, Pharma Drug Company Ltd. paid for 1 month of rent for the warehouse room, which has a monthly cost of $1100.

532    Kola-Nut Ltd is a corporation which sells soft drinks.  This month, Kola-Nut Ltd paid for 1 month of rent for their company's office space. Each month, the rent owing was $17000.

533    Kola-Nut Ltd is an organization which specializes in providing their customers with soft drinks.  This month, Kola-Nut Ltd paid for 1 month of rent for the warehouse room, which has a monthly cost of $1200.

534    Kola-Nut Ltd provides their customers with soft drinks.  This week, Kola-Nut Ltd purchased 4470 batches of soda bottles which were placed into the warehouse, and which had a per-unit cost of $1800.

535    Grand Convention Ltd offers their customers a wide range of banquet hall rentals for corporate meetings.  This month, Grand Convention Ltd paid for 1 month of rent for their company's office space. Each month, the rent owing was $15000.

536    Jameson & Jameson is a company which offers their customers a wide selection of soap products.  Today Jameson & Jameson signed up for a loan with a 5% interest rate, and so the bank immediately transferred cash to the company in the amount of $112000.

537    NY Fitness sells various gym memberships for professional sports teams.  This December, NY Fitness recognized 1 year of depreciation on a building which had a total useful life of 25 years, and which had originally been bought for $974000.

538    Pharma Drug Company Ltd. is an organization which specializes in providing their customers with medications.  This January, Pharma Drug Company Ltd. has made an advance payment to cover the next 12 months of utility bills, which have a monthly cost of $2600.

539    Pharma Drug Company Ltd. sells several different types of medications. Today Pharma Drug Company Ltd. signed up for a loan with a 5% interest rate, and so the bank immediately transferred cash to the company in the amount of $109000.

540    AC&C Ltd. sells various cell phone plans. This January, AC&C Ltd. has made an advance payment to cover the next 12 months of utility bills, which have a monthly cost of $2200.

541    David & Johnson is a corporation which sells legal services. David & Johnson has just provided 1900 large orders which had been paid for in advance last year. Each order was in the amount of $2300.

542    Kola-Nut Ltd sells several different types of soft drinks. This week, Kola-Nut Ltd purchased 3370 batches of soda bottles which were placed into the warehouse, and which had a per-unit cost of $2700.

543    Grand Convention Ltd is a company which offers their customers a wide selection of banquet hall rentals for corporate meetings. This month, Grand Convention Ltd paid for 1 month of rent for their company's office space. Each month, the rent owing was $16000.

544    NBG Media Corporation is an organization which specializes in providing their customers with broadcasting services for advertising agencies. Today NBG Media Corporation signed up for a loan with a 5% interest rate, and so the bank immediately transferred cash to the company in the amount of $73000.

545    Mount Tessory Academy sells several different types of private school education. Mount Tessory Academy has just provided 1100 large orders which had been paid for in advance last year. Each order was in the amount of $1400.

546    Fairway Malls is a privately-held corporation which focuses on their niche of premium retail spaces in their shopping centers. This month, Fairway Malls paid 1 monthly loan repayment towards their long-term note payable. The interest portion was 60% of the payment. The total amount paid in cash was $23000.

547    Pharma Drug Company Ltd. is a market leader that is well-known for their brand of medications. Today Pharma Drug Company Ltd. signed up for a loan with a 5% interest rate, and so the bank immediately transferred cash to the company in the amount of $20000.

548    Fairway Malls is a corporation which sells retail spaces in their shopping centers. Today, Fairway Malls received payment upfront for 1600 large orders which will not be provided until early next year. Each order was in the amount of $2500.

549    Sprike Inc is a market leader that is well-known for their brand of athletic apparel. This week, Sprike Inc purchased 4490 batches of athletic t-shirts which were placed into the warehouse, and which had a per-unit cost of $1100.

550    Jameson & Jameson is a corporation which sells soap products. This week, Jameson & Jameson purchased 3920 truckloads of bars of soap which were placed into the warehouse, and which had a per-unit cost of $2400.

551    LA Met Theatre Company sells various live theatrical performances. This January, LA Met Theatre Company has made an advance payment to cover the next 12 months of utility bills, which have a monthly cost of $1600.

552    McGerald's is a privately-held corporation which focuses on their niche of premium fast food meals. Today, McGerald's bought equipment which has a 5 year useful life, and which had a cost of $21000.

553    Jameson & Jameson sells various soap products. Today Jameson & Jameson signed up for a loan with a 5% interest rate, and so the bank immediately transferred cash to the company in the amount of $37000.

554    Comedy 253 sells various live performances of stand-up comedy. Today, Comedy 253 received payment upfront for 1900 large orders which will not be provided until early next year. Each order was in the amount of $1500.

555    NY Fitness is a company which offers their customers a wide selection of gym memberships for professional sports teams. NY Fitness has just purchased a building using cash, which has an expected useful life of 30 years, and which had a total cost of $459000.

556    McGerald's offers their customers a wide range of fast food meals. This December, McGerald's recognized 1 year of depreciation on a building which had a total useful life of 25 years, and which had originally been bought for $280000.

557    NY Fitness is a company which offers their customers a wide selection of gym memberships for professional sports teams. This December, NY Fitness recognized 1 year of depreciation on a building which had a total useful life of 25 years, and which had originally been bought for $618000.

558    AC&C Ltd. sells several different types of cell phone plans. This month, AC&C Ltd. has estimated that 5% of the accounts receivable might not end up being collectable, based on past experience. The accounts receivable will need to be adjusted from its current balance of $38000.

559    A to Z Event Guru Ltd is a market leader that is well-known for their brand of start-to-finish event planning services for large gatherings. This month, A to Z Event Guru Ltd must amortize 1 month worth of utility bills which they had prepaid at the beginning of the year. The amount that they had paid upfront for the year was $12000.

560    Grand Convention Ltd is a company which offers their customers a wide selection of banquet hall rentals for corporate meetings. This month, Grand Convention Ltd paid for 1 month of rent for their company's office space. Each month, the rent owing was $9000.

561    David & Johnson is a market leader that is well-known for their brand of legal services. This December, David & Johnson recognized 1 year of depreciation on a building which had a total useful life of 25 years, and which had originally been bought for $74000.

562    Comedy 253 sells several different types of live performances of stand-up comedy. Comedy 253 has just provided 1600 large orders which had been paid for in advance last year. Each order was in the amount of $1400.

563    A to Z Event Guru Ltd sells several different types of start-to-finish event planning services for large gatherings. This week, A to Z Event Guru Ltd paid each of the 1000 staff members their bi-weekly wages, which per person had a cost of $2200.

564    Mount Tessory Academy sells several different types of private school education. Today, Mount Tessory Academy has paid cash to their supplier to fully pay off their account payable balance, which was $96000.

565    LA Met Theatre Company is an organization which specializes in providing their customers with live theatrical performances. This December, LA Met Theatre Company recognized 1 year of depreciation on equipment which had a total useful life of 10 years, and which had originally cost $190000.

566    A to Z Event Guru Ltd provides their customers with start-to-finish event planning services for large gatherings. This week, A to Z Event Guru Ltd paid each of the 2440 staff members their bi-weekly wages, which per person had a cost of $1500.

567    Fairway Malls is a corporation which sells retail spaces in their shopping centers. This week, Fairway Malls paid each of the 3650 staff members their bi-weekly wages, which per person had a cost of $1000.

568    Cirque du Lune offers their customers a wide range of circus performances. This month, Cirque du Lune paid for 1 month of rent for their company's office space. Each month, the rent owing was $17000.

569    Comedy 253 sells several different types of live performances of stand-up comedy. This December, Comedy 253 recognized 1 year of depreciation on a building which had a total useful life of 25 years, and which had originally been bought for $565000.

570     Payday Now is a company which offers their customers a wide selection of short-term loan arrangements. This month, Payday Now must amortize 1 month worth of utility bills which they had prepaid at the beginning of the year. The amount that they had paid upfront for the year was $38400.

571     Jameson & Jameson sells several different types of soap products. This month, Jameson & Jameson paid for 1 month of rent for the warehouse room, which has a monthly cost of $2300.

572     Grand Convention Ltd offers their customers a wide range of banquet hall rentals for corporate meetings. This month, Grand Convention Ltd paid for 1 month of rent for their company's office space. Each month, the rent owing was $21000.

573     Comedy 253 is a corporation which sells live performances of stand-up comedy. This January, Comedy 253 has made an advance payment to cover the next 12 months of utility bills, which have a monthly cost of $1700.

574     Sprike Inc is a corporation which sells athletic apparel. Sprike Inc has just purchased a building using cash, which has an expected useful life of 30 years, and which had a total cost of $74000.

575     Kola-Nut Ltd is an organization which specializes in providing their customers with soft drinks. Today, Kola-Nut Ltd received an upfront payment for 1700 batches of soda bottles which will be provided to the customer 6 months from now. The payment for each was $2100.

576     Paytech Ltd sells several different types of payroll transaction processing services. This January, Paytech Ltd has made an advance payment to cover the next 12 months of utility bills, which have a monthly cost of $1400.

577     Grand Convention Ltd is a privately-held corporation which focuses on their niche of premium banquet hall rentals for corporate meetings. This month, Grand Convention Ltd must amortize 1 month worth of utility bills which they had prepaid at the beginning of the year. The amount that they had paid upfront for the year was $21600.

578     Pharma Drug Company Ltd. sells various medications. Today Pharma Drug Company Ltd. sold 19100 batches of pills which had a 30% mark-up. They had originally been bought from their suppliers for a unit cost of $1950.

579     Mr. Mop is a corporation which sells household cleaners. Today Mr. Mop sold 27600 tons of cleaning solution which had a 30% mark-up. They had originally been bought from their suppliers for a unit cost of $1150.

580     Pharma Drug Company Ltd. sells various medications. Pharma Drug Company Ltd. has just purchased a building using cash, which has an expected useful life of 30 years, and which had a total cost of $50000.

581 Mount Tessory Academy is a market leader that is well-known for their brand of private school education. This December, Mount Tessory Academy recognized 1 year of depreciation on equipment which had a total useful life of 10 years, and which had originally cost $230000.

582 Toyonda is a corporation which sells cars. Today Toyonda signed up for a loan with a 5% interest rate, and so the bank immediately transferred cash to the company in the amount of $97000.

583 Kola-Nut Ltd is a privately-held corporation which focuses on their niche of premium soft drinks. This month, Kola-Nut Ltd accepted 17800 batches of soda bottles which were returned by customers. These products had been marked up by 35% and they had originally been bought at a per-unit cost of $2700.

584 LA Met Theatre Company offers their customers a wide range of live theatrical performances. This year, LA Met Theatre Company has provided 2200 shows each of which earned revenues of $1160.

585 Mr. Mop sells various household cleaners. Today Mr. Mop sold 44500 tons of cleaning solution which had a 30% mark-up. They had originally been bought from their suppliers for a unit cost of $2560.

586 Mr. Mop is a privately-held corporation which focuses on their niche of premium household cleaners. This month, Mr. Mop paid 1 monthly loan repayment towards their long-term note payable. The interest portion was 60% of the payment. The total amount paid in cash was $21000.

587 Club Disco is a corporation which sells dance venue rentals for large family gatherings. This January, Club Disco has made an advance payment to cover the next 12 months of utility bills, which have a monthly cost of $1200.

588 David & Johnson provides their customers with legal services. Today, David & Johnson has paid cash to their supplier to fully pay off their account payable balance, which was $9000.

589 McGerald's sells various fast food meals. This December, McGerald's recognized 1 year of depreciation on equipment which had a total useful life of 10 years, and which had originally cost $120000.

590 Comedy 253 is a market leader that is well-known for their brand of live performances of stand-up comedy. This year, Comedy 253 has provided 1000 shows each of which earned revenues of $1110.

591     Paytech Ltd is a privately-held corporation which focuses on their niche of premium payroll transaction processing services. This January, Paytech Ltd has made an advance payment to cover the next 12 months of utility bills, which have a monthly cost of $1000.

592     Jameson & Jameson is an organization which specializes in providing their customers with soap products. This week, Jameson & Jameson purchased 1390 truckloads of bars of soap which were placed into the warehouse, and which had a per-unit cost of $1700.

593     Sprike Inc sells various athletic apparel. This December, Sprike Inc recognized 1 year of depreciation on a building which had a total useful life of 25 years, and which had originally been bought for $297000.

594     Club Disco provides their customers with dance venue rentals for large family gatherings. This December, Club Disco has paid each of the company's 1100 owners an annual dividend in the amount of $26000.

595     Paytech Ltd is a corporation which sells payroll transaction processing services. Today, Paytech Ltd bought equipment which has a 5 year useful life, and which had a cost of $22000.

596     LA Met Theatre Company is a company which offers their customers a wide selection of live theatrical performances. This week, LA Met Theatre Company paid each of the 1630 staff members their bi-weekly wages, which per person had a cost of $1000.

597     Cirque du Lune sells several different types of circus performances. This month, Cirque du Lune paid 1 monthly loan repayment towards their long-term note payable. The interest portion was 60% of the payment. The total amount paid in cash was $11000.

598     NBG Media Corporation is a privately-held corporation which focuses on their niche of premium broadcasting services for advertising agencies. This December, NBG Media Corporation recognized 1 year of depreciation on equipment which had a total useful life of 10 years, and which had originally cost $80000.

599     A to Z Event Guru Ltd is a market leader that is well-known for their brand of start-to-finish event planning services for large gatherings. This month, A to Z Event Guru Ltd must amortize 1 month worth of utility bills which they had prepaid at the beginning of the year. The amount that they had paid upfront for the year was $12000.

600     David & Johnson sells various legal services. This year, David & Johnson has provided 1700 billable hours each of which earned revenues of $2600.

601 Comedy 253 sells various live performances of stand-up comedy. This month, Comedy 253 must amortize 1 month worth of utility bills which they had prepaid at the beginning of the year. The amount that they had paid upfront for the year was $12000.

602 Cirque du Lune sells several different types of circus performances. Today, Cirque du Lune bought equipment which has a 5 year useful life, and which had a cost of $14000.

603 Jameson & Jameson is a market leader that is well-known for their brand of soap products. Today, Jameson & Jameson received an upfront payment for 5850 truckloads of bars of soap which will be provided to the customer 6 months from now. The payment for each was $2500.

604 David & Johnson sells several different types of legal services. This January, David & Johnson has made an advance payment to cover the next 12 months of utility bills, which have a monthly cost of $1600.

605 Jameson & Jameson is a corporation which sells soap products. This month, Jameson & Jameson has estimated that 20% of the accounts receivable might not end up being collectable, based on past experience. The accounts receivable will need to be adjusted from its current balance of $91000.

606 Payday Now is an organization which specializes in providing their customers with short-term loan arrangements. This January, Payday Now has made an advance payment to cover the next 12 months of utility bills, which have a monthly cost of $2700.

607 Payday Now is a privately-held corporation which focuses on their niche of premium short-term loan arrangements. This week, Payday Now paid each of the 3940 staff members their bi-weekly wages, which per person had a cost of $1900.

608 Payday Now sells several different types of short-term loan arrangements. Payday Now has just provided 1600 large orders which had been paid for in advance last year. Each order was in the amount of $2700.

609 A to Z Event Guru Ltd is a market leader that is well-known for their brand of start-to-finish event planning services for large gatherings. This January, A to Z Event Guru Ltd has made an advance payment to cover the next 12 months of utility bills, which have a monthly cost of $1800.

610 Jameson & Jameson sells several different types of soap products. Today, Jameson & Jameson bought equipment which has a 5 year useful life, and which had a cost of $22000.

611 Kola-Nut Ltd is a corporation which sells soft drinks. This month, Kola-Nut Ltd has estimated that 30% of the accounts receivable might not end up being collectable, based on past experience. The accounts receivable will need to be adjusted from its current balance of $95000.

612 Comedy 253 provides their customers with live performances of stand-up comedy. This month, Comedy 253 paid for 1 month of rent for their company's office space. Each month, the rent owing was $21000.

613 Mr. Mop is a company which offers their customers a wide selection of household cleaners. Today, Mr. Mop received an upfront payment for 5540 tons of cleaning solution which will be provided to the customer 6 months from now. The payment for each was $2600.

614 Air America is a market leader that is well-known for their brand of global flights. Air America has just received a cash payment for the full amount that this customer owed to the company for all of their purchases to date. The outstanding balance which has now been paid was $15000.

615 Pharma Drug Company Ltd. sells several different types of medications. This month, Pharma Drug Company Ltd. paid for 1 month of rent for the warehouse room, which has a monthly cost of $2800.

616 Sprike Inc is a corporation which sells athletic apparel. This week, Sprike Inc purchased 4660 batches of athletic t-shirts which were placed into the warehouse, and which had a per-unit cost of $1900.

617 Pharma Drug Company Ltd. is a company which offers their customers a wide selection of medications. This month, Pharma Drug Company Ltd. paid for 1 month of rent for the warehouse room, which has a monthly cost of $2400.

618 Air America is a corporation which sells global flights. This month, Air America paid 1 monthly loan repayment towards their long-term note payable. The interest portion was 60% of the payment. The total amount paid in cash was $11000.

619 Cirque du Lune is a company which offers their customers a wide selection of circus performances. Cirque du Lune has just received a cash payment for the full amount that this customer owed to the company for all of their purchases to date. The outstanding balance which has now been paid was $45000.

620 Club Disco provides their customers with dance venue rentals for large family gatherings. This year, Club Disco has provided 1800 evening rentals each of which earned revenues of $2610.

621    Cirque du Lune is a privately-held corporation which focuses on their niche of premium circus performances. Cirque du Lune has just provided 1600 large orders which had been paid for in advance last year. Each order was in the amount of $1800.

622    Jameson & Jameson is an organization which specializes in providing their customers with soap products. This December, Jameson & Jameson recognized 1 year of depreciation on equipment which had a total useful life of 10 years, and which had originally cost $150000.

623    Mr. Mop sells several different types of household cleaners. This month, Mr. Mop paid for 1 month of rent for the warehouse room, which has a monthly cost of $1300.

624    AC&C Ltd. is an organization which specializes in providing their customers with cell phone plans. Today AC&C Ltd. signed up for a loan with a 5% interest rate, and so the bank immediately transferred cash to the company in the amount of $34000.

625    AC&C Ltd. is a market leader that is well-known for their brand of cell phone plans. This December, AC&C Ltd. has paid each of the company's 1500 owners an annual dividend in the amount of $8000.

626    Fairway Malls sells various retail spaces in their shopping centers. This December, Fairway Malls recognized 1 year of depreciation on equipment which had a total useful life of 10 years, and which had originally cost $130000.

627    NBG Media Corporation is a market leader that is well-known for their brand of broadcasting services for advertising agencies. Today, NBG Media Corporation has paid cash to their supplier to fully pay off their account payable balance, which was $31000.

628    Toyonda is a corporation which sells cars. Today, Toyonda bought equipment which has a 5 year useful life, and which had a cost of $11000.

629    Mount Tessory Academy sells various private school education subscriptions. This December, Mount Tessory Academy recognized 1 year of depreciation on a building which had a total useful life of 25 years, and which had originally been bought for $178000.

630    Kola-Nut Ltd is a company which offers their customers a wide selection of soft drinks. Kola-Nut Ltd has just purchased a building using cash, which has an expected useful life of 30 years, and which had a total cost of $233000.

631    David & Johnson is a corporation which sells legal services. Today, David & Johnson received payment upfront for 2100 large orders which will not be provided until early next year. Each order was in the amount of $2700.

632    NY Fitness provides their customers with gym memberships for professional sports teams. NY Fitness has just provided 2400 large orders which had been paid for in advance last year. Each order was in the amount of $2100.

633    Hogtown Records is a corporation which sells audio services for local musicians to record their music albums. This month, Hogtown Records paid for 1 month of rent for their company's office space. Each month, the rent owing was $20000.

634    Jameson & Jameson sells several different types of soap products. This month, Jameson & Jameson paid 1 monthly loan repayment towards their long-term note payable. The interest portion was 60% of the payment. The total amount paid in cash was $17000.

635    Comedy 253 provides their customers with live performances of stand-up comedy. This December, Comedy 253 recognized 1 year of depreciation on a building which had a total useful life of 25 years, and which had originally been bought for $805000.

636    Fairway Malls is a privately-held corporation which focuses on their niche of premium retail spaces in their shopping centers. Today, Fairway Malls bought equipment which has a 5 year useful life, and which had a cost of $25000.

637    Payday Now sells various short-term loan arrangements. Payday Now has just provided 1200 large orders which had been paid for in advance last year. Each order was in the amount of $1500.

638    Pharma Drug Company Ltd. sells various medications. This week, Pharma Drug Company Ltd. purchased 2730 batches of pills which were placed into the warehouse, and which had a per-unit cost of $2000.

639    Mr. Mop is a company which offers their customers a wide selection of household cleaners. This January, Mr. Mop has made an advance payment to cover the next 12 months of utility bills, which have a monthly cost of $1000.

640    Hogtown Records is a privately-held corporation which focuses on their niche of premium audio services for local musicians to record their music albums. Today, Hogtown Records received payment upfront for 2200 large orders which will not be provided until early next year. Each order was in the amount of $2700.

641    Payday Now sells several different types of short-term loan arrangements. This January, Payday Now has made an advance payment to cover the next 12 months of utility bills, which have a monthly cost of $1100.

642     Jameson & Jameson is a company which offers their customers a wide selection of soap products.  Today Jameson & Jameson sold 20300 truckloads of bars of soap which had a 30% mark-up. They had originally been bought from their suppliers for a unit cost of $1370.

643     Fairway Malls offers their customers a wide range of retail spaces in their shopping centers.  This month, Fairway Malls paid for 1 month of rent for their company's office space. Each month, the rent owing was $11000.

644     Comedy 253 sells various live performances of stand-up comedy.  Today, Comedy 253 bought equipment which has a 5 year useful life, and which had a cost of $15000.

645     Mount Tessory Academy sells several different types of private school education. Today, Mount Tessory Academy received payment upfront for 1100 large orders which will not be provided until early next year. Each order was in the amount of $1800.

646     Sprike Inc provides their customers with athletic apparel.  This month, Sprike Inc paid for 1 month of rent for the warehouse room, which has a monthly cost of $1500.

647     Pharma Drug Company Ltd. sells several different types of medications.  Today, Pharma Drug Company Ltd. received an upfront payment for 4810 batches of pills which will be provided to the customer 6 months from now. The payment for each was $1900.

648     LA Met Theatre Company is an organization which specializes in providing their customers with live theatrical performances.  LA Met Theatre Company has just purchased a building using cash, which has an expected useful life of 30 years, and which had a total cost of $772000.

649     Mr. Mop is a company which offers their customers a wide selection of household cleaners.  Today Mr. Mop sold 38100 tons of cleaning solution which had a 30% mark-up. They had originally been bought from their suppliers for a unit cost of $1780.

650     Fairway Malls sells several different types of retail spaces in their shopping centers.  This month, Fairway Malls must amortize 1 month worth of utility bills which they had prepaid at the beginning of the year. The amount that they had paid upfront for the year was $13200.

651     David & Johnson sells various legal services.  This year, David & Johnson has provided 1600 billable hours each of which earned revenues of $1810.

652 AC&C Ltd. sells various cell phone plans. This month, AC&C Ltd. has estimated that 25% of the accounts receivable might not end up being collectable, based on past experience. The accounts receivable will need to be adjusted from its current balance of $93000.

653 Mr. Mop provides their customers with household cleaners. This month, Mr. Mop paid for 1 month of rent for the warehouse room, which has a monthly cost of $1800.

654 Fairway Malls is a corporation which sells retail spaces in their shopping centers. This year, Fairway Malls has provided 1400 monthly retail space rentals each of which earned revenues of $1440.

655 Sprike Inc provides their customers with athletic apparel. Today, Sprike Inc received an upfront payment for 5760 batches of athletic t-shirts which will be provided to the customer 6 months from now. The payment for each was $2100.

656 Hogtown Records offers their customers a wide range of audio services for local musicians to record their music albums. Today, Hogtown Records bought equipment which has a 5 year useful life, and which had a cost of $26000.

657 Mr. Mop sells several different types of household cleaners. Mr. Mop has just purchased a building using cash, which has an expected useful life of 30 years, and which had a total cost of $808000.

658 Fairway Malls provides their customers with retail spaces in their shopping centers. This week, Fairway Malls paid each of the 2690 staff members their bi-weekly wages, which per person had a cost of $1700.

659 Cirque du Lune sells various circus performances. Cirque du Lune has just purchased a building using cash, which has an expected useful life of 30 years, and which had a total cost of $362000.

660 Kola-Nut Ltd provides their customers with soft drinks. This month, Kola-Nut Ltd must amortize 1 month worth of utility bills which they had prepaid at the beginning of the year. The amount that they had paid upfront for the year was $28800.

661 LA Met Theatre Company is a privately-held corporation which focuses on their niche of premium live theatrical performances. This December, LA Met Theatre Company has paid each of the company's 1000 owners an annual dividend in the amount of $24000.

662 Cirque du Lune is a privately-held corporation which focuses on their niche of premium circus performances. Today Cirque du Lune signed up for a loan with a 5% interest rate, and so the bank immediately transferred cash to the company in the amount of $49000.

663     Mr. Mop is a company which offers their customers a wide selection of household cleaners. This month, Mr. Mop accepted 11000 tons of cleaning solution which were returned by customers. These products had been marked up by 35% and they had originally been bought at a per-unit cost of $1000.

664     Toyonda is an organization which specializes in providing their customers with cars. Today, Toyonda has paid cash to their supplier to fully pay off their account payable balance, which was $63000.

665     LA Met Theatre Company is an organization which specializes in providing their customers with live theatrical performances. This January, LA Met Theatre Company has made an advance payment to cover the next 12 months of utility bills, which have a monthly cost of $1400.

666     Sprike Inc provides their customers with athletic apparel. Today Sprike Inc sold 8700 batches of athletic t-shirts which had a 30% mark-up. They had originally been bought from their suppliers for a unit cost of $1490.

667     NY Fitness offers their customers a wide range of gym memberships for professional sports teams. NY Fitness has just provided 1500 large orders which had been paid for in advance last year. Each order was in the amount of $2600.

668     Grand Convention Ltd is a market leader that is well-known for their brand of banquet hall rentals for corporate meetings. This month, Grand Convention Ltd has estimated that 5% of the accounts receivable might not end up being collectable, based on past experience. The accounts receivable will need to be adjusted from its current balance of $54000.

669     NY Fitness is a company which offers their customers a wide selection of gym memberships for professional sports teams. This year, NY Fitness has provided 1000 team memberships each of which earned revenues of $2890.

670     Fairway Malls is a privately-held corporation which focuses on their niche of premium retail spaces in their shopping centers. This week, Fairway Malls paid each of the 3280 staff members their bi-weekly wages, which per person had a cost of $1100.

671     Club Disco sells various dance venue rentals for large family gatherings. This January, Club Disco has made an advance payment to cover the next 12 months of utility bills, which have a monthly cost of $2300.

672     Kola-Nut Ltd is a corporation which sells soft drinks. This month, Kola-Nut Ltd paid for 1 month of rent for the warehouse room, which has a monthly cost of $2500.

673    Pharma Drug Company Ltd. is a market leader that is well-known for their brand of medications. This month, Pharma Drug Company Ltd. paid for 1 month of rent for the warehouse room, which has a monthly cost of $1500.

674    Fairway Malls is a company which offers their customers a wide selection of retail spaces in their shopping centers. This year, Fairway Malls has provided 1200 monthly retail space rentals each of which earned revenues of $1410.

675    Pharma Drug Company Ltd. is a market leader that is well-known for their brand of medications. This month, Pharma Drug Company Ltd. accepted 21600 batches of pills which were returned by customers. These products had been marked up by 35% and they had originally been bought at a per-unit cost of $2800.

676    LA Met Theatre Company is a privately-held corporation which focuses on their niche of premium live theatrical performances. Today LA Met Theatre Company signed up for a loan with a 5% interest rate, and so the bank immediately transferred cash to the company in the amount of $84000.

677    Pharma Drug Company Ltd. is a market leader that is well-known for their brand of medications. Today Pharma Drug Company Ltd. sold 51800 batches of pills which had a 30% mark-up. They had originally been bought from their suppliers for a unit cost of $2000.

678    Club Disco is a corporation which sells dance venue rentals for large family gatherings. This December, Club Disco recognized 1 year of depreciation on a building which had a total useful life of 25 years, and which had originally been bought for $960000.

679    Jameson & Jameson is a corporation which sells soap products. This month, Jameson & Jameson paid for 1 month of rent for their company's office space. Each month, the rent owing was $15000.

680    Kola-Nut Ltd is an organization which specializes in providing their customers with soft drinks. This week, Kola-Nut Ltd purchased 5470 batches of soda bottles which were placed into the warehouse, and which had a per-unit cost of $2700.

681    Paytech Ltd is a privately-held corporation which focuses on their niche of premium payroll transaction processing services. This month, Paytech Ltd has estimated that 10% of the accounts receivable might not end up being collectable, based on past experience. The accounts receivable will need to be adjusted from its current balance of $89000.

682  LA Met Theatre Company is a corporation which sells live theatrical performances. LA Met Theatre Company has just received a cash payment for the full amount that this customer owed to the company for all of their purchases to date. The outstanding balance which has now been paid was $86000.

683  Comedy 253 sells various live performances of stand-up comedy. This January, Comedy 253 has made an advance payment to cover the next 12 months of utility bills, which have a monthly cost of $2500.

684  Grand Convention Ltd is a market leader that is well-known for their brand of banquet hall rentals for corporate meetings. This December, Grand Convention Ltd recognized 1 year of depreciation on equipment which had a total useful life of 10 years, and which had originally cost $220000.

685  Paytech Ltd is an organization which specializes in providing their customers with payroll transaction processing services. This December, Paytech Ltd has paid each of the company's 1700 owners an annual dividend in the amount of $13000.

686  Fairway Malls is a corporation which sells retail spaces in their shopping centers. This year, Fairway Malls has provided 2400 monthly retail space rentals each of which earned revenues of $1250.

687  Jameson & Jameson is a corporation which sells soap products. This month, Jameson & Jameson accepted 28200 truckloads of bars of soap which were returned by customers. These products had been marked up by 35% and they had originally been bought at a per-unit cost of $1400.

688  Kola-Nut Ltd is a company which offers their customers a wide selection of soft drinks. Today, Kola-Nut Ltd received an upfront payment for 3930 batches of soda bottles which will be provided to the customer 6 months from now. The payment for each was $1100.

689  Mr. Mop is a privately-held corporation which focuses on their niche of premium household cleaners. Today, Mr. Mop received an upfront payment for 1150 tons of cleaning solution which will be provided to the customer 6 months from now. The payment for each was $2000.

690  NBG Media Corporation is a market leader that is well-known for their brand of broadcasting services for advertising agencies. This month, NBG Media Corporation must amortize 1 month worth of utility bills which they had prepaid at the beginning of the year. The amount that they had paid upfront for the year was $36000.

691  NY Fitness sells several different types of gym memberships for professional sports teams. Today, NY Fitness received payment upfront for 2400 large orders which will not be provided until early next year. Each order was in the amount of $2800.

692    Jameson & Jameson is a corporation which sells soap products. This December, Jameson & Jameson has paid each of the company's 1200 owners an annual dividend in the amount of $17000.

693    Sprike Inc is a company which offers their customers a wide selection of athletic apparel. Today, Sprike Inc received an upfront payment for 5170 batches of athletic t-shirts which will be provided to the customer 6 months from now. The payment for each was $2700.

694    Payday Now is a privately-held corporation which focuses on their niche of premium short-term loan arrangements. This month, Payday Now has estimated that 30% of the accounts receivable might not end up being collectable, based on past experience. The accounts receivable will need to be adjusted from its current balance of $28000.

695    Comedy 253 is a corporation which sells live performances of stand-up comedy. Today, Comedy 253 has paid cash to their supplier to fully pay off their account payable balance, which was $47000.

696    Payday Now is an organization which specializes in providing their customers with short-term loan arrangements. This year, Payday Now has provided 1900 payday loans each of which earned revenues of $1500.

697    Pharma Drug Company Ltd. is an organization which specializes in providing their customers with medications. This month, Pharma Drug Company Ltd. paid for 1 month of rent for the warehouse room, which has a monthly cost of $1100.

698    NY Fitness sells several different types of gym memberships for professional sports teams. Today, NY Fitness received payment upfront for 2300 large orders which will not be provided until early next year. Each order was in the amount of $2400.

699    Air America is an organization which specializes in providing their customers with global flights. Today, Air America received payment upfront for 2000 large orders which will not be provided until early next year. Each order was in the amount of $1700.

700    A to Z Event Guru Ltd is a corporation which sells start-to-finish event planning services for large gatherings. This month, A to Z Event Guru Ltd paid for 1 month of rent for their company's office space. Each month, the rent owing was $17000.

701    Pharma Drug Company Ltd. is a market leader that is well-known for their brand of medications. This month, Pharma Drug Company Ltd. accepted 4000 batches of pills which were returned by customers. These products had been marked up by 35% and they had originally been bought at a per-unit cost of $1600.

702     Sprike Inc is a company which offers their customers a wide selection of athletic apparel. This month, Sprike Inc must amortize 1 month worth of utility bills which they had prepaid at the beginning of the year. The amount that they had paid upfront for the year was $20400.

703     Jameson & Jameson is a privately-held corporation which focuses on their niche of premium soap products. Today Jameson & Jameson sold 45900 truckloads of bars of soap which had a 30% mark-up. They had originally been bought from their suppliers for a unit cost of $1960.

704     Grand Convention Ltd is a privately-held corporation which focuses on their niche of premium banquet hall rentals for corporate meetings. Grand Convention Ltd has just received a cash payment for the full amount that this customer owed to the company for all of their purchases to date. The outstanding balance which has now been paid was $37000.

705     Kola-Nut Ltd sells various soft drinks. This month, Kola-Nut Ltd paid for 1 month of rent for the warehouse room, which has a monthly cost of $1900.

706     Mr. Mop sells various household cleaners. This week, Mr. Mop purchased 1960 tons of cleaning solution which were placed into the warehouse, and which had a per-unit cost of $1300.

707     Payday Now sells various short-term loan arrangements. This month, Payday Now must amortize 1 month worth of utility bills which they had prepaid at the beginning of the year. The amount that they had paid upfront for the year was $30000.

708     Pharma Drug Company Ltd. offers their customers a wide range of medications. This week, Pharma Drug Company Ltd. purchased 3080 batches of pills which were placed into the warehouse, and which had a per-unit cost of $1500.

709     Sprike Inc offers their customers a wide range of athletic apparel. This month, Sprike Inc accepted 3300 batches of athletic t-shirts which were returned by customers. These products had been marked up by 35% and they had originally been bought at a per-unit cost of $2000.

710     Jameson & Jameson sells various soap products. This week, Jameson & Jameson paid each of the 3750 staff members their bi-weekly wages, which per person had a cost of $1500.

711     David & Johnson is a market leader that is well-known for their brand of legal services. Today David & Johnson signed up for a loan with a 5% interest rate, and so the bank immediately transferred cash to the company in the amount of $113000.

712    NBG Media Corporation is a company which offers their customers a wide selection of broadcasting services for advertising agencies. This December, NBG Media Corporation recognized 1 year of depreciation on a building which had a total useful life of 25 years, and which had originally been bought for $688000.

713    Kola-Nut Ltd is a corporation which sells soft drinks. This December, Kola-Nut Ltd has paid each of the company's 1500 owners an annual dividend in the amount of $23000.

714    Kola-Nut Ltd sells several different types of soft drinks. Kola-Nut Ltd has just received a cash payment for the full amount that this customer owed to the company for all of their purchases to date. The outstanding balance which has now been paid was $46000.

715    Mount Tessory Academy is a privately-held corporation which focuses on their niche of premium private school education. This December, Mount Tessory Academy recognized 1 year of depreciation on equipment which had a total useful life of 10 years, and which had originally cost $100000.

716    Hogtown Records sells several different types of audio services for local musicians to record their music albums. Today, Hogtown Records bought equipment which has a 5 year useful life, and which had a cost of $19000.

717    Comedy 253 is a corporation which sells live performances of stand-up comedy. Comedy 253 has just received a cash payment for the full amount that this customer owed to the company for all of their purchases to date. The outstanding balance which has now been paid was $8000.

718    LA Met Theatre Company is a company which offers their customers a wide selection of live theatrical performances. LA Met Theatre Company has just purchased a building using cash, which has an expected useful life of 30 years, and which had a total cost of $218000.

719    Kola-Nut Ltd sells various soft drinks. Today Kola-Nut Ltd sold 19300 batches of soda bottles which had a 30% mark-up. They had originally been bought from their suppliers for a unit cost of $1070.

720    Pharma Drug Company Ltd. sells several different types of medications. This month, Pharma Drug Company Ltd. paid 1 monthly loan repayment towards their long-term note payable. The interest portion was 60% of the payment. The total amount paid in cash was $25000.

721    Hogtown Records provides their customers with audio services for local musicians to record their music albums. Today, Hogtown Records received payment upfront for 1600 large orders which will not be provided until early next year. Each order was in the amount of $1300.

722 Pharma Drug Company Ltd. provides their customers with medications. Today Pharma Drug Company Ltd. sold 47800 batches of pills which had a 30% mark-up. They had originally been bought from their suppliers for a unit cost of $2100.

723 Sprike Inc sells several different types of athletic apparel. This January, Sprike Inc has made an advance payment to cover the next 12 months of utility bills, which have a monthly cost of $2100.

724 Pharma Drug Company Ltd. provides their customers with medications. This month, Pharma Drug Company Ltd. accepted 29200 batches of pills which were returned by customers. These products had been marked up by 35% and they had originally been bought at a per-unit cost of $1900.

725 Sprike Inc is an organization which specializes in providing their customers with athletic apparel. This month, Sprike Inc paid for 1 month of rent for the warehouse room, which has a monthly cost of $2100.

726 Kola-Nut Ltd offers their customers a wide range of soft drinks. This month, Kola-Nut Ltd paid for 1 month of rent for the warehouse room, which has a monthly cost of $1600.

727 Jameson & Jameson is a market leader that is well-known for their brand of soap products. This December, Jameson & Jameson recognized 1 year of depreciation on equipment which had a total useful life of 10 years, and which had originally cost $180000.

728 Cirque du Lune provides their customers with circus performances. This December, Cirque du Lune has paid each of the company's 1500 owners an annual dividend in the amount of $12000.

729 David & Johnson is a corporation which sells legal services. Today, David & Johnson received payment upfront for 1100 large orders which will not be provided until early next year. Each order was in the amount of $2300.

730 Payday Now provides their customers with short-term loan arrangements. This month, Payday Now paid for 1 month of rent for their company's office space. Each month, the rent owing was $10000.

731 Paytech Ltd sells several different types of payroll transaction processing services. This month, Paytech Ltd has estimated that 25% of the accounts receivable might not end up being collectable, based on past experience. The accounts receivable will need to be adjusted from its current balance of $64000.

732 Club Disco is a market leader that is well-known for their brand of dance venue rentals for large family gatherings. Today, Club Disco bought equipment which has a 5 year useful life, and which had a cost of $10000.

733 Club Disco is a corporation which sells dance venue rentals for large family gatherings. Club Disco has just received a cash payment for the full amount that this customer owed to the company for all of their purchases to date. The outstanding balance which has now been paid was $65000.

734 Mr. Mop is a privately-held corporation which focuses on their niche of premium household cleaners. Today, Mr. Mop received an upfront payment for 4870 tons of cleaning solution which will be provided to the customer 6 months from now. The payment for each was $1100.

735 Jameson & Jameson sells various soap products. This month, Jameson & Jameson paid for 1 month of rent for the warehouse room, which has a monthly cost of $1700.

736 Fairway Malls is a company which offers their customers a wide selection of retail spaces in their shopping centers. This December, Fairway Malls recognized 1 year of depreciation on equipment which had a total useful life of 10 years, and which had originally cost $200000.

737 Fairway Malls is a market leader that is well-known for their brand of retail spaces in their shopping centers. Fairway Malls has just received a cash payment for the full amount that this customer owed to the company for all of their purchases to date. The outstanding balance which has now been paid was $13000.

738 Comedy 253 provides their customers with live performances of stand-up comedy. This year, Comedy 253 has provided 1600 shows each of which earned revenues of $1900.

739 Sprike Inc sells various athletic apparel. This month, Sprike Inc paid for 1 month of rent for the warehouse room, which has a monthly cost of $1100.

740 LA Met Theatre Company is a market leader that is well-known for their brand of live theatrical performances. This week, LA Met Theatre Company paid each of the 1540 staff members their bi-weekly wages, which per person had a cost of $1600.

741 Toyonda is a corporation which sells cars. This month, Toyonda must amortize 1 month worth of utility bills which they had prepaid at the beginning of the year. The amount that they had paid upfront for the year was $28800.

742 Mr. Mop sells several different types of household cleaners. Today, Mr. Mop received an upfront payment for 3610 tons of cleaning solution which will be provided to the customer 6 months from now. The payment for each was $2700.

743 Paytech Ltd is a company which offers their customers a wide selection of payroll transaction processing services. This December, Paytech Ltd recognized 1 year of depreciation on a building which had a total useful life of 25 years, and which had originally been bought for $72000.

744 Jameson & Jameson is an organization which specializes in providing their customers with soap products. This week, Jameson & Jameson purchased 5620 truckloads of bars of soap which were placed into the warehouse, and which had a per-unit cost of $2600.

745 Paytech Ltd sells various payroll transaction processing services. Today, Paytech Ltd received payment upfront for 2100 large orders which will not be provided until early next year. Each order was in the amount of $2000.

746 Payday Now is a company which offers their customers a wide selection of short-term loan arrangements. Today, Payday Now has paid cash to their supplier to fully pay off their account payable balance, which was $21000.

747 Jameson & Jameson is a company which offers their customers a wide selection of soap products. Today, Jameson & Jameson has paid cash to their supplier to fully pay off their account payable balance, which was $32000.

748 Mr. Mop offers their customers a wide range of household cleaners. Today, Mr. Mop received an upfront payment for 2410 tons of cleaning solution which will be provided to the customer 6 months from now. The payment for each was $1500.

749 Pharma Drug Company Ltd. provides their customers with medications. This month, Pharma Drug Company Ltd. accepted 7600 batches of pills which were returned by customers. These products had been marked up by 35% and they had originally been bought at a per-unit cost of $2400.

750 LA Met Theatre Company is a company which offers their customers a wide selection of live theatrical performances. LA Met Theatre Company has just received a cash payment for the full amount that this customer owed to the company for all of their purchases to date. The outstanding balance which has now been paid was $65000.

751 Sprike Inc offers their customers a wide range of athletic apparel. This week, Sprike Inc purchased 3460 batches of athletic t-shirts which were placed into the warehouse, and which had a per-unit cost of $1000.

752 McGerald's offers their customers a wide range of fast food meals. Today, McGerald's has paid cash to their supplier to fully pay off their account payable balance, which was $65000.

753    Pharma Drug Company Ltd. offers their customers a wide range of medications. This month, Pharma Drug Company Ltd. accepted 16900 batches of pills which were returned by customers. These products had been marked up by 35% and they had originally been bought at a per-unit cost of $2500.

754    Sprike Inc is a privately-held corporation which focuses on their niche of premium athletic apparel.  This week, Sprike Inc purchased 2760 batches of athletic t-shirts which were placed into the warehouse, and which had a per-unit cost of $1600.

755    Comedy 253 is a corporation which sells live performances of stand-up comedy. Today, Comedy 253 received payment upfront for 1800 large orders which will not be provided until early next year. Each order was in the amount of $2400.

756    Paytech Ltd is a privately-held corporation which focuses on their niche of premium payroll transaction processing services.  This year, Paytech Ltd has provided 1800 batches of transactions for the current period each of which earned revenues of $2350.

757    Kola-Nut Ltd sells various soft drinks.  Today Kola-Nut Ltd sold 37000 batches of soda bottles which had a 30% mark-up. They had originally been bought from their suppliers for a unit cost of $1740.

758    Jameson & Jameson is an organization which specializes in providing their customers with soap products.  This month, Jameson & Jameson paid for 1 month of rent for the warehouse room, which has a monthly cost of $1000.

759    Club Disco provides their customers with dance venue rentals for large family gatherings.  Club Disco has just provided 1400 large orders which had been paid for in advance last year. Each order was in the amount of $2400.

760    Mr. Mop provides their customers with household cleaners. This month, Mr. Mop has estimated that 30% of the accounts receivable might not end up being collectable, based on past experience. The accounts receivable will need to be adjusted from its current balance of $57000.

761    Mr. Mop is a market leader that is well-known for their brand of household cleaners. This December, Mr. Mop has paid each of the company's 2100 owners an annual dividend in the amount of $26000.

762    LA Met Theatre Company is a corporation which sells live theatrical performances.  This month, LA Met Theatre Company paid 1 monthly loan repayment towards their long-term note payable. The interest portion was 60% of the payment. The total amount paid in cash was $18000.

763 Fairway Malls sells various retail spaces in their shopping centers. Today, Fairway Malls has paid cash to their supplier to fully pay off their account payable balance, which was $88000.

764 Mr. Mop is a company which offers their customers a wide selection of household cleaners. This month, Mr. Mop paid 1 monthly loan repayment towards their long-term note payable. The interest portion was 60% of the payment. The total amount paid in cash was $20000.

765 Fairway Malls is a market leader that is well-known for their brand of retail spaces in their shopping centers. Today Fairway Malls signed up for a loan with a 5% interest rate, and so the bank immediately transferred cash to the company in the amount of $72000.

766 David & Johnson is a privately-held corporation which focuses on their niche of premium legal services. David & Johnson has just received a cash payment for the full amount that this customer owed to the company for all of their purchases to date. The outstanding balance which has now been paid was $24000.

767 Cirque du Lune offers their customers a wide range of circus performances. Today, Cirque du Lune received payment upfront for 1600 large orders which will not be provided until early next year. Each order was in the amount of $2200.

768 Kola-Nut Ltd offers their customers a wide range of soft drinks. This month, Kola-Nut Ltd accepted 26000 batches of soda bottles which were returned by customers. These products had been marked up by 35% and they had originally been bought at a per-unit cost of $1200.

769 A to Z Event Guru Ltd is a company which offers their customers a wide selection of start-to-finish event planning services for large gatherings. This week, A to Z Event Guru Ltd paid each of the 3400 staff members their bi-weekly wages, which per person had a cost of $2800.

770 Kola-Nut Ltd sells various soft drinks. This December, Kola-Nut Ltd recognized 1 year of depreciation on equipment which had a total useful life of 10 years, and which had originally cost $160000.

771 Jameson & Jameson is an organization which specializes in providing their customers with soap products. This December, Jameson & Jameson recognized 1 year of depreciation on a building which had a total useful life of 25 years, and which had originally been bought for $752000.

772 Kola-Nut Ltd is a corporation which sells soft drinks. Today Kola-Nut Ltd sold 46700 batches of soda bottles which had a 30% mark-up. They had originally been bought from their suppliers for a unit cost of $1200.

773     Kola-Nut Ltd sells several different types of soft drinks. This December, Kola-Nut Ltd recognized 1 year of depreciation on equipment which had a total useful life of 10 years, and which had originally cost $220000.

774     Air America sells various global flights. Air America has just provided 2200 large orders which had been paid for in advance last year. Each order was in the amount of $2200.

775     Paytech Ltd provides their customers with payroll transaction processing services. This month, Paytech Ltd must amortize 1 month worth of utility bills which they had prepaid at the beginning of the year. The amount that they had paid upfront for the year was $34800.

776     Mr. Mop is a privately-held corporation which focuses on their niche of premium household cleaners. This December, Mr. Mop recognized 1 year of depreciation on a building which had a total useful life of 25 years, and which had originally been bought for $576000.

777     Kola-Nut Ltd is a privately-held corporation which focuses on their niche of premium soft drinks. This month, Kola-Nut Ltd has estimated that 15% of the accounts receivable might not end up being collectable, based on past experience. The accounts receivable will need to be adjusted from its current balance of $30000.

778     Mr. Mop is an organization which specializes in providing their customers with household cleaners. This month, Mr. Mop paid for 1 month of rent for their company's office space. Each month, the rent owing was $12000.

779     Sprike Inc sells several different types of athletic apparel. Sprike Inc has just received a cash payment for the full amount that this customer owed to the company for all of their purchases to date. The outstanding balance which has now been paid was $90000.

780     Pharma Drug Company Ltd. is an organization which specializes in providing their customers with medications. Today Pharma Drug Company Ltd. sold 36700 batches of pills which had a 30% mark-up. They had originally been bought from their suppliers for a unit cost of $2920.

781     NBG Media Corporation is a market leader that is well-known for their brand of broadcasting services for advertising agencies. Today, NBG Media Corporation has paid cash to their supplier to fully pay off their account payable balance, which was $89000.

782     NY Fitness is an organization which specializes in providing their customers with gym memberships for professional sports teams. This month, NY Fitness paid for 1 month of rent for their company's office space. Each month, the rent owing was $12000.

783 Kola-Nut Ltd is a company which offers their customers a wide selection of soft drinks. Today, Kola-Nut Ltd received an upfront payment for 5270 batches of soda bottles which will be provided to the customer 6 months from now. The payment for each was $1300.

784 Payday Now provides their customers with short-term loan arrangements. This month, Payday Now has estimated that 20% of the accounts receivable might not end up being collectable, based on past experience. The accounts receivable will need to be adjusted from its current balance of $26000.

785 Mr. Mop is a market leader that is well-known for their brand of household cleaners. This December, Mr. Mop has paid each of the company's 1100 owners an annual dividend in the amount of $9000.

786 A to Z Event Guru Ltd is a market leader that is well-known for their brand of start-to-finish event planning services for large gatherings. This month, A to Z Event Guru Ltd paid for 1 month of rent for their company's office space. Each month, the rent owing was $19000.

787 Paytech Ltd sells various payroll transaction processing services. Paytech Ltd has just purchased a building using cash, which has an expected useful life of 30 years, and which had a total cost of $292000.

788 Air America offers their customers a wide range of global flights. Air America has just provided 1000 large orders which had been paid for in advance last year. Each order was in the amount of $2400.

789 Pharma Drug Company Ltd. sells several different types of medications. Pharma Drug Company Ltd. has just purchased a building using cash, which has an expected useful life of 30 years, and which had a total cost of $709000.

790 Comedy 253 is a company which offers their customers a wide selection of live performances of stand-up comedy. This year, Comedy 253 has provided 2100 shows each of which earned revenues of $2680.

791 David & Johnson sells several different types of legal services. David & Johnson has just provided 1300 large orders which had been paid for in advance last year. Each order was in the amount of $2400.

792 Kola-Nut Ltd is a corporation which sells soft drinks. Today Kola-Nut Ltd sold 19300 batches of soda bottles which had a 30% mark-up. They had originally been bought from their suppliers for a unit cost of $2920.

793 Pharma Drug Company Ltd. is a corporation which sells medications. This week, Pharma Drug Company Ltd. purchased 3900 batches of pills which were placed into the warehouse, and which had a per-unit cost of $2500.

794    Club Disco is an organization which specializes in providing their customers with dance venue rentals for large family gatherings. This year, Club Disco has provided 2300 evening rentals each of which earned revenues of $1300.

795    Comedy 253 is a privately-held corporation which focuses on their niche of premium live performances of stand-up comedy. This month, Comedy 253 paid for 1 month of rent for their company's office space. Each month, the rent owing was $26000.

796    Kola-Nut Ltd is an organization which specializes in providing their customers with soft drinks. Today Kola-Nut Ltd sold 26600 batches of soda bottles which had a 30% mark-up. They had originally been bought from their suppliers for a unit cost of $2310.

797    Pharma Drug Company Ltd. is a privately-held corporation which focuses on their niche of premium medications. This month, Pharma Drug Company Ltd. accepted 7800 batches of pills which were returned by customers. These products had been marked up by 35% and they had originally been bought at a per-unit cost of $1700.

798    Hogtown Records is a company which offers their customers a wide selection of audio services for local musicians to record their music albums. This year, Hogtown Records has provided 2300 albums each of which earned revenues of $1010.

799    AC&C Ltd. sells several different types of cell phone plans. This December, AC&C Ltd. recognized 1 year of depreciation on a building which had a total useful life of 25 years, and which had originally been bought for $891000.

800    Pharma Drug Company Ltd. sells various medications. Today, Pharma Drug Company Ltd. received an upfront payment for 2700 batches of pills which will be provided to the customer 6 months from now. The payment for each was $2000.

801    AC&C Ltd. is a corporation which sells cell phone plans. AC&C Ltd. has just received a cash payment for the full amount that this customer owed to the company for all of their purchases to date. The outstanding balance which has now been paid was $77000.

802    Sprike Inc provides their customers with athletic apparel. This month, Sprike Inc paid for 1 month of rent for their company's office space. Each month, the rent owing was $10000.

803    McGerald's is an organization which specializes in providing their customers with fast food meals. This December, McGerald's recognized 1 year of depreciation on a building which had a total useful life of 25 years, and which had originally been bought for $46000.

804 McGerald's is a market leader that is well-known for their brand of fast food meals. Today, McGerald's has paid cash to their supplier to fully pay off their account payable balance, which was $80000.

805 LA Met Theatre Company is an organization which specializes in providing their customers with live theatrical performances. This month, LA Met Theatre Company paid for 1 month of rent for their company's office space. Each month, the rent owing was $12000.

806 Pharma Drug Company Ltd. is a privately-held corporation which focuses on their niche of premium medications. Today Pharma Drug Company Ltd. sold 12100 batches of pills which had a 30% mark-up. They had originally been bought from their suppliers for a unit cost of $1630.

807 Air America is a market leader that is well-known for their brand of global flights. This December, Air America recognized 1 year of depreciation on equipment which had a total useful life of 10 years, and which had originally cost $170000.

808 NY Fitness sells several different types of gym memberships for professional sports teams. This month, NY Fitness paid for 1 month of rent for their company's office space. Each month, the rent owing was $26000.

809 NBG Media Corporation offers their customers a wide range of broadcasting services for advertising agencies. This month, NBG Media Corporation must amortize 1 month worth of utility bills which they had prepaid at the beginning of the year. The amount that they had paid upfront for the year was $45600.

810 Pharma Drug Company Ltd. offers their customers a wide range of medications. This month, Pharma Drug Company Ltd. accepted 14300 batches of pills which were returned by customers. These products had been marked up by 35% and they had originally been bought at a per-unit cost of $1600.

811 Mr. Mop offers their customers a wide range of household cleaners. This month, Mr. Mop paid for 1 month of rent for their company's office space. Each month, the rent owing was $16000.

812 Grand Convention Ltd is a corporation which sells banquet hall rentals for corporate meetings. This year, Grand Convention Ltd has provided 2100 corporate events each of which earned revenues of $2240.

813 Club Disco is a privately-held corporation which focuses on their niche of premium dance venue rentals for large family gatherings. This December, Club Disco recognized 1 year of depreciation on equipment which had a total useful life of 10 years, and which had originally cost $180000.

814 Club Disco is a corporation which sells dance venue rentals for large family gatherings. Today, Club Disco received payment upfront for 1000 large orders which will not be provided until early next year. Each order was in the amount of $1400.

815 Kola-Nut Ltd is a corporation which sells soft drinks. This week, Kola-Nut Ltd purchased 1400 batches of soda bottles which were placed into the warehouse, and which had a per-unit cost of $2800.

816 Jameson & Jameson provides their customers with soap products. This January, Jameson & Jameson has made an advance payment to cover the next 12 months of utility bills, which have a monthly cost of $1300.

817 Mr. Mop offers their customers a wide range of household cleaners. This month, Mr. Mop must amortize 1 month worth of utility bills which they had prepaid at the beginning of the year. The amount that they had paid upfront for the year was $19200.

818 David & Johnson offers their customers a wide range of legal services. Today, David & Johnson received payment upfront for 1600 large orders which will not be provided until early next year. Each order was in the amount of $1500.

819 Kola-Nut Ltd provides their customers with soft drinks. This December, Kola-Nut Ltd recognized 1 year of depreciation on a building which had a total useful life of 25 years, and which had originally been bought for $215000.

820 David & Johnson provides their customers with legal services. This month, David & Johnson paid for 1 month of rent for their company's office space. Each month, the rent owing was $25000.

821 A to Z Event Guru Ltd sells several different types of start-to-finish event planning services for large gatherings. This December, A to Z Event Guru Ltd recognized 1 year of depreciation on a building which had a total useful life of 25 years, and which had originally been bought for $314000.

822 Pharma Drug Company Ltd. is a company which offers their customers a wide selection of medications. This month, Pharma Drug Company Ltd. has estimated that 20% of the accounts receivable might not end up being collectable, based on past experience. The accounts receivable will need to be adjusted from its current balance of $102000.

823 Mount Tessory Academy is a company which offers their customers a wide selection of private school education. This December, Mount Tessory Academy recognized 1 year of depreciation on a building which had a total useful life of 25 years, and which had originally been bought for $219000.

824 Fairway Malls is an organization which specializes in providing their customers with retail spaces in their shopping centers. This month, Fairway Malls paid 1 monthly loan repayment towards their long-term note payable. The interest portion was 60% of the payment. The total amount paid in cash was $26000.

825 Air America offers their customers a wide range of global flights. This December, Air America has paid each of the company's 1900 owners an annual dividend in the amount of $12000.

826 Toyonda sells several different types of cars. This December, Toyonda recognized 1 year of depreciation on a building which had a total useful life of 25 years, and which had originally been bought for $385000.

827 Mr. Mop sells various household cleaners. Today, Mr. Mop bought equipment which has a 5 year useful life, and which had a cost of $22000.

828 Kola-Nut Ltd is an organization which specializes in providing their customers with soft drinks. Today Kola-Nut Ltd signed up for a loan with a 5% interest rate, and so the bank immediately transferred cash to the company in the amount of $32000.

829 A to Z Event Guru Ltd is a corporation which sells start-to-finish event planning services for large gatherings. Today A to Z Event Guru Ltd signed up for a loan with a 5% interest rate, and so the bank immediately transferred cash to the company in the amount of $77000.

830 Kola-Nut Ltd is a corporation which sells soft drinks. This week, Kola-Nut Ltd purchased 4630 batches of soda bottles which were placed into the warehouse, and which had a per-unit cost of $2700.

831 Fairway Malls provides their customers with retail spaces in their shopping centers. This month, Fairway Malls must amortize 1 month worth of utility bills which they had prepaid at the beginning of the year. The amount that they had paid upfront for the year was $13200.

832 NBG Media Corporation provides their customers with broadcasting services for advertising agencies. Today, NBG Media Corporation bought equipment which has a 5 year useful life, and which had a cost of $15000.

833 Pharma Drug Company Ltd. is a company which offers their customers a wide selection of medications. Today, Pharma Drug Company Ltd. received an upfront payment for 3360 batches of pills which will be provided to the customer 6 months from now. The payment for each was $2800.

834    NBG Media Corporation is a privately-held corporation which focuses on their niche of premium broadcasting services for advertising agencies. This December, NBG Media Corporation recognized 1 year of depreciation on a building which had a total useful life of 25 years, and which had originally been bought for $845000.

835    Mr. Mop offers their customers a wide range of household cleaners. This month, Mr. Mop paid for 1 month of rent for their company's office space. Each month, the rent owing was $8000.

836    Sprike Inc is a privately-held corporation which focuses on their niche of premium athletic apparel. This month, Sprike Inc paid for 1 month of rent for the warehouse room, which has a monthly cost of $2300.

837    NY Fitness offers their customers a wide range of gym memberships for professional sports teams. This December, NY Fitness recognized 1 year of depreciation on a building which had a total useful life of 25 years, and which had originally been bought for $158000.

838    Cirque du Lune sells several different types of circus performances. This year, Cirque du Lune has provided 2000 shows each of which earned revenues of $1360.

839    Mr. Mop provides their customers with household cleaners. This month, Mr. Mop paid for 1 month of rent for their company's office space. Each month, the rent owing was $8000.

840    Jameson & Jameson offers their customers a wide range of soap products. Today Jameson & Jameson sold 41900 truckloads of bars of soap which had a 30% mark-up. They had originally been bought from their suppliers for a unit cost of $1670.

841    Cirque du Lune is a privately-held corporation which focuses on their niche of premium circus performances. This year, Cirque du Lune has provided 1000 shows each of which earned revenues of $2910.

842    Fairway Malls provides their customers with retail spaces in their shopping centers. Today Fairway Malls signed up for a loan with a 5% interest rate, and so the bank immediately transferred cash to the company in the amount of $102000.

843    Pharma Drug Company Ltd. is a company which offers their customers a wide selection of medications. This week, Pharma Drug Company Ltd. purchased 4260 batches of pills which were placed into the warehouse, and which had a per-unit cost of $2200.

844 AC&C Ltd. sells various cell phone plans. AC&C Ltd. has just provided 1900 large orders which had been paid for in advance last year. Each order was in the amount of $1000.

845 Mr. Mop sells various household cleaners. Today, Mr. Mop received an upfront payment for 1120 tons of cleaning solution which will be provided to the customer 6 months from now. The payment for each was $1000.

846 Grand Convention Ltd sells several different types of banquet hall rentals for corporate meetings. Grand Convention Ltd has just purchased a building using cash, which has an expected useful life of 30 years, and which had a total cost of $424000.

847 Jameson & Jameson is a corporation which sells soap products. This week, Jameson & Jameson purchased 1470 truckloads of bars of soap which were placed into the warehouse, and which had a per-unit cost of $1400.

848 NY Fitness is an organization which specializes in providing their customers with gym memberships for professional sports teams. This year, NY Fitness has provided 2300 team memberships each of which earned revenues of $1690.

849 Pharma Drug Company Ltd. is a privately-held corporation which focuses on their niche of premium medications. Today, Pharma Drug Company Ltd. received an upfront payment for 2260 batches of pills which will be provided to the customer 6 months from now. The payment for each was $2600.

850 David & Johnson is a privately-held corporation which focuses on their niche of premium legal services. Today, David & Johnson received payment upfront for 2300 large orders which will not be provided until early next year. Each order was in the amount of $1700.

851 AC&C Ltd. provides their customers with cell phone plans. This year, AC&C Ltd. has provided 1600 monthly cell phone service each of which earned revenues of $2800.

852 NY Fitness is a market leader that is well-known for their brand of gym memberships for professional sports teams. Today, NY Fitness received payment upfront for 2300 large orders which will not be provided until early next year. Each order was in the amount of $2100.

853 AC&C Ltd. is a market leader that is well-known for their brand of cell phone plans. Today, AC&C Ltd. has paid cash to their supplier to fully pay off their account payable balance, which was $18000.

854 Toyonda sells various cars. This January, Toyonda has made an advance payment to cover the next 12 months of utility bills, which have a monthly cost of $2200.

855 Pharma Drug Company Ltd. is a corporation which sells medications. This week, Pharma Drug Company Ltd. purchased 4580 batches of pills which were placed into the warehouse, and which had a per-unit cost of $1100.

856 Comedy 253 offers their customers a wide range of live performances of stand-up comedy. Today, Comedy 253 bought equipment which has a 5 year useful life, and which had a cost of $18000.

857 Grand Convention Ltd is a market leader that is well-known for their brand of banquet hall rentals for corporate meetings. This month, Grand Convention Ltd has estimated that 15% of the accounts receivable might not end up being collectable, based on past experience. The accounts receivable will need to be adjusted from its current balance of $85000.

858 Grand Convention Ltd provides their customers with banquet hall rentals for corporate meetings. This month, Grand Convention Ltd must amortize 1 month worth of utility bills which they had prepaid at the beginning of the year. The amount that they had paid upfront for the year was $37200.

859 Kola-Nut Ltd sells several different types of soft drinks. This month, Kola-Nut Ltd accepted 18400 batches of soda bottles which were returned by customers. These products had been marked up by 35% and they had originally been bought at a per-unit cost of $1300.

860 Cirque du Lune offers their customers a wide range of circus performances. This month, Cirque du Lune has estimated that 25% of the accounts receivable might not end up being collectable, based on past experience. The accounts receivable will need to be adjusted from its current balance of $48000.

861 Club Disco is a privately-held corporation which focuses on their niche of premium dance venue rentals for large family gatherings. This December, Club Disco recognized 1 year of depreciation on equipment which had a total useful life of 10 years, and which had originally cost $180000.

862 Pharma Drug Company Ltd. provides their customers with medications. This month, Pharma Drug Company Ltd. has estimated that 25% of the accounts receivable might not end up being collectable, based on past experience. The accounts receivable will need to be adjusted from its current balance of $89000.

863 Hogtown Records sells several different types of audio services for local musicians to record their music albums. This January, Hogtown Records has made an advance payment to cover the next 12 months of utility bills, which have a monthly cost of $1000.

864 Comedy 253 is a privately-held corporation which focuses on their niche of premium live performances of stand-up comedy. Comedy 253 has just received a cash payment for the full amount that this customer owed to the company for all of their purchases to date. The outstanding balance which has now been paid was $91000.

865 Kola-Nut Ltd is a corporation which sells soft drinks. Today Kola-Nut Ltd sold 4600 batches of soda bottles which had a 30% mark-up. They had originally been bought from their suppliers for a unit cost of $2520.

866 Payday Now is a privately-held corporation which focuses on their niche of premium short-term loan arrangements. Today, Payday Now received payment upfront for 1800 large orders which will not be provided until early next year. Each order was in the amount of $2700.

867 AC&C Ltd. is a privately-held corporation which focuses on their niche of premium cell phone plans. This month, AC&C Ltd. must amortize 1 month worth of utility bills which they had prepaid at the beginning of the year. The amount that they had paid upfront for the year was $19200.

868 Payday Now is a privately-held corporation which focuses on their niche of premium short-term loan arrangements. This January, Payday Now has made an advance payment to cover the next 12 months of utility bills, which have a monthly cost of $1000.

869 NBG Media Corporation sells several different types of broadcasting services for advertising agencies. NBG Media Corporation has just received a cash payment for the full amount that this customer owed to the company for all of their purchases to date. The outstanding balance which has now been paid was $35000.

870 Kola-Nut Ltd sells several different types of soft drinks. This month, Kola-Nut Ltd paid 1 monthly loan repayment towards their long-term note payable. The interest portion was 60% of the payment. The total amount paid in cash was $19000.

871 Hogtown Records provides their customers with audio services for local musicians to record their music albums. This month, Hogtown Records paid for 1 month of rent for their company's office space. Each month, the rent owing was $21000.

872 Toyonda provides their customers with cars. Today, Toyonda bought equipment which has a 5 year useful life, and which had a cost of $20000.

873 Payday Now is a corporation which sells short-term loan arrangements. This January, Payday Now has made an advance payment to cover the next 12 months of utility bills, which have a monthly cost of $1200.

874 Hogtown Records is a corporation which sells audio services for local musicians to record their music albums. Hogtown Records has just purchased a building using cash, which has an expected useful life of 30 years, and which had a total cost of $469000.

875 Air America is a privately-held corporation which focuses on their niche of premium global flights. This January, Air America has made an advance payment to cover the next 12 months of utility bills, which have a monthly cost of $2700.

876 Air America sells various global flights. This month, Air America has estimated that 10% of the accounts receivable might not end up being collectable, based on past experience. The accounts receivable will need to be adjusted from its current balance of $28000.

877 Pharma Drug Company Ltd. is a market leader that is well-known for their brand of medications. This January, Pharma Drug Company Ltd. has made an advance payment to cover the next 12 months of utility bills, which have a monthly cost of $1100.

878 Mr. Mop sells various household cleaners. This month, Mr. Mop accepted 3000 tons of cleaning solution which were returned by customers. These products had been marked up by 35% and they had originally been bought at a per-unit cost of $2100.

879 Sprike Inc is an organization which specializes in providing their customers with athletic apparel. This month, Sprike Inc paid for 1 month of rent for the warehouse room, which has a monthly cost of $1500.

880 Pharma Drug Company Ltd. is a corporation which sells medications. Today, Pharma Drug Company Ltd. received an upfront payment for 1590 batches of pills which will be provided to the customer 6 months from now. The payment for each was $2100.

881 Grand Convention Ltd sells several different types of banquet hall rentals for corporate meetings. This month, Grand Convention Ltd paid 1 monthly loan repayment towards their long-term note payable. The interest portion was 60% of the payment. The total amount paid in cash was $18000.

882 Jameson & Jameson is a company which offers their customers a wide selection of soap products. This month, Jameson & Jameson paid for 1 month of rent for the warehouse room, which has a monthly cost of $1900.

883 Payday Now is a company which offers their customers a wide selection of short-term loan arrangements. This month, Payday Now has estimated that 10% of the accounts receivable might not end up being collectable, based on past experience. The accounts receivable will need to be adjusted from its current balance of $100000.

884 Mr. Mop is an organization which specializes in providing their customers with household cleaners. This month, Mr. Mop paid for 1 month of rent for the warehouse room, which has a monthly cost of $2500.

885 Air America is an organization which specializes in providing their customers with global flights. Air America has just received a cash payment for the full amount that this customer owed to the company for all of their purchases to date. The outstanding balance which has now been paid was $39000.

886 Comedy 253 offers their customers a wide range of live performances of stand-up comedy. Today, Comedy 253 has paid cash to their supplier to fully pay off their account payable balance, which was $65000.

887 AC&C Ltd. offers their customers a wide range of cell phone plans. AC&C Ltd. has just received a cash payment for the full amount that this customer owed to the company for all of their purchases to date. The outstanding balance which has now been paid was $35000.

888 A to Z Event Guru Ltd offers their customers a wide range of start-to-finish event planning services for large gatherings. This December, A to Z Event Guru Ltd recognized 1 year of depreciation on equipment which had a total useful life of 10 years, and which had originally cost $110000.

889 Grand Convention Ltd is a company which offers their customers a wide selection of banquet hall rentals for corporate meetings. Today Grand Convention Ltd signed up for a loan with a 5% interest rate, and so the bank immediately transferred cash to the company in the amount of $70000.

890 Hogtown Records sells several different types of audio services for local musicians to record their music albums. This December, Hogtown Records has paid each of the company's 2400 owners an annual dividend in the amount of $8000.

891 Fairway Malls offers their customers a wide range of retail spaces in their shopping centers. This January, Fairway Malls has made an advance payment to cover the next 12 months of utility bills, which have a monthly cost of $1000.

892 Fairway Malls sells various retail spaces in their shopping centers. This December, Fairway Malls recognized 1 year of depreciation on a building which had a total useful life of 25 years, and which had originally been bought for $636000.

893    Club Disco provides their customers with dance venue rentals for large family gatherings. This month, Club Disco must amortize 1 month worth of utility bills which they had prepaid at the beginning of the year. The amount that they had paid upfront for the year was $14400.

894    NBG Media Corporation is a corporation which sells broadcasting services for advertising agencies. This month, NBG Media Corporation paid for 1 month of rent for their company's office space. Each month, the rent owing was $11000.

895    NY Fitness is an organization which specializes in providing their customers with gym memberships for professional sports teams. This December, NY Fitness recognized 1 year of depreciation on a building which had a total useful life of 25 years, and which had originally been bought for $587000.

896    Comedy 253 is an organization which specializes in providing their customers with live performances of stand-up comedy. This month, Comedy 253 paid 1 monthly loan repayment towards their long-term note payable. The interest portion was 60% of the payment. The total amount paid in cash was $17000.

897    Kola-Nut Ltd is an organization which specializes in providing their customers with soft drinks. Today, Kola-Nut Ltd received an upfront payment for 2610 batches of soda bottles which will be provided to the customer 6 months from now. The payment for each was $1100.

898    David & Johnson is a company which offers their customers a wide selection of legal services. David & Johnson has just purchased a building using cash, which has an expected useful life of 30 years, and which had a total cost of $908000.

899    Mount Tessory Academy provides their customers with private school education. This year, Mount Tessory Academy has provided 2000 annual tuition memberships each of which earned revenues of $2030.

900    Paytech Ltd is a market leader that is well-known for their brand of payroll transaction processing services. This December, Paytech Ltd recognized 1 year of depreciation on equipment which had a total useful life of 10 years, and which had originally cost $110000.

901    Mount Tessory Academy is a corporation which sells private school education. This December, Mount Tessory Academy has paid each of the company's 1100 owners an annual dividend in the amount of $9000.

902    Pharma Drug Company Ltd. is a company which offers their customers a wide selection of medications. Today, Pharma Drug Company Ltd. received an upfront payment for 3650 batches of pills which will be provided to the customer 6 months from now. The payment for each was $1400.

903     Sprike Inc is a corporation which sells athletic apparel. Today, Sprike Inc received an upfront payment for 1790 batches of athletic t-shirts which will be provided to the customer 6 months from now. The payment for each was $2500.

904     Sprike Inc sells various athletic apparel. This January, Sprike Inc has made an advance payment to cover the next 12 months of utility bills, which have a monthly cost of $1500.

905     Mount Tessory Academy offers their customers a wide range of private school education. Today, Mount Tessory Academy has paid cash to their supplier to fully pay off their account payable balance, which was $96000.

906     Pharma Drug Company Ltd. is a privately-held corporation which focuses on their niche of premium medications. This month, Pharma Drug Company Ltd. accepted 5900 batches of pills which were returned by customers. These products had been marked up by 35% and they had originally been bought at a per-unit cost of $1400.

907     LA Met Theatre Company is a privately-held corporation which focuses on their niche of premium live theatrical performances. Today LA Met Theatre Company signed up for a loan with a 5% interest rate, and so the bank immediately transferred cash to the company in the amount of $104000.

908     Fairway Malls sells various retail spaces in their shopping centers. This December, Fairway Malls recognized 1 year of depreciation on equipment which had a total useful life of 10 years, and which had originally cost $210000.

909     Mr. Mop is a privately-held corporation which focuses on their niche of premium household cleaners. This month, Mr. Mop paid for 1 month of rent for the warehouse room, which has a monthly cost of $1700.

910     A to Z Event Guru Ltd offers their customers a wide range of start-to-finish event planning services for large gatherings. Today, A to Z Event Guru Ltd has paid cash to their supplier to fully pay off their account payable balance, which was $72000.

911     Mr. Mop is a privately-held corporation which focuses on their niche of premium household cleaners. Today Mr. Mop sold 41300 tons of cleaning solution which had a 30% mark-up. They had originally been bought from their suppliers for a unit cost of $2960.

912     Kola-Nut Ltd is a privately-held corporation which focuses on their niche of premium soft drinks. Today, Kola-Nut Ltd received an upfront payment for 3040 batches of soda bottles which will be provided to the customer 6 months from now. The payment for each was $1200.

913     NY Fitness is an organization which specializes in providing their customers with gym memberships for professional sports teams. NY Fitness has just received a cash payment for the full amount that this customer owed to the company for all of their purchases to date. The outstanding balance which has now been paid was $71000.

914     Fairway Malls offers their customers a wide range of retail spaces in their shopping centers. Fairway Malls has just purchased a building using cash, which has an expected useful life of 30 years, and which had a total cost of $831000.

915     McGerald's sells several different types of fast food meals. Today McGerald's signed up for a loan with a 5% interest rate, and so the bank immediately transferred cash to the company in the amount of $34000.

916     Sprike Inc offers their customers a wide range of athletic apparel. Today, Sprike Inc bought equipment which has a 5 year useful life, and which had a cost of $15000.

917     Jameson & Jameson sells several different types of soap products. Jameson & Jameson has just purchased a building using cash, which has an expected useful life of 30 years, and which had a total cost of $912000.

918     Jameson & Jameson is a company which offers their customers a wide selection of soap products. This week, Jameson & Jameson purchased 4460 truckloads of bars of soap which were placed into the warehouse, and which had a per-unit cost of $2300.

919     Club Disco offers their customers a wide range of dance venue rentals for large family gatherings. This year, Club Disco has provided 1800 evening rentals each of which earned revenues of $2520.

920     Pharma Drug Company Ltd. is an organization which specializes in providing their customers with medications. This month, Pharma Drug Company Ltd. has estimated that 5% of the accounts receivable might not end up being collectable, based on past experience. The accounts receivable will need to be adjusted from its current balance of $77000.

921     Mr. Mop is a corporation which sells household cleaners. This week, Mr. Mop purchased 3430 tons of cleaning solution which were placed into the warehouse, and which had a per-unit cost of $1900.

922     Hogtown Records sells several different types of audio services for local musicians to record their music albums. This month, Hogtown Records must amortize 1 month worth of utility bills which they had prepaid at the beginning of the year. The amount that they had paid upfront for the year was $44400.

923     Kola-Nut Ltd is a corporation which sells soft drinks. Today, Kola-Nut Ltd has paid cash to their supplier to fully pay off their account payable balance, which was $64000.

924     Jameson & Jameson provides their customers with soap products. This month, Jameson & Jameson accepted 17700 truckloads of bars of soap which were returned by customers. These products had been marked up by 35% and they had originally been bought at a per-unit cost of $1300.

925     Mr. Mop offers their customers a wide range of household cleaners. This month, Mr. Mop must amortize 1 month worth of utility bills which they had prepaid at the beginning of the year. The amount that they had paid upfront for the year was $13200.

926     Fairway Malls sells several different types of retail spaces in their shopping centers. This month, Fairway Malls has estimated that 5% of the accounts receivable might not end up being collectable, based on past experience. The accounts receivable will need to be adjusted from its current balance of $74000.

927     AC&C Ltd. is a company which offers their customers a wide selection of cell phone plans. This month, AC&C Ltd. paid for 1 month of rent for their company's office space. Each month, the rent owing was $18000.

928     NBG Media Corporation offers their customers a wide range of broadcasting services for advertising agencies. This month, NBG Media Corporation paid 1 monthly loan repayment towards their long-term note payable. The interest portion was 60% of the payment. The total amount paid in cash was $26000.

929     David & Johnson sells several different types of legal services. Today, David & Johnson received payment upfront for 2300 large orders which will not be provided until early next year. Each order was in the amount of $2100.

930     Club Disco sells various dance venue rentals for large family gatherings. Club Disco has just provided 1400 large orders which had been paid for in advance last year. Each order was in the amount of $2400.

931     Kola-Nut Ltd sells various soft drinks. This month, Kola-Nut Ltd paid for 1 month of rent for the warehouse room, which has a monthly cost of $1200.

932     McGerald's sells various fast food meals. This month, McGerald's has estimated that 10% of the accounts receivable might not end up being collectable, based on past experience. The accounts receivable will need to be adjusted from its current balance of $82000.

933 Pharma Drug Company Ltd. offers their customers a wide range of medications. This month, Pharma Drug Company Ltd. paid 1 monthly loan repayment towards their long-term note payable. The interest portion was 60% of the payment. The total amount paid in cash was $17000.

934 McGerald's sells various fast food meals. Today McGerald's signed up for a loan with a 5% interest rate, and so the bank immediately transferred cash to the company in the amount of $27000.

935 Mount Tessory Academy is a market leader that is well-known for their brand of private school education. This month, Mount Tessory Academy must amortize 1 month worth of utility bills which they had prepaid at the beginning of the year. The amount that they had paid upfront for the year was $18000.

936 Comedy 253 is a privately-held corporation which focuses on their niche of premium live performances of stand-up comedy. Comedy 253 has just provided 1600 large orders which had been paid for in advance last year. Each order was in the amount of $2700.

937 Air America is a privately-held corporation which focuses on their niche of premium global flights. This December, Air America has paid each of the company's 1500 owners an annual dividend in the amount of $16000.

938 Grand Convention Ltd is a privately-held corporation which focuses on their niche of premium banquet hall rentals for corporate meetings. This December, Grand Convention Ltd has paid each of the company's 1200 owners an annual dividend in the amount of $22000.

939 NY Fitness is a market leader that is well-known for their brand of gym memberships for professional sports teams. This month, NY Fitness must amortize 1 month worth of utility bills which they had prepaid at the beginning of the year. The amount that they had paid upfront for the year was $40800.

940 Payday Now offers their customers a wide range of short-term loan arrangements. This month, Payday Now must amortize 1 month worth of utility bills which they had prepaid at the beginning of the year. The amount that they had paid upfront for the year was $13200.

941 Jameson & Jameson sells various soap products. This month, Jameson & Jameson must amortize 1 month worth of utility bills which they had prepaid at the beginning of the year. The amount that they had paid upfront for the year was $39600.

942 Mount Tessory Academy sells various private school education subscriptions. Today Mount Tessory Academy signed up for a loan with a 5% interest rate, and so the bank immediately transferred cash to the company in the amount of $57000.

943    LA Met Theatre Company is an organization which specializes in providing their customers with live theatrical performances. Today LA Met Theatre Company signed up for a loan with a 5% interest rate, and so the bank immediately transferred cash to the company in the amount of $37000.

944    NY Fitness offers their customers a wide range of gym memberships for professional sports teams. This January, NY Fitness has made an advance payment to cover the next 12 months of utility bills, which have a monthly cost of $2700.

945    LA Met Theatre Company is a market leader that is well-known for their brand of live theatrical performances. Today, LA Met Theatre Company bought equipment which has a 5 year useful life, and which had a cost of $12000.

946    NBG Media Corporation offers their customers a wide range of broadcasting services for advertising agencies. Today, NBG Media Corporation has paid cash to their supplier to fully pay off their account payable balance, which was $45000.

947    Fairway Malls is a corporation which sells retail spaces in their shopping centers. Today, Fairway Malls received payment upfront for 1900 large orders which will not be provided until early next year. Each order was in the amount of $2800.

948    NY Fitness is a market leader that is well-known for their brand of gym memberships for professional sports teams. This January, NY Fitness has made an advance payment to cover the next 12 months of utility bills, which have a monthly cost of $1300.

949    LA Met Theatre Company is a corporation which sells live theatrical performances. This December, LA Met Theatre Company recognized 1 year of depreciation on equipment which had a total useful life of 10 years, and which had originally cost $220000.

950    Club Disco offers their customers a wide range of dance venue rentals for large family gatherings. This December, Club Disco recognized 1 year of depreciation on a building which had a total useful life of 25 years, and which had originally been bought for $437000.

951    NY Fitness sells various gym memberships for professional sports teams. Today, NY Fitness received payment upfront for 1500 large orders which will not be provided until early next year. Each order was in the amount of $2300.

952    Grand Convention Ltd is a market leader that is well-known for their brand of banquet hall rentals for corporate meetings. This week, Grand Convention Ltd paid each of the 3810 staff members their bi-weekly wages, which per person had a cost of $2600.

953     Jameson & Jameson is a corporation which sells soap products. This month, Jameson & Jameson accepted 17000 truckloads of bars of soap which were returned by customers. These products had been marked up by 35% and they had originally been bought at a per-unit cost of $1400.

954     Jameson & Jameson offers their customers a wide range of soap products. This December, Jameson & Jameson has paid each of the company's 1700 owners an annual dividend in the amount of $18000.

955     AC&C Ltd. sells several different types of cell phone plans. Today AC&C Ltd. signed up for a loan with a 5% interest rate, and so the bank immediately transferred cash to the company in the amount of $75000.

956     Kola-Nut Ltd offers their customers a wide range of soft drinks. This month, Kola-Nut Ltd paid for 1 month of rent for the warehouse room, which has a monthly cost of $1800.

957     A to Z Event Guru Ltd is a corporation which sells start-to-finish event planning services for large gatherings. This week, A to Z Event Guru Ltd paid each of the 3350 staff members their bi-weekly wages, which per person had a cost of $1300.

958     Comedy 253 provides their customers with live performances of stand-up comedy. Comedy 253 has just received a cash payment for the full amount that this customer owed to the company for all of their purchases to date. The outstanding balance which has now been paid was $15000.

959     NY Fitness is an organization which specializes in providing their customers with gym memberships for professional sports teams. This month, NY Fitness paid for 1 month of rent for their company's office space. Each month, the rent owing was $12000.

960     Mr. Mop is a corporation which sells household cleaners. This month, Mr. Mop accepted 20700 tons of cleaning solution which were returned by customers. These products had been marked up by 35% and they had originally been bought at a per-unit cost of $2700.

961     Jameson & Jameson is an organization which specializes in providing their customers with soap products. This month, Jameson & Jameson paid for 1 month of rent for the warehouse room, which has a monthly cost of $1200.

962     LA Met Theatre Company provides their customers with live theatrical performances. This week, LA Met Theatre Company paid each of the 2150 staff members their bi-weekly wages, which per person had a cost of $2200.

963 Kola-Nut Ltd offers their customers a wide range of soft drinks. This month, Kola-Nut Ltd accepted 24900 batches of soda bottles which were returned by customers. These products had been marked up by 35% and they had originally been bought at a per-unit cost of $2100.

964 Comedy 253 is a company which offers their customers a wide selection of live performances of stand-up comedy. Comedy 253 has just purchased a building using cash, which has an expected useful life of 30 years, and which had a total cost of $644000.

965 Payday Now offers their customers a wide range of short-term loan arrangements. Payday Now has just provided 1000 large orders which had been paid for in advance last year. Each order was in the amount of $2000.

966 Jameson & Jameson is a market leader that is well-known for their brand of soap products. This December, Jameson & Jameson recognized 1 year of depreciation on equipment which had a total useful life of 10 years, and which had originally cost $190000.

967 Sprike Inc is a corporation which sells athletic apparel. Today, Sprike Inc received an upfront payment for 3540 batches of athletic t-shirts which will be provided to the customer 6 months from now. The payment for each was $2600.

968 Air America is an organization which specializes in providing their customers with global flights. This month, Air America paid 1 monthly loan repayment towards their long-term note payable. The interest portion was 60% of the payment. The total amount paid in cash was $22000.

969 Toyonda sells several different types of cars. This month, Toyonda paid 1 monthly loan repayment towards their long-term note payable. The interest portion was 60% of the payment. The total amount paid in cash was $16000.

970 Mr. Mop offers their customers a wide range of household cleaners. This month, Mr. Mop accepted 2800 tons of cleaning solution which were returned by customers. These products had been marked up by 35% and they had originally been bought at a per-unit cost of $1300.

971 David & Johnson is a market leader that is well-known for their brand of legal services. This month, David & Johnson paid 1 monthly loan repayment towards their long-term note payable. The interest portion was 60% of the payment. The total amount paid in cash was $13000.

972 Air America is a market leader that is well-known for their brand of global flights. This January, Air America has made an advance payment to cover the next 12 months of utility bills, which have a monthly cost of $1600.

973 McGerald's is a market leader that is well-known for their brand of fast food meals. McGerald's has just provided 1900 large orders which had been paid for in advance last year. Each order was in the amount of $2800.

974 Comedy 253 is an organization which specializes in providing their customers with live performances of stand-up comedy. This month, Comedy 253 must amortize 1 month worth of utility bills which they had prepaid at the beginning of the year. The amount that they had paid upfront for the year was $32400.

975 Mount Tessory Academy offers their customers a wide range of private school education. Today, Mount Tessory Academy has paid cash to their supplier to fully pay off their account payable balance, which was $80000.

976 Pharma Drug Company Ltd. sells various medications. This month, Pharma Drug Company Ltd. paid for 1 month of rent for the warehouse room, which has a monthly cost of $2100.

977 Cirque du Lune is an organization which specializes in providing their customers with circus performances. This December, Cirque du Lune recognized 1 year of depreciation on a building which had a total useful life of 25 years, and which had originally been bought for $770000.

978 Mr. Mop is a privately-held corporation which focuses on their niche of premium household cleaners. Mr. Mop has just received a cash payment for the full amount that this customer owed to the company for all of their purchases to date. The outstanding balance which has now been paid was $82000.

979 Kola-Nut Ltd is an organization which specializes in providing their customers with soft drinks. Today, Kola-Nut Ltd received an upfront payment for 1090 batches of soda bottles which will be provided to the customer 6 months from now. The payment for each was $1900.

980 Pharma Drug Company Ltd. offers their customers a wide range of medications. This month, Pharma Drug Company Ltd. must amortize 1 month worth of utility bills which they had prepaid at the beginning of the year. The amount that they had paid upfront for the year was $22800.

981 Jameson & Jameson is a privately-held corporation which focuses on their niche of premium soap products. This week, Jameson & Jameson purchased 3670 truckloads of bars of soap which were placed into the warehouse, and which had a per-unit cost of $1500.

982 NY Fitness is a corporation which sells gym memberships for professional sports teams. Today NY Fitness signed up for a loan with a 5% interest rate, and so the bank immediately transferred cash to the company in the amount of $42000.

983 Kola-Nut Ltd is a company which offers their customers a wide selection of soft drinks. Today Kola-Nut Ltd signed up for a loan with a 5% interest rate, and so the bank immediately transferred cash to the company in the amount of $111000.

984 Pharma Drug Company Ltd. provides their customers with medications. Today Pharma Drug Company Ltd. signed up for a loan with a 5% interest rate, and so the bank immediately transferred cash to the company in the amount of $111000.

985 Grand Convention Ltd is a market leader that is well-known for their brand of banquet hall rentals for corporate meetings. This December, Grand Convention Ltd recognized 1 year of depreciation on equipment which had a total useful life of 10 years, and which had originally cost $110000.

986 Fairway Malls sells various retail spaces in their shopping centers. Today, Fairway Malls received payment upfront for 2000 large orders which will not be provided until early next year. Each order was in the amount of $2200.

987 Sprike Inc provides their customers with athletic apparel. Today Sprike Inc sold 29900 batches of athletic t-shirts which had a 30% mark-up. They had originally been bought from their suppliers for a unit cost of $1190.

988 Jameson & Jameson offers their customers a wide range of soap products. This month, Jameson & Jameson paid for 1 month of rent for the warehouse room, which has a monthly cost of $2100.

989 Kola-Nut Ltd is a privately-held corporation which focuses on their niche of premium soft drinks. This month, Kola-Nut Ltd paid for 1 month of rent for the warehouse room, which has a monthly cost of $1900.

990 Toyonda offers their customers a wide range of cars. This January, Toyonda has made an advance payment to cover the next 12 months of utility bills, which have a monthly cost of $2200.

991 Mr. Mop provides their customers with household cleaners. This week, Mr. Mop purchased 2010 tons of cleaning solution which were placed into the warehouse, and which had a per-unit cost of $1200.

992 Toyonda is a market leader that is well-known for their brand of cars. Today, Toyonda bought equipment which has a 5 year useful life, and which had a cost of $20000.

993 Fairway Malls sells several different types of retail spaces in their shopping centers. This month, Fairway Malls has estimated that 20% of the accounts receivable might not end up being collectable, based on past experience. The accounts receivable will need to be adjusted from its current balance of $73000.

994 AC&C Ltd. sells various cell phone plans. This January, AC&C Ltd. has made an advance payment to cover the next 12 months of utility bills, which have a monthly cost of $1500.

995 Kola-Nut Ltd is a corporation which sells soft drinks. Today, Kola-Nut Ltd has paid cash to their supplier to fully pay off their account payable balance, which was $57000.

996 A to Z Event Guru Ltd is a corporation which sells start-to-finish event planning services for large gatherings. This month, A to Z Event Guru Ltd paid 1 monthly loan repayment towards their long-term note payable. The interest portion was 60% of the payment. The total amount paid in cash was $19000.

997 Club Disco is an organization which specializes in providing their customers with dance venue rentals for large family gatherings. This December, Club Disco has paid each of the company's 1300 owners an annual dividend in the amount of $8000.

998 Cirque du Lune is a market leader that is well-known for their brand of circus performances. Today, Cirque du Lune received payment upfront for 1100 large orders which will not be provided until early next year. Each order was in the amount of $1300.

999 McGerald's sells several different types of fast food meals. Today, McGerald's received payment upfront for 1900 large orders which will not be provided until early next year. Each order was in the amount of $2400.

1000 Air America sells various global flights. Today, Air America has paid cash to their supplier to fully pay off their account payable balance, which was $9000.

**SOLUTIONS:**

1      David & Johnson sells various legal services.  This January, David & Johnson has made an advance payment to cover the next 12 months of utility bills, which have a monthly cost of $2400.

DR Prepaid Expense $28,800   CR Cash $28,800

The prepaid expense (asset) account has increased, and the cash (asset) account has decreased by: 12 months x $2,400 per month = $28,800 for the year.

2      Paytech Ltd sells various payroll transaction processing services.  This January, Paytech Ltd has made an advance payment to cover the next 12 months of utility bills, which have a monthly cost of $1200.

DR Prepaid Expense $14,400   CR Cash $14,400

The prepaid expense (asset) account has increased, and the cash (asset) account has decreased by: 12 months x $1,200 per month = $14,400 for the year.

3      Club Disco is a company which offers their customers a wide selection of dance venue rentals for large family gatherings.  Club Disco has just received a cash payment for the full amount that this customer owed to the company for all of their purchases to date. The outstanding balance which has now been paid was $75000.

DR Cash $75,000   CR Accounts Receivable $75,000

The cash (asset) account has increased, and the accounts receivable (asset) account has decreased by $75,000.

4      Mr. Mop provides their customers with household cleaners.  Mr. Mop has just received a cash payment for the full amount that this customer owed to the company for all of their purchases to date. The outstanding balance which has now been paid was $35000.

DR Cash $35,000   CR Accounts Receivable $35,000

The cash (asset) account has increased, and the accounts receivable (asset) account has decreased by $35,000.

5    A to Z Event Guru Ltd sells various start-to-finish event planning services for large gatherings. This January, A to Z Event Guru Ltd has made an advance payment to cover the next 12 months of utility bills, which have a monthly cost of $2400.

DR Prepaid Expense $28,800    CR Cash $28,800

The prepaid expense (asset) account has increased, and the cash (asset) account has decreased by: 12 months x $2,400 per month = $28,800 for the year.

6    Mr. Mop is a market leader that is well-known for their brand of household cleaners. This month, Mr. Mop has estimated that 10% of the accounts receivable might not end up being collectable, based on past experience. The accounts receivable will need to be adjusted from its current balance of $21000.

DR Bad Debt expense $2,100    CR Allowance for Doubtful Accounts $2,100

The bad debts (expense) and the allowance for doubtful accounts (contra-asset) have both increased by: 10% x $21,000 = $2,100

7    David & Johnson is an organization which specializes in providing their customers with legal services. David & Johnson has just provided 2300 large orders which had been paid for in advance last year. Each order was in the amount of $1900.

DR Unearned Revenue $4,370,000    CR Sales $4,370,000

The unearned revenue (liability) account has decreased and the and the sales (revenue) account has increased by: 2300 large orders x $1,900 = $4,370,000

8    Hogtown Records is a company which offers their customers a wide selection of audio services for local musicians to record their music albums. Hogtown Records has just received a cash payment for the full amount that this customer owed to the company for all of their purchases to date. The outstanding balance which has now been paid was $33000.

DR Cash $33,000    CR Accounts Receivable $33,000

The cash (asset) account has increased, and the accounts receivable (asset) account has decreased by $33,000.

9    Mr. Mop is a corporation which sells household cleaners.  Today Mr. Mop sold 31800 tons of cleaning solution which had a 30% mark-up. They had originally been bought from their suppliers for a unit cost of $2350.

DR Accounts Receivable $97,149,000    DR Cost of Goods Sold $74,730,000
CR Sales $97,149,000    CR Inventory $74,730,000

This transaction increases the accounts receivable (asset) account, the sales (revenue) account, and the cost of goods sold (expense) account. The inventory (asset) account has decreased. 31800 tons of cleaning solution x $2,350 = $74,730,000.  The 30% markup applies to the sales and accounts receivable amounts, i.e. $74,730,000 x 1.30 = $97,149,000

10   Pharma Drug Company Ltd. is a privately-held corporation which focuses on their niche of premium medications.  This month, Pharma Drug Company Ltd. has estimated that 20% of the accounts receivable might not end up being collectable, based on past experience. The accounts receivable will need to be adjusted from its current balance of $73000.

DR Bad Debt expense $14,600    CR Allowance for Doubtful Accounts $14,600

The bad debts (expense) and the allowance for doubtful accounts (contra-asset) have both increased by: 20% x $73,000 = $14,600

11   Kola-Nut Ltd is a corporation which sells soft drinks.  This month, Kola-Nut Ltd must amortize 1 month worth of utility bills which they had prepaid at the beginning of the year. The amount that they had paid upfront for the year was $18000.

DR Utilities expense $1,500    CR Prepaid Expense $1,500

The utilities (expense) account has increased and the prepaid expense (asset) account has decreased by: $18,000 for the year, divided by 12 months = $1,500

12   Paytech Ltd sells various payroll transaction processing services.  Today Paytech Ltd signed up for a loan with a 5% interest rate, and so the bank immediately transferred cash to the company in the amount of $89000.

DR Cash $89,000    CR Loan Payable $89,000

The cash (asset) and the loan payable (liability) accounts have both increased by: $89,000. The interest rate does not affect this initial accounting entry, but it will be used for the calculation of interest expense when repayments are made in the future toward this loan.

13    Hogtown Records sells various audio services for local musicians to record their music albums. This month, Hogtown Records must amortize 1 month worth of utility bills which they had prepaid at the beginning of the year. The amount that they had paid upfront for the year was $28800.

DR Utilities expense $2,400    CR Prepaid Expense $2,400

The utilities (expense) account has increased and the prepaid expense (asset) account has decreased by: $28,800 for the year, divided by 12 months = $2,400

14    Jameson & Jameson is a company which offers their customers a wide selection of soap products. This month, Jameson & Jameson paid for 1 month of rent for their company's office space. Each month, the rent owing was $18000.

DR Rent expense $18,000    CR Accounts Payable $18,000

The rent (expense) and the accounts payable (liability) accounts are both increased by one month's worth of rent, which is $18,000.

15    Sprike Inc is a market leader that is well-known for their brand of athletic apparel. This December, Sprike Inc recognized 1 year of depreciation on a building which had a total useful life of 25 years, and which had originally been bought for $752000.

DR Depreciation expense $30,080    CR Accumulated Depreciation $30,080

The depreciation (expense) account and the accumulated depreciation (contra-asset) accounts have both increased by: $752,000 divided by 25 years = $30,080 depreciation per year.

16    Jameson & Jameson provides their customers with soap products. Today Jameson & Jameson sold 38300 truckloads of bars of soap which had a 30% mark-up. They had originally been bought from their suppliers for a unit cost of $1910.

DR Accounts Receivable $95,098,900    DR Cost of Goods Sold $73,153,000
CR Sales $95,098,900    CR Inventory $73,153,000

This transaction increases the accounts receivable (asset) account, the sales (revenue) account, and the cost of goods sold (expense) account. The inventory (asset) account has decreased. 38300 truckloads of bars of soap x $1,910 = $73,153,000. The 30% markup applies to the sales and accounts receivable amounts, i.e. $73,153,000 x 1.30 = $95,098,900

17   McGerald's sells several different types of fast food meals. This December, McGerald's has paid each of the company's 1300 owners an annual dividend in the amount of $18000.

DR Retained Earnings $23,400,000   CR Cash $23,400,000

The retained earnings (equity) and the cash accounts have both decreased by: 1300 owners x $18,000 = $23,400,000

18   Air America is a company which offers their customers a wide selection of global flights. This January, Air America has made an advance payment to cover the next 12 months of utility bills, which have a monthly cost of $2500.

DR Prepaid Expense $30,000   CR Cash $30,000

The prepaid expense (asset) account has increased, and the cash (asset) account has decreased by: 12 months x $2,500 per month = $30,000 for the year.

19   Payday Now is a market leader that is well-known for their brand of short-term loan arrangements. Today Payday Now signed up for a loan with a 5% interest rate, and so the bank immediately transferred cash to the company in the amount of $115000.

DR Cash $115,000   CR Loan Payable $115,000

The cash (asset) and the loan payable (liability) accounts have both increased by: $115,000. The interest rate does not affect this initial accounting entry, but it will be used for the calculation of interest expense when repayments are made in the future toward this loan.

20   Club Disco sells various dance venue rentals for large family gatherings. This December, Club Disco recognized 1 year of depreciation on a building which had a total useful life of 25 years, and which had originally been bought for $42000.

DR Depreciation expense $1,680   CR Accumulated Depreciation $1,680

The depreciation (expense) account and the accumulated depreciation (contra-asset) accounts have both increased by: $42,000 divided by 25 years = $1,680 depreciation per year.

21   Pharma Drug Company Ltd. is a company which offers their customers a wide selection of medications.  This week, Pharma Drug Company Ltd. purchased 3820 batches of pills which were placed into the warehouse, and which had a per-unit cost of $2200.

DR Inventory $8,404,000    CR Accounts Payable $8,404,000

There was an increase in the inventory (asset) account, and also an increase in the accounts payable (liability) account. 3820 batches of pills x $2,200 = $8,404,000

22   McGerald's provides their customers with fast food meals.  Today McGerald's signed up for a loan with a 5% interest rate, and so the bank immediately transferred cash to the company in the amount of $100000.

DR Cash $100,000    CR Loan Payable $100,000

The cash (asset) and the loan payable (liability) accounts have both increased by: $100,000. The interest rate does not affect this initial accounting entry, but it will be used for the calculation of interest expense when repayments are made in the future toward this loan.

23   Air America is a privately-held corporation which focuses on their niche of premium global flights.  Today, Air America has paid cash to their supplier to fully pay off their account payable balance, which was $70000.

DR Accounts Payable $70,000    CR Cash $70,000

The accounts payable (liability) and cash (asset) accounts have both increased by $70,000.

24   Grand Convention Ltd is a company which offers their customers a wide selection of banquet hall rentals for corporate meetings.  Today Grand Convention Ltd signed up for a loan with a 5% interest rate, and so the bank immediately transferred cash to the company in the amount of $57000.

DR Cash $57,000    CR Loan Payable $57,000

The cash (asset) and the loan payable (liability) accounts have both increased by: $57,000. The interest rate does not affect this initial accounting entry, but it will be used for the calculation of interest expense when repayments are made in the future toward this loan.

25    Kola-Nut Ltd is a privately-held corporation which focuses on their niche of premium soft drinks. This December, Kola-Nut Ltd recognized 1 year of depreciation on a building which had a total useful life of 25 years, and which had originally been bought for $525000.

DR Depreciation expense $21,000    CR Accumulated Depreciation $21,000

The depreciation (expense) account and the accumulated depreciation (contra-asset) accounts have both increased by: $525,000 divided by 25 years = $21,000 depreciation per year.

26    Pharma Drug Company Ltd. is a corporation which sells medications. This week, Pharma Drug Company Ltd. purchased 2260 batches of pills which were placed into the warehouse, and which had a per-unit cost of $2800.

DR Inventory $6,328,000    CR Accounts Payable $6,328,000

There was an increase in the inventory (asset) account, and also an increase in the accounts payable (liability) account. 2260 batches of pills x $2,800 = $6,328,000

27    Jameson & Jameson is an organization which specializes in providing their customers with soap products. This December, Jameson & Jameson recognized 1 year of depreciation on equipment which had a total useful life of 10 years, and which had originally cost $90000.

DR Depreciation expense $9,000    CR Accumulated Depreciation $9,000

The depreciation (expense) account and the accumulated depreciation (contra-asset) accounts have both increased by: $90,000 divided by 10 years = $9,000 depreciation per year.

28    Pharma Drug Company Ltd. sells several different types of medications. This month, Pharma Drug Company Ltd. paid for 1 month of rent for the warehouse room, which has a monthly cost of $2600.

DR Rent expense $2,600    CR Accounts Payable $2,600

The rent (expense) and the accounts payable (liability) accounts are both increased by one month's worth of rent, which is $2,600.

29    Toyonda is a corporation which sells cars. Today, Toyonda has paid cash to their supplier to fully pay off their account payable balance, which was $82000.

DR Accounts Payable $82,000    CR Cash $82,000

The accounts payable (liability) and cash (asset) accounts have both increased by $82,000.

30    Mount Tessory Academy is a privately-held corporation which focuses on their niche of premium private school education. Mount Tessory Academy has just provided 1200 large orders which had been paid for in advance last year. Each order was in the amount of $2100.

DR Unearned Revenue $2,520,000    CR Sales $2,520,000

The unearned revenue (liability) account has decreased and the and the sales (revenue) account has increased by: 1200 large orders x $2,100 = $2,520,000

31    Payday Now is a market leader that is well-known for their brand of short-term loan arrangements. This month, Payday Now paid for 1 month of rent for their company's office space. Each month, the rent owing was $26000.

DR Rent expense $26,000    CR Accounts Payable $26,000

The rent (expense) and the accounts payable (liability) accounts are both increased by one month's worth of rent, which is $26,000.

32    A to Z Event Guru Ltd is a market leader that is well-known for their brand of start-to-finish event planning services for large gatherings. This January, A to Z Event Guru Ltd has made an advance payment to cover the next 12 months of utility bills, which have a monthly cost of $1700.

DR Prepaid Expense $20,400    CR Cash $20,400

The prepaid expense (asset) account has increased, and the cash (asset) account has decreased by: 12 months x $1,700 per month = $20,400 for the year.

33    Kola-Nut Ltd is a market leader that is well-known for their brand of soft drinks. This month, Kola-Nut Ltd accepted 7700 batches of soda bottles which were returned by customers. These products had been marked up by 35% and they had originally been bought at a per-unit cost of $1200.

DR Sales Returns $12,474,000    DR Inventory $9,240,000    CR Accounts Receivable $12,474,000    CR Cost of Goods Sold $9,240,000

This transaction increases the sales returns (contra-revenue) account, and the inventory (asset) account. The accounts receivable (asset) account and the cost of goods sold (expense) account have both decreased. 7700 batches of soda bottles x $1,200 = $9,240,000. The 35% markup applies to the sales returns and accounts receivable amounts, i.e. $9,240,000 x 1.35 = $12,474,000

34    Pharma Drug Company Ltd. sells several different types of medications.  Today Pharma Drug Company Ltd. sold 44600 batches of pills which had a 30% mark-up. They had originally been bought from their suppliers for a unit cost of $2070.

DR Accounts Receivable $120,018,600    DR Cost of Goods Sold $92,322,000 CR Sales $120,018,600    CR Inventory $92,322,000

This transaction increases the accounts receivable (asset) account, the sales (revenue) account, and the cost of goods sold (expense) account. The inventory (asset) account has decreased. 44600 batches of pills x $2,070 = $92,322,000. The 30% markup applies to the sales and accounts receivable amounts, i.e. $92,322,000 x 1.30 = $120,018,600

35    Cirque du Lune is an organization which specializes in providing their customers with circus performances.  This December, Cirque du Lune recognized 1 year of depreciation on equipment which had a total useful life of 10 years, and which had originally cost $200000.

DR Depreciation expense $20,000    CR Accumulated Depreciation $20,000

The depreciation (expense) account and the accumulated depreciation (contra-asset) accounts have both increased by: $200,000 divided by 10 years = $20,000 depreciation per year.

36    Toyonda is a company which offers their customers a wide selection of cars. Today, Toyonda has paid cash to their supplier to fully pay off their account payable balance, which was $29000.

DR Accounts Payable $29,000    CR Cash $29,000

The accounts payable (liability) and cash (asset) accounts have both increased by $29,000.

37    Kola-Nut Ltd provides their customers with soft drinks. This week, Kola-Nut Ltd purchased 4080 batches of soda bottles which were placed into the warehouse, and which had a per-unit cost of $2400.

DR Inventory $9,792,000    CR Accounts Payable $9,792,000

There was an increase in the inventory (asset) account, and also an increase in the accounts payable (liability) account. 4080 batches of soda bottles x $2,400 = $9,792,000

38    NY Fitness is an organization which specializes in providing their customers with gym memberships for professional sports teams. Today, NY Fitness received payment upfront for 1100 large orders which will not be provided until early next year. Each order was in the amount of $1500.

DR Cash $1,650,000    CR Unearned Revenue $1,650,000

The cash (asset) and the unearned revenue (liability) accounts have both increased by: 1100 large orders x $1,500 = $1,650,000

39    LA Met Theatre Company is an organization which specializes in providing their customers with live theatrical performances. This month, LA Met Theatre Company has estimated that 20% of the accounts receivable might not end up being collectable, based on past experience. The accounts receivable will need to be adjusted from its current balance of $53000.

DR Bad Debt expense $10,600    CR Allowance for Doubtful Accounts $10,600

The bad debts (expense) and the allowance for doubtful accounts (contra-asset) have both increased by: 20% x $53,000 = $10,600

40    Pharma Drug Company Ltd. offers their customers a wide range of medications. This month, Pharma Drug Company Ltd. paid 1 monthly loan repayment towards their long-term note payable. The interest portion was 60% of the payment. The total amount paid in cash was $14000.

DR Interest Expense $8,400    DR Loan Payable $5,600    CR Cash $14,000

The interest (expense) account has increased by $14,000 x 0.6 = $8,400. The loan payable (liability) has decreased by $14,000 x 0.4 = $5,600. The cash (asset) account has decreased by the full amount of the payment, which is $14,000

41    David & Johnson is a market leader that is well-known for their brand of legal services. David & Johnson has just purchased a building using cash, which has an expected useful life of 30 years, and which had a total cost of $1013000.

DR Building $1,013,000    CR Cash $1,013,000

The building (asset) account has increased, and the cash (asset) account has decreased by: $1,013,000. The useful life does not affect this original accounting entry, but it will be used to calculate depreciation of the asset in the future.

42    Jameson & Jameson is an organization which specializes in providing their customers with soap products. This month, Jameson & Jameson paid for 1 month of rent for the warehouse room, which has a monthly cost of $2200.

DR Rent expense $2,200    CR Accounts Payable $2,200

The rent (expense) and the accounts payable (liability) accounts are both increased by one month's worth of rent, which is $2,200.

43    NY Fitness is an organization which specializes in providing their customers with gym memberships for professional sports teams. This year, NY Fitness has provided 1300 team memberships each of which earned revenues of $2370.

DR Accounts Receivable $3,081,000    CR Sales $3,081,000

The accounts receivable (asset) and the sales (revenue) accounts have both increased by: 1300 team memberships x $2,370 = $3,081,000

44    NY Fitness offers their customers a wide range of gym memberships for professional sports teams. NY Fitness has just received a cash payment for the full amount that this customer owed to the company for all of their purchases to date. The outstanding balance which has now been paid was $69000.

DR Cash $69,000    CR Accounts Receivable $69,000

The cash (asset) account has increased, and the accounts receivable (asset) account has decreased by $69,000.

45    Mr. Mop provides their customers with household cleaners. Today, Mr. Mop received an upfront payment for 1390 tons of cleaning solution which will be provided to the customer 6 months from now. The payment for each was $2600.

DR Cash $3,614,000    CR Unearned Revenue $3,614,000

The cash (asset) and the unearned revenue (liability) accounts have both increased by: 1390 tons of cleaning solution x $2,600 = $3,614,000

46    Jameson & Jameson is a market leader that is well-known for their brand of soap products. This month, Jameson & Jameson paid for 1 month of rent for the warehouse room, which has a monthly cost of $1000.

DR Rent expense $1,000    CR Accounts Payable $1,000

The rent (expense) and the accounts payable (liability) accounts are both increased by one month's worth of rent, which is $1,000.

47    A to Z Event Guru Ltd sells several different types of start-to-finish event planning services for large gatherings. This month, A to Z Event Guru Ltd must amortize 1 month worth of utility bills which they had prepaid at the beginning of the year. The amount that they had paid upfront for the year was $21600.

DR Utilities expense $1,800    CR Prepaid Expense $1,800

The utilities (expense) account has increased and the prepaid expense (asset) account has decreased by: $21,600 for the year, divided by 12 months = $1,800

48    Sprike Inc is a corporation which sells athletic apparel. This month, Sprike Inc accepted 6100 batches of athletic t-shirts which were returned by customers. These products had been marked up by 35% and they had originally been bought at a per-unit cost of $2400.

DR Sales Returns $19,764,000    DR Inventory $14,640,000    CR Accounts Receivable $19,764,000    CR Cost of Goods Sold $14,640,000

This transaction increases the sales returns (contra-revenue) account, and the inventory (asset) account. The accounts receivable (asset) account and the cost of goods sold (expense) account have both decreased. 6100 batches of athletic t-shirts x $2,400 = $14,640,000. The 35% markup applies to the sales returns and accounts receivable amounts, i.e. $14,640,000 x 1.35 = $19,764,000

49    Fairway Malls is a company which offers their customers a wide selection of retail spaces in their shopping centers. This year, Fairway Malls has provided 2200 monthly retail space rentals each of which earned revenues of $2440.

DR Accounts Receivable $5,368,000    CR Sales $5,368,000

The accounts receivable (asset) and the sales (revenue) accounts have both increased by: 2200 monthly retail space rentals x $2,440 = $5,368,000

50      AC&C Ltd. is a privately-held corporation which focuses on their niche of premium cell phone plans.  AC&C Ltd. has just received a cash payment for the full amount that this customer owed to the company for all of their purchases to date. The outstanding balance which has now been paid was $59000.

DR Cash $59,000    CR Accounts Receivable $59,000

The cash (asset) account has increased, and the accounts receivable (asset) account has decreased by $59,000.

51      Payday Now is a privately-held corporation which focuses on their niche of premium short-term loan arrangements.  Today, Payday Now has paid cash to their supplier to fully pay off their account payable balance, which was $26000.

DR Accounts Payable $26,000    CR Cash $26,000

The accounts payable (liability) and cash (asset) accounts have both increased by $26,000.

52      Grand Convention Ltd is a corporation which sells banquet hall rentals for corporate meetings.  Today, Grand Convention Ltd has paid cash to their supplier to fully pay off their account payable balance, which was $64000.

DR Accounts Payable $64,000    CR Cash $64,000

The accounts payable (liability) and cash (asset) accounts have both increased by $64,000.

53      Mr. Mop is a privately-held corporation which focuses on their niche of premium household cleaners.  This month, Mr. Mop paid for 1 month of rent for the warehouse room, which has a monthly cost of $1600.

DR Rent expense $1,600    CR Accounts Payable $1,600

The rent (expense) and the accounts payable (liability) accounts are both increased by one month's worth of rent, which is $1,600.

54      Sprike Inc provides their customers with athletic apparel.  This month, Sprike Inc paid for 1 month of rent for the warehouse room, which has a monthly cost of $2600.

DR Rent expense $2,600    CR Accounts Payable $2,600

The rent (expense) and the accounts payable (liability) accounts are both increased by one month's worth of rent, which is $2,600.

55    McGerald's offers their customers a wide range of fast food meals.  This year, McGerald's has provided 1700 burger combos each of which earned revenues of $2060.

DR Accounts Receivable $3,502,000    CR Sales $3,502,000

The accounts receivable (asset) and the sales (revenue) accounts have both increased by: 1700 burger combos x $2,060 = $3,502,000

56    Comedy 253 provides their customers with live performances of stand-up comedy.  This month, Comedy 253 paid 1 monthly loan repayment towards their long-term note payable. The interest portion was 60% of the payment. The total amount paid in cash was $23000.

DR Interest Expense $13,800    DR Loan Payable $9,200    CR Cash $23,000

The interest (expense) account has increased by $23,000 x 0.6 = $13,800. The loan payable (liability) has decreased by $23,000 x 0.4 = $9,200. The cash (asset) account has decreased by the full amount of the payment, which is $23,000

57    Paytech Ltd sells several different types of payroll transaction processing services.  Today, Paytech Ltd received payment upfront for 1700 large orders which will not be provided until early next year. Each order was in the amount of $2200.

DR Cash $3,740,000    CR Unearned Revenue $3,740,000

The cash (asset) and the unearned revenue (liability) accounts have both increased by: 1700 large orders x $2,200 = $3,740,000

58    Pharma Drug Company Ltd. is a privately-held corporation which focuses on their niche of premium medications.  This month, Pharma Drug Company Ltd. paid for 1 month of rent for their company's office space. Each month, the rent owing was $20000.

DR Rent expense $20,000    CR Accounts Payable $20,000

The rent (expense) and the accounts payable (liability) accounts are both increased by one month's worth of rent, which is $20,000.

59    Paytech Ltd is a company which offers their customers a wide selection of payroll transaction processing services. This month, Paytech Ltd has estimated that 30% of the accounts receivable might not end up being collectable, based on past experience. The accounts receivable will need to be adjusted from its current balance of $44000.

DR Bad Debt expense $13,200    CR Allowance for Doubtful Accounts $13,200

The bad debts (expense) and the allowance for doubtful accounts (contra-asset) have both increased by: 30% x $44,000 = $13,200

60    Club Disco is a company which offers their customers a wide selection of dance venue rentals for large family gatherings. Today, Club Disco received payment upfront for 2000 large orders which will not be provided until early next year. Each order was in the amount of $1900.

DR Cash $3,800,000    CR Unearned Revenue $3,800,000

The cash (asset) and the unearned revenue (liability) accounts have both increased by: 2000 large orders x $1,900 = $3,800,000

61    Mount Tessory Academy is a corporation which sells private school education. This December, Mount Tessory Academy has paid each of the company's 2100 owners an annual dividend in the amount of $23000.

DR Retained Earnings $48,300,000    CR Cash $48,300,000

The retained earnings (equity) and the cash accounts have both decreased by: 2100 owners x $23,000 = $48,300,000

62    Payday Now sells various short-term loan arrangements. This month, Payday Now paid for 1 month of rent for their company's office space. Each month, the rent owing was $13000.

DR Rent expense $13,000    CR Accounts Payable $13,000

The rent (expense) and the accounts payable (liability) accounts are both increased by one month's worth of rent, which is $13,000.

63    Payday Now is an organization which specializes in providing their customers with short-term loan arrangements. This year, Payday Now has provided 1100 payday loans each of which earned revenues of $1900.

DR Accounts Receivable $2,090,000    CR Sales $2,090,000

The accounts receivable (asset) and the sales (revenue) accounts have both increased by: 1100 payday loans x $1,900 = $2,090,000

64    Fairway Malls offers their customers a wide range of retail spaces in their
      shopping centers.  This month, Fairway Malls paid 1 monthly loan repayment
      towards their long-term note payable. The interest portion was 60% of the
      payment. The total amount paid in cash was $25000.

      DR Interest Expense $15,000    DR Loan Payable $10,000    CR Cash $25,000

      The interest (expense) account has increased by $25,000 x 0.6 = $15,000. The
      loan payable (liability) has decreased by $25,000 x 0.4 = $10,000. The cash
      (asset) account has decreased by the full amount of the payment, which is
      $25,000

65    Kola-Nut Ltd is a market leader that is well-known for their brand of soft drinks.
      Today Kola-Nut Ltd sold 5900 batches of soda bottles which had a 30% mark-up.
      They had originally been bought from their suppliers for a unit cost of $2910.

      DR Accounts Receivable $22,319,700    DR Cost of Goods Sold $17,169,000
      CR Sales $22,319,700    CR Inventory $17,169,000

      This transaction increases the accounts receivable (asset) account, the sales
      (revenue) account, and the cost of goods sold (expense) account. The inventory
      (asset) account has decreased. 5900 batches of soda bottles x $2,910 =
      $17,169,000.  The 30% markup applies to the sales and accounts receivable
      amounts, i.e. $17,169,000 x 1.30 = $22,319,700

66    Grand Convention Ltd sells several different types of banquet hall rentals for
      corporate meetings.  This month, Grand Convention Ltd paid for 1 month of rent
      for their company's office space. Each month, the rent owing was $16000.

      DR Rent expense $16,000    CR Accounts Payable $16,000

      The rent (expense) and the accounts payable (liability) accounts are both
      increased by one month's worth of rent, which is $16,000.

67    Pharma Drug Company Ltd. offers their customers a wide range of medications.
      Pharma Drug Company Ltd. has just purchased a building using cash, which has
      an expected useful life of 30 years, and which had a total cost of $802000.

      DR Building $802,000    CR Cash $802,000

      The building (asset) account has increased, and the cash (asset) account has
      decreased by: $802,000. The useful life does not affect this original accounting
      entry, but it will be used to calculate depreciation of the asset in the future.

68    Payday Now is a privately-held corporation which focuses on their niche of premium short-term loan arrangements. Today Payday Now signed up for a loan with a 5% interest rate, and so the bank immediately transferred cash to the company in the amount of $34000.

DR Cash $34,000    CR Loan Payable $34,000

The cash (asset) and the loan payable (liability) accounts have both increased by: $34,000. The interest rate does not affect this initial accounting entry, but it will be used for the calculation of interest expense when repayments are made in the future toward this loan.

69    David & Johnson is a market leader that is well-known for their brand of legal services. This month, David & Johnson paid 1 monthly loan repayment towards their long-term note payable. The interest portion was 60% of the payment. The total amount paid in cash was $9000.

DR Interest Expense $5,400    DR Loan Payable $3,600    CR Cash $9,000

The interest (expense) account has increased by $9,000 x 0.6 = $5,400. The loan payable (liability) has decreased by $9,000 x 0.4 = $3,600. The cash (asset) account has decreased by the full amount of the payment, which is $9,000

70    NY Fitness sells several different types of gym memberships for professional sports teams. This January, NY Fitness has made an advance payment to cover the next 12 months of utility bills, which have a monthly cost of $1600.

DR Prepaid Expense $19,200    CR Cash $19,200

The prepaid expense (asset) account has increased, and the cash (asset) account has decreased by: 12 months x $1,600 per month = $19,200 for the year.

71    Jameson & Jameson is a privately-held corporation which focuses on their niche of premium soap products. This month, Jameson & Jameson paid for 1 month of rent for the warehouse room, which has a monthly cost of $1900.

DR Rent expense $1,900    CR Accounts Payable $1,900

The rent (expense) and the accounts payable (liability) accounts are both increased by one month's worth of rent, which is $1,900.

72 Mount Tessory Academy sells various private school education subscriptions. Mount Tessory Academy has just received a cash payment for the full amount that this customer owed to the company for all of their purchases to date. The outstanding balance which has now been paid was $34000.

DR Cash $34,000    CR Accounts Receivable $34,000

The cash (asset) account has increased, and the accounts receivable (asset) account has decreased by $34,000.

73 Jameson & Jameson is a privately-held corporation which focuses on their niche of premium soap products.  This month, Jameson & Jameson paid for 1 month of rent for their company's office space. Each month, the rent owing was $20000.

DR Rent expense $20,000    CR Accounts Payable $20,000

The rent (expense) and the accounts payable (liability) accounts are both increased by one month's worth of rent, which is $20,000.

74 Mr. Mop is a market leader that is well-known for their brand of household cleaners.  This month, Mr. Mop accepted 6500 tons of cleaning solution which were returned by customers. These products had been marked up by 35% and they had originally been bought at a per-unit cost of $1500.

DR Sales Returns $13,162,500    DR Inventory $9,750,000    CR Accounts Receivable $13,162,500    CR Cost of Goods Sold $9,750,000

This transaction increases the sales returns (contra-revenue) account, and the inventory (asset) account. The accounts receivable (asset) account and the cost of goods sold (expense) account have both decreased. 6500 tons of cleaning solution x $1,500 = $9,750,000. The 35% markup applies to the sales returns and accounts receivable amounts, i.e. $9,750,000 x 1.35 = $13,162,500

75 Grand Convention Ltd sells several different types of banquet hall rentals for corporate meetings.  This December, Grand Convention Ltd recognized 1 year of depreciation on equipment which had a total useful life of 10 years, and which had originally cost $130000.

DR Depreciation expense $13,000    CR Accumulated Depreciation $13,000

The depreciation (expense) account and the accumulated depreciation (contra-asset) accounts have both increased by: $130,000 divided by 10 years = $13,000 depreciation per year.

76    Club Disco is a company which offers their customers a wide selection of dance
      venue rentals for large family gatherings.  This year, Club Disco has provided
      1100 evening rentals each of which earned revenues of $1050.

      DR Accounts Receivable $1,155,000    CR Sales $1,155,000

      The accounts receivable (asset) and the sales (revenue) accounts have both
      increased by: 1100 evening rentals x $1,050 = $1,155,000

77    Hogtown Records is a market leader that is well-known for their brand of audio
      services for local musicians to record their music albums.  Hogtown Records has
      just purchased a building using cash, which has an expected useful life of 30
      years, and which had a total cost of $193000.

      DR Building $193,000    CR Cash $193,000

      The building (asset) account has increased, and the cash (asset) account has
      decreased by: $193,000. The useful life does not affect this original accounting
      entry, but it will be used to calculate depreciation of the asset in the future.

78    Payday Now sells various short-term loan arrangements.  This month, Payday
      Now paid for 1 month of rent for their company's office space. Each month, the
      rent owing was $26000.

      DR Rent expense $26,000    CR Accounts Payable $26,000

      The rent (expense) and the accounts payable (liability) accounts are both
      increased by one month's worth of rent, which is $26,000.

79    Sprike Inc is a privately-held corporation which focuses on their niche of premium
      athletic apparel.  Today, Sprike Inc received an upfront payment for 4800
      batches of athletic t-shirts which will be provided to the customer 6 months from
      now. The payment for each was $2100.

      DR Cash $10,080,000    CR Unearned Revenue $10,080,000

      The cash (asset) and the unearned revenue (liability) accounts have both
      increased by: 4800 batches of athletic t-shirts x $2,100 = $10,080,000

80      David & Johnson offers their customers a wide range of legal services. Today David & Johnson signed up for a loan with a 5% interest rate, and so the bank immediately transferred cash to the company in the amount of $117000.

DR Cash $117,000    CR Loan Payable $117,000

The cash (asset) and the loan payable (liability) accounts have both increased by: $117,000. The interest rate does not affect this initial accounting entry, but it will be used for the calculation of interest expense when repayments are made in the future toward this loan.

81      Payday Now is a company which offers their customers a wide selection of short-term loan arrangements. Today Payday Now signed up for a loan with a 5% interest rate, and so the bank immediately transferred cash to the company in the amount of $41000.

DR Cash $41,000    CR Loan Payable $41,000

The cash (asset) and the loan payable (liability) accounts have both increased by: $41,000. The interest rate does not affect this initial accounting entry, but it will be used for the calculation of interest expense when repayments are made in the future toward this loan.

82      Mr. Mop is a privately-held corporation which focuses on their niche of premium household cleaners. Today Mr. Mop sold 19800 tons of cleaning solution which had a 30% mark-up. They had originally been bought from their suppliers for a unit cost of $2840.

DR Accounts Receivable $73,101,600    DR Cost of Goods Sold $56,232,000
CR Sales $73,101,600    CR Inventory $56,232,000

This transaction increases the accounts receivable (asset) account, the sales (revenue) account, and the cost of goods sold (expense) account. The inventory (asset) account has decreased. 19800 tons of cleaning solution x $2,840 = $56,232,000. The 30% markup applies to the sales and accounts receivable amounts, i.e. $56,232,000 x 1.30 = $73,101,600

83      Kola-Nut Ltd is a company which offers their customers a wide selection of soft drinks. Kola-Nut Ltd has just purchased a building using cash, which has an expected useful life of 30 years, and which had a total cost of $792000.

DR Building $792,000    CR Cash $792,000

The building (asset) account has increased, and the cash (asset) account has decreased by: $792,000. The useful life does not affect this original accounting entry, but it will be used to calculate depreciation of the asset in the future.

84    Mr. Mop sells several different types of household cleaners. This week, Mr. Mop purchased 3010 tons of cleaning solution which were placed into the warehouse, and which had a per-unit cost of $1800.

DR Inventory $5,418,000   CR Accounts Payable $5,418,000

There was an increase in the inventory (asset) account, and also an increase in the accounts payable (liability) account. 3010 tons of cleaning solution x $1,800 = $5,418,000

85    Mount Tessory Academy is a company which offers their customers a wide selection of private school education. Mount Tessory Academy has just provided 1100 large orders which had been paid for in advance last year. Each order was in the amount of $1200.

DR Unearned Revenue $1,320,000    CR Sales $1,320,000

The unearned revenue (liability) account has decreased and the and the sales (revenue) account has increased by: 1100 large orders x $1,200 = $1,320,000

86    McGerald's provides their customers with fast food meals. This month, McGerald's must amortize 1 month worth of utility bills which they had prepaid at the beginning of the year. The amount that they had paid upfront for the year was $12000.

DR Utilities expense $1,000   CR Prepaid Expense $1,000

The utilities (expense) account has increased and the prepaid expense (asset) account has decreased by: $12,000 for the year, divided by 12 months = $1,000

87    Kola-Nut Ltd is an organization which specializes in providing their customers with soft drinks. This month, Kola-Nut Ltd paid 1 monthly loan repayment towards their long-term note payable. The interest portion was 60% of the payment. The total amount paid in cash was $24000.

DR Interest Expense $14,400   DR Loan Payable $9,600   CR Cash $24,000

The interest (expense) account has increased by $24,000 x 0.6 = $14,400. The loan payable (liability) has decreased by $24,000 x 0.4 = $9,600. The cash (asset) account has decreased by the full amount of the payment, which is $24,000

88    Jameson & Jameson is a privately-held corporation which focuses on their niche of premium soap products. Today, Jameson & Jameson bought equipment which has a 5 year useful life, and which had a cost of $11000.

DR Equipment $11,000    CR Accounts Payable $11,000

The equipment (asset) and the accounts payable (liability) accounts have both increased by: $11,000. The useful life does not affect this original accounting entry, but it will be used to calculate depreciation of the asset in the future.

89    Club Disco is an organization which specializes in providing their customers with dance venue rentals for large family gatherings. This month, Club Disco must amortize 1 month worth of utility bills which they had prepaid at the beginning of the year. The amount that they had paid upfront for the year was $22800.

DR Utilities expense $1,900    CR Prepaid Expense $1,900

The utilities (expense) account has increased and the prepaid expense (asset) account has decreased by: $22,800 for the year, divided by 12 months = $1,900

90    Grand Convention Ltd is a company which offers their customers a wide selection of banquet hall rentals for corporate meetings. This December, Grand Convention Ltd recognized 1 year of depreciation on equipment which had a total useful life of 10 years, and which had originally cost $170000.

DR Depreciation expense $17,000    CR Accumulated Depreciation $17,000

The depreciation (expense) account and the accumulated depreciation (contra-asset) accounts have both increased by: $170,000 divided by 10 years = $17,000 depreciation per year.

91    A to Z Event Guru Ltd is a privately-held corporation which focuses on their niche of premium start-to-finish event planning services for large gatherings. A to Z Event Guru Ltd has just purchased a building using cash, which has an expected useful life of 30 years, and which had a total cost of $398000.

DR Building $398,000    CR Cash $398,000

The building (asset) account has increased, and the cash (asset) account has decreased by: $398,000. The useful life does not affect this original accounting entry, but it will be used to calculate depreciation of the asset in the future.

92   Cirque du Lune sells several different types of circus performances. This month, Cirque du Lune paid 1 monthly loan repayment towards their long-term note payable. The interest portion was 60% of the payment. The total amount paid in cash was $21000.

DR Interest Expense $12,600   DR Loan Payable $8,400   CR Cash $21,000

The interest (expense) account has increased by $21,000 x 0.6 = $12,600. The loan payable (liability) has decreased by $21,000 x 0.4 = $8,400. The cash (asset) account has decreased by the full amount of the payment, which is $21,000

93   Payday Now is a corporation which sells short-term loan arrangements. This month, Payday Now paid for 1 month of rent for their company's office space. Each month, the rent owing was $9000.

DR Rent expense $9,000   CR Accounts Payable $9,000

The rent (expense) and the accounts payable (liability) accounts are both increased by one month's worth of rent, which is $9,000.

94   Club Disco is a company which offers their customers a wide selection of dance venue rentals for large family gatherings. This month, Club Disco has estimated that 10% of the accounts receivable might not end up being collectable, based on past experience. The accounts receivable will need to be adjusted from its current balance of $23000.

DR Bad Debt expense $2,300   CR Allowance for Doubtful Accounts $2,300

The bad debts (expense) and the allowance for doubtful accounts (contra-asset) have both increased by: 10% x $23,000 = $2,300

95   Mr. Mop sells several different types of household cleaners. Today Mr. Mop sold 9600 tons of cleaning solution which had a 30% mark-up. They had originally been bought from their suppliers for a unit cost of $2950.

DR Accounts Receivable $36,816,000   DR Cost of Goods Sold $28,320,000
CR Sales $36,816,000   CR Inventory $28,320,000

This transaction increases the accounts receivable (asset) account, the sales (revenue) account, and the cost of goods sold (expense) account. The inventory (asset) account has decreased. 9600 tons of cleaning solution x $2,950 = $28,320,000. The 30% markup applies to the sales and accounts receivable amounts, i.e. $28,320,000 x 1.30 = $36,816,000

96    Toyonda sells various cars. This month, Toyonda must amortize 1 month worth of utility bills which they had prepaid at the beginning of the year. The amount that they had paid upfront for the year was $37200.

DR Utilities expense $3,100    CR Prepaid Expense $3,100

The utilities (expense) account has increased and the prepaid expense (asset) account has decreased by: $37,200 for the year, divided by 12 months = $3,100

97    Kola-Nut Ltd is a corporation which sells soft drinks. Kola-Nut Ltd has just purchased a building using cash, which has an expected useful life of 30 years, and which had a total cost of $768000.

DR Building $768,000    CR Cash $768,000

The building (asset) account has increased, and the cash (asset) account has decreased by: $768,000. The useful life does not affect this original accounting entry, but it will be used to calculate depreciation of the asset in the future.

98    Pharma Drug Company Ltd. offers their customers a wide range of medications. This week, Pharma Drug Company Ltd. purchased 1340 batches of pills which were placed into the warehouse, and which had a per-unit cost of $1000.

DR Inventory $1,340,000    CR Accounts Payable $1,340,000

There was an increase in the inventory (asset) account, and also an increase in the accounts payable (liability) account. 1340 batches of pills x $1,000 = $1,340,000

99    Paytech Ltd is a privately-held corporation which focuses on their niche of premium payroll transaction processing services. Paytech Ltd has just received a cash payment for the full amount that this customer owed to the company for all of their purchases to date. The outstanding balance which has now been paid was $75000.

DR Cash $75,000    CR Accounts Receivable $75,000

The cash (asset) account has increased, and the accounts receivable (asset) account has decreased by $75,000.

100  Sprike Inc offers their customers a wide range of athletic apparel. Sprike Inc has just received a cash payment for the full amount that this customer owed to the company for all of their purchases to date. The outstanding balance which has now been paid was $53000.

DR Cash $53,000    CR Accounts Receivable $53,000

The cash (asset) account has increased, and the accounts receivable (asset) account has decreased by $53,000.

101  David & Johnson is a privately-held corporation which focuses on their niche of premium legal services. David & Johnson has just purchased a building using cash, which has an expected useful life of 30 years, and which had a total cost of $153000.

DR Building $153,000    CR Cash $153,000

The building (asset) account has increased, and the cash (asset) account has decreased by: $153,000. The useful life does not affect this original accounting entry, but it will be used to calculate depreciation of the asset in the future.

102  Club Disco offers their customers a wide range of dance venue rentals for large family gatherings. Club Disco has just provided 1200 large orders which had been paid for in advance last year. Each order was in the amount of $1400.

DR Unearned Revenue $1,680,000    CR Sales $1,680,000

The unearned revenue (liability) account has decreased and the and the sales (revenue) account has increased by: 1200 large orders x $1,400 = $1,680,000

103  A to Z Event Guru Ltd offers their customers a wide range of start-to-finish event planning services for large gatherings. A to Z Event Guru Ltd has just provided 2300 large orders which had been paid for in advance last year. Each order was in the amount of $1500.

DR Unearned Revenue $3,450,000    CR Sales $3,450,000

The unearned revenue (liability) account has decreased and the and the sales (revenue) account has increased by: 2300 large orders x $1,500 = $3,450,000

104   David & Johnson sells several different types of legal services.  David & Johnson has just purchased a building using cash, which has an expected useful life of 30 years, and which had a total cost of $844000.

DR Building $844,000    CR Cash $844,000

The building (asset) account has increased, and the cash (asset) account has decreased by: $844,000. The useful life does not affect this original accounting entry, but it will be used to calculate depreciation of the asset in the future.

105   AC&C Ltd. is a corporation which sells cell phone plans.  This December, AC&C Ltd. has paid each of the company's 1700 owners an annual dividend in the amount of $16000.

DR Retained Earnings $27,200,000    CR Cash $27,200,000

The retained earnings (equity) and the cash accounts have both decreased by: 1700 owners x $16,000 = $27,200,000

106   McGerald's is a privately-held corporation which focuses on their niche of premium fast food meals.  This week, McGerald's paid each of the 2020 staff members their bi-weekly wages, which per person had a cost of $2200.

DR Wage expense $4,444,000    CR Accounts Payable $4,444,000

The wage (expense) and the accounts payable (liability) accounts have both increased by: 2020 staff members x $2,200 = $4,444,000

107   Payday Now is a privately-held corporation which focuses on their niche of premium short-term loan arrangements.  Today Payday Now signed up for a loan with a 5% interest rate, and so the bank immediately transferred cash to the company in the amount of $102000.

DR Cash $102,000    CR Loan Payable $102,000

The cash (asset) and the loan payable (liability) accounts have both increased by: $102,000. The interest rate does not affect this initial accounting entry, but it will be used for the calculation of interest expense when repayments are made in the future toward this loan.

108     Cirque du Lune is a market leader that is well-known for their brand of circus performances. This January, Cirque du Lune has made an advance payment to cover the next 12 months of utility bills, which have a monthly cost of $1000.

DR Prepaid Expense $12,000    CR Cash $12,000

The prepaid expense (asset) account has increased, and the cash (asset) account has decreased by: 12 months x $1,000 per month = $12,000 for the year.

109     Sprike Inc is a corporation which sells athletic apparel. This month, Sprike Inc paid for 1 month of rent for the warehouse room, which has a monthly cost of $2400.

DR Rent expense $2,400    CR Accounts Payable $2,400

The rent (expense) and the accounts payable (liability) accounts are both increased by one month's worth of rent, which is $2,400.

110     Fairway Malls sells various retail spaces in their shopping centers. This month, Fairway Malls must amortize 1 month worth of utility bills which they had prepaid at the beginning of the year. The amount that they had paid upfront for the year was $33600.

DR Utilities expense $2,800    CR Prepaid Expense $2,800

The utilities (expense) account has increased and the prepaid expense (asset) account has decreased by: $33,600 for the year, divided by 12 months = $2,800

111     Club Disco is a privately-held corporation which focuses on their niche of premium dance venue rentals for large family gatherings. Club Disco has just received a cash payment for the full amount that this customer owed to the company for all of their purchases to date. The outstanding balance which has now been paid was $64000.

DR Cash $64,000    CR Accounts Receivable $64,000

The cash (asset) account has increased, and the accounts receivable (asset) account has decreased by $64,000.

112   Sprike Inc is a market leader that is well-known for their brand of athletic apparel. Today, Sprike Inc received an upfront payment for 5850 batches of athletic t-shirts which will be provided to the customer 6 months from now. The payment for each was $2500.

DR Cash $14,625,000    CR Unearned Revenue $14,625,000

The cash (asset) and the unearned revenue (liability) accounts have both increased by: 5850 batches of athletic t-shirts x $2,500 = $14,625,000

113   Air America is a company which offers their customers a wide selection of global flights.  Air America has just provided 2200 large orders which had been paid for in advance last year. Each order was in the amount of $2200.

DR Unearned Revenue $4,840,000    CR Sales $4,840,000

The unearned revenue (liability) account has decreased and the and the sales (revenue) account has increased by: 2200 large orders x $2,200 = $4,840,000

114   Kola-Nut Ltd is an organization which specializes in providing their customers with soft drinks.  This week, Kola-Nut Ltd purchased 4400 batches of soda bottles which were placed into the warehouse, and which had a per-unit cost of $2200.

DR Inventory $9,680,000    CR Accounts Payable $9,680,000

There was an increase in the inventory (asset) account, and also an increase in the accounts payable (liability) account. 4400 batches of soda bottles x $2,200 = $9,680,000

115   Mr. Mop is a privately-held corporation which focuses on their niche of premium household cleaners.  Today Mr. Mop signed up for a loan with a 5% interest rate, and so the bank immediately transferred cash to the company in the amount of $69000.

DR Cash $69,000    CR Loan Payable $69,000

The cash (asset) and the loan payable (liability) accounts have both increased by: $69,000. The interest rate does not affect this initial accounting entry, but it will be used for the calculation of interest expense when repayments are made in the future toward this loan.

116 Cirque du Lune is a privately-held corporation which focuses on their niche of premium circus performances. This January, Cirque du Lune has made an advance payment to cover the next 12 months of utility bills, which have a monthly cost of $1100.

DR Prepaid Expense $13,200 CR Cash $13,200

The prepaid expense (asset) account has increased, and the cash (asset) account has decreased by: 12 months x $1,100 per month = $13,200 for the year.

117 AC&C Ltd. is a company which offers their customers a wide selection of cell phone plans. Today, AC&C Ltd. has paid cash to their supplier to fully pay off their account payable balance, which was $19000.

DR Accounts Payable $19,000 CR Cash $19,000

The accounts payable (liability) and cash (asset) accounts have both increased by $19,000.

118 Payday Now sells various short-term loan arrangements. This year, Payday Now has provided 1100 payday loans each of which earned revenues of $1370.

DR Accounts Receivable $1,507,000 CR Sales $1,507,000

The accounts receivable (asset) and the sales (revenue) accounts have both increased by: 1100 payday loans x $1,370 = $1,507,000

119 LA Met Theatre Company is an organization which specializes in providing their customers with live theatrical performances. Today, LA Met Theatre Company bought equipment which has a 5 year useful life, and which had a cost of $11000.

DR Equipment $11,000 CR Accounts Payable $11,000

The equipment (asset) and the accounts payable (liability) accounts have both increased by: $11,000. The useful life does not affect this original accounting entry, but it will be used to calculate depreciation of the asset in the future.

120 Kola-Nut Ltd is a corporation which sells soft drinks. This December, Kola-Nut Ltd has paid each of the company's 1300 owners an annual dividend in the amount of $20000.

DR Retained Earnings $26,000,000 CR Cash $26,000,000

The retained earnings (equity) and the cash accounts have both decreased by: 1300 owners x $20,000 = $26,000,000

121    Pharma Drug Company Ltd. offers their customers a wide range of medications. This December, Pharma Drug Company Ltd. recognized 1 year of depreciation on a building which had a total useful life of 25 years, and which had originally been bought for $927000.

DR Depreciation expense $37,080    CR Accumulated Depreciation $37,080

The depreciation (expense) account and the accumulated depreciation (contra-asset) accounts have both increased by: $927,000 divided by 25 years = $37,080 depreciation per year.

122    LA Met Theatre Company sells various live theatrical performances. Today LA Met Theatre Company signed up for a loan with a 5% interest rate, and so the bank immediately transferred cash to the company in the amount of $75000.

DR Cash $75,000    CR Loan Payable $75,000

The cash (asset) and the loan payable (liability) accounts have both increased by: $75,000. The interest rate does not affect this initial accounting entry, but it will be used for the calculation of interest expense when repayments are made in the future toward this loan.

123    Grand Convention Ltd provides their customers with banquet hall rentals for corporate meetings. Today, Grand Convention Ltd received payment upfront for 1600 large orders which will not be provided until early next year. Each order was in the amount of $2000.

DR Cash $3,200,000    CR Unearned Revenue $3,200,000

The cash (asset) and the unearned revenue (liability) accounts have both increased by: 1600 large orders x $2,000 = $3,200,000

124    Hogtown Records sells various audio services for local musicians to record their music albums. This month, Hogtown Records paid 1 monthly loan repayment towards their long-term note payable. The interest portion was 60% of the payment. The total amount paid in cash was $24000.

DR Interest Expense $14,400    DR Loan Payable $9,600    CR Cash $24,000

The interest (expense) account has increased by $24,000 x 0.6 = $14,400. The loan payable (liability) has decreased by $24,000 x 0.4 = $9,600. The cash (asset) account has decreased by the full amount of the payment, which is $24,000

125     Jameson & Jameson is a corporation which sells soap products. Today, Jameson & Jameson received an upfront payment for 3350 truckloads of bars of soap which will be provided to the customer 6 months from now. The payment for each was $1900.

DR Cash $6,365,000    CR Unearned Revenue $6,365,000

The cash (asset) and the unearned revenue (liability) accounts have both increased by: 3350 truckloads of bars of soap x $1,900 = $6,365,000

126     Air America is a company which offers their customers a wide selection of global flights. Today, Air America bought equipment which has a 5 year useful life, and which had a cost of $10000.

DR Equipment $10,000    CR Accounts Payable $10,000

The equipment (asset) and the accounts payable (liability) accounts have both increased by: $10,000. The useful life does not affect this original accounting entry, but it will be used to calculate depreciation of the asset in the future.

127     Comedy 253 provides their customers with live performances of stand-up comedy. This month, Comedy 253 has estimated that 5% of the accounts receivable might not end up being collectable, based on past experience. The accounts receivable will need to be adjusted from its current balance of $25000.

DR Bad Debt expense $1,250    CR Allowance for Doubtful Accounts $1,250

The bad debts (expense) and the allowance for doubtful accounts (contra-asset) have both increased by: 5% x $25,000 = $1,250

128     Club Disco is an organization which specializes in providing their customers with dance venue rentals for large family gatherings. Today, Club Disco has paid cash to their supplier to fully pay off their account payable balance, which was $37000.

DR Accounts Payable $37,000    CR Cash $37,000

The accounts payable (liability) and cash (asset) accounts have both increased by $37,000.

134

129   Air America provides their customers with global flights. Today Air America signed up for a loan with a 5% interest rate, and so the bank immediately transferred cash to the company in the amount of $61000.

DR Cash $61,000   CR Loan Payable $61,000

The cash (asset) and the loan payable (liability) accounts have both increased by: $61,000. The interest rate does not affect this initial accounting entry, but it will be used for the calculation of interest expense when repayments are made in the future toward this loan.

130   McGerald's sells various fast food meals. This December, McGerald's recognized 1 year of depreciation on equipment which had a total useful life of 10 years, and which had originally cost $220000.

DR Depreciation expense $22,000   CR Accumulated Depreciation $22,000

The depreciation (expense) account and the accumulated depreciation (contra-asset) accounts have both increased by: $220,000 divided by 10 years = $22,000 depreciation per year.

131   A to Z Event Guru Ltd is a company which offers their customers a wide selection of start-to-finish event planning services for large gatherings. This December, A to Z Event Guru Ltd recognized 1 year of depreciation on equipment which had a total useful life of 10 years, and which had originally cost $230000.

DR Depreciation expense $23,000   CR Accumulated Depreciation $23,000

The depreciation (expense) account and the accumulated depreciation (contra-asset) accounts have both increased by: $230,000 divided by 10 years = $23,000 depreciation per year.

132   Payday Now is a privately-held corporation which focuses on their niche of premium short-term loan arrangements. This December, Payday Now recognized 1 year of depreciation on a building which had a total useful life of 25 years, and which had originally been bought for $707000.

DR Depreciation expense $28,280   CR Accumulated Depreciation $28,280

The depreciation (expense) account and the accumulated depreciation (contra-asset) accounts have both increased by: $707,000 divided by 25 years = $28,280 depreciation per year.

133     Mount Tessory Academy is a company which offers their customers a wide
        selection of private school education.  Mount Tessory Academy has just
        purchased a building using cash, which has an expected useful life of 30 years,
        and which had a total cost of $541000.

        DR Building $541,000    CR Cash $541,000

        The building (asset) account has increased, and the cash (asset) account has
        decreased by: $541,000. The useful life does not affect this original accounting
        entry, but it will be used to calculate depreciation of the asset in the future.

134     Grand Convention Ltd sells various banquet hall rentals for corporate meetings.
        Grand Convention Ltd has just received a cash payment for the full amount that
        this customer owed to the company for all of their purchases to date. The
        outstanding balance which has now been paid was $74000.

        DR Cash $74,000    CR Accounts Receivable $74,000

        The cash (asset) account has increased, and the accounts receivable (asset)
        account has decreased by $74,000.

135     Pharma Drug Company Ltd. is an organization which specializes in providing
        their customers with medications.  Today, Pharma Drug Company Ltd. has paid
        cash to their supplier to fully pay off their account payable balance, which was
        $49000.

        DR Accounts Payable $49,000    CR Cash $49,000

        The accounts payable (liability) and cash (asset) accounts have both increased
        by $49,000.

136     Club Disco is an organization which specializes in providing their customers with
        dance venue rentals for large family gatherings.  Today, Club Disco has paid
        cash to their supplier to fully pay off their account payable balance, which was
        $60000.

        DR Accounts Payable $60,000    CR Cash $60,000

        The accounts payable (liability) and cash (asset) accounts have both increased
        by $60,000.

137    Mount Tessory Academy is a company which offers their customers a wide
       selection of private school education.  Mount Tessory Academy has just received
       a cash payment for the full amount that this customer owed to the company for
       all of their purchases to date. The outstanding balance which has now been paid
       was $71000.

       DR Cash $71,000    CR Accounts Receivable $71,000

       The cash (asset) account has increased, and the accounts receivable (asset)
       account has decreased by $71,000.

138    NBG Media Corporation is a company which offers their customers a wide
       selection of broadcasting services for advertising agencies.  This January, NBG
       Media Corporation has made an advance payment to cover the next 12 months
       of utility bills, which have a monthly cost of $1900.

       DR Prepaid Expense $22,800    CR Cash $22,800

       The prepaid expense (asset) account has increased, and the cash (asset)
       account has decreased by: 12 months x $1,900 per month = $22,800 for the
       year.

139    David & Johnson sells various legal services.  Today, David & Johnson received
       payment upfront for 1300 large orders which will not be provided until early next
       year. Each order was in the amount of $2000.

       DR Cash $2,600,000    CR Unearned Revenue $2,600,000

       The cash (asset) and the unearned revenue (liability) accounts have both
       increased by: 1300 large orders x $2,000 = $2,600,000

140    Kola-Nut Ltd offers their customers a wide range of soft drinks.  This week, Kola-
       Nut Ltd purchased 3260 batches of soda bottles which were placed into the
       warehouse, and which had a per-unit cost of $2700.

       DR Inventory $8,802,000    CR Accounts Payable $8,802,000

       There was an increase in the inventory (asset) account, and also an increase in
       the accounts payable (liability) account. 3260 batches of soda bottles x $2,700 =
       $8,802,000

141     Kola-Nut Ltd offers their customers a wide range of soft drinks. Today Kola-Nut Ltd sold 9600 batches of soda bottles which had a 30% mark-up. They had originally been bought from their suppliers for a unit cost of $1290.

DR Accounts Receivable $16,099,200    DR Cost of Goods Sold $12,384,000
CR Sales $16,099,200    CR Inventory $12,384,000

This transaction increases the accounts receivable (asset) account, the sales (revenue) account, and the cost of goods sold (expense) account. The inventory (asset) account has decreased. 9600 batches of soda bottles x $1,290 = $12,384,000. The 30% markup applies to the sales and accounts receivable amounts, i.e. $12,384,000 x 1.30 = $16,099,200

142     Kola-Nut Ltd is an organization which specializes in providing their customers with soft drinks. This month, Kola-Nut Ltd has estimated that 15% of the accounts receivable might not end up being collectable, based on past experience. The accounts receivable will need to be adjusted from its current balance of $55000.

DR Bad Debt expense $8,250    CR Allowance for Doubtful Accounts $8,250

The bad debts (expense) and the allowance for doubtful accounts (contra-asset) have both increased by: 15% x $55,000 = $8,250

143     Jameson & Jameson provides their customers with soap products. This month, Jameson & Jameson paid 1 monthly loan repayment towards their long-term note payable. The interest portion was 60% of the payment. The total amount paid in cash was $20000.

DR Interest Expense $12,000    DR Loan Payable $8,000    CR Cash $20,000

The interest (expense) account has increased by $20,000 x 0.6 = $12,000. The loan payable (liability) has decreased by $20,000 x 0.4 = $8,000. The cash (asset) account has decreased by the full amount of the payment, which is $20,000

144     Sprike Inc is a privately-held corporation which focuses on their niche of premium athletic apparel. Today, Sprike Inc bought equipment which has a 5 year useful life, and which had a cost of $24000.

DR Equipment $24,000    CR Accounts Payable $24,000

The equipment (asset) and the accounts payable (liability) accounts have both increased by: $24,000. The useful life does not affect this original accounting entry, but it will be used to calculate depreciation of the asset in the future.

145   Mr. Mop is a privately-held corporation which focuses on their niche of premium household cleaners. This month, Mr. Mop paid for 1 month of rent for the warehouse room, which has a monthly cost of $2100.

DR Rent expense $2,100   CR Accounts Payable $2,100

The rent (expense) and the accounts payable (liability) accounts are both increased by one month's worth of rent, which is $2,100.

146   AC&C Ltd. is a company which offers their customers a wide selection of cell phone plans. This year, AC&C Ltd. has provided 2300 monthly cell phone service each of which earned revenues of $1880.

DR Accounts Receivable $4,324,000   CR Sales $4,324,000

The accounts receivable (asset) and the sales (revenue) accounts have both increased by: 2300 monthly cell phone service x $1,880 = $4,324,000

147   Jameson & Jameson sells various soap products. This month, Jameson & Jameson paid for 1 month of rent for the warehouse room, which has a monthly cost of $1200.

DR Rent expense $1,200   CR Accounts Payable $1,200

The rent (expense) and the accounts payable (liability) accounts are both increased by one month's worth of rent, which is $1,200.

148   Hogtown Records is a company which offers their customers a wide selection of audio services for local musicians to record their music albums. Today, Hogtown Records bought equipment which has a 5 year useful life, and which had a cost of $19000.

DR Equipment $19,000   CR Accounts Payable $19,000

The equipment (asset) and the accounts payable (liability) accounts have both increased by: $19,000. The useful life does not affect this original accounting entry, but it will be used to calculate depreciation of the asset in the future.

149   Pharma Drug Company Ltd. is a market leader that is well-known for their brand of medications. This month, Pharma Drug Company Ltd. paid for 1 month of rent for the warehouse room, which has a monthly cost of $1600.

DR Rent expense $1,600   CR Accounts Payable $1,600

The rent (expense) and the accounts payable (liability) accounts are both increased by one month's worth of rent, which is $1,600.

150     Club Disco provides their customers with dance venue rentals for large family gatherings. This December, Club Disco has paid each of the company's 2200 owners an annual dividend in the amount of $11000.

DR Retained Earnings $24,200,000     CR Cash $24,200,000

The retained earnings (equity) and the cash accounts have both decreased by: 2200 owners x $11,000 = $24,200,000

151     LA Met Theatre Company is a privately-held corporation which focuses on their niche of premium live theatrical performances. This year, LA Met Theatre Company has provided 1400 shows each of which earned revenues of $1030.

DR Accounts Receivable $1,442,000     CR Sales $1,442,000

The accounts receivable (asset) and the sales (revenue) accounts have both increased by: 1400 shows x $1,030 = $1,442,000

152     Club Disco is a corporation which sells dance venue rentals for large family gatherings. This December, Club Disco has paid each of the company's 1800 owners an annual dividend in the amount of $17000.

DR Retained Earnings $30,600,000     CR Cash $30,600,000

The retained earnings (equity) and the cash accounts have both decreased by: 1800 owners x $17,000 = $30,600,000

153     Pharma Drug Company Ltd. is a privately-held corporation which focuses on their niche of premium medications. Today Pharma Drug Company Ltd. sold 5900 batches of pills which had a 30% mark-up. They had originally been bought from their suppliers for a unit cost of $1230.

DR Accounts Receivable $9,434,100     DR Cost of Goods Sold $7,257,000     CR Sales $9,434,100     CR Inventory $7,257,000

This transaction increases the accounts receivable (asset) account, the sales (revenue) account, and the cost of goods sold (expense) account. The inventory (asset) account has decreased. 5900 batches of pills x $1,230 = $7,257,000. The 30% markup applies to the sales and accounts receivable amounts, i.e. $7,257,000 x 1.30 = $9,434,100

154 Club Disco is a corporation which sells dance venue rentals for large family gatherings. Club Disco has just purchased a building using cash, which has an expected useful life of 30 years, and which had a total cost of $385000.

DR Building $385,000    CR Cash $385,000

The building (asset) account has increased, and the cash (asset) account has decreased by: $385,000. The useful life does not affect this original accounting entry, but it will be used to calculate depreciation of the asset in the future.

155 Pharma Drug Company Ltd. is a privately-held corporation which focuses on their niche of premium medications. This month, Pharma Drug Company Ltd. accepted 4400 batches of pills which were returned by customers. These products had been marked up by 35% and they had originally been bought at a per-unit cost of $1400.

DR Sales Returns $8,316,000    DR Inventory $6,160,000    CR Accounts Receivable $8,316,000    CR Cost of Goods Sold $6,160,000

This transaction increases the sales returns (contra-revenue) account, and the inventory (asset) account. The accounts receivable (asset) account and the cost of goods sold (expense) account have both decreased. 4400 batches of pills x $1,400 = $6,160,000. The 35% markup applies to the sales returns and accounts receivable amounts, i.e. $6,160,000 x 1.35 = $8,316,000

156 Kola-Nut Ltd sells various soft drinks. This month, Kola-Nut Ltd accepted 18900 batches of soda bottles which were returned by customers. These products had been marked up by 35% and they had originally been bought at a per-unit cost of $1500.

DR Sales Returns $38,272,500    DR Inventory $28,350,000    CR Accounts Receivable $38,272,500    CR Cost of Goods Sold $28,350,000

This transaction increases the sales returns (contra-revenue) account, and the inventory (asset) account. The accounts receivable (asset) account and the cost of goods sold (expense) account have both decreased. 18900 batches of soda bottles x $1,500 = $28,350,000. The 35% markup applies to the sales returns and accounts receivable amounts, i.e. $28,350,000 x 1.35 = $38,272,500

157     Jameson & Jameson is a corporation which sells soap products.  This month, Jameson & Jameson accepted 10300 truckloads of bars of soap which were returned by customers. These products had been marked up by 35% and they had originally been bought at a per-unit cost of $1500.

DR Sales Returns $20,857,500    DR Inventory $15,450,000    CR Accounts Receivable $20,857,500    CR Cost of Goods Sold $15,450,000

This transaction increases the sales returns (contra-revenue) account, and the inventory (asset) account. The accounts receivable (asset) account and the cost of goods sold (expense) account have both decreased. 10300 truckloads of bars of soap x $1,500 = $15,450,000. The 35% markup applies to the sales returns and accounts receivable amounts, i.e. $15,450,000 x 1.35 = $20,857,500

158     Kola-Nut Ltd is a privately-held corporation which focuses on their niche of premium soft drinks.  Today, Kola-Nut Ltd received an upfront payment for 2700 batches of soda bottles which will be provided to the customer 6 months from now. The payment for each was $2200.

DR Cash $5,940,000    CR Unearned Revenue $5,940,000

The cash (asset) and the unearned revenue (liability) accounts have both increased by: 2700 batches of soda bottles x $2,200 = $5,940,000

159     Kola-Nut Ltd is a market leader that is well-known for their brand of soft drinks. This week, Kola-Nut Ltd purchased 3620 batches of soda bottles which were placed into the warehouse, and which had a per-unit cost of $1500.

DR Inventory $5,430,000    CR Accounts Payable $5,430,000

There was an increase in the inventory (asset) account, and also an increase in the accounts payable (liability) account. 3620 batches of soda bottles x $1,500 = $5,430,000

160     Jameson & Jameson offers their customers a wide range of soap products.  This month, Jameson & Jameson paid for 1 month of rent for the warehouse room, which has a monthly cost of $1000.

DR Rent expense $1,000    CR Accounts Payable $1,000

The rent (expense) and the accounts payable (liability) accounts are both increased by one month's worth of rent, which is $1,000.

161     LA Met Theatre Company is an organization which specializes in providing their customers with live theatrical performances. This year, LA Met Theatre Company has provided 1700 shows each of which earned revenues of $1780.

DR Accounts Receivable $3,026,000     CR Sales $3,026,000

The accounts receivable (asset) and the sales (revenue) accounts have both increased by: 1700 shows x $1,780 = $3,026,000

162     Paytech Ltd is a company which offers their customers a wide selection of payroll transaction processing services. Today, Paytech Ltd has paid cash to their supplier to fully pay off their account payable balance, which was $82000.

DR Accounts Payable $82,000     CR Cash $82,000

The accounts payable (liability) and cash (asset) accounts have both increased by $82,000.

163     Sprike Inc is a privately-held corporation which focuses on their niche of premium athletic apparel. This month, Sprike Inc accepted 1300 batches of athletic t-shirts which were returned by customers. These products had been marked up by 35% and they had originally been bought at a per-unit cost of $1200.

DR Sales Returns $2,106,000     DR Inventory $1,560,000     CR Accounts Receivable $2,106,000     CR Cost of Goods Sold $1,560,000

This transaction increases the sales returns (contra-revenue) account, and the inventory (asset) account. The accounts receivable (asset) account and the cost of goods sold (expense) account have both decreased. 1300 batches of athletic t-shirts x $1,200 = $1,560,000. The 35% markup applies to the sales returns and accounts receivable amounts, i.e. $1,560,000 x 1.35 = $2,106,000

164     Pharma Drug Company Ltd. sells various medications. This month, Pharma Drug Company Ltd. paid for 1 month of rent for the warehouse room, which has a monthly cost of $2500.

DR Rent expense $2,500     CR Accounts Payable $2,500

The rent (expense) and the accounts payable (liability) accounts are both increased by one month's worth of rent, which is $2,500.

165    Jameson & Jameson is a company which offers their customers a wide selection
       of soap products. Today, Jameson & Jameson received an upfront payment for
       1420 truckloads of bars of soap which will be provided to the customer 6 months
       from now. The payment for each was $2300.

       DR Cash $3,266,000    CR Unearned Revenue $3,266,000

       The cash (asset) and the unearned revenue (liability) accounts have both
       increased by: 1420 truckloads of bars of soap x $2,300 = $3,266,000

166    Air America is a privately-held corporation which focuses on their niche of
       premium global flights. Air America has just purchased a building using cash,
       which has an expected useful life of 30 years, and which had a total cost of
       $512000.

       DR Building $512,000    CR Cash $512,000

       The building (asset) account has increased, and the cash (asset) account has
       decreased by: $512,000. The useful life does not affect this original accounting
       entry, but it will be used to calculate depreciation of the asset in the future.

167    Cirque du Lune is an organization which specializes in providing their customers
       with circus performances. This month, Cirque du Lune paid 1 monthly loan
       repayment towards their long-term note payable. The interest portion was 60% of
       the payment. The total amount paid in cash was $25000.

       DR Interest Expense $15,000    DR Loan Payable $10,000    CR Cash $25,000

       The interest (expense) account has increased by $25,000 x 0.6 = $15,000. The
       loan payable (liability) has decreased by $25,000 x 0.4 = $10,000. The cash
       (asset) account has decreased by the full amount of the payment, which is
       $25,000

168    Hogtown Records offers their customers a wide range of audio services for local
       musicians to record their music albums. This December, Hogtown Records has
       paid each of the company's 2100 owners an annual dividend in the amount of
       $26000.

       DR Retained Earnings $54,600,000    CR Cash $54,600,000

       The retained earnings (equity) and the cash accounts have both decreased by:
       2100 owners x $26,000 = $54,600,000

169     Kola-Nut Ltd sells several different types of soft drinks.  This December, Kola-Nut Ltd recognized 1 year of depreciation on equipment which had a total useful life of 10 years, and which had originally cost $180000.

DR Depreciation expense $18,000     CR Accumulated Depreciation $18,000

The depreciation (expense) account and the accumulated depreciation (contra-asset) accounts have both increased by: $180,000 divided by 10 years = $18,000 depreciation per year.

170     Hogtown Records provides their customers with audio services for local musicians to record their music albums.  This December, Hogtown Records recognized 1 year of depreciation on a building which had a total useful life of 25 years, and which had originally been bought for $434000.

DR Depreciation expense $17,360     CR Accumulated Depreciation $17,360

The depreciation (expense) account and the accumulated depreciation (contra-asset) accounts have both increased by: $434,000 divided by 25 years = $17,360 depreciation per year.

171     Kola-Nut Ltd is a corporation which sells soft drinks.  This month, Kola-Nut Ltd paid for 1 month of rent for the warehouse room, which has a monthly cost of $2400.

DR Rent expense $2,400     CR Accounts Payable $2,400

The rent (expense) and the accounts payable (liability) accounts are both increased by one month's worth of rent, which is $2,400.

172     Cirque du Lune sells various circus performances.  This year, Cirque du Lune has provided 1700 shows each of which earned revenues of $2470.

DR Accounts Receivable $4,199,000     CR Sales $4,199,000

The accounts receivable (asset) and the sales (revenue) accounts have both increased by: 1700 shows x $2,470 = $4,199,000

173    Comedy 253 is a market leader that is well-known for their brand of live performances of stand-up comedy. This December, Comedy 253 recognized 1 year of depreciation on equipment which had a total useful life of 10 years, and which had originally cost $150000.

DR Depreciation expense $15,000    CR Accumulated Depreciation $15,000

The depreciation (expense) account and the accumulated depreciation (contra-asset) accounts have both increased by: $150,000 divided by 10 years = $15,000 depreciation per year.

174    Club Disco is a privately-held corporation which focuses on their niche of premium dance venue rentals for large family gatherings. This December, Club Disco recognized 1 year of depreciation on a building which had a total useful life of 25 years, and which had originally been bought for $249000.

DR Depreciation expense $9,960    CR Accumulated Depreciation $9,960

The depreciation (expense) account and the accumulated depreciation (contra-asset) accounts have both increased by: $249,000 divided by 25 years = $9,960 depreciation per year.

175    Jameson & Jameson sells several different types of soap products. This month, Jameson & Jameson paid for 1 month of rent for the warehouse room, which has a monthly cost of $1800.

DR Rent expense $1,800    CR Accounts Payable $1,800

The rent (expense) and the accounts payable (liability) accounts are both increased by one month's worth of rent, which is $1,800.

176    Grand Convention Ltd sells various banquet hall rentals for corporate meetings. This month, Grand Convention Ltd must amortize 1 month worth of utility bills which they had prepaid at the beginning of the year. The amount that they had paid upfront for the year was $30000.

DR Utilities expense $2,500    CR Prepaid Expense $2,500

The utilities (expense) account has increased and the prepaid expense (asset) account has decreased by: $30,000 for the year, divided by 12 months = $2,500

177     Hogtown Records is a privately-held corporation which focuses on their niche of premium audio services for local musicians to record their music albums. This month, Hogtown Records paid for 1 month of rent for their company's office space. Each month, the rent owing was $20000.

DR Rent expense $20,000    CR Accounts Payable $20,000

The rent (expense) and the accounts payable (liability) accounts are both increased by one month's worth of rent, which is $20,000.

178     Jameson & Jameson is a market leader that is well-known for their brand of soap products. Today Jameson & Jameson sold 10400 truckloads of bars of soap which had a 30% mark-up. They had originally been bought from their suppliers for a unit cost of $2370.

DR Accounts Receivable $32,042,400    DR Cost of Goods Sold $24,648,000
CR Sales $32,042,400    CR Inventory $24,648,000

This transaction increases the accounts receivable (asset) account, the sales (revenue) account, and the cost of goods sold (expense) account. The inventory (asset) account has decreased. 10400 truckloads of bars of soap x $2,370 = $24,648,000.  The 30% markup applies to the sales and accounts receivable amounts, i.e. $24,648,000 x 1.30 = $32,042,400

179     Paytech Ltd sells various payroll transaction processing services. Today, Paytech Ltd bought equipment which has a 5 year useful life, and which had a cost of $11000.

DR Equipment $11,000    CR Accounts Payable $11,000

The equipment (asset) and the accounts payable (liability) accounts have both increased by: $11,000. The useful life does not affect this original accounting entry, but it will be used to calculate depreciation of the asset in the future.

180     A to Z Event Guru Ltd provides their customers with start-to-finish event planning services for large gatherings.  A to Z Event Guru Ltd has just purchased a building using cash, which has an expected useful life of 30 years, and which had a total cost of $726000.

DR Building $726,000    CR Cash $726,000

The building (asset) account has increased, and the cash (asset) account has decreased by: $726,000. The useful life does not affect this original accounting entry, but it will be used to calculate depreciation of the asset in the future.

181 AC&C Ltd. sells various cell phone plans. This week, AC&C Ltd. paid each of the 2910 staff members their bi-weekly wages, which per person had a cost of $1500.

DR Wage expense $4,365,000   CR Accounts Payable $4,365,000

The wage (expense) and the accounts payable (liability) accounts have both increased by: 2910 staff members x $1,500 = $4,365,000

182 Paytech Ltd sells various payroll transaction processing services. Today, Paytech Ltd received payment upfront for 2400 large orders which will not be provided until early next year. Each order was in the amount of $1100.

DR Cash $2,640,000   CR Unearned Revenue $2,640,000

The cash (asset) and the unearned revenue (liability) accounts have both increased by: 2400 large orders x $1,100 = $2,640,000

183 Hogtown Records provides their customers with audio services for local musicians to record their music albums. This December, Hogtown Records has paid each of the company's 1200 owners an annual dividend in the amount of $23000.

DR Retained Earnings $27,600,000   CR Cash $27,600,000

The retained earnings (equity) and the cash accounts have both decreased by: 1200 owners x $23,000 = $27,600,000

184 Jameson & Jameson is a privately-held corporation which focuses on their niche of premium soap products. Today Jameson & Jameson sold 9400 truckloads of bars of soap which had a 30% mark-up. They had originally been bought from their suppliers for a unit cost of $2490.

DR Accounts Receivable $30,427,800   DR Cost of Goods Sold $23,406,000
CR Sales $30,427,800   CR Inventory $23,406,000

This transaction increases the accounts receivable (asset) account, the sales (revenue) account, and the cost of goods sold (expense) account. The inventory (asset) account has decreased. 9400 truckloads of bars of soap x $2,490 = $23,406,000. The 30% markup applies to the sales and accounts receivable amounts, i.e. $23,406,000 x 1.30 = $30,427,800

185    Pharma Drug Company Ltd. is an organization which specializes in providing their customers with medications. Today Pharma Drug Company Ltd. sold 48600 batches of pills which had a 30% mark-up. They had originally been bought from their suppliers for a unit cost of $1020.

DR Accounts Receivable $64,443,600    DR Cost of Goods Sold $49,572,000
CR Sales $64,443,600    CR Inventory $49,572,000

This transaction increases the accounts receivable (asset) account, the sales (revenue) account, and the cost of goods sold (expense) account. The inventory (asset) account has decreased. 48600 batches of pills x $1,020 = $49,572,000. The 30% markup applies to the sales and accounts receivable amounts, i.e. $49,572,000 x 1.30 = $64,443,600

186    Hogtown Records provides their customers with audio services for local musicians to record their music albums. This December, Hogtown Records has paid each of the company's 1100 owners an annual dividend in the amount of $21000.

DR Retained Earnings $23,100,000    CR Cash $23,100,000

The retained earnings (equity) and the cash accounts have both decreased by: 1100 owners x $21,000 = $23,100,000

187    Paytech Ltd is a market leader that is well-known for their brand of payroll transaction processing services. Today, Paytech Ltd has paid cash to their supplier to fully pay off their account payable balance, which was $54000.

DR Accounts Payable $54,000    CR Cash $54,000

The accounts payable (liability) and cash (asset) accounts have both increased by $54,000.

188    Mr. Mop offers their customers a wide range of household cleaners. This January, Mr. Mop has made an advance payment to cover the next 12 months of utility bills, which have a monthly cost of $1900.

DR Prepaid Expense $22,800    CR Cash $22,800

The prepaid expense (asset) account has increased, and the cash (asset) account has decreased by: 12 months x $1,900 per month = $22,800 for the year.

189 A to Z Event Guru Ltd is an organization which specializes in providing their customers with start-to-finish event planning services for large gatherings. A to Z Event Guru Ltd has just purchased a building using cash, which has an expected useful life of 30 years, and which had a total cost of $579000.

DR Building $579,000    CR Cash $579,000

The building (asset) account has increased, and the cash (asset) account has decreased by: $579,000. The useful life does not affect this original accounting entry, but it will be used to calculate depreciation of the asset in the future.

190 NY Fitness is a privately-held corporation which focuses on their niche of premium gym memberships for professional sports teams. This December, NY Fitness has paid each of the company's 1600 owners an annual dividend in the amount of $9000.

DR Retained Earnings $14,400,000    CR Cash $14,400,000

The retained earnings (equity) and the cash accounts have both decreased by: 1600 owners x $9,000 = $14,400,000

191 Mr. Mop is a market leader that is well-known for their brand of household cleaners. Today Mr. Mop signed up for a loan with a 5% interest rate, and so the bank immediately transferred cash to the company in the amount of $27000.

DR Cash $27,000    CR Loan Payable $27,000

The cash (asset) and the loan payable (liability) accounts have both increased by: $27,000. The interest rate does not affect this initial accounting entry, but it will be used for the calculation of interest expense when repayments are made in the future toward this loan.

192 Grand Convention Ltd is a corporation which sells banquet hall rentals for corporate meetings. Grand Convention Ltd has just received a cash payment for the full amount that this customer owed to the company for all of their purchases to date. The outstanding balance which has now been paid was $92000.

DR Cash $92,000    CR Accounts Receivable $92,000

The cash (asset) account has increased, and the accounts receivable (asset) account has decreased by $92,000.

193 Mount Tessory Academy is a privately-held corporation which focuses on their niche of premium private school education. Mount Tessory Academy has just received a cash payment for the full amount that this customer owed to the company for all of their purchases to date. The outstanding balance which has now been paid was $33000.

DR Cash $33,000    CR Accounts Receivable $33,000

The cash (asset) account has increased, and the accounts receivable (asset) account has decreased by $33,000.

194 Comedy 253 offers their customers a wide range of live performances of stand-up comedy. This year, Comedy 253 has provided 2100 shows each of which earned revenues of $1220.

DR Accounts Receivable $2,562,000    CR Sales $2,562,000

The accounts receivable (asset) and the sales (revenue) accounts have both increased by: 2100 shows x $1,220 = $2,562,000

195 Jameson & Jameson offers their customers a wide range of soap products. This month, Jameson & Jameson accepted 29700 truckloads of bars of soap which were returned by customers. These products had been marked up by 35% and they had originally been bought at a per-unit cost of $1800.

DR Sales Returns $72,171,000    DR Inventory $53,460,000    CR Accounts Receivable $72,171,000    CR Cost of Goods Sold $53,460,000

This transaction increases the sales returns (contra-revenue) account, and the inventory (asset) account. The accounts receivable (asset) account and the cost of goods sold (expense) account have both decreased. 29700 truckloads of bars of soap x $1,800 = $53,460,000. The 35% markup applies to the sales returns and accounts receivable amounts, i.e. $53,460,000 x 1.35 = $72,171,000

196 McGerald's is an organization which specializes in providing their customers with fast food meals. This January, McGerald's has made an advance payment to cover the next 12 months of utility bills, which have a monthly cost of $1300.

DR Prepaid Expense $15,600    CR Cash $15,600

The prepaid expense (asset) account has increased, and the cash (asset) account has decreased by: 12 months x $1,300 per month = $15,600 for the year.

197    Sprike Inc sells several different types of athletic apparel. This month, Sprike Inc accepted 7300 batches of athletic t-shirts which were returned by customers. These products had been marked up by 35% and they had originally been bought at a per-unit cost of $2800.

DR Sales Returns $27,594,000    DR Inventory $20,440,000    CR Accounts Receivable $27,594,000    CR Cost of Goods Sold $20,440,000

This transaction increases the sales returns (contra-revenue) account, and the inventory (asset) account. The accounts receivable (asset) account and the cost of goods sold (expense) account have both decreased. 7300 batches of athletic t-shirts x $2,800 = $20,440,000. The 35% markup applies to the sales returns and accounts receivable amounts, i.e. $20,440,000 x 1.35 = $27,594,000

198    Sprike Inc provides their customers with athletic apparel. This month, Sprike Inc must amortize 1 month worth of utility bills which they had prepaid at the beginning of the year. The amount that they had paid upfront for the year was $30000.

DR Utilities expense $2,500    CR Prepaid Expense $2,500

The utilities (expense) account has increased and the prepaid expense (asset) account has decreased by: $30,000 for the year, divided by 12 months = $2,500

199    AC&C Ltd. sells several different types of cell phone plans. This month, AC&C Ltd. paid for 1 month of rent for their company's office space. Each month, the rent owing was $12000.

DR Rent expense $12,000    CR Accounts Payable $12,000

The rent (expense) and the accounts payable (liability) accounts are both increased by one month's worth of rent, which is $12,000.

200    Air America is a corporation which sells global flights. This December, Air America recognized 1 year of depreciation on a building which had a total useful life of 25 years, and which had originally been bought for $754000.

DR Depreciation expense $30,160    CR Accumulated Depreciation $30,160

The depreciation (expense) account and the accumulated depreciation (contra-asset) accounts have both increased by: $754,000 divided by 25 years = $30,160 depreciation per year.

201    David & Johnson sells several different types of legal services.  Today, David & Johnson received payment upfront for 1000 large orders which will not be provided until early next year. Each order was in the amount of $2700.

DR Cash $2,700,000    CR Unearned Revenue $2,700,000

The cash (asset) and the unearned revenue (liability) accounts have both increased by: 1000 large orders x $2,700 = $2,700,000

202    NBG Media Corporation sells various broadcasting services for advertising agencies.  This January, NBG Media Corporation has made an advance payment to cover the next 12 months of utility bills, which have a monthly cost of $2700.

DR Prepaid Expense $32,400    CR Cash $32,400

The prepaid expense (asset) account has increased, and the cash (asset) account has decreased by: 12 months x $2,700 per month = $32,400 for the year.

203    Sprike Inc is a corporation which sells athletic apparel.  Today, Sprike Inc received an upfront payment for 2290 batches of athletic t-shirts which will be provided to the customer 6 months from now. The payment for each was $1800.

DR Cash $4,122,000    CR Unearned Revenue $4,122,000

The cash (asset) and the unearned revenue (liability) accounts have both increased by: 2290 batches of athletic t-shirts x $1,800 = $4,122,000

204    Fairway Malls is a market leader that is well-known for their brand of retail spaces in their shopping centers.  This December, Fairway Malls recognized 1 year of depreciation on a building which had a total useful life of 25 years, and which had originally been bought for $35000.

DR Depreciation expense $1,400    CR Accumulated Depreciation $1,400

The depreciation (expense) account and the accumulated depreciation (contra-asset) accounts have both increased by: $35,000 divided by 25 years = $1,400 depreciation per year.

205 Toyonda is a market leader that is well-known for their brand of cars. Today Toyonda signed up for a loan with a 5% interest rate, and so the bank immediately transferred cash to the company in the amount of $49000.

DR Cash $49,000   CR Loan Payable $49,000

The cash (asset) and the loan payable (liability) accounts have both increased by: $49,000. The interest rate does not affect this initial accounting entry, but it will be used for the calculation of interest expense when repayments are made in the future toward this loan.

206 David & Johnson offers their customers a wide range of legal services. David & Johnson has just provided 2200 large orders which had been paid for in advance last year. Each order was in the amount of $2300.

DR Unearned Revenue $5,060,000   CR Sales $5,060,000

The unearned revenue (liability) account has decreased and the and the sales (revenue) account has increased by: 2200 large orders x $2,300 = $5,060,000

207 NBG Media Corporation offers their customers a wide range of broadcasting services for advertising agencies. Today NBG Media Corporation signed up for a loan with a 5% interest rate, and so the bank immediately transferred cash to the company in the amount of $92000.

DR Cash $92,000   CR Loan Payable $92,000

The cash (asset) and the loan payable (liability) accounts have both increased by: $92,000. The interest rate does not affect this initial accounting entry, but it will be used for the calculation of interest expense when repayments are made in the future toward this loan.

208 Pharma Drug Company Ltd. sells several different types of medications. Today, Pharma Drug Company Ltd. has paid cash to their supplier to fully pay off their account payable balance, which was $46000.

DR Accounts Payable $46,000   CR Cash $46,000

The accounts payable (liability) and cash (asset) accounts have both increased by $46,000.

209 Hogtown Records is a corporation which sells audio services for local musicians to record their music albums. This week, Hogtown Records paid each of the 3710 staff members their bi-weekly wages, which per person had a cost of $1300.

DR Wage expense $4,823,000    CR Accounts Payable $4,823,000

The wage (expense) and the accounts payable (liability) accounts have both increased by: 3710 staff members x $1,300 = $4,823,000

210 Hogtown Records provides their customers with audio services for local musicians to record their music albums. Today, Hogtown Records has paid cash to their supplier to fully pay off their account payable balance, which was $41000.

DR Accounts Payable $41,000    CR Cash $41,000

The accounts payable (liability) and cash (asset) accounts have both increased by $41,000.

211 Club Disco sells various dance venue rentals for large family gatherings. Today, Club Disco received payment upfront for 2400 large orders which will not be provided until early next year. Each order was in the amount of $1300.

DR Cash $3,120,000    CR Unearned Revenue $3,120,000

The cash (asset) and the unearned revenue (liability) accounts have both increased by: 2400 large orders x $1,300 = $3,120,000

212 AC&C Ltd. is a corporation which sells cell phone plans. This December, AC&C Ltd. recognized 1 year of depreciation on equipment which had a total useful life of 10 years, and which had originally cost $140000.

DR Depreciation expense $14,000    CR Accumulated Depreciation $14,000

The depreciation (expense) account and the accumulated depreciation (contra-asset) accounts have both increased by: $140,000 divided by 10 years = $14,000 depreciation per year.

213 Mr. Mop sells several different types of household cleaners. This January, Mr. Mop has made an advance payment to cover the next 12 months of utility bills, which have a monthly cost of $1500.

DR Prepaid Expense $18,000    CR Cash $18,000

The prepaid expense (asset) account has increased, and the cash (asset) account has decreased by: 12 months x $1,500 per month = $18,000 for the year.

214 Club Disco is an organization which specializes in providing their customers with dance venue rentals for large family gatherings. This year, Club Disco has provided 2400 evening rentals each of which earned revenues of $2100.

DR Accounts Receivable $5,040,000    CR Sales $5,040,000

The accounts receivable (asset) and the sales (revenue) accounts have both increased by: 2400 evening rentals x $2,100 = $5,040,000

215 Mount Tessory Academy is a corporation which sells private school education. This month, Mount Tessory Academy paid 1 monthly loan repayment towards their long-term note payable. The interest portion was 60% of the payment. The total amount paid in cash was $24000.

DR Interest Expense $14,400    DR Loan Payable $9,600    CR Cash $24,000

The interest (expense) account has increased by $24,000 x 0.6 = $14,400. The loan payable (liability) has decreased by $24,000 x 0.4 = $9,600. The cash (asset) account has decreased by the full amount of the payment, which is $24,000

216 AC&C Ltd. is a corporation which sells cell phone plans. This month, AC&C Ltd. has estimated that 15% of the accounts receivable might not end up being collectable, based on past experience. The accounts receivable will need to be adjusted from its current balance of $43000.

DR Bad Debt expense $6,450    CR Allowance for Doubtful Accounts $6,450

The bad debts (expense) and the allowance for doubtful accounts (contra-asset) have both increased by: 15% x $43,000 = $6,450

217 Mr. Mop is a market leader that is well-known for their brand of household cleaners. This month, Mr. Mop paid for 1 month of rent for the warehouse room, which has a monthly cost of $2700.

DR Rent expense $2,700    CR Accounts Payable $2,700

The rent (expense) and the accounts payable (liability) accounts are both increased by one month's worth of rent, which is $2,700.

218    Pharma Drug Company Ltd. provides their customers with medications. This
       week, Pharma Drug Company Ltd. purchased 4550 batches of pills which were
       placed into the warehouse, and which had a per-unit cost of $2800.

       DR Inventory $12,740,000    CR Accounts Payable $12,740,000

       There was an increase in the inventory (asset) account, and also an increase in
       the accounts payable (liability) account. 4550 batches of pills x $2,800 =
       $12,740,000

219    Sprike Inc sells several different types of athletic apparel.  Sprike Inc has just
       purchased a building using cash, which has an expected useful life of 30 years,
       and which had a total cost of $818000.

       DR Building $818,000    CR Cash $818,000

       The building (asset) account has increased, and the cash (asset) account has
       decreased by: $818,000. The useful life does not affect this original accounting
       entry, but it will be used to calculate depreciation of the asset in the future.

220    Jameson & Jameson provides their customers with soap products.  Today
       Jameson & Jameson signed up for a loan with a 5% interest rate, and so the
       bank immediately transferred cash to the company in the amount of $85000.

       DR Cash $85,000    CR Loan Payable $85,000

       The cash (asset) and the loan payable (liability) accounts have both increased
       by: $85,000. The interest rate does not affect this initial accounting entry, but it
       will be used for the calculation of interest expense when repayments are made in
       the future toward this loan.

221    Jameson & Jameson provides their customers with soap products.  This month,
       Jameson & Jameson paid 1 monthly loan repayment towards their long-term
       note payable. The interest portion was 60% of the payment. The total amount
       paid in cash was $17000.

       DR Interest Expense $10,200    DR Loan Payable $6,800    CR Cash $17,000

       The interest (expense) account has increased by $17,000 x 0.6 = $10,200. The
       loan payable (liability) has decreased by $17,000 x 0.4 = $6,800. The cash
       (asset) account has decreased by the full amount of the payment, which is
       $17,000

222    Pharma Drug Company Ltd. provides their customers with medications. Today Pharma Drug Company Ltd. sold 38600 batches of pills which had a 30% mark-up. They had originally been bought from their suppliers for a unit cost of $1910.

DR Accounts Receivable $95,843,800   DR Cost of Goods Sold $73,726,000
CR Sales $95,843,800   CR Inventory $73,726,000

This transaction increases the accounts receivable (asset) account, the sales (revenue) account, and the cost of goods sold (expense) account. The inventory (asset) account has decreased. 38600 batches of pills x $1,910 = $73,726,000. The 30% markup applies to the sales and accounts receivable amounts, i.e. $73,726,000 x 1.30 = $95,843,800

223    Fairway Malls sells several different types of retail spaces in their shopping centers. This month, Fairway Malls paid for 1 month of rent for their company's office space. Each month, the rent owing was $21000.

DR Rent expense $21,000   CR Accounts Payable $21,000

The rent (expense) and the accounts payable (liability) accounts are both increased by one month's worth of rent, which is $21,000.

224    LA Met Theatre Company is a privately-held corporation which focuses on their niche of premium live theatrical performances. This year, LA Met Theatre Company has provided 1100 shows each of which earned revenues of $2930.

DR Accounts Receivable $3,223,000   CR Sales $3,223,000

The accounts receivable (asset) and the sales (revenue) accounts have both increased by: 1100 shows x $2,930 = $3,223,000

225    Cirque du Lune sells several different types of circus performances. This December, Cirque du Lune has paid each of the company's 1900 owners an annual dividend in the amount of $24000.

DR Retained Earnings $45,600,000   CR Cash $45,600,000

The retained earnings (equity) and the cash accounts have both decreased by: 1900 owners x $24,000 = $45,600,000

226 Paytech Ltd is a privately-held corporation which focuses on their niche of premium payroll transaction processing services. This month, Paytech Ltd paid 1 monthly loan repayment towards their long-term note payable. The interest portion was 60% of the payment. The total amount paid in cash was $20000.

DR Interest Expense $12,000   DR Loan Payable $8,000   CR Cash $20,000

The interest (expense) account has increased by $20,000 x 0.6 = $12,000. The loan payable (liability) has decreased by $20,000 x 0.4 = $8,000. The cash (asset) account has decreased by the full amount of the payment, which is $20,000

227 Toyonda offers their customers a wide range of cars. Today, Toyonda has paid cash to their supplier to fully pay off their account payable balance, which was $41000.

DR Accounts Payable $41,000   CR Cash $41,000

The accounts payable (liability) and cash (asset) accounts have both increased by $41,000.

228 Mr. Mop provides their customers with household cleaners. This month, Mr. Mop paid for 1 month of rent for the warehouse room, which has a monthly cost of $2700.

DR Rent expense $2,700   CR Accounts Payable $2,700

The rent (expense) and the accounts payable (liability) accounts are both increased by one month's worth of rent, which is $2,700.

229 Jameson & Jameson is a company which offers their customers a wide selection of soap products. This week, Jameson & Jameson purchased 2700 truckloads of bars of soap which were placed into the warehouse, and which had a per-unit cost of $2600.

DR Inventory $7,020,000   CR Accounts Payable $7,020,000

There was an increase in the inventory (asset) account, and also an increase in the accounts payable (liability) account. 2700 truckloads of bars of soap x $2,600 = $7,020,000

230 Air America offers their customers a wide range of global flights. Today, Air America has paid cash to their supplier to fully pay off their account payable balance, which was $11000.

DR Accounts Payable $11,000   CR Cash $11,000

The accounts payable (liability) and cash (asset) accounts have both increased by $11,000.

231 Sprike Inc is an organization which specializes in providing their customers with athletic apparel. Today Sprike Inc sold 3400 batches of athletic t-shirts which had a 30% mark-up. They had originally been bought from their suppliers for a unit cost of $1880.

DR Accounts Receivable $8,309,600   DR Cost of Goods Sold $6,392,000   CR Sales $8,309,600   CR Inventory $6,392,000

This transaction increases the accounts receivable (asset) account, the sales (revenue) account, and the cost of goods sold (expense) account. The inventory (asset) account has decreased. 3400 batches of athletic t-shirts x $1,880 = $6,392,000. The 30% markup applies to the sales and accounts receivable amounts, i.e. $6,392,000 x 1.30 = $8,309,600

232 Comedy 253 is a corporation which sells live performances of stand-up comedy. This month, Comedy 253 paid 1 monthly loan repayment towards their long-term note payable. The interest portion was 60% of the payment. The total amount paid in cash was $12000.

DR Interest Expense $7,200   DR Loan Payable $4,800   CR Cash $12,000

The interest (expense) account has increased by $12,000 x 0.6 = $7,200. The loan payable (liability) has decreased by $12,000 x 0.4 = $4,800. The cash (asset) account has decreased by the full amount of the payment, which is $12,000

233 Payday Now is an organization which specializes in providing their customers with short-term loan arrangements. Today Payday Now signed up for a loan with a 5% interest rate, and so the bank immediately transferred cash to the company in the amount of $33000.

DR Cash $33,000   CR Loan Payable $33,000

The cash (asset) and the loan payable (liability) accounts have both increased by: $33,000. The interest rate does not affect this initial accounting entry, but it will be used for the calculation of interest expense when repayments are made in the future toward this loan.

234    David & Johnson is an organization which specializes in providing their customers with legal services. This January, David & Johnson has made an advance payment to cover the next 12 months of utility bills, which have a monthly cost of $1800.

DR Prepaid Expense $21,600    CR Cash $21,600

The prepaid expense (asset) account has increased, and the cash (asset) account has decreased by: 12 months x $1,800 per month = $21,600 for the year.

235    Mount Tessory Academy provides their customers with private school education. This month, Mount Tessory Academy must amortize 1 month worth of utility bills which they had prepaid at the beginning of the year. The amount that they had paid upfront for the year was $45600.

DR Utilities expense $3,800    CR Prepaid Expense $3,800

The utilities (expense) account has increased and the prepaid expense (asset) account has decreased by: $45,600 for the year, divided by 12 months = $3,800

236    Jameson & Jameson sells various soap products. This month, Jameson & Jameson paid for 1 month of rent for the warehouse room, which has a monthly cost of $2000.

DR Rent expense $2,000    CR Accounts Payable $2,000

The rent (expense) and the accounts payable (liability) accounts are both increased by one month's worth of rent, which is $2,000.

237    Paytech Ltd is a company which offers their customers a wide selection of payroll transaction processing services. This month, Paytech Ltd has estimated that 10% of the accounts receivable might not end up being collectable, based on past experience. The accounts receivable will need to be adjusted from its current balance of $95000.

DR Bad Debt expense $9,500    CR Allowance for Doubtful Accounts $9,500

The bad debts (expense) and the allowance for doubtful accounts (contra-asset) have both increased by: 10% x $95,000 = $9,500

238    Sprike Inc is a market leader that is well-known for their brand of athletic apparel. Sprike Inc has just purchased a building using cash, which has an expected useful life of 30 years, and which had a total cost of $864000.

DR Building $864,000    CR Cash $864,000

The building (asset) account has increased, and the cash (asset) account has decreased by: $864,000. The useful life does not affect this original accounting entry, but it will be used to calculate depreciation of the asset in the future.

239    Mr. Mop offers their customers a wide range of household cleaners. This month, Mr. Mop accepted 2900 tons of cleaning solution which were returned by customers. These products had been marked up by 35% and they had originally been bought at a per-unit cost of $2800.

DR Sales Returns $10,962,000    DR Inventory $8,120,000    CR Accounts Receivable $10,962,000    CR Cost of Goods Sold $8,120,000

This transaction increases the sales returns (contra-revenue) account, and the inventory (asset) account. The accounts receivable (asset) account and the cost of goods sold (expense) account have both decreased. 2900 tons of cleaning solution x $2,800 = $8,120,000. The 35% markup applies to the sales returns and accounts receivable amounts, i.e. $8,120,000 x 1.35 = $10,962,000

240    A to Z Event Guru Ltd sells various start-to-finish event planning services for large gatherings. This month, A to Z Event Guru Ltd has estimated that 10% of the accounts receivable might not end up being collectable, based on past experience. The accounts receivable will need to be adjusted from its current balance of $45000.

DR Bad Debt expense $4,500    CR Allowance for Doubtful Accounts $4,500

The bad debts (expense) and the allowance for doubtful accounts (contra-asset) have both increased by: 10% x $45,000 = $4,500

241    Cirque du Lune is a company which offers their customers a wide selection of circus performances. This December, Cirque du Lune recognized 1 year of depreciation on equipment which had a total useful life of 10 years, and which had originally cost $80000.

DR Depreciation expense $8,000    CR Accumulated Depreciation $8,000

The depreciation (expense) account and the accumulated depreciation (contra-asset) accounts have both increased by: $80,000 divided by 10 years = $8,000 depreciation per year.

242    Hogtown Records is an organization which specializes in providing their customers with audio services for local musicians to record their music albums. This December, Hogtown Records recognized 1 year of depreciation on equipment which had a total useful life of 10 years, and which had originally cost $200000.

DR Depreciation expense $20,000    CR Accumulated Depreciation $20,000

The depreciation (expense) account and the accumulated depreciation (contra-asset) accounts have both increased by: $200,000 divided by 10 years = $20,000 depreciation per year.

243    NY Fitness is a market leader that is well-known for their brand of gym memberships for professional sports teams. This year, NY Fitness has provided 1200 team memberships each of which earned revenues of $1760.

DR Accounts Receivable $2,112,000    CR Sales $2,112,000

The accounts receivable (asset) and the sales (revenue) accounts have both increased by: 1200 team memberships x $1,760 = $2,112,000

244    Pharma Drug Company Ltd. is an organization which specializes in providing their customers with medications. This week, Pharma Drug Company Ltd. paid each of the 3620 staff members their bi-weekly wages, which per person had a cost of $1800.

DR Wage expense $6,516,000    CR Accounts Payable $6,516,000

The wage (expense) and the accounts payable (liability) accounts have both increased by: 3620 staff members x $1,800 = $6,516,000

245    Grand Convention Ltd offers their customers a wide range of banquet hall rentals for corporate meetings. Today Grand Convention Ltd signed up for a loan with a 5% interest rate, and so the bank immediately transferred cash to the company in the amount of $65000.

DR Cash $65,000    CR Loan Payable $65,000

The cash (asset) and the loan payable (liability) accounts have both increased by: $65,000. The interest rate does not affect this initial accounting entry, but it will be used for the calculation of interest expense when repayments are made in the future toward this loan.

246 Fairway Malls is a company which offers their customers a wide selection of retail spaces in their shopping centers. This December, Fairway Malls recognized 1 year of depreciation on equipment which had a total useful life of 10 years, and which had originally cost $120000.

DR Depreciation expense $12,000    CR Accumulated Depreciation $12,000

The depreciation (expense) account and the accumulated depreciation (contra-asset) accounts have both increased by: $120,000 divided by 10 years = $12,000 depreciation per year.

247 LA Met Theatre Company is a company which offers their customers a wide selection of live theatrical performances. Today, LA Met Theatre Company received payment upfront for 1600 large orders which will not be provided until early next year. Each order was in the amount of $2700.

DR Cash $4,320,000    CR Unearned Revenue $4,320,000

The cash (asset) and the unearned revenue (liability) accounts have both increased by: 1600 large orders x $2,700 = $4,320,000

248 Kola-Nut Ltd is a company which offers their customers a wide selection of soft drinks. This month, Kola-Nut Ltd paid for 1 month of rent for the warehouse room, which has a monthly cost of $2600.

DR Rent expense $2,600    CR Accounts Payable $2,600

The rent (expense) and the accounts payable (liability) accounts are both increased by one month's worth of rent, which is $2,600.

249 David & Johnson is a market leader that is well-known for their brand of legal services. This December, David & Johnson recognized 1 year of depreciation on a building which had a total useful life of 25 years, and which had originally been bought for $308000.

DR Depreciation expense $12,320    CR Accumulated Depreciation $12,320

The depreciation (expense) account and the accumulated depreciation (contra-asset) accounts have both increased by: $308,000 divided by 25 years = $12,320 depreciation per year.

250 McGerald's sells several different types of fast food meals. Today McGerald's signed up for a loan with a 5% interest rate, and so the bank immediately transferred cash to the company in the amount of $89000.

DR Cash $89,000   CR Loan Payable $89,000

The cash (asset) and the loan payable (liability) accounts have both increased by: $89,000. The interest rate does not affect this initial accounting entry, but it will be used for the calculation of interest expense when repayments are made in the future toward this loan.

251 Club Disco is a market leader that is well-known for their brand of dance venue rentals for large family gatherings. This December, Club Disco recognized 1 year of depreciation on a building which had a total useful life of 25 years, and which had originally been bought for $326000.

DR Depreciation expense $13,040   CR Accumulated Depreciation $13,040

The depreciation (expense) account and the accumulated depreciation (contra-asset) accounts have both increased by: $326,000 divided by 25 years = $13,040 depreciation per year.

252 Fairway Malls offers their customers a wide range of retail spaces in their shopping centers. This month, Fairway Malls paid 1 monthly loan repayment towards their long-term note payable. The interest portion was 60% of the payment. The total amount paid in cash was $9000.

DR Interest Expense $5,400   DR Loan Payable $3,600   CR Cash $9,000

The interest (expense) account has increased by $9,000 x 0.6 = $5,400. The loan payable (liability) has decreased by $9,000 x 0.4 = $3,600. The cash (asset) account has decreased by the full amount of the payment, which is $9,000

253 Sprike Inc is a company which offers their customers a wide selection of athletic apparel. Sprike Inc has just purchased a building using cash, which has an expected useful life of 30 years, and which had a total cost of $177000.

DR Building $177,000   CR Cash $177,000

The building (asset) account has increased, and the cash (asset) account has decreased by: $177,000. The useful life does not affect this original accounting entry, but it will be used to calculate depreciation of the asset in the future.

254    NBG Media Corporation sells several different types of broadcasting services for advertising agencies. Today, NBG Media Corporation bought equipment which has a 5 year useful life, and which had a cost of $10000.

DR Equipment $10,000    CR Accounts Payable $10,000

The equipment (asset) and the accounts payable (liability) accounts have both increased by: $10,000. The useful life does not affect this original accounting entry, but it will be used to calculate depreciation of the asset in the future.

255    Mr. Mop provides their customers with household cleaners. This December, Mr. Mop recognized 1 year of depreciation on a building which had a total useful life of 25 years, and which had originally been bought for $891000.

DR Depreciation expense $35,640    CR Accumulated Depreciation $35,640

The depreciation (expense) account and the accumulated depreciation (contra-asset) accounts have both increased by: $891,000 divided by 25 years = $35,640 depreciation per year.

256    Grand Convention Ltd is an organization which specializes in providing their customers with banquet hall rentals for corporate meetings. This December, Grand Convention Ltd recognized 1 year of depreciation on equipment which had a total useful life of 10 years, and which had originally cost $210000.

DR Depreciation expense $21,000    CR Accumulated Depreciation $21,000

The depreciation (expense) account and the accumulated depreciation (contra-asset) accounts have both increased by: $210,000 divided by 10 years = $21,000 depreciation per year.

257    Club Disco sells several different types of dance venue rentals for large family gatherings. Club Disco has just provided 1700 large orders which had been paid for in advance last year. Each order was in the amount of $1500.

DR Unearned Revenue $2,550,000    CR Sales $2,550,000

The unearned revenue (liability) account has decreased and the and the sales (revenue) account has increased by: 1700 large orders x $1,500 = $2,550,000

258    Air America sells several different types of global flights.  Today, Air America bought equipment which has a 5 year useful life, and which had a cost of $16000.

DR Equipment $16,000    CR Accounts Payable $16,000

The equipment (asset) and the accounts payable (liability) accounts have both increased by: $16,000. The useful life does not affect this original accounting entry, but it will be used to calculate depreciation of the asset in the future.

259    Hogtown Records sells several different types of audio services for local musicians to record their music albums.  This month, Hogtown Records must amortize 1 month worth of utility bills which they had prepaid at the beginning of the year. The amount that they had paid upfront for the year was $18000.

DR Utilities expense $1,500    CR Prepaid Expense $1,500

The utilities (expense) account has increased and the prepaid expense (asset) account has decreased by: $18,000 for the year, divided by 12 months = $1,500

260    Toyonda is a market leader that is well-known for their brand of cars.  This January, Toyonda has made an advance payment to cover the next 12 months of utility bills, which have a monthly cost of $1300.

DR Prepaid Expense $15,600    CR Cash $15,600

The prepaid expense (asset) account has increased, and the cash (asset) account has decreased by: 12 months x $1,300 per month = $15,600 for the year.

261    LA Met Theatre Company is an organization which specializes in providing their customers with live theatrical performances.  This year, LA Met Theatre Company has provided 1100 shows each of which earned revenues of $1080.

DR Accounts Receivable $1,188,000    CR Sales $1,188,000

The accounts receivable (asset) and the sales (revenue) accounts have both increased by: 1100 shows x $1,080 = $1,188,000

262    Toyonda sells several different types of cars. This December, Toyonda recognized 1 year of depreciation on a building which had a total useful life of 25 years, and which had originally been bought for $464000.

DR Depreciation expense $18,560    CR Accumulated Depreciation $18,560

The depreciation (expense) account and the accumulated depreciation (contra-asset) accounts have both increased by: $464,000 divided by 25 years = $18,560 depreciation per year.

263    A to Z Event Guru Ltd is a privately-held corporation which focuses on their niche of premium start-to-finish event planning services for large gatherings. This year, A to Z Event Guru Ltd has provided 1600 events each of which earned revenues of $2390.

DR Accounts Receivable $3,824,000    CR Sales $3,824,000

The accounts receivable (asset) and the sales (revenue) accounts have both increased by: 1600 events x $2,390 = $3,824,000

264    Cirque du Lune is a corporation which sells circus performances. Today Cirque du Lune signed up for a loan with a 5% interest rate, and so the bank immediately transferred cash to the company in the amount of $84000.

DR Cash $84,000    CR Loan Payable $84,000

The cash (asset) and the loan payable (liability) accounts have both increased by: $84,000. The interest rate does not affect this initial accounting entry, but it will be used for the calculation of interest expense when repayments are made in the future toward this loan.

265    Jameson & Jameson is a company which offers their customers a wide selection of soap products. This December, Jameson & Jameson recognized 1 year of depreciation on a building which had a total useful life of 25 years, and which had originally been bought for $459000.

DR Depreciation expense $18,360    CR Accumulated Depreciation $18,360

The depreciation (expense) account and the accumulated depreciation (contra-asset) accounts have both increased by: $459,000 divided by 25 years = $18,360 depreciation per year.

266    Pharma Drug Company Ltd. sells several different types of medications. Today Pharma Drug Company Ltd. sold 44300 batches of pills which had a 30% mark-up. They had originally been bought from their suppliers for a unit cost of $2170.

DR Accounts Receivable $124,970,300    DR Cost of Goods Sold $96,131,000
CR Sales $124,970,300    CR Inventory $96,131,000

This transaction increases the accounts receivable (asset) account, the sales (revenue) account, and the cost of goods sold (expense) account. The inventory (asset) account has decreased. 44300 batches of pills x $2,170 = $96,131,000. The 30% markup applies to the sales and accounts receivable amounts, i.e. $96,131,000 x 1.30 = $124,970,300

267    Kola-Nut Ltd sells various soft drinks. This week, Kola-Nut Ltd purchased 2220 batches of soda bottles which were placed into the warehouse, and which had a per-unit cost of $1000.

DR Inventory $2,220,000    CR Accounts Payable $2,220,000

There was an increase in the inventory (asset) account, and also an increase in the accounts payable (liability) account. 2220 batches of soda bottles x $1,000 = $2,220,000

268    Toyonda provides their customers with cars. This month, Toyonda paid 1 monthly loan repayment towards their long-term note payable. The interest portion was 60% of the payment. The total amount paid in cash was $23000.

DR Interest Expense $13,800    DR Loan Payable $9,200    CR Cash $23,000

The interest (expense) account has increased by $23,000 x 0.6 = $13,800. The loan payable (liability) has decreased by $23,000 x 0.4 = $9,200. The cash (asset) account has decreased by the full amount of the payment, which is $23,000

269    Air America sells various global flights. This December, Air America recognized 1 year of depreciation on a building which had a total useful life of 25 years, and which had originally been bought for $461000.

DR Depreciation expense $18,440    CR Accumulated Depreciation $18,440

The depreciation (expense) account and the accumulated depreciation (contra-asset) accounts have both increased by: $461,000 divided by 25 years = $18,440 depreciation per year.

270    Paytech Ltd sells several different types of payroll transaction processing services. This December, Paytech Ltd has paid each of the company's 1100 owners an annual dividend in the amount of $19000.

DR Retained Earnings $20,900,000    CR Cash $20,900,000

The retained earnings (equity) and the cash accounts have both decreased by: 1100 owners x $19,000 = $20,900,000

271    Fairway Malls provides their customers with retail spaces in their shopping centers. This month, Fairway Malls paid for 1 month of rent for their company's office space. Each month, the rent owing was $16000.

DR Rent expense $16,000    CR Accounts Payable $16,000

The rent (expense) and the accounts payable (liability) accounts are both increased by one month's worth of rent, which is $16,000.

272    Hogtown Records sells various audio services for local musicians to record their music albums. This December, Hogtown Records recognized 1 year of depreciation on equipment which had a total useful life of 10 years, and which had originally cost $230000.

DR Depreciation expense $23,000    CR Accumulated Depreciation $23,000

The depreciation (expense) account and the accumulated depreciation (contra-asset) accounts have both increased by: $230,000 divided by 10 years = $23,000 depreciation per year.

273    Pharma Drug Company Ltd. is an organization which specializes in providing their customers with medications. Today Pharma Drug Company Ltd. sold 52700 batches of pills which had a 30% mark-up. They had originally been bought from their suppliers for a unit cost of $2630.

DR Accounts Receivable $180,181,300    DR Cost of Goods Sold $138,601,000
CR Sales $180,181,300    CR Inventory $138,601,000

This transaction increases the accounts receivable (asset) account, the sales (revenue) account, and the cost of goods sold (expense) account. The inventory (asset) account has decreased. 52700 batches of pills x $2,630 = $138,601,000. The 30% markup applies to the sales and accounts receivable amounts, i.e. $138,601,000 x 1.30 = $180,181,300

274   A to Z Event Guru Ltd offers their customers a wide range of start-to-finish event planning services for large gatherings.  A to Z Event Guru Ltd has just provided 1600 large orders which had been paid for in advance last year. Each order was in the amount of $2700.

DR Unearned Revenue $4,320,000    CR Sales $4,320,000

The unearned revenue (liability) account has decreased and the and the sales (revenue) account has increased by: 1600 large orders x $2,700 = $4,320,000

275   Kola-Nut Ltd sells several different types of soft drinks.  This month, Kola-Nut Ltd paid for 1 month of rent for the warehouse room, which has a monthly cost of $1400.

DR Rent expense $1,400    CR Accounts Payable $1,400

The rent (expense) and the accounts payable (liability) accounts are both increased by one month's worth of rent, which is $1,400.

276   Sprike Inc sells several different types of athletic apparel.  This month, Sprike Inc has estimated that 15% of the accounts receivable might not end up being collectable, based on past experience. The accounts receivable will need to be adjusted from its current balance of $25000.

DR Bad Debt expense $3,750    CR Allowance for Doubtful Accounts $3,750

The bad debts (expense) and the allowance for doubtful accounts (contra-asset) have both increased by: 15% x $25,000 = $3,750

277   AC&C Ltd. sells several different types of cell phone plans.  This December, AC&C Ltd. recognized 1 year of depreciation on a building which had a total useful life of 25 years, and which had originally been bought for $615000.

DR Depreciation expense $24,600    CR Accumulated Depreciation $24,600

The depreciation (expense) account and the accumulated depreciation (contra-asset) accounts have both increased by: $615,000 divided by 25 years = $24,600 depreciation per year.

278   Air America provides their customers with global flights.  This year, Air America has provided 1400 flights each of which earned revenues of $2920.

DR Accounts Receivable $4,088,000    CR Sales $4,088,000

The accounts receivable (asset) and the sales (revenue) accounts have both increased by: 1400 flights x $2,920 = $4,088,000

279 Sprike Inc is a corporation which sells athletic apparel. This month, Sprike Inc has estimated that 5% of the accounts receivable might not end up being collectable, based on past experience. The accounts receivable will need to be adjusted from its current balance of $50000.

DR Bad Debt expense $2,500    CR Allowance for Doubtful Accounts $2,500

The bad debts (expense) and the allowance for doubtful accounts (contra-asset) have both increased by: 5% x $50,000 = $2,500

280 Mr. Mop offers their customers a wide range of household cleaners. This month, Mr. Mop accepted 25900 tons of cleaning solution which were returned by customers. These products had been marked up by 35% and they had originally been bought at a per-unit cost of $1500.

DR Sales Returns $52,447,500    DR Inventory $38,850,000    CR Accounts Receivable $52,447,500    CR Cost of Goods Sold $38,850,000

This transaction increases the sales returns (contra-revenue) account, and the inventory (asset) account. The accounts receivable (asset) account and the cost of goods sold (expense) account have both decreased. 25900 tons of cleaning solution x $1,500 = $38,850,000. The 35% markup applies to the sales returns and accounts receivable amounts, i.e. $38,850,000 x 1.35 = $52,447,500

281 Sprike Inc is a corporation which sells athletic apparel. Today, Sprike Inc received an upfront payment for 3060 batches of athletic t-shirts which will be provided to the customer 6 months from now. The payment for each was $1500.

DR Cash $4,590,000    CR Unearned Revenue $4,590,000

The cash (asset) and the unearned revenue (liability) accounts have both increased by: 3060 batches of athletic t-shirts x $1,500 = $4,590,000

282 Pharma Drug Company Ltd. offers their customers a wide range of medications. Today, Pharma Drug Company Ltd. received an upfront payment for 1950 batches of pills which will be provided to the customer 6 months from now. The payment for each was $2000.

DR Cash $3,900,000    CR Unearned Revenue $3,900,000

The cash (asset) and the unearned revenue (liability) accounts have both increased by: 1950 batches of pills x $2,000 = $3,900,000

283 Jameson & Jameson is an organization which specializes in providing their customers with soap products. This month, Jameson & Jameson accepted 10800 truckloads of bars of soap which were returned by customers. These products had been marked up by 35% and they had originally been bought at a per-unit cost of $2700.

DR Sales Returns $39,366,000   DR Inventory $29,160,000   CR Accounts Receivable $39,366,000   CR Cost of Goods Sold $29,160,000

This transaction increases the sales returns (contra-revenue) account, and the inventory (asset) account. The accounts receivable (asset) account and the cost of goods sold (expense) account have both decreased. 10800 truckloads of bars of soap x $2,700 = $29,160,000. The 35% markup applies to the sales returns and accounts receivable amounts, i.e. $29,160,000 x 1.35 = $39,366,000

284 Jameson & Jameson offers their customers a wide range of soap products. Today Jameson & Jameson sold 35400 truckloads of bars of soap which had a 30% mark-up. They had originally been bought from their suppliers for a unit cost of $1330.

DR Accounts Receivable $61,206,600   DR Cost of Goods Sold $47,082,000
CR Sales $61,206,600   CR Inventory $47,082,000

This transaction increases the accounts receivable (asset) account, the sales (revenue) account, and the cost of goods sold (expense) account. The inventory (asset) account has decreased. 35400 truckloads of bars of soap x $1,330 = $47,082,000. The 30% markup applies to the sales and accounts receivable amounts, i.e. $47,082,000 x 1.30 = $61,206,600

285 Fairway Malls is a privately-held corporation which focuses on their niche of premium retail spaces in their shopping centers. Fairway Malls has just purchased a building using cash, which has an expected useful life of 30 years, and which had a total cost of $23000.

DR Building $23,000   CR Cash $23,000

The building (asset) account has increased, and the cash (asset) account has decreased by: $23,000. The useful life does not affect this original accounting entry, but it will be used to calculate depreciation of the asset in the future.

286     Mr. Mop is a privately-held corporation which focuses on their niche of premium household cleaners. Today, Mr. Mop bought equipment which has a 5 year useful life, and which had a cost of $20000.

DR Equipment $20,000    CR Accounts Payable $20,000

The equipment (asset) and the accounts payable (liability) accounts have both increased by: $20,000. The useful life does not affect this original accounting entry, but it will be used to calculate depreciation of the asset in the future.

287     Payday Now sells several different types of short-term loan arrangements. This month, Payday Now must amortize 1 month worth of utility bills which they had prepaid at the beginning of the year. The amount that they had paid upfront for the year was $22800.

DR Utilities expense $1,900    CR Prepaid Expense $1,900

The utilities (expense) account has increased and the prepaid expense (asset) account has decreased by: $22,800 for the year, divided by 12 months = $1,900

288     Payday Now is a market leader that is well-known for their brand of short-term loan arrangements. This December, Payday Now has paid each of the company's 2300 owners an annual dividend in the amount of $20000.

DR Retained Earnings $46,000,000    CR Cash $46,000,000

The retained earnings (equity) and the cash accounts have both decreased by: 2300 owners x $20,000 = $46,000,000

289     Fairway Malls is an organization which specializes in providing their customers with retail spaces in their shopping centers. Fairway Malls has just purchased a building using cash, which has an expected useful life of 30 years, and which had a total cost of $323000.

DR Building $323,000    CR Cash $323,000

The building (asset) account has increased, and the cash (asset) account has decreased by: $323,000. The useful life does not affect this original accounting entry, but it will be used to calculate depreciation of the asset in the future.

290 AC&C Ltd. sells several different types of cell phone plans. Today, AC&C Ltd. received payment upfront for 1600 large orders which will not be provided until early next year. Each order was in the amount of $2600.

DR Cash $4,160,000   CR Unearned Revenue $4,160,000

The cash (asset) and the unearned revenue (liability) accounts have both increased by: 1600 large orders x $2,600 = $4,160,000

291 Jameson & Jameson sells various soap products. This month, Jameson & Jameson paid for 1 month of rent for the warehouse room, which has a monthly cost of $2700.

DR Rent expense $2,700   CR Accounts Payable $2,700

The rent (expense) and the accounts payable (liability) accounts are both increased by one month's worth of rent, which is $2,700.

292 Payday Now is a market leader that is well-known for their brand of short-term loan arrangements. This month, Payday Now paid for 1 month of rent for their company's office space. Each month, the rent owing was $18000.

DR Rent expense $18,000   CR Accounts Payable $18,000

The rent (expense) and the accounts payable (liability) accounts are both increased by one month's worth of rent, which is $18,000.

293 Hogtown Records is a market leader that is well-known for their brand of audio services for local musicians to record their music albums. Today, Hogtown Records bought equipment which has a 5 year useful life, and which had a cost of $17000.

DR Equipment $17,000   CR Accounts Payable $17,000

The equipment (asset) and the accounts payable (liability) accounts have both increased by: $17,000. The useful life does not affect this original accounting entry, but it will be used to calculate depreciation of the asset in the future.

294 Sprike Inc sells several different types of athletic apparel. This month, Sprike Inc paid for 1 month of rent for the warehouse room, which has a monthly cost of $2300.

DR Rent expense $2,300   CR Accounts Payable $2,300

The rent (expense) and the accounts payable (liability) accounts are both increased by one month's worth of rent, which is $2,300.

295     Pharma Drug Company Ltd. is a market leader that is well-known for their brand of medications. This month, Pharma Drug Company Ltd. paid for 1 month of rent for the warehouse room, which has a monthly cost of $2800.

DR Rent expense $2,800    CR Accounts Payable $2,800

The rent (expense) and the accounts payable (liability) accounts are both increased by one month's worth of rent, which is $2,800.

296     Toyonda offers their customers a wide range of cars. This week, Toyonda paid each of the 1290 staff members their bi-weekly wages, which per person had a cost of $1300.

DR Wage expense $1,677,000    CR Accounts Payable $1,677,000

The wage (expense) and the accounts payable (liability) accounts have both increased by: 1290 staff members x $1,300 = $1,677,000

297     Club Disco is a company which offers their customers a wide selection of dance venue rentals for large family gatherings. This month, Club Disco paid for 1 month of rent for their company's office space. Each month, the rent owing was $22000.

DR Rent expense $22,000    CR Accounts Payable $22,000

The rent (expense) and the accounts payable (liability) accounts are both increased by one month's worth of rent, which is $22,000.

298     NY Fitness is a privately-held corporation which focuses on their niche of premium gym memberships for professional sports teams. NY Fitness has just purchased a building using cash, which has an expected useful life of 30 years, and which had a total cost of $373000.

DR Building $373,000    CR Cash $373,000

The building (asset) account has increased, and the cash (asset) account has decreased by: $373,000. The useful life does not affect this original accounting entry, but it will be used to calculate depreciation of the asset in the future.

299 Payday Now is an organization which specializes in providing their customers with short-term loan arrangements. This week, Payday Now paid each of the 1070 staff members their bi-weekly wages, which per person had a cost of $2700.

DR Wage expense $2,889,000    CR Accounts Payable $2,889,000

The wage (expense) and the accounts payable (liability) accounts have both increased by: 1070 staff members x $2,700 = $2,889,000

300 Sprike Inc offers their customers a wide range of athletic apparel. This week, Sprike Inc purchased 4480 batches of athletic t-shirts which were placed into the warehouse, and which had a per-unit cost of $2300.

DR Inventory $10,304,000    CR Accounts Payable $10,304,000

There was an increase in the inventory (asset) account, and also an increase in the accounts payable (liability) account. 4480 batches of athletic t-shirts x $2,300 = $10,304,000

301 Kola-Nut Ltd is a market leader that is well-known for their brand of soft drinks. Today Kola-Nut Ltd sold 35900 batches of soda bottles which had a 30% mark-up. They had originally been bought from their suppliers for a unit cost of $2770.

DR Accounts Receivable $129,275,900    DR Cost of Goods Sold $99,443,000
CR Sales $129,275,900    CR Inventory $99,443,000

This transaction increases the accounts receivable (asset) account, the sales (revenue) account, and the cost of goods sold (expense) account. The inventory (asset) account has decreased. 35900 batches of soda bottles x $2,770 = $99,443,000.  The 30% markup applies to the sales and accounts receivable amounts, i.e. $99,443,000 x 1.30 = $129,275,900

302 Sprike Inc is an organization which specializes in providing their customers with athletic apparel. Today, Sprike Inc received an upfront payment for 4580 batches of athletic t-shirts which will be provided to the customer 6 months from now. The payment for each was $2400.

DR Cash $10,992,000    CR Unearned Revenue $10,992,000

The cash (asset) and the unearned revenue (liability) accounts have both increased by: 4580 batches of athletic t-shirts x $2,400 = $10,992,000

303    David & Johnson offers their customers a wide range of legal services. This month, David & Johnson has estimated that 5% of the accounts receivable might not end up being collectable, based on past experience. The accounts receivable will need to be adjusted from its current balance of $34000.

DR Bad Debt expense $1,700    CR Allowance for Doubtful Accounts $1,700

The bad debts (expense) and the allowance for doubtful accounts (contra-asset) have both increased by: 5% x $34,000 = $1,700

304    McGerald's sells various fast food meals. McGerald's has just purchased a building using cash, which has an expected useful life of 30 years, and which had a total cost of $360000.

DR Building $360,000    CR Cash $360,000

The building (asset) account has increased, and the cash (asset) account has decreased by: $360,000. The useful life does not affect this original accounting entry, but it will be used to calculate depreciation of the asset in the future.

305    Air America is a corporation which sells global flights. This December, Air America recognized 1 year of depreciation on equipment which had a total useful life of 10 years, and which had originally cost $80000.

DR Depreciation expense $8,000    CR Accumulated Depreciation $8,000

The depreciation (expense) account and the accumulated depreciation (contra-asset) accounts have both increased by: $80,000 divided by 10 years = $8,000 depreciation per year.

306    NBG Media Corporation is an organization which specializes in providing their customers with broadcasting services for advertising agencies. Today, NBG Media Corporation has paid cash to their supplier to fully pay off their account payable balance, which was $30000.

DR Accounts Payable $30,000    CR Cash $30,000

The accounts payable (liability) and cash (asset) accounts have both increased by $30,000.

307 McGerald's is a market leader that is well-known for their brand of fast food meals. This December, McGerald's has paid each of the company's 1800 owners an annual dividend in the amount of $15000.

DR Retained Earnings $27,000,000    CR Cash $27,000,000

The retained earnings (equity) and the cash accounts have both decreased by: 1800 owners x $15,000 = $27,000,000

308 Fairway Malls sells various retail spaces in their shopping centers. This month, Fairway Malls paid for 1 month of rent for their company's office space. Each month, the rent owing was $22000.

DR Rent expense $22,000    CR Accounts Payable $22,000

The rent (expense) and the accounts payable (liability) accounts are both increased by one month's worth of rent, which is $22,000.

309 Kola-Nut Ltd sells several different types of soft drinks. Today Kola-Nut Ltd sold 39100 batches of soda bottles which had a 30% mark-up. They had originally been bought from their suppliers for a unit cost of $1220.

DR Accounts Receivable $62,012,600    DR Cost of Goods Sold $47,702,000
CR Sales $62,012,600    CR Inventory $47,702,000

This transaction increases the accounts receivable (asset) account, the sales (revenue) account, and the cost of goods sold (expense) account. The inventory (asset) account has decreased. 39100 batches of soda bottles x $1,220 = $47,702,000. The 30% markup applies to the sales and accounts receivable amounts, i.e. $47,702,000 x 1.30 = $62,012,600

310 NY Fitness is a privately-held corporation which focuses on their niche of premium gym memberships for professional sports teams. This week, NY Fitness paid each of the 2760 staff members their bi-weekly wages, which per person had a cost of $1400.

DR Wage expense $3,864,000    CR Accounts Payable $3,864,000

The wage (expense) and the accounts payable (liability) accounts have both increased by: 2760 staff members x $1,400 = $3,864,000

311 AC&C Ltd. sells various cell phone plans. This December, AC&C Ltd. recognized 1 year of depreciation on a building which had a total useful life of 25 years, and which had originally been bought for $801000.

DR Depreciation expense $32,040    CR Accumulated Depreciation $32,040

The depreciation (expense) account and the accumulated depreciation (contra-asset) accounts have both increased by: $801,000 divided by 25 years = $32,040 depreciation per year.

312 Grand Convention Ltd sells various banquet hall rentals for corporate meetings. This December, Grand Convention Ltd recognized 1 year of depreciation on equipment which had a total useful life of 10 years, and which had originally cost $100000.

DR Depreciation expense $10,000    CR Accumulated Depreciation $10,000

The depreciation (expense) account and the accumulated depreciation (contra-asset) accounts have both increased by: $100,000 divided by 10 years = $10,000 depreciation per year.

313 Comedy 253 is a privately-held corporation which focuses on their niche of premium live performances of stand-up comedy. This December, Comedy 253 recognized 1 year of depreciation on equipment which had a total useful life of 10 years, and which had originally cost $200000.

DR Depreciation expense $20,000    CR Accumulated Depreciation $20,000

The depreciation (expense) account and the accumulated depreciation (contra-asset) accounts have both increased by: $200,000 divided by 10 years = $20,000 depreciation per year.

314 Paytech Ltd is a corporation which sells payroll transaction processing services. This month, Paytech Ltd must amortize 1 month worth of utility bills which they had prepaid at the beginning of the year. The amount that they had paid upfront for the year was $42000.

DR Utilities expense $3,500    CR Prepaid Expense $3,500

The utilities (expense) account has increased and the prepaid expense (asset) account has decreased by: $42,000 for the year, divided by 12 months = $3,500

315    Kola-Nut Ltd sells several different types of soft drinks. This month, Kola-Nut Ltd paid 1 monthly loan repayment towards their long-term note payable. The interest portion was 60% of the payment. The total amount paid in cash was $12000.

DR Interest Expense $7,200    DR Loan Payable $4,800    CR Cash $12,000

The interest (expense) account has increased by $12,000 x 0.6 = $7,200. The loan payable (liability) has decreased by $12,000 x 0.4 = $4,800. The cash (asset) account has decreased by the full amount of the payment, which is $12,000

316    Jameson & Jameson sells various soap products. Today Jameson & Jameson signed up for a loan with a 5% interest rate, and so the bank immediately transferred cash to the company in the amount of $96000.

DR Cash $96,000    CR Loan Payable $96,000

The cash (asset) and the loan payable (liability) accounts have both increased by: $96,000. The interest rate does not affect this initial accounting entry, but it will be used for the calculation of interest expense when repayments are made in the future toward this loan.

317    Mr. Mop is a privately-held corporation which focuses on their niche of premium household cleaners. This month, Mr. Mop paid for 1 month of rent for the warehouse room, which has a monthly cost of $1100.

DR Rent expense $1,100    CR Accounts Payable $1,100

The rent (expense) and the accounts payable (liability) accounts are both increased by one month's worth of rent, which is $1,100.

318    Fairway Malls is a market leader that is well-known for their brand of retail spaces in their shopping centers. This December, Fairway Malls recognized 1 year of depreciation on equipment which had a total useful life of 10 years, and which had originally cost $190000.

DR Depreciation expense $19,000    CR Accumulated Depreciation $19,000

The depreciation (expense) account and the accumulated depreciation (contra-asset) accounts have both increased by: $190,000 divided by 10 years = $19,000 depreciation per year.

319    Kola-Nut Ltd is an organization which specializes in providing their customers with soft drinks. Today, Kola-Nut Ltd has paid cash to their supplier to fully pay off their account payable balance, which was $26000.

DR Accounts Payable $26,000    CR Cash $26,000

The accounts payable (liability) and cash (asset) accounts have both increased by $26,000.

320    Sprike Inc offers their customers a wide range of athletic apparel. This December, Sprike Inc recognized 1 year of depreciation on a building which had a total useful life of 25 years, and which had originally been bought for $61000.

DR Depreciation expense $2,440    CR Accumulated Depreciation $2,440

The depreciation (expense) account and the accumulated depreciation (contra-asset) accounts have both increased by: $61,000 divided by 25 years = $2,440 depreciation per year.

321    Mr. Mop provides their customers with household cleaners. Today, Mr. Mop received an upfront payment for 5090 tons of cleaning solution which will be provided to the customer 6 months from now. The payment for each was $2000.

DR Cash $10,180,000    CR Unearned Revenue $10,180,000

The cash (asset) and the unearned revenue (liability) accounts have both increased by: 5090 tons of cleaning solution x $2,000 = $10,180,000

322    Pharma Drug Company Ltd. is a market leader that is well-known for their brand of medications. This week, Pharma Drug Company Ltd. purchased 5510 batches of pills which were placed into the warehouse, and which had a per-unit cost of $1300.

DR Inventory $7,163,000    CR Accounts Payable $7,163,000

There was an increase in the inventory (asset) account, and also an increase in the accounts payable (liability) account. 5510 batches of pills x $1,300 = $7,163,000

323     A to Z Event Guru Ltd is a company which offers their customers a wide selection of start-to-finish event planning services for large gatherings. This year, A to Z Event Guru Ltd has provided 1000 events each of which earned revenues of $1910.

DR Accounts Receivable $1,910,000     CR Sales $1,910,000

The accounts receivable (asset) and the sales (revenue) accounts have both increased by: 1000 events x $1,910 = $1,910,000

324     Sprike Inc is a corporation which sells athletic apparel. Today, Sprike Inc bought equipment which has a 5 year useful life, and which had a cost of $8000.

DR Equipment $8,000     CR Accounts Payable $8,000

The equipment (asset) and the accounts payable (liability) accounts have both increased by: $8,000. The useful life does not affect this original accounting entry, but it will be used to calculate depreciation of the asset in the future.

325     Mount Tessory Academy offers their customers a wide range of private school education. This December, Mount Tessory Academy has paid each of the company's 1600 owners an annual dividend in the amount of $16000.

DR Retained Earnings $25,600,000     CR Cash $25,600,000

The retained earnings (equity) and the cash accounts have both decreased by: 1600 owners x $16,000 = $25,600,000

326     Comedy 253 is a company which offers their customers a wide selection of live performances of stand-up comedy. This year, Comedy 253 has provided 2200 shows each of which earned revenues of $1080.

DR Accounts Receivable $2,376,000     CR Sales $2,376,000

The accounts receivable (asset) and the sales (revenue) accounts have both increased by: 2200 shows x $1,080 = $2,376,000

327     Toyonda is a corporation which sells cars. This December, Toyonda recognized 1 year of depreciation on equipment which had a total useful life of 10 years, and which had originally cost $150000.

DR Depreciation expense $15,000     CR Accumulated Depreciation $15,000

The depreciation (expense) account and the accumulated depreciation (contra-asset) accounts have both increased by: $150,000 divided by 10 years = $15,000 depreciation per year.

328    Grand Convention Ltd sells several different types of banquet hall rentals for corporate meetings.  Today, Grand Convention Ltd bought equipment which has a 5 year useful life, and which had a cost of $24000.

DR Equipment $24,000    CR Accounts Payable $24,000

The equipment (asset) and the accounts payable (liability) accounts have both increased by: $24,000. The useful life does not affect this original accounting entry, but it will be used to calculate depreciation of the asset in the future.

329    NY Fitness is a privately-held corporation which focuses on their niche of premium gym memberships for professional sports teams.  This January, NY Fitness has made an advance payment to cover the next 12 months of utility bills, which have a monthly cost of $2000.

DR Prepaid Expense $24,000    CR Cash $24,000

The prepaid expense (asset) account has increased, and the cash (asset) account has decreased by: 12 months x $2,000 per month = $24,000 for the year.

330    Mr. Mop offers their customers a wide range of household cleaners.  Today, Mr. Mop received an upfront payment for 1420 tons of cleaning solution which will be provided to the customer 6 months from now. The payment for each was $1600.

DR Cash $2,272,000    CR Unearned Revenue $2,272,000

The cash (asset) and the unearned revenue (liability) accounts have both increased by: 1420 tons of cleaning solution x $1,600 = $2,272,000

331    Jameson & Jameson is a company which offers their customers a wide selection of soap products.  This month, Jameson & Jameson accepted 27900 truckloads of bars of soap which were returned by customers. These products had been marked up by 35% and they had originally been bought at a per-unit cost of $2300.

DR Sales Returns $86,629,500    DR Inventory $64,170,000    CR Accounts Receivable $86,629,500    CR Cost of Goods Sold $64,170,000

This transaction increases the sales returns (contra-revenue) account, and the inventory (asset) account. The accounts receivable (asset) account and the cost of goods sold (expense) account have both decreased. 27900 truckloads of bars of soap x $2,300 = $64,170,000. The 35% markup applies to the sales returns and accounts receivable amounts, i.e. $64,170,000 x 1.35 = $86,629,500

332     Kola-Nut Ltd is a market leader that is well-known for their brand of soft drinks. This month, Kola-Nut Ltd accepted 29400 batches of soda bottles which were returned by customers. These products had been marked up by 35% and they had originally been bought at a per-unit cost of $1300.

DR Sales Returns $51,597,000    DR Inventory $38,220,000    CR Accounts Receivable $51,597,000    CR Cost of Goods Sold $38,220,000

This transaction increases the sales returns (contra-revenue) account, and the inventory (asset) account. The accounts receivable (asset) account and the cost of goods sold (expense) account have both decreased. 29400 batches of soda bottles x $1,300 = $38,220,000. The 35% markup applies to the sales returns and accounts receivable amounts, i.e. $38,220,000 x 1.35 = $51,597,000

333     Pharma Drug Company Ltd. is an organization which specializes in providing their customers with medications. This month, Pharma Drug Company Ltd. paid for 1 month of rent for the warehouse room, which has a monthly cost of $1000.

DR Rent expense $1,000    CR Accounts Payable $1,000

The rent (expense) and the accounts payable (liability) accounts are both increased by one month's worth of rent, which is $1,000.

334     NY Fitness sells various gym memberships for professional sports teams. Today, NY Fitness received payment upfront for 1800 large orders which will not be provided until early next year. Each order was in the amount of $2500.

DR Cash $4,500,000    CR Unearned Revenue $4,500,000

The cash (asset) and the unearned revenue (liability) accounts have both increased by: 1800 large orders x $2,500 = $4,500,000

335     NBG Media Corporation is a company which offers their customers a wide selection of broadcasting services for advertising agencies. This week, NBG Media Corporation paid each of the 1230 staff members their bi-weekly wages, which per person had a cost of $2100.

DR Wage expense $2,583,000    CR Accounts Payable $2,583,000

The wage (expense) and the accounts payable (liability) accounts have both increased by: 1230 staff members x $2,100 = $2,583,000

336    A to Z Event Guru Ltd is an organization which specializes in providing their customers with start-to-finish event planning services for large gatherings. Today, A to Z Event Guru Ltd has paid cash to their supplier to fully pay off their account payable balance, which was $69000.

DR Accounts Payable $69,000    CR Cash $69,000

The accounts payable (liability) and cash (asset) accounts have both increased by $69,000.

337    Pharma Drug Company Ltd. provides their customers with medications. Pharma Drug Company Ltd. has just received a cash payment for the full amount that this customer owed to the company for all of their purchases to date. The outstanding balance which has now been paid was $92000.

DR Cash $92,000    CR Accounts Receivable $92,000

The cash (asset) account has increased, and the accounts receivable (asset) account has decreased by $92,000.

338    A to Z Event Guru Ltd is a privately-held corporation which focuses on their niche of premium start-to-finish event planning services for large gatherings. A to Z Event Guru Ltd has just provided 1500 large orders which had been paid for in advance last year. Each order was in the amount of $1800.

DR Unearned Revenue $2,700,000    CR Sales $2,700,000

The unearned revenue (liability) account has decreased and the and the sales (revenue) account has increased by: 1500 large orders x $1,800 = $2,700,000

339    A to Z Event Guru Ltd is a company which offers their customers a wide selection of start-to-finish event planning services for large gatherings. Today, A to Z Event Guru Ltd received payment upfront for 1800 large orders which will not be provided until early next year. Each order was in the amount of $1600.

DR Cash $2,880,000    CR Unearned Revenue $2,880,000

The cash (asset) and the unearned revenue (liability) accounts have both increased by: 1800 large orders x $1,600 = $2,880,000

340 Mr. Mop is a company which offers their customers a wide selection of household cleaners. Today, Mr. Mop has paid cash to their supplier to fully pay off their account payable balance, which was $13000.

DR Accounts Payable $13,000    CR Cash $13,000

The accounts payable (liability) and cash (asset) accounts have both increased by $13,000.

341 Mount Tessory Academy is a corporation which sells private school education. This December, Mount Tessory Academy recognized 1 year of depreciation on equipment which had a total useful life of 10 years, and which had originally cost $110000.

DR Depreciation expense $11,000    CR Accumulated Depreciation $11,000

The depreciation (expense) account and the accumulated depreciation (contra-asset) accounts have both increased by: $110,000 divided by 10 years = $11,000 depreciation per year.

342 Kola-Nut Ltd sells several different types of soft drinks. This week, Kola-Nut Ltd purchased 1490 batches of soda bottles which were placed into the warehouse, and which had a per-unit cost of $1200.

DR Inventory $1,788,000    CR Accounts Payable $1,788,000

There was an increase in the inventory (asset) account, and also an increase in the accounts payable (liability) account. 1490 batches of soda bottles x $1,200 = $1,788,000

343 Hogtown Records is an organization which specializes in providing their customers with audio services for local musicians to record their music albums. This year, Hogtown Records has provided 1400 albums each of which earned revenues of $2260.

DR Accounts Receivable $3,164,000    CR Sales $3,164,000

The accounts receivable (asset) and the sales (revenue) accounts have both increased by: 1400 albums x $2,260 = $3,164,000

344 Sprike Inc is a corporation which sells athletic apparel. This month, Sprike Inc accepted 20600 batches of athletic t-shirts which were returned by customers. These products had been marked up by 35% and they had originally been bought at a per-unit cost of $2200.

DR Sales Returns $61,182,000   DR Inventory $45,320,000   CR Accounts Receivable $61,182,000   CR Cost of Goods Sold $45,320,000

This transaction increases the sales returns (contra-revenue) account, and the inventory (asset) account. The accounts receivable (asset) account and the cost of goods sold (expense) account have both decreased. 20600 batches of athletic t-shirts x $2,200 = $45,320,000. The 35% markup applies to the sales returns and accounts receivable amounts, i.e. $45,320,000 x 1.35 = $61,182,000

345 Cirque du Lune is a privately-held corporation which focuses on their niche of premium circus performances. This December, Cirque du Lune has paid each of the company's 2400 owners an annual dividend in the amount of $25000.

DR Retained Earnings $60,000,000   CR Cash $60,000,000

The retained earnings (equity) and the cash accounts have both decreased by: 2400 owners x $25,000 = $60,000,000

346 David & Johnson is a company which offers their customers a wide selection of legal services. Today, David & Johnson bought equipment which has a 5 year useful life, and which had a cost of $14000.

DR Equipment $14,000   CR Accounts Payable $14,000

The equipment (asset) and the accounts payable (liability) accounts have both increased by: $14,000. The useful life does not affect this original accounting entry, but it will be used to calculate depreciation of the asset in the future.

347 Pharma Drug Company Ltd. is a privately-held corporation which focuses on their niche of premium medications. This month, Pharma Drug Company Ltd. must amortize 1 month worth of utility bills which they had prepaid at the beginning of the year. The amount that they had paid upfront for the year was $13200.

DR Utilities expense $1,100   CR Prepaid Expense $1,100

The utilities (expense) account has increased and the prepaid expense (asset) account has decreased by: $13,200 for the year, divided by 12 months = $1,100

348     Mr. Mop is an organization which specializes in providing their customers with household cleaners. This month, Mr. Mop accepted 23300 tons of cleaning solution which were returned by customers. These products had been marked up by 35% and they had originally been bought at a per-unit cost of $1300.

DR Sales Returns $40,891,500    DR Inventory $30,290,000    CR Accounts Receivable $40,891,500    CR Cost of Goods Sold $30,290,000

This transaction increases the sales returns (contra-revenue) account, and the inventory (asset) account. The accounts receivable (asset) account and the cost of goods sold (expense) account have both decreased. 23300 tons of cleaning solution x $1,300 = $30,290,000. The 35% markup applies to the sales returns and accounts receivable amounts, i.e. $30,290,000 x 1.35 = $40,891,500

349     Mount Tessory Academy offers their customers a wide range of private school education. This year, Mount Tessory Academy has provided 1400 annual tuition memberships each of which earned revenues of $2420.

DR Accounts Receivable $3,388,000    CR Sales $3,388,000

The accounts receivable (asset) and the sales (revenue) accounts have both increased by: 1400 annual tuition memberships x $2,420 = $3,388,000

350     Pharma Drug Company Ltd. sells several different types of medications. Today, Pharma Drug Company Ltd. received an upfront payment for 3730 batches of pills which will be provided to the customer 6 months from now. The payment for each was $2600.

DR Cash $9,698,000    CR Unearned Revenue $9,698,000

The cash (asset) and the unearned revenue (liability) accounts have both increased by: 3730 batches of pills x $2,600 = $9,698,000

351     Kola-Nut Ltd sells various soft drinks. This month, Kola-Nut Ltd accepted 20200 batches of soda bottles which were returned by customers. These products had been marked up by 35% and they had originally been bought at a per-unit cost of $1000.

DR Sales Returns $27,270,000    DR Inventory $20,200,000    CR Accounts Receivable $27,270,000    CR Cost of Goods Sold $20,200,000

This transaction increases the sales returns (contra-revenue) account, and the inventory (asset) account. The accounts receivable (asset) account and the cost of goods sold (expense) account have both decreased. 20200 batches of soda bottles x $1,000 = $20,200,000. The 35% markup applies to the sales returns and accounts receivable amounts, i.e. $20,200,000 x 1.35 = $27,270,000

352    Payday Now is an organization which specializes in providing their customers with short-term loan arrangements. Today Payday Now signed up for a loan with a 5% interest rate, and so the bank immediately transferred cash to the company in the amount of $44000.

DR Cash $44,000    CR Loan Payable $44,000

The cash (asset) and the loan payable (liability) accounts have both increased by: $44,000. The interest rate does not affect this initial accounting entry, but it will be used for the calculation of interest expense when repayments are made in the future toward this loan.

353    Mr. Mop is a corporation which sells household cleaners. This week, Mr. Mop purchased 3760 tons of cleaning solution which were placed into the warehouse, and which had a per-unit cost of $1200.

DR Inventory $4,512,000    CR Accounts Payable $4,512,000

There was an increase in the inventory (asset) account, and also an increase in the accounts payable (liability) account. 3760 tons of cleaning solution x $1,200 = $4,512,000

354    NY Fitness is a privately-held corporation which focuses on their niche of premium gym memberships for professional sports teams. This December, NY Fitness has paid each of the company's 2100 owners an annual dividend in the amount of $21000.

DR Retained Earnings $44,100,000    CR Cash $44,100,000

The retained earnings (equity) and the cash accounts have both decreased by: 2100 owners x $21,000 = $44,100,000

355    Jameson & Jameson is an organization which specializes in providing their customers with soap products. Today Jameson & Jameson sold 45300 truckloads of bars of soap which had a 30% mark-up. They had originally been bought from their suppliers for a unit cost of $1480.

DR Accounts Receivable $87,157,200    DR Cost of Goods Sold $67,044,000
CR Sales $87,157,200    CR Inventory $67,044,000

This transaction increases the accounts receivable (asset) account, the sales (revenue) account, and the cost of goods sold (expense) account. The inventory (asset) account has decreased. 45300 truckloads of bars of soap x $1,480 = $67,044,000. The 30% markup applies to the sales and accounts receivable amounts, i.e. $67,044,000 x 1.30 = $87,157,200

356     Pharma Drug Company Ltd. is an organization which specializes in providing their customers with medications. This week, Pharma Drug Company Ltd. purchased 2020 batches of pills which were placed into the warehouse, and which had a per-unit cost of $1500.

DR Inventory $3,030,000    CR Accounts Payable $3,030,000

There was an increase in the inventory (asset) account, and also an increase in the accounts payable (liability) account. 2020 batches of pills x $1,500 = $3,030,000

357     Mount Tessory Academy offers their customers a wide range of private school education. Today Mount Tessory Academy signed up for a loan with a 5% interest rate, and so the bank immediately transferred cash to the company in the amount of $112000.

DR Cash $112,000    CR Loan Payable $112,000

The cash (asset) and the loan payable (liability) accounts have both increased by: $112,000. The interest rate does not affect this initial accounting entry, but it will be used for the calculation of interest expense when repayments are made in the future toward this loan.

358     Fairway Malls is a company which offers their customers a wide selection of retail spaces in their shopping centers. This December, Fairway Malls recognized 1 year of depreciation on a building which had a total useful life of 25 years, and which had originally been bought for $81000.

DR Depreciation expense $3,240    CR Accumulated Depreciation $3,240

The depreciation (expense) account and the accumulated depreciation (contra-asset) accounts have both increased by: $81,000 divided by 25 years = $3,240 depreciation per year.

359     Cirque du Lune is a privately-held corporation which focuses on their niche of premium circus performances. This December, Cirque du Lune recognized 1 year of depreciation on a building which had a total useful life of 25 years, and which had originally been bought for $211000.

DR Depreciation expense $8,440    CR Accumulated Depreciation $8,440

The depreciation (expense) account and the accumulated depreciation (contra-asset) accounts have both increased by: $211,000 divided by 25 years = $8,440 depreciation per year.

360    Kola-Nut Ltd is a company which offers their customers a wide selection of soft drinks.  Today Kola-Nut Ltd sold 15400 batches of soda bottles which had a 30% mark-up. They had originally been bought from their suppliers for a unit cost of $2950.

DR Accounts Receivable $59,059,000    DR Cost of Goods Sold $45,430,000
CR Sales $59,059,000    CR Inventory $45,430,000

This transaction increases the accounts receivable (asset) account, the sales (revenue) account, and the cost of goods sold (expense) account. The inventory (asset) account has decreased. 15400 batches of soda bottles x $2,950 = $45,430,000.  The 30% markup applies to the sales and accounts receivable amounts, i.e. $45,430,000 x 1.30 = $59,059,000

361    Kola-Nut Ltd offers their customers a wide range of soft drinks.  This December, Kola-Nut Ltd has paid each of the company's 1300 owners an annual dividend in the amount of $26000.

DR Retained Earnings $33,800,000    CR Cash $33,800,000

The retained earnings (equity) and the cash accounts have both decreased by: 1300 owners x $26,000 = $33,800,000

362    Comedy 253 is an organization which specializes in providing their customers with live performances of stand-up comedy.  This month, Comedy 253 has estimated that 10% of the accounts receivable might not end up being collectable, based on past experience. The accounts receivable will need to be adjusted from its current balance of $45000.

DR Bad Debt expense $4,500    CR Allowance for Doubtful Accounts $4,500

The bad debts (expense) and the allowance for doubtful accounts (contra-asset) have both increased by: 10% x $45,000 = $4,500

363    Kola-Nut Ltd is a corporation which sells soft drinks.  Today Kola-Nut Ltd sold 5800 batches of soda bottles which had a 30% mark-up. They had originally been bought from their suppliers for a unit cost of $1430.

DR Accounts Receivable $10,782,200    DR Cost of Goods Sold $8,294,000
CR Sales $10,782,200    CR Inventory $8,294,000

This transaction increases the accounts receivable (asset) account, the sales (revenue) account, and the cost of goods sold (expense) account. The inventory (asset) account has decreased. 5800 batches of soda bottles x $1,430 = $8,294,000.  The 30% markup applies to the sales and accounts receivable amounts, i.e. $8,294,000 x 1.30 = $10,782,200

364 Pharma Drug Company Ltd. provides their customers with medications. This month, Pharma Drug Company Ltd. accepted 20400 batches of pills which were returned by customers. These products had been marked up by 35% and they had originally been bought at a per-unit cost of $2000.

DR Sales Returns $55,080,000 DR Inventory $40,800,000 CR Accounts Receivable $55,080,000 CR Cost of Goods Sold $40,800,000

This transaction increases the sales returns (contra-revenue) account, and the inventory (asset) account. The accounts receivable (asset) account and the cost of goods sold (expense) account have both decreased. 20400 batches of pills x $2,000 = $40,800,000. The 35% markup applies to the sales returns and accounts receivable amounts, i.e. $40,800,000 x 1.35 = $55,080,000

365 Payday Now offers their customers a wide range of short-term loan arrangements. Today, Payday Now received payment upfront for 2100 large orders which will not be provided until early next year. Each order was in the amount of $2400.

DR Cash $5,040,000 CR Unearned Revenue $5,040,000

The cash (asset) and the unearned revenue (liability) accounts have both increased by: 2100 large orders x $2,400 = $5,040,000

366 Mount Tessory Academy offers their customers a wide range of private school education. Today, Mount Tessory Academy received payment upfront for 1600 large orders which will not be provided until early next year. Each order was in the amount of $1900.

DR Cash $3,040,000 CR Unearned Revenue $3,040,000

The cash (asset) and the unearned revenue (liability) accounts have both increased by: 1600 large orders x $1,900 = $3,040,000

367 Cirque du Lune offers their customers a wide range of circus performances. This month, Cirque du Lune has estimated that 5% of the accounts receivable might not end up being collectable, based on past experience. The accounts receivable will need to be adjusted from its current balance of $20000.

DR Bad Debt expense $1,000 CR Allowance for Doubtful Accounts $1,000

The bad debts (expense) and the allowance for doubtful accounts (contra-asset) have both increased by: 5% x $20,000 = $1,000

368     Kola-Nut Ltd is a market leader that is well-known for their brand of soft drinks. Today Kola-Nut Ltd signed up for a loan with a 5% interest rate, and so the bank immediately transferred cash to the company in the amount of $86000.

DR Cash $86,000    CR Loan Payable $86,000

The cash (asset) and the loan payable (liability) accounts have both increased by: $86,000. The interest rate does not affect this initial accounting entry, but it will be used for the calculation of interest expense when repayments are made in the future toward this loan.

369     Mr. Mop offers their customers a wide range of household cleaners.  Today, Mr. Mop bought equipment which has a 5 year useful life, and which had a cost of $20000.

DR Equipment $20,000    CR Accounts Payable $20,000

The equipment (asset) and the accounts payable (liability) accounts have both increased by: $20,000. The useful life does not affect this original accounting entry, but it will be used to calculate depreciation of the asset in the future.

370     David & Johnson sells several different types of legal services.  This month, David & Johnson must amortize 1 month worth of utility bills which they had prepaid at the beginning of the year. The amount that they had paid upfront for the year was $19200.

DR Utilities expense $1,600    CR Prepaid Expense $1,600

The utilities (expense) account has increased and the prepaid expense (asset) account has decreased by: $19,200 for the year, divided by 12 months = $1,600

371     Paytech Ltd is a corporation which sells payroll transaction processing services. This year, Paytech Ltd has provided 2000 batches of transactions for the current period each of which earned revenues of $2860.

DR Accounts Receivable $5,720,000    CR Sales $5,720,000

The accounts receivable (asset) and the sales (revenue) accounts have both increased by: 2000 batches of transactions for the current period x $2,860 = $5,720,000

372     NBG Media Corporation is an organization which specializes in providing their customers with broadcasting services for advertising agencies.  NBG Media Corporation has just received a cash payment for the full amount that this customer owed to the company for all of their purchases to date. The outstanding balance which has now been paid was $69000.

DR Cash $69,000    CR Accounts Receivable $69,000

The cash (asset) account has increased, and the accounts receivable (asset) account has decreased by $69,000.

373     Sprike Inc is a market leader that is well-known for their brand of athletic apparel. This month, Sprike Inc accepted 4700 batches of athletic t-shirts which were returned by customers. These products had been marked up by 35% and they had originally been bought at a per-unit cost of $1300.

DR Sales Returns $8,248,500    DR Inventory $6,110,000    CR Accounts Receivable $8,248,500    CR Cost of Goods Sold $6,110,000

This transaction increases the sales returns (contra-revenue) account, and the inventory (asset) account. The accounts receivable (asset) account and the cost of goods sold (expense) account have both decreased. 4700 batches of athletic t-shirts x $1,300 = $6,110,000. The 35% markup applies to the sales returns and accounts receivable amounts, i.e. $6,110,000 x 1.35 = $8,248,500

374     Mount Tessory Academy is a company which offers their customers a wide selection of private school education.  This December, Mount Tessory Academy recognized 1 year of depreciation on a building which had a total useful life of 25 years, and which had originally been bought for $168000.

DR Depreciation expense $6,720    CR Accumulated Depreciation $6,720

The depreciation (expense) account and the accumulated depreciation (contra-asset) accounts have both increased by: $168,000 divided by 25 years = $6,720 depreciation per year.

375     Comedy 253 is an organization which specializes in providing their customers with live performances of stand-up comedy.  Today, Comedy 253 received payment upfront for 2100 large orders which will not be provided until early next year. Each order was in the amount of $1100.

DR Cash $2,310,000    CR Unearned Revenue $2,310,000

The cash (asset) and the unearned revenue (liability) accounts have both increased by: 2100 large orders x $1,100 = $2,310,000

376  Paytech Ltd offers their customers a wide range of payroll transaction processing services. Today, Paytech Ltd received payment upfront for 1900 large orders which will not be provided until early next year. Each order was in the amount of $1400.

DR Cash $2,660,000   CR Unearned Revenue $2,660,000

The cash (asset) and the unearned revenue (liability) accounts have both increased by: 1900 large orders x $1,400 = $2,660,000

377  Sprike Inc sells several different types of athletic apparel.  Today Sprike Inc sold 11200 batches of athletic t-shirts which had a 30% mark-up. They had originally been bought from their suppliers for a unit cost of $2050.

DR Accounts Receivable $29,848,000   DR Cost of Goods Sold $22,960,000
CR Sales $29,848,000   CR Inventory $22,960,000

This transaction increases the accounts receivable (asset) account, the sales (revenue) account, and the cost of goods sold (expense) account. The inventory (asset) account has decreased. 11200 batches of athletic t-shirts x $2,050 = $22,960,000.  The 30% markup applies to the sales and accounts receivable amounts, i.e. $22,960,000 x 1.30 = $29,848,000

378  Pharma Drug Company Ltd. sells several different types of medications.  This week, Pharma Drug Company Ltd. paid each of the 3760 staff members their bi-weekly wages, which per person had a cost of $2400.

DR Wage expense $9,024,000   CR Accounts Payable $9,024,000

The wage (expense) and the accounts payable (liability) accounts have both increased by: 3760 staff members x $2,400 = $9,024,000

379  Hogtown Records is an organization which specializes in providing their customers with audio services for local musicians to record their music albums. This January, Hogtown Records has made an advance payment to cover the next 12 months of utility bills, which have a monthly cost of $1200.

DR Prepaid Expense $14,400   CR Cash $14,400

The prepaid expense (asset) account has increased, and the cash (asset) account has decreased by: 12 months x $1,200 per month = $14,400 for the year.

380    McGerald's provides their customers with fast food meals. This year, McGerald's has provided 1100 burger combos each of which earned revenues of $1790.

DR Accounts Receivable $1,969,000   CR Sales $1,969,000

The accounts receivable (asset) and the sales (revenue) accounts have both increased by: 11/1 /2urger combos x $1,790 = $1,969,000

381    Cirque du Lune is a market leader that is well-known for their brand of circus performances. This December, Cirque du Lune has paid each of the company's 2000 owners an annual dividend in the amount of $18000.

DR Retained Earnings $36,000,000   CR Cash $36,000,000

The retained earnings (equity) and the cash accounts have both decreased by: 2000 owners x $18,000 = $36,000,000

382    Kola-Nut Ltd is a market leader that is well-known for their brand of soft drinks. This month, Kola-Nut Ltd paid for 1 month of rent for the warehouse room, which has a monthly cost of $1300.

DR Rent expense $1,300   CR Accounts Payable $1,300

The rent (expense) and the accounts payable (liability) accounts are both increased by one month's worth of rent, which is $1,300.

383    Kola-Nut Ltd is a privately-held corporation which focuses on their niche of premium soft drinks. Kola-Nut Ltd has just received a cash payment for the full amount that this customer owed to the company for all of their purchases to date. The outstanding balance which has now been paid was $87000.

DR Cash $87,000   CR Accounts Receivable $87,000

The cash (asset) account has increased, and the accounts receivable (asset) account has decreased by $87,000.

384    McGerald's offers their customers a wide range of fast food meals. This year, McGerald's has provided 1500 burger combos each of which earned revenues of $1660.

DR Accounts Receivable $2,490,000   CR Sales $2,490,000

The accounts receivable (asset) and the sales (revenue) accounts have both increased by: 15/1 /2urger combos x $1,660 = $2,490,000

385  LA Met Theatre Company is an organization which specializes in providing their customers with live theatrical performances. This January, LA Met Theatre Company has made an advance payment to cover the next 12 months of utility bills, which have a monthly cost of $1800.

DR Prepaid Expense $21,600   CR Cash $21,600

The prepaid expense (asset) account has increased, and the cash (asset) account has decreased by: 12 months x $1,800 per month = $21,600 for the year.

386  Mr. Mop is a corporation which sells household cleaners. Today, Mr. Mop received an upfront payment for 5160 tons of cleaning solution which will be provided to the customer 6 months from now. The payment for each was $1100.

DR Cash $5,676,000   CR Unearned Revenue $5,676,000

The cash (asset) and the unearned revenue (liability) accounts have both increased by: 5160 tons of cleaning solution x $1,100 = $5,676,000

387  Sprike Inc is an organization which specializes in providing their customers with athletic apparel. This month, Sprike Inc paid for 1 month of rent for the warehouse room, which has a monthly cost of $1500.

DR Rent expense $1,500   CR Accounts Payable $1,500

The rent (expense) and the accounts payable (liability) accounts are both increased by one month's worth of rent, which is $1,500.

388  Jameson & Jameson is an organization which specializes in providing their customers with soap products. This week, Jameson & Jameson paid each of the 1800 staff members their bi-weekly wages, which per person had a cost of $1500.

DR Wage expense $2,700,000   CR Accounts Payable $2,700,000

The wage (expense) and the accounts payable (liability) accounts have both increased by: 1800 staff members x $1,500 = $2,700,000

389  Kola-Nut Ltd sells various soft drinks. This month, Kola-Nut Ltd paid for 1 month of rent for their company's office space. Each month, the rent owing was $11000.

DR Rent expense $11,000   CR Accounts Payable $11,000

The rent (expense) and the accounts payable (liability) accounts are both increased by one month's worth of rent, which is $11,000.

390 Sprike Inc sells various athletic apparel. Today Sprike Inc sold 50500 batches of athletic t-shirts which had a 30% mark-up. They had originally been bought from their suppliers for a unit cost of $2370.

DR Accounts Receivable $155,590,500   DR Cost of Goods Sold $119,685,000
CR Sales $155,590,500   CR Inventory $119,685,000

This transaction increases the accounts receivable (asset) account, the sales (revenue) account, and the cost of goods sold (expense) account. The inventory (asset) account has decreased. 50500 batches of athletic t-shirts x $2,370 = $119,685,000. The 30% markup applies to the sales and accounts receivable amounts, i.e. $119,685,000 x 1.30 = $155,590,500

391 Pharma Drug Company Ltd. is a corporation which sells medications. This December, Pharma Drug Company Ltd. recognized 1 year of depreciation on equipment which had a total useful life of 10 years, and which had originally cost $140000.

DR Depreciation expense $14,000   CR Accumulated Depreciation $14,000

The depreciation (expense) account and the accumulated depreciation (contra-asset) accounts have both increased by: $140,000 divided by 10 years = $14,000 depreciation per year.

392 Kola-Nut Ltd is a corporation which sells soft drinks. This month, Kola-Nut Ltd accepted 20100 batches of soda bottles which were returned by customers. These products had been marked up by 35% and they had originally been bought at a per-unit cost of $2200.

DR Sales Returns $59,697,000   DR Inventory $44,220,000   CR Accounts Receivable $59,697,000   CR Cost of Goods Sold $44,220,000

This transaction increases the sales returns (contra-revenue) account, and the inventory (asset) account. The accounts receivable (asset) account and the cost of goods sold (expense) account have both decreased. 20100 batches of soda bottles x $2,200 = $44,220,000. The 35% markup applies to the sales returns and accounts receivable amounts, i.e. $44,220,000 x 1.35 = $59,697,000

393    Sprike Inc sells various athletic apparel.  Today Sprike Inc signed up for a loan with a 5% interest rate, and so the bank immediately transferred cash to the company in the amount of $82000.

DR Cash $82,000    CR Loan Payable $82,000

The cash (asset) and the loan payable (liability) accounts have both increased by: $82,000. The interest rate does not affect this initial accounting entry, but it will be used for the calculation of interest expense when repayments are made in the future toward this loan.

394    Air America sells several different types of global flights.  Today Air America signed up for a loan with a 5% interest rate, and so the bank immediately transferred cash to the company in the amount of $112000.

DR Cash $112,000    CR Loan Payable $112,000

The cash (asset) and the loan payable (liability) accounts have both increased by: $112,000. The interest rate does not affect this initial accounting entry, but it will be used for the calculation of interest expense when repayments are made in the future toward this loan.

395    A to Z Event Guru Ltd is a company which offers their customers a wide selection of start-to-finish event planning services for large gatherings.  A to Z Event Guru Ltd has just provided 2400 large orders which had been paid for in advance last year. Each order was in the amount of $2600.

DR Unearned Revenue $6,240,000    CR Sales $6,240,000

The unearned revenue (liability) account has decreased and the and the sales (revenue) account has increased by: 24/1 /2arge orders x $2,600 = $6,240,000

396    Paytech Ltd is a privately-held corporation which focuses on their niche of premium payroll transaction processing services.  Paytech Ltd has just provided 2100 large orders which had been paid for in advance last year. Each order was in the amount of $2000.

DR Unearned Revenue $4,200,000    CR Sales $4,200,000

The unearned revenue (liability) account has decreased and the and the sales (revenue) account has increased by: 21/1 /2arge orders x $2,000 = $4,200,000

397    Mount Tessory Academy offers their customers a wide range of private school education. Mount Tessory Academy has just received a cash payment for the full amount that this customer owed to the company for all of their purchases to date. The outstanding balance which has now been paid was $57000.

DR Cash $57,000    CR Accounts Receivable $57,000

The cash (asset) account has increased, and the accounts receivable (asset) account has decreased by $57,000.

398    Kola-Nut Ltd offers their customers a wide range of soft drinks. This month, Kola-Nut Ltd paid for 1 month of rent for the warehouse room, which has a monthly cost of $1900.

DR Rent expense $1,900    CR Accounts Payable $1,900

The rent (expense) and the accounts payable (liability) accounts are both increased by one month's worth of rent, which is $1,900.

399    Mr. Mop is a privately-held corporation which focuses on their niche of premium household cleaners. Today Mr. Mop sold 6600 tons of cleaning solution which had a 30% mark-up. They had originally been bought from their suppliers for a unit cost of $1060.

DR Accounts Receivable $9,094,800    DR Cost of Goods Sold $6,996,000    CR Sales $9,094,800    CR Inventory $6,996,000

This transaction increases the accounts receivable (asset) account, the sales (revenue) account, and the cost of goods sold (expense) account. The inventory (asset) account has decreased. 6600 tons of cleaning solution x $1,060 = $6,996,000. The 30% markup applies to the sales and accounts receivable amounts, i.e. $6,996,000 x 1.30 = $9,094,800

400    Cirque du Lune offers their customers a wide range of circus performances. This December, Cirque du Lune recognized 1 year of depreciation on a building which had a total useful life of 25 years, and which had originally been bought for $69000.

DR Depreciation expense $2,760    CR Accumulated Depreciation $2,760

The depreciation (expense) account and the accumulated depreciation (contra-asset) accounts have both increased by: $69,000 divided by 25 years = $2,760 depreciation per year.

401   Cirque du Lune is a company which offers their customers a wide selection of circus performances. Today, Cirque du Lune bought equipment which has a 5 year useful life, and which had a cost of $22000.

DR Equipment $22,000   CR Accounts Payable $22,000

The equipment (asset) and the accounts payable (liability) accounts have both increased by: $22,000. The useful life does not affect this original accounting entry, but it will be used to calculate depreciation of the asset in the future.

402   NBG Media Corporation is a corporation which sells broadcasting services for advertising agencies. This December, NBG Media Corporation has paid each of the company's 1900 owners an annual dividend in the amount of $26000.

DR Retained Earnings $49,400,000   CR Cash $49,400,000

The retained earnings (equity) and the cash accounts have both decreased by: 1900 owners x $26,000 = $49,400,000

403   Payday Now is a market leader that is well-known for their brand of short-term loan arrangements. Payday Now has just received a cash payment for the full amount that this customer owed to the company for all of their purchases to date. The outstanding balance which has now been paid was $69000.

DR Cash $69,000   CR Accounts Receivable $69,000

The cash (asset) account has increased, and the accounts receivable (asset) account has decreased by $69,000.

404   Sprike Inc is a company which offers their customers a wide selection of athletic apparel. Today Sprike Inc sold 16200 batches of athletic t-shirts which had a 30% mark-up. They had originally been bought from their suppliers for a unit cost of $2780.

DR Accounts Receivable $58,546,800   DR Cost of Goods Sold $45,036,000
CR Sales $58,546,800   CR Inventory $45,036,000

This transaction increases the accounts receivable (asset) account, the sales (revenue) account, and the cost of goods sold (expense) account. The inventory (asset) account has decreased. 16200 batches of athletic t-shirts x $2,780 = $45,036,000. The 30% markup applies to the sales and accounts receivable amounts, i.e. $45,036,000 x 1.30 = $58,546,800

405    Paytech Ltd offers their customers a wide range of payroll transaction processing services.  Today, Paytech Ltd received payment upfront for 1100 large orders which will not be provided until early next year. Each order was in the amount of $1500.

DR Cash $1,650,000    CR Unearned Revenue $1,650,000

The cash (asset) and the unearned revenue (liability) accounts have both increased by: 1100 large orders x $1,500 = $1,650,000

406    Cirque du Lune sells several different types of circus performances.  Today Cirque du Lune signed up for a loan with a 5% interest rate, and so the bank immediately transferred cash to the company in the amount of $84000.

DR Cash $84,000    CR Loan Payable $84,000

The cash (asset) and the loan payable (liability) accounts have both increased by: $84,000. The interest rate does not affect this initial accounting entry, but it will be used for the calculation of interest expense when repayments are made in the future toward this loan.

407    LA Met Theatre Company is an organization which specializes in providing their customers with live theatrical performances.  Today, LA Met Theatre Company has paid cash to their supplier to fully pay off their account payable balance, which was $47000.

DR Accounts Payable $47,000    CR Cash $47,000

The accounts payable (liability) and cash (asset) accounts have both increased by $47,000.

408    Club Disco is a privately-held corporation which focuses on their niche of premium dance venue rentals for large family gatherings.  This year, Club Disco has provided 1900 evening rentals each of which earned revenues of $2670.

DR Accounts Receivable $5,073,000    CR Sales $5,073,000

The accounts receivable (asset) and the sales (revenue) accounts have both increased by: 19/1 /2vening rentals x $2,670 = $5,073,000

409    Club Disco sells various dance venue rentals for large family gatherings. This December, Club Disco recognized 1 year of depreciation on a building which had a total useful life of 25 years, and which had originally been bought for $854000.

DR Depreciation expense $34,160    CR Accumulated Depreciation $34,160

The depreciation (expense) account and the accumulated depreciation (contra-asset) accounts have both increased by: $854,000 divided by 25 years = $34,160 depreciation per year.

410    Cirque du Lune sells several different types of circus performances. This year, Cirque du Lune has provided 1700 shows each of which earned revenues of $1590.

DR Accounts Receivable $2,703,000    CR Sales $2,703,000

The accounts receivable (asset) and the sales (revenue) accounts have both increased by: 17/1 /2hows x $1,590 = $2,703,000

411    Mr. Mop provides their customers with household cleaners. Mr. Mop has just purchased a building using cash, which has an expected useful life of 30 years, and which had a total cost of $805000.

DR Building $805,000    CR Cash $805,000

The building (asset) account has increased, and the cash (asset) account has decreased by: $805,000. The useful life does not affect this original accounting entry, but it will be used to calculate depreciation of the asset in the future.

412    NBG Media Corporation offers their customers a wide range of broadcasting services for advertising agencies. This month, NBG Media Corporation paid for 1 month of rent for their company's office space. Each month, the rent owing was $19000.

DR Rent expense $19,000    CR Accounts Payable $19,000

The rent (expense) and the accounts payable (liability) accounts are both increased by one month's worth of rent, which is $19,000.

413    Paytech Ltd is an organization which specializes in providing their customers with payroll transaction processing services. This December, Paytech Ltd recognized 1 year of depreciation on equipment which had a total useful life of 10 years, and which had originally cost $110000.

DR Depreciation expense $11,000    CR Accumulated Depreciation $11,000

The depreciation (expense) account and the accumulated depreciation (contra-asset) accounts have both increased by: $110,000 divided by 10 years = $11,000 depreciation per year.

414    Payday Now is a privately-held corporation which focuses on their niche of premium short-term loan arrangements. This month, Payday Now paid 1 monthly loan repayment towards their long-term note payable. The interest portion was 60% of the payment. The total amount paid in cash was $17000.

DR Interest Expense $10,200    DR Loan Payable $6,800    CR Cash $17,000

The interest (expense) account has increased by $17,000 x 0.6 = $10,200. The loan payable (liability) has decreased by $17,000 x 0.4 = $6,800. The cash (asset) account has decreased by the full amount of the payment, which is $17,000

415    NBG Media Corporation sells several different types of broadcasting services for advertising agencies. NBG Media Corporation has just purchased a building using cash, which has an expected useful life of 30 years, and which had a total cost of $383000.

DR Building $383,000    CR Cash $383,000

The building (asset) account has increased, and the cash (asset) account has decreased by: $383,000. The useful life does not affect this original accounting entry, but it will be used to calculate depreciation of the asset in the future.

416    Mr. Mop sells several different types of household cleaners. Mr. Mop has just received a cash payment for the full amount that this customer owed to the company for all of their purchases to date. The outstanding balance which has now been paid was $15000.

DR Cash $15,000    CR Accounts Receivable $15,000

The cash (asset) account has increased, and the accounts receivable (asset) account has decreased by $15,000.

417  Pharma Drug Company Ltd. sells several different types of medications. This December, Pharma Drug Company Ltd. has paid each of the company's 1900 owners an annual dividend in the amount of $12000.

DR Retained Earnings $22,800,000    CR Cash $22,800,000

The retained earnings (equity) and the cash accounts have both decreased by: 1900 owners x $12,000 = $22,800,000

418  Cirque du Lune sells various circus performances. This year, Cirque du Lune has provided 1800 shows each of which earned revenues of $1500.

DR Accounts Receivable $2,700,000    CR Sales $2,700,000

The accounts receivable (asset) and the sales (revenue) accounts have both increased by: 18/1 /2hows x $1,500 = $2,700,000

419  NY Fitness is a company which offers their customers a wide selection of gym memberships for professional sports teams. Today, NY Fitness bought equipment which has a 5 year useful life, and which had a cost of $11000.

DR Equipment $11,000    CR Accounts Payable $11,000

The equipment (asset) and the accounts payable (liability) accounts have both increased by: $11,000. The useful life does not affect this original accounting entry, but it will be used to calculate depreciation of the asset in the future.

420  LA Met Theatre Company is a privately-held corporation which focuses on their niche of premium live theatrical performances. LA Met Theatre Company has just provided 2200 large orders which had been paid for in advance last year. Each order was in the amount of $2800.

DR Unearned Revenue $6,160,000    CR Sales $6,160,000

The unearned revenue (liability) account has decreased and the and the sales (revenue) account has increased by: 22/1 /2arge orders x $2,800 = $6,160,000

421  Paytech Ltd is a privately-held corporation which focuses on their niche of premium payroll transaction processing services. This December, Paytech Ltd has paid each of the company's 1900 owners an annual dividend in the amount of $23000.

DR Retained Earnings $43,700,000    CR Cash $43,700,000

The retained earnings (equity) and the cash accounts have both decreased by: 1900 owners x $23,000 = $43,700,000

422 McGerald's is a company which offers their customers a wide selection of fast food meals. This December, McGerald's recognized 1 year of depreciation on equipment which had a total useful life of 10 years, and which had originally cost $110000.

DR Depreciation expense $11,000    CR Accumulated Depreciation $11,000

The depreciation (expense) account and the accumulated depreciation (contra-asset) accounts have both increased by: $110,000 divided by 10 years = $11,000 depreciation per year.

423 LA Met Theatre Company is a market leader that is well-known for their brand of live theatrical performances. LA Met Theatre Company has just received a cash payment for the full amount that this customer owed to the company for all of their purchases to date. The outstanding balance which has now been paid was $39000.

DR Cash $39,000    CR Accounts Receivable $39,000

The cash (asset) account has increased, and the accounts receivable (asset) account has decreased by $39,000.

424 Jameson & Jameson is a corporation which sells soap products. This week, Jameson & Jameson purchased 2070 truckloads of bars of soap which were placed into the warehouse, and which had a per-unit cost of $2700.

DR Inventory $5,589,000    CR Accounts Payable $5,589,000

There was an increase in the inventory (asset) account, and also an increase in the accounts payable (liability) account. 2070 truckloads of bars of soap x $2,700 = $5,589,000

425 Paytech Ltd sells various payroll transaction processing services. This year, Paytech Ltd has provided 2200 batches of transactions for the current period each of which earned revenues of $2240.

DR Accounts Receivable $4,928,000    CR Sales $4,928,000

The accounts receivable (asset) and the sales (revenue) accounts have both increased by: 22/1 /2atches of transactions for the current period x $2,240 = $4,928,000

426     Sprike Inc is a privately-held corporation which focuses on their niche of premium athletic apparel. This month, Sprike Inc paid 1 monthly loan repayment towards their long-term note payable. The interest portion was 60% of the payment. The total amount paid in cash was $15000.

DR Interest Expense $9,000    DR Loan Payable $6,000    CR Cash $15,000

The interest (expense) account has increased by $15,000 x 0.6 = $9,000. The loan payable (liability) has decreased by $15,000 x 0.4 = $6,000. The cash (asset) account has decreased by the full amount of the payment, which is $15,000

427     Comedy 253 sells several different types of live performances of stand-up comedy. This December, Comedy 253 recognized 1 year of depreciation on a building which had a total useful life of 25 years, and which had originally been bought for $376000.

DR Depreciation expense $15,040    CR Accumulated Depreciation $15,040

The depreciation (expense) account and the accumulated depreciation (contra-asset) accounts have both increased by: $376,000 divided by 25 years = $15,040 depreciation per year.

428     Toyonda is an organization which specializes in providing their customers with cars. This December, Toyonda recognized 1 year of depreciation on a building which had a total useful life of 25 years, and which had originally been bought for $220000.

DR Depreciation expense $8,800    CR Accumulated Depreciation $8,800

The depreciation (expense) account and the accumulated depreciation (contra-asset) accounts have both increased by: $220,000 divided by 25 years = $8,800 depreciation per year.

429     Comedy 253 sells various live performances of stand-up comedy. Today, Comedy 253 received payment upfront for 2200 large orders which will not be provided until early next year. Each order was in the amount of $2300.

DR Cash $5,060,000    CR Unearned Revenue $5,060,000

The cash (asset) and the unearned revenue (liability) accounts have both increased by: 2200 large orders x $2,300 = $5,060,000

430　Toyonda sells various cars.  This January, Toyonda has made an advance payment to cover the next 12 months of utility bills, which have a monthly cost of $2000.

DR Prepaid Expense $24,000　CR Cash $24,000

The prepaid expense (asset) account has increased, and the cash (asset) account has decreased by: 12 months x $2,000 per month = $24,000 for the year.

431　Grand Convention Ltd is an organization which specializes in providing their customers with banquet hall rentals for corporate meetings.  Grand Convention Ltd has just provided 2400 large orders which had been paid for in advance last year. Each order was in the amount of $2200.

DR Unearned Revenue $5,280,000　CR Sales $5,280,000

The unearned revenue (liability) account has decreased and the and the sales (revenue) account has increased by: 24/1 /2arge orders x $2,200 = $5,280,000

432　Club Disco sells various dance venue rentals for large family gatherings.  Today, Club Disco bought equipment which has a 5 year useful life, and which had a cost of $17000.

DR Equipment $17,000　CR Accounts Payable $17,000

The equipment (asset) and the accounts payable (liability) accounts have both increased by: $17,000. The useful life does not affect this original accounting entry, but it will be used to calculate depreciation of the asset in the future.

433　A to Z Event Guru Ltd is a company which offers their customers a wide selection of start-to-finish event planning services for large gatherings.  This January, A to Z Event Guru Ltd has made an advance payment to cover the next 12 months of utility bills, which have a monthly cost of $1000.

DR Prepaid Expense $12,000　CR Cash $12,000

The prepaid expense (asset) account has increased, and the cash (asset) account has decreased by: 12 months x $1,000 per month = $12,000 for the year.

434 David & Johnson is a corporation which sells legal services. This year, David & Johnson has provided 2000 billable hours each of which earned revenues of $2100.

DR Accounts Receivable $4,200,000    CR Sales $4,200,000

The accounts receivable (asset) and the sales (revenue) accounts have both increased by: 20/1 /2illable hours x $2,100 = $4,200,000

435 Sprike Inc sells several different types of athletic apparel. This month, Sprike Inc paid 1 monthly loan repayment towards their long-term note payable. The interest portion was 60% of the payment. The total amount paid in cash was $24000.

DR Interest Expense $14,400    DR Loan Payable $9,600    CR Cash $24,000

The interest (expense) account has increased by $24,000 x 0.6 = $14,400. The loan payable (liability) has decreased by $24,000 x 0.4 = $9,600. The cash (asset) account has decreased by the full amount of the payment, which is $24,000

436 Fairway Malls offers their customers a wide range of retail spaces in their shopping centers. Fairway Malls has just received a cash payment for the full amount that this customer owed to the company for all of their purchases to date. The outstanding balance which has now been paid was $75000.

DR Cash $75,000    CR Accounts Receivable $75,000

The cash (asset) account has increased, and the accounts receivable (asset) account has decreased by $75,000.

437 Pharma Drug Company Ltd. is a privately-held corporation which focuses on their niche of premium medications. Today Pharma Drug Company Ltd. sold 32900 batches of pills which had a 30% mark-up. They had originally been bought from their suppliers for a unit cost of $1460.

DR Accounts Receivable $62,444,200    DR Cost of Goods Sold $48,034,000
CR Sales $62,444,200    CR Inventory $48,034,000

This transaction increases the accounts receivable (asset) account, the sales (revenue) account, and the cost of goods sold (expense) account. The inventory (asset) account has decreased. 32900 batches of pills x $1,460 = $48,034,000. The 30% markup applies to the sales and accounts receivable amounts, i.e. $48,034,000 x 1.30 = $62,444,200

438     Kola-Nut Ltd is a company which offers their customers a wide selection of soft drinks. This month, Kola-Nut Ltd must amortize 1 month worth of utility bills which they had prepaid at the beginning of the year. The amount that they had paid upfront for the year was $43200.

DR Utilities expense $3,600    CR Prepaid Expense $3,600

The utilities (expense) account has increased and the prepaid expense (asset) account has decreased by: $43,200 for the year, divided by 12 months = $3,600

439     Pharma Drug Company Ltd. offers their customers a wide range of medications. This month, Pharma Drug Company Ltd. accepted 5900 batches of pills which were returned by customers. These products had been marked up by 35% and they had originally been bought at a per-unit cost of $1400.

DR Sales Returns $11,151,000    DR Inventory $8,260,000    CR Accounts Receivable $11,151,000    CR Cost of Goods Sold $8,260,000

This transaction increases the sales returns (contra-revenue) account, and the inventory (asset) account. The accounts receivable (asset) account and the cost of goods sold (expense) account have both decreased. 5900 batches of pills x $1,400 = $8,260,000. The 35% markup applies to the sales returns and accounts receivable amounts, i.e. $8,260,000 x 1.35 = $11,151,000

440     Kola-Nut Ltd is a company which offers their customers a wide selection of soft drinks. Today, Kola-Nut Ltd received an upfront payment for 4020 batches of soda bottles which will be provided to the customer 6 months from now. The payment for each was $1500.

DR Cash $6,030,000    CR Unearned Revenue $6,030,000

The cash (asset) and the unearned revenue (liability) accounts have both increased by: 4020 batches of soda bottles x $1,500 = $6,030,000

441     LA Met Theatre Company is a privately-held corporation which focuses on their niche of premium live theatrical performances. LA Met Theatre Company has just purchased a building using cash, which has an expected useful life of 30 years, and which had a total cost of $392000.

DR Building $392,000    CR Cash $392,000

The building (asset) account has increased, and the cash (asset) account has decreased by: $392,000. The useful life does not affect this original accounting entry, but it will be used to calculate depreciation of the asset in the future.

442    Mount Tessory Academy sells several different types of private school education. This month, Mount Tessory Academy has estimated that 20% of the accounts receivable might not end up being collectable, based on past experience. The accounts receivable will need to be adjusted from its current balance of $86000.

DR Bad Debt expense $17,200   CR Allowance for Doubtful Accounts $17,200

The bad debts (expense) and the allowance for doubtful accounts (contra-asset) have both increased by: 20% x $86,000 = $17,200

443    NY Fitness provides their customers with gym memberships for professional sports teams. This January, NY Fitness has made an advance payment to cover the next 12 months of utility bills, which have a monthly cost of $2800.

DR Prepaid Expense $33,600   CR Cash $33,600

The prepaid expense (asset) account has increased, and the cash (asset) account has decreased by: 12 months x $2,800 per month = $33,600 for the year.

444    Hogtown Records is a privately-held corporation which focuses on their niche of premium audio services for local musicians to record their music albums. Today, Hogtown Records bought equipment which has a 5 year useful life, and which had a cost of $17000.

DR Equipment $17,000   CR Accounts Payable $17,000

The equipment (asset) and the accounts payable (liability) accounts have both increased by: $17,000. The useful life does not affect this original accounting entry, but it will be used to calculate depreciation of the asset in the future.

445    Grand Convention Ltd provides their customers with banquet hall rentals for corporate meetings. Today, Grand Convention Ltd received payment upfront for 2300 large orders which will not be provided until early next year. Each order was in the amount of $1800.

DR Cash $4,140,000   CR Unearned Revenue $4,140,000

The cash (asset) and the unearned revenue (liability) accounts have both increased by: 2300 large orders x $1,800 = $4,140,000

446    AC&C Ltd. is an organization which specializes in providing their customers with cell phone plans. This week, AC&C Ltd. paid each of the 1770 staff members their bi-weekly wages, which per person had a cost of $2200.

DR Wage expense $3,894,000    CR Accounts Payable $3,894,000

The wage (expense) and the accounts payable (liability) accounts have both increased by: 1770 staff members x $2,200 = $3,894,000

447    Hogtown Records sells various audio services for local musicians to record their music albums. Today Hogtown Records signed up for a loan with a 5% interest rate, and so the bank immediately transferred cash to the company in the amount of $93000.

DR Cash $93,000    CR Loan Payable $93,000

The cash (asset) and the loan payable (liability) accounts have both increased by: $93,000. The interest rate does not affect this initial accounting entry, but it will be used for the calculation of interest expense when repayments are made in the future toward this loan.

448    Paytech Ltd is a privately-held corporation which focuses on their niche of premium payroll transaction processing services. Paytech Ltd has just provided 1900 large orders which had been paid for in advance last year. Each order was in the amount of $1000.

DR Unearned Revenue $1,900,000    CR Sales $1,900,000

The unearned revenue (liability) account has decreased and the and the sales (revenue) account has increased by: 19/1 /2arge orders x $1,000 = $1,900,000

449    Grand Convention Ltd provides their customers with banquet hall rentals for corporate meetings. This December, Grand Convention Ltd has paid each of the company's 2100 owners an annual dividend in the amount of $21000.

DR Retained Earnings $44,100,000    CR Cash $44,100,000

The retained earnings (equity) and the cash accounts have both decreased by: 2100 owners x $21,000 = $44,100,000

450     Pharma Drug Company Ltd. sells various medications. Today Pharma Drug
        Company Ltd. sold 40100 batches of pills which had a 30% mark-up. They had
        originally been bought from their suppliers for a unit cost of $1680.

        DR Accounts Receivable $87,578,400    DR Cost of Goods Sold $67,368,000
        CR Sales $87,578,400    CR Inventory $67,368,000

        This transaction increases the accounts receivable (asset) account, the sales
        (revenue) account, and the cost of goods sold (expense) account. The inventory
        (asset) account has decreased. 40100 batches of pills x $1,680 = $67,368,000.
        The 30% markup applies to the sales and accounts receivable amounts, i.e.
        $67,368,000 x 1.30 = $87,578,400

451     Jameson & Jameson is a market leader that is well-known for their brand of soap
        products. Today Jameson & Jameson sold 48700 truckloads of bars of soap
        which had a 30% mark-up. They had originally been bought from their suppliers
        for a unit cost of $2870.

        DR Accounts Receivable $181,699,700    DR Cost of Goods Sold $139,769,000
        CR Sales $181,699,700    CR Inventory $139,769,000

        This transaction increases the accounts receivable (asset) account, the sales
        (revenue) account, and the cost of goods sold (expense) account. The inventory
        (asset) account has decreased. 48700 truckloads of bars of soap x $2,870 =
        $139,769,000. The 30% markup applies to the sales and accounts receivable
        amounts, i.e. $139,769,000 x 1.30 = $181,699,700

452     Club Disco is a market leader that is well-known for their brand of dance venue
        rentals for large family gatherings. This week, Club Disco paid each of the 1240
        staff members their bi-weekly wages, which per person had a cost of $1900.

        DR Wage expense $2,356,000    CR Accounts Payable $2,356,000

        The wage (expense) and the accounts payable (liability) accounts have both
        increased by: 1240 staff members x $1,900 = $2,356,000

453     Hogtown Records is a privately-held corporation which focuses on their niche of
        premium audio services for local musicians to record their music albums.
        Hogtown Records has just provided 1500 large orders which had been paid for in
        advance last year. Each order was in the amount of $1600.

        DR Unearned Revenue $2,400,000    CR Sales $2,400,000

        The unearned revenue (liability) account has decreased and the and the sales
        (revenue) account has increased by: 15/1 /2arge orders x $1,600 = $2,400,000

454    Pharma Drug Company Ltd. is a company which offers their customers a wide selection of medications.  This December, Pharma Drug Company Ltd. recognized 1 year of depreciation on equipment which had a total useful life of 10 years, and which had originally cost $130000.

DR Depreciation expense $13,000    CR Accumulated Depreciation $13,000

The depreciation (expense) account and the accumulated depreciation (contra-asset) accounts have both increased by: $130,000 divided by 10 years = $13,000 depreciation per year.

455    Club Disco is a market leader that is well-known for their brand of dance venue rentals for large family gatherings.  Today, Club Disco bought equipment which has a 5 year useful life, and which had a cost of $23000.

DR Equipment $23,000    CR Accounts Payable $23,000

The equipment (asset) and the accounts payable (liability) accounts have both increased by: $23,000. The useful life does not affect this original accounting entry, but it will be used to calculate depreciation of the asset in the future.

456    NBG Media Corporation sells several different types of broadcasting services for advertising agencies.  This week, NBG Media Corporation paid each of the 3820 staff members their bi-weekly wages, which per person had a cost of $1700.

DR Wage expense $6,494,000    CR Accounts Payable $6,494,000

The wage (expense) and the accounts payable (liability) accounts have both increased by: 3820 staff members x $1,700 = $6,494,000

457    Air America is a company which offers their customers a wide selection of global flights.  Air America has just purchased a building using cash, which has an expected useful life of 30 years, and which had a total cost of $944000.

DR Building $944,000    CR Cash $944,000

The building (asset) account has increased, and the cash (asset) account has decreased by: $944,000. The useful life does not affect this original accounting entry, but it will be used to calculate depreciation of the asset in the future.

458     Mount Tessory Academy sells various private school education subscriptions. Mount Tessory Academy has just provided 1700 large orders which had been paid for in advance last year. Each order was in the amount of $1100.

DR Unearned Revenue $1,870,000    CR Sales $1,870,000

The unearned revenue (liability) account has decreased and the and the sales (revenue) account has increased by: 17/1 /2arge orders x $1,100 = $1,870,000

459     Kola-Nut Ltd is a corporation which sells soft drinks.  This December, Kola-Nut Ltd recognized 1 year of depreciation on a building which had a total useful life of 25 years, and which had originally been bought for $742000.

DR Depreciation expense $29,680    CR Accumulated Depreciation $29,680

The depreciation (expense) account and the accumulated depreciation (contra-asset) accounts have both increased by: $742,000 divided by 25 years = $29,680 depreciation per year.

460     Fairway Malls is a company which offers their customers a wide selection of retail spaces in their shopping centers.  Today, Fairway Malls bought equipment which has a 5 year useful life, and which had a cost of $13000.

DR Equipment $13,000    CR Accounts Payable $13,000

The equipment (asset) and the accounts payable (liability) accounts have both increased by: $13,000. The useful life does not affect this original accounting entry, but it will be used to calculate depreciation of the asset in the future.

461     Fairway Malls is a privately-held corporation which focuses on their niche of premium retail spaces in their shopping centers.  This month, Fairway Malls paid 1 monthly loan repayment towards their long-term note payable. The interest portion was 60% of the payment. The total amount paid in cash was $20000.

DR Interest Expense $12,000    DR Loan Payable $8,000    CR Cash $20,000

The interest (expense) account has increased by $20,000 x 0.6 = $12,000. The loan payable (liability) has decreased by $20,000 x 0.4 = $8,000. The cash (asset) account has decreased by the full amount of the payment, which is $20,000

462    Hogtown Records provides their customers with audio services for local musicians to record their music albums. Today, Hogtown Records has paid cash to their supplier to fully pay off their account payable balance, which was $19000.

DR Accounts Payable $19,000    CR Cash $19,000

The accounts payable (liability) and cash (asset) accounts have both increased by $19,000.

463    Sprike Inc is a company which offers their customers a wide selection of athletic apparel. This December, Sprike Inc recognized 1 year of depreciation on a building which had a total useful life of 25 years, and which had originally been bought for $728000.

DR Depreciation expense $29,120    CR Accumulated Depreciation $29,120

The depreciation (expense) account and the accumulated depreciation (contra-asset) accounts have both increased by: $728,000 divided by 25 years = $29,120 depreciation per year.

464    Mount Tessory Academy is a corporation which sells private school education. Mount Tessory Academy has just received a cash payment for the full amount that this customer owed to the company for all of their purchases to date. The outstanding balance which has now been paid was $55000.

DR Cash $55,000    CR Accounts Receivable $55,000

The cash (asset) account has increased, and the accounts receivable (asset) account has decreased by $55,000.

465    Jameson & Jameson is a company which offers their customers a wide selection of soap products. This month, Jameson & Jameson accepted 21500 truckloads of bars of soap which were returned by customers. These products had been marked up by 35% and they had originally been bought at a per-unit cost of $1600.

DR Sales Returns $46,440,000    DR Inventory $34,400,000    CR Accounts Receivable $46,440,000    CR Cost of Goods Sold $34,400,000

This transaction increases the sales returns (contra-revenue) account, and the inventory (asset) account. The accounts receivable (asset) account and the cost of goods sold (expense) account have both decreased. 21500 truckloads of bars of soap x $1,600 = $34,400,000. The 35% markup applies to the sales returns and accounts receivable amounts, i.e. $34,400,000 x 1.35 = $46,440,000

466 NY Fitness is a market leader that is well-known for their brand of gym memberships for professional sports teams. This year, NY Fitness has provided 1500 team memberships each of which earned revenues of $2170.

DR Accounts Receivable $3,255,000    CR Sales $3,255,000

The accounts receivable (asset) and the sales (revenue) accounts have both increased by: 15/1 /2eam memberships x $2,170 = $3,255,000

467 Air America is a corporation which sells global flights. This year, Air America has provided 1000 flights each of which earned revenues of $2380.

DR Accounts Receivable $2,380,000    CR Sales $2,380,000

The accounts receivable (asset) and the sales (revenue) accounts have both increased by: 10/1 /2lights x $2,380 = $2,380,000

468 Kola-Nut Ltd is an organization which specializes in providing their customers with soft drinks. This week, Kola-Nut Ltd purchased 5840 batches of soda bottles which were placed into the warehouse, and which had a per-unit cost of $2200.

DR Inventory $12,848,000    CR Accounts Payable $12,848,000

There was an increase in the inventory (asset) account, and also an increase in the accounts payable (liability) account. 5840 batches of soda bottles x $2,200 = $12,848,000

469 Hogtown Records is an organization which specializes in providing their customers with audio services for local musicians to record their music albums. This December, Hogtown Records has paid each of the company's 1700 owners an annual dividend in the amount of $15000.

DR Retained Earnings $25,500,000    CR Cash $25,500,000

The retained earnings (equity) and the cash accounts have both decreased by: 1700 owners x $15,000 = $25,500,000

470 A to Z Event Guru Ltd is a market leader that is well-known for their brand of start-to-finish event planning services for large gatherings. This month, A to Z Event Guru Ltd paid for 1 month of rent for their company's office space. Each month, the rent owing was $17000.

DR Rent expense $17,000    CR Accounts Payable $17,000

The rent (expense) and the accounts payable (liability) accounts are both increased by one month's worth of rent, which is $17,000.

218

471    Jameson & Jameson sells several different types of soap products. Jameson & Jameson has just purchased a building using cash, which has an expected useful life of 30 years, and which had a total cost of $141000.

DR Building $141,000    CR Cash $141,000

The building (asset) account has increased, and the cash (asset) account has decreased by: $141,000. The useful life does not affect this original accounting entry, but it will be used to calculate depreciation of the asset in the future.

472    Sprike Inc is a privately-held corporation which focuses on their niche of premium athletic apparel. This month, Sprike Inc paid for 1 month of rent for the warehouse room, which has a monthly cost of $1800.

DR Rent expense $1,800    CR Accounts Payable $1,800

The rent (expense) and the accounts payable (liability) accounts are both increased by one month's worth of rent, which is $1,800.

473    Grand Convention Ltd is a corporation which sells banquet hall rentals for corporate meetings. This December, Grand Convention Ltd has paid each of the company's 1900 owners an annual dividend in the amount of $23000.

DR Retained Earnings $43,700,000    CR Cash $43,700,000

The retained earnings (equity) and the cash accounts have both decreased by: 1900 owners x $23,000 = $43,700,000

474    Jameson & Jameson is an organization which specializes in providing their customers with soap products. Today Jameson & Jameson sold 48800 truckloads of bars of soap which had a 30% mark-up. They had originally been bought from their suppliers for a unit cost of $2150.

DR Accounts Receivable $136,396,000    DR Cost of Goods Sold $104,920,000
CR Sales $136,396,000    CR Inventory $104,920,000

This transaction increases the accounts receivable (asset) account, the sales (revenue) account, and the cost of goods sold (expense) account. The inventory (asset) account has decreased. 48800 truckloads of bars of soap x $2,150 = $104,920,000. The 30% markup applies to the sales and accounts receivable amounts, i.e. $104,920,000 x 1.30 = $136,396,000

475 Air America sells various global flights. Today Air America signed up for a loan with a 5% interest rate, and so the bank immediately transferred cash to the company in the amount of $65000.

DR Cash $65,000    CR Loan Payable $65,000

The cash (asset) and the loan payable (liability) accounts have both increased by: $65,000. The interest rate does not affect this initial accounting entry, but it will be used for the calculation of interest expense when repayments are made in the future toward this loan.

476 Sprike Inc is an organization which specializes in providing their customers with athletic apparel. This December, Sprike Inc has paid each of the company's 1100 owners an annual dividend in the amount of $9000.

DR Retained Earnings $9,900,000    CR Cash $9,900,000

The retained earnings (equity) and the cash accounts have both decreased by: 1100 owners x $9,000 = $9,900,000

477 McGerald's is a corporation which sells fast food meals. This month, McGerald's has estimated that 10% of the accounts receivable might not end up being collectable, based on past experience. The accounts receivable will need to be adjusted from its current balance of $22000.

DR Bad Debt expense $2,200    CR Allowance for Doubtful Accounts $2,200

The bad debts (expense) and the allowance for doubtful accounts (contra-asset) have both increased by: 10% x $22,000 = $2,200

478 Hogtown Records is a corporation which sells audio services for local musicians to record their music albums. Today, Hogtown Records bought equipment which has a 5 year useful life, and which had a cost of $14000.

DR Equipment $14,000    CR Accounts Payable $14,000

The equipment (asset) and the accounts payable (liability) accounts have both increased by: $14,000. The useful life does not affect this original accounting entry, but it will be used to calculate depreciation of the asset in the future.

479      Jameson & Jameson is a company which offers their customers a wide selection of soap products. This month, Jameson & Jameson has estimated that 25% of the accounts receivable might not end up being collectable, based on past experience. The accounts receivable will need to be adjusted from its current balance of $22000.

DR Bad Debt expense $5,500     CR Allowance for Doubtful Accounts $5,500

The bad debts (expense) and the allowance for doubtful accounts (contra-asset) have both increased by: 25% x $22,000 = $5,500

480      Kola-Nut Ltd sells several different types of soft drinks. This month, Kola-Nut Ltd paid 1 monthly loan repayment towards their long-term note payable. The interest portion was 60% of the payment. The total amount paid in cash was $17000.

DR Interest Expense $10,200     DR Loan Payable $6,800     CR Cash $17,000

The interest (expense) account has increased by $17,000 x 0.6 = $10,200. The loan payable (liability) has decreased by $17,000 x 0.4 = $6,800. The cash (asset) account has decreased by the full amount of the payment, which is $17,000

481      McGerald's sells various fast food meals. Today, McGerald's received payment upfront for 2300 large orders which will not be provided until early next year. Each order was in the amount of $1500.

DR Cash $3,450,000     CR Unearned Revenue $3,450,000

The cash (asset) and the unearned revenue (liability) accounts have both increased by: 2300 large orders x $1,500 = $3,450,000

482      Jameson & Jameson is a corporation which sells soap products. Today Jameson & Jameson sold 44900 truckloads of bars of soap which had a 30% mark-up. They had originally been bought from their suppliers for a unit cost of $2230.

DR Accounts Receivable $130,165,100     DR Cost of Goods Sold $100,127,000
CR Sales $130,165,100     CR Inventory $100,127,000

This transaction increases the accounts receivable (asset) account, the sales (revenue) account, and the cost of goods sold (expense) account. The inventory (asset) account has decreased. 44900 truckloads of bars of soap x $2,230 = $100,127,000. The 30% markup applies to the sales and accounts receivable amounts, i.e. $100,127,000 x 1.30 = $130,165,100

483  Jameson & Jameson sells various soap products. Today Jameson & Jameson sold 28400 truckloads of bars of soap which had a 30% mark-up. They had originally been bought from their suppliers for a unit cost of $2480.

DR Accounts Receivable $91,561,600   DR Cost of Goods Sold $70,432,000
CR Sales $91,561,600   CR Inventory $70,432,000

This transaction increases the accounts receivable (asset) account, the sales (revenue) account, and the cost of goods sold (expense) account. The inventory (asset) account has decreased. 28400 truckloads of bars of soap x $2,480 = $70,432,000. The 30% markup applies to the sales and accounts receivable amounts, i.e. $70,432,000 x 1.30 = $91,561,600

484  Jameson & Jameson sells various soap products. This month, Jameson & Jameson paid 1 monthly loan repayment towards their long-term note payable. The interest portion was 60% of the payment. The total amount paid in cash was $24000.

DR Interest Expense $14,400   DR Loan Payable $9,600   CR Cash $24,000

The interest (expense) account has increased by $24,000 x 0.6 = $14,400. The loan payable (liability) has decreased by $24,000 x 0.4 = $9,600. The cash (asset) account has decreased by the full amount of the payment, which is $24,000

485  Mr. Mop is an organization which specializes in providing their customers with household cleaners. This week, Mr. Mop purchased 4300 tons of cleaning solution which were placed into the warehouse, and which had a per-unit cost of $1500.

DR Inventory $6,450,000   CR Accounts Payable $6,450,000

There was an increase in the inventory (asset) account, and also an increase in the accounts payable (liability) account. 4300 tons of cleaning solution x $1,500 = $6,450,000

486  Jameson & Jameson offers their customers a wide range of soap products. This month, Jameson & Jameson paid for 1 month of rent for the warehouse room, which has a monthly cost of $2600.

DR Rent expense $2,600   CR Accounts Payable $2,600

The rent (expense) and the accounts payable (liability) accounts are both increased by one month's worth of rent, which is $2,600.

487    Paytech Ltd is a corporation which sells payroll transaction processing services. This January, Paytech Ltd has made an advance payment to cover the next 12 months of utility bills, which have a monthly cost of $1800.

DR Prepaid Expense $21,600   CR Cash $21,600

The prepaid expense (asset) account has increased, and the cash (asset) account has decreased by: 12 months x $1,800 per month = $21,600 for the year.

488    Cirque du Lune provides their customers with circus performances. This January, Cirque du Lune has made an advance payment to cover the next 12 months of utility bills, which have a monthly cost of $2700.

DR Prepaid Expense $32,400   CR Cash $32,400

The prepaid expense (asset) account has increased, and the cash (asset) account has decreased by: 12 months x $2,700 per month = $32,400 for the year.

489    Mount Tessory Academy sells several different types of private school education. Mount Tessory Academy has just received a cash payment for the full amount that this customer owed to the company for all of their purchases to date. The outstanding balance which has now been paid was $40000.

DR Cash $40,000   CR Accounts Receivable $40,000

The cash (asset) account has increased, and the accounts receivable (asset) account has decreased by $40,000.

490    Sprike Inc is a market leader that is well-known for their brand of athletic apparel. Today Sprike Inc sold 27300 batches of athletic t-shirts which had a 30% mark-up. They had originally been bought from their suppliers for a unit cost of $1020.

DR Accounts Receivable $36,199,800   DR Cost of Goods Sold $27,846,000
CR Sales $36,199,800   CR Inventory $27,846,000

This transaction increases the accounts receivable (asset) account, the sales (revenue) account, and the cost of goods sold (expense) account. The inventory (asset) account has decreased. 27300 batches of athletic t-shirts x $1,020 = $27,846,000. The 30% markup applies to the sales and accounts receivable amounts, i.e. $27,846,000 x 1.30 = $36,199,800

491 Comedy 253 sells several different types of live performances of stand-up comedy. This December, Comedy 253 has paid each of the company's 1100 owners an annual dividend in the amount of $14000.

DR Retained Earnings $15,400,000    CR Cash $15,400,000

The retained earnings (equity) and the cash accounts have both decreased by: 1100 owners x $14,000 = $15,400,000

492 Kola-Nut Ltd sells several different types of soft drinks. This December, Kola-Nut Ltd recognized 1 year of depreciation on equipment which had a total useful life of 10 years, and which had originally cost $190000.

DR Depreciation expense $19,000    CR Accumulated Depreciation $19,000

The depreciation (expense) account and the accumulated depreciation (contra-asset) accounts have both increased by: $190,000 divided by 10 years = $19,000 depreciation per year.

493 Comedy 253 sells various live performances of stand-up comedy. This December, Comedy 253 recognized 1 year of depreciation on equipment which had a total useful life of 10 years, and which had originally cost $110000.

DR Depreciation expense $11,000    CR Accumulated Depreciation $11,000

The depreciation (expense) account and the accumulated depreciation (contra-asset) accounts have both increased by: $110,000 divided by 10 years = $11,000 depreciation per year.

494 Jameson & Jameson is a corporation which sells soap products. This week, Jameson & Jameson paid each of the 1420 staff members their bi-weekly wages, which per person had a cost of $2500.

DR Wage expense $3,550,000    CR Accounts Payable $3,550,000

The wage (expense) and the accounts payable (liability) accounts have both increased by: 1420 staff members x $2,500 = $3,550,000

495 Paytech Ltd is an organization which specializes in providing their customers with payroll transaction processing services. This December, Paytech Ltd has paid each of the company's 1400 owners an annual dividend in the amount of $12000.

DR Retained Earnings $16,800,000    CR Cash $16,800,000

The retained earnings (equity) and the cash accounts have both decreased by: 1400 owners x $12,000 = $16,800,000

496    NBG Media Corporation is a market leader that is well-known for their brand of broadcasting services for advertising agencies. Today, NBG Media Corporation has paid cash to their supplier to fully pay off their account payable balance, which was $33000.

DR Accounts Payable $33,000    CR Cash $33,000

The accounts payable (liability) and cash (asset) accounts have both increased by $33,000.

497    Toyonda offers their customers a wide range of cars. This December, Toyonda has paid each of the company's 1600 owners an annual dividend in the amount of $17000.

DR Retained Earnings $27,200,000    CR Cash $27,200,000

The retained earnings (equity) and the cash accounts have both decreased by: 1600 owners x $17,000 = $27,200,000

498    Grand Convention Ltd is a corporation which sells banquet hall rentals for corporate meetings. This January, Grand Convention Ltd has made an advance payment to cover the next 12 months of utility bills, which have a monthly cost of $2800.

DR Prepaid Expense $33,600    CR Cash $33,600

The prepaid expense (asset) account has increased, and the cash (asset) account has decreased by: 12 months x $2,800 per month = $33,600 for the year.

499    Grand Convention Ltd is a market leader that is well-known for their brand of banquet hall rentals for corporate meetings. Today, Grand Convention Ltd bought equipment which has a 5 year useful life, and which had a cost of $18000.

DR Equipment $18,000    CR Accounts Payable $18,000

The equipment (asset) and the accounts payable (liability) accounts have both increased by: $18,000. The useful life does not affect this original accounting entry, but it will be used to calculate depreciation of the asset in the future.

500    Kola-Nut Ltd provides their customers with soft drinks. Today Kola-Nut Ltd sold 37200 batches of soda bottles which had a 30% mark-up. They had originally been bought from their suppliers for a unit cost of $1370.

DR Accounts Receivable $66,253,200    DR Cost of Goods Sold $50,964,000
CR Sales $66,253,200    CR Inventory $50,964,000

This transaction increases the accounts receivable (asset) account, the sales (revenue) account, and the cost of goods sold (expense) account. The inventory (asset) account has decreased. 37200 batches of soda bottles x $1,370 = $50,964,000. The 30% markup applies to the sales and accounts receivable amounts, i.e. $50,964,000 x 1.30 = $66,253,200

501    Hogtown Records is a company which offers their customers a wide selection of audio services for local musicians to record their music albums. This month, Hogtown Records paid 1 monthly loan repayment towards their long-term note payable. The interest portion was 60% of the payment. The total amount paid in cash was $24000.

DR Interest Expense $14,400    DR Loan Payable $9,600    CR Cash $24,000

The interest (expense) account has increased by $24,000 x 0.6 = $14,400. The loan payable (liability) has decreased by $24,000 x 0.4 = $9,600. The cash (asset) account has decreased by the full amount of the payment, which is $24,000

502    Jameson & Jameson is a market leader that is well-known for their brand of soap products. Today Jameson & Jameson sold 44800 truckloads of bars of soap which had a 30% mark-up. They had originally been bought from their suppliers for a unit cost of $1440.

DR Accounts Receivable $83,865,600    DR Cost of Goods Sold $64,512,000
CR Sales $83,865,600    CR Inventory $64,512,000

This transaction increases the accounts receivable (asset) account, the sales (revenue) account, and the cost of goods sold (expense) account. The inventory (asset) account has decreased. 44800 truckloads of bars of soap x $1,440 = $64,512,000. The 30% markup applies to the sales and accounts receivable amounts, i.e. $64,512,000 x 1.30 = $83,865,600

503 Mr. Mop is a company which offers their customers a wide selection of household cleaners. This month, Mr. Mop has estimated that 15% of the accounts receivable might not end up being collectable, based on past experience. The accounts receivable will need to be adjusted from its current balance of $79000.

DR Bad Debt expense $11,850    CR Allowance for Doubtful Accounts $11,850

The bad debts (expense) and the allowance for doubtful accounts (contra-asset) have both increased by: 15% x $79,000 = $11,850

504 Hogtown Records is a company which offers their customers a wide selection of audio services for local musicians to record their music albums. This December, Hogtown Records has paid each of the company's 2400 owners an annual dividend in the amount of $15000.

DR Retained Earnings $36,000,000    CR Cash $36,000,000

The retained earnings (equity) and the cash accounts have both decreased by: 2400 owners x $15,000 = $36,000,000

505 Pharma Drug Company Ltd. is a market leader that is well-known for their brand of medications. Today Pharma Drug Company Ltd. sold 23800 batches of pills which had a 30% mark-up. They had originally been bought from their suppliers for a unit cost of $2410.

DR Accounts Receivable $74,565,400    DR Cost of Goods Sold $57,358,000
CR Sales $74,565,400    CR Inventory $57,358,000

This transaction increases the accounts receivable (asset) account, the sales (revenue) account, and the cost of goods sold (expense) account. The inventory (asset) account has decreased. 23800 batches of pills x $2,410 = $57,358,000. The 30% markup applies to the sales and accounts receivable amounts, i.e. $57,358,000 x 1.30 = $74,565,400

506 AC&C Ltd. provides their customers with cell phone plans. This year, AC&C Ltd. has provided 1300 monthly cell phone service each of which earned revenues of $1260.

DR Accounts Receivable $1,638,000    CR Sales $1,638,000

The accounts receivable (asset) and the sales (revenue) accounts have both increased by: 13/1 /2onthly cell phone service x $1,260 = $1,638,000

507 Paytech Ltd is an organization which specializes in providing their customers with payroll transaction processing services. This month, Paytech Ltd paid 1 monthly loan repayment towards their long-term note payable. The interest portion was 60% of the payment. The total amount paid in cash was $18000.

DR Interest Expense $10,800   DR Loan Payable $7,200   CR Cash $18,000

The interest (expense) account has increased by $18,000 x 0.6 = $10,800. The loan payable (liability) has decreased by $18,000 x 0.4 = $7,200. The cash (asset) account has decreased by the full amount of the payment, which is $18,000

508 David & Johnson provides their customers with legal services. Today, David & Johnson has paid cash to their supplier to fully pay off their account payable balance, which was $76000.

DR Accounts Payable $76,000   CR Cash $76,000

The accounts payable (liability) and cash (asset) accounts have both increased by $76,000.

509 Kola-Nut Ltd offers their customers a wide range of soft drinks. Today, Kola-Nut Ltd received an upfront payment for 2140 batches of soda bottles which will be provided to the customer 6 months from now. The payment for each was $2400.

DR Cash $5,136,000   CR Unearned Revenue $5,136,000

The cash (asset) and the unearned revenue (liability) accounts have both increased by: 2140 batches of soda bottles x $2,400 = $5,136,000

510 Mr. Mop is a privately-held corporation which focuses on their niche of premium household cleaners. Today, Mr. Mop received an upfront payment for 4690 tons of cleaning solution which will be provided to the customer 6 months from now. The payment for each was $2000.

DR Cash $9,380,000   CR Unearned Revenue $9,380,000

The cash (asset) and the unearned revenue (liability) accounts have both increased by: 4690 tons of cleaning solution x $2,000 = $9,380,000

511 Toyonda is a market leader that is well-known for their brand of cars. This December, Toyonda recognized 1 year of depreciation on a building which had a total useful life of 25 years, and which had originally been bought for $522000.

DR Depreciation expense $20,880    CR Accumulated Depreciation $20,880

The depreciation (expense) account and the accumulated depreciation (contra-asset) accounts have both increased by: $522,000 divided by 25 years = $20,880 depreciation per year.

512 NY Fitness is a corporation which sells gym memberships for professional sports teams. This month, NY Fitness has estimated that 5% of the accounts receivable might not end up being collectable, based on past experience. The accounts receivable will need to be adjusted from its current balance of $42000.

DR Bad Debt expense $2,100    CR Allowance for Doubtful Accounts $2,100

The bad debts (expense) and the allowance for doubtful accounts (contra-asset) have both increased by: 5% x $42,000 = $2,100

513 NY Fitness offers their customers a wide range of gym memberships for professional sports teams. This January, NY Fitness has made an advance payment to cover the next 12 months of utility bills, which have a monthly cost of $2000.

DR Prepaid Expense $24,000    CR Cash $24,000

The prepaid expense (asset) account has increased, and the cash (asset) account has decreased by: 12 months x $2,000 per month = $24,000 for the year.

514 Sprike Inc provides their customers with athletic apparel. Sprike Inc has just received a cash payment for the full amount that this customer owed to the company for all of their purchases to date. The outstanding balance which has now been paid was $70000.

DR Cash $70,000    CR Accounts Receivable $70,000

The cash (asset) account has increased, and the accounts receivable (asset) account has decreased by $70,000.

515    NBG Media Corporation is a company which offers their customers a wide selection of broadcasting services for advertising agencies. This month, NBG Media Corporation must amortize 1 month worth of utility bills which they had prepaid at the beginning of the year. The amount that they had paid upfront for the year was $18000.

DR Utilities expense $1,500    CR Prepaid Expense $1,500

The utilities (expense) account has increased and the prepaid expense (asset) account has decreased by: $18,000 for the year, divided by 12 months = $1,500

516    David & Johnson is a company which offers their customers a wide selection of legal services. This month, David & Johnson must amortize 1 month worth of utility bills which they had prepaid at the beginning of the year. The amount that they had paid upfront for the year was $21600.

DR Utilities expense $1,800    CR Prepaid Expense $1,800

The utilities (expense) account has increased and the prepaid expense (asset) account has decreased by: $21,600 for the year, divided by 12 months = $1,800

517    Pharma Drug Company Ltd. is a corporation which sells medications. Today Pharma Drug Company Ltd. sold 15200 batches of pills which had a 30% mark-up. They had originally been bought from their suppliers for a unit cost of $1450.

DR Accounts Receivable $28,652,000    DR Cost of Goods Sold $22,040,000
CR Sales $28,652,000    CR Inventory $22,040,000

This transaction increases the accounts receivable (asset) account, the sales (revenue) account, and the cost of goods sold (expense) account. The inventory (asset) account has decreased. 15200 batches of pills x $1,450 = $22,040,000. The 30% markup applies to the sales and accounts receivable amounts, i.e. $22,040,000 x 1.30 = $28,652,000

518    Cirque du Lune is a market leader that is well-known for their brand of circus performances. Today, Cirque du Lune bought equipment which has a 5 year useful life, and which had a cost of $11000.

DR Equipment $11,000    CR Accounts Payable $11,000

The equipment (asset) and the accounts payable (liability) accounts have both increased by: $11,000. The useful life does not affect this original accounting entry, but it will be used to calculate depreciation of the asset in the future.

230

519    Club Disco is an organization which specializes in providing their customers with dance venue rentals for large family gatherings. This January, Club Disco has made an advance payment to cover the next 12 months of utility bills, which have a monthly cost of $2300.

DR Prepaid Expense $27,600    CR Cash $27,600

The prepaid expense (asset) account has increased, and the cash (asset) account has decreased by: 12 months x $2,300 per month = $27,600 for the year.

520    Cirque du Lune provides their customers with circus performances. This month, Cirque du Lune has estimated that 30% of the accounts receivable might not end up being collectable, based on past experience. The accounts receivable will need to be adjusted from its current balance of $66000.

DR Bad Debt expense $19,800    CR Allowance for Doubtful Accounts $19,800

The bad debts (expense) and the allowance for doubtful accounts (contra-asset) have both increased by: 30% x $66,000 = $19,800

521    LA Met Theatre Company is a market leader that is well-known for their brand of live theatrical performances. This December, LA Met Theatre Company recognized 1 year of depreciation on a building which had a total useful life of 25 years, and which had originally been bought for $910000.

DR Depreciation expense $36,400    CR Accumulated Depreciation $36,400

The depreciation (expense) account and the accumulated depreciation (contra-asset) accounts have both increased by: $910,000 divided by 25 years = $36,400 depreciation per year.

522    AC&C Ltd. provides their customers with cell phone plans. This month, AC&C Ltd. paid for 1 month of rent for their company's office space. Each month, the rent owing was $15000.

DR Rent expense $15,000    CR Accounts Payable $15,000

The rent (expense) and the accounts payable (liability) accounts are both increased by one month's worth of rent, which is $15,000.

523 Comedy 253 sells various live performances of stand-up comedy. Today, Comedy 253 received payment upfront for 1700 large orders which will not be provided until early next year. Each order was in the amount of $1900.

DR Cash $3,230,000    CR Unearned Revenue $3,230,000

The cash (asset) and the unearned revenue (liability) accounts have both increased by: 1700 large orders x $1,900 = $3,230,000

524 Kola-Nut Ltd offers their customers a wide range of soft drinks. This week, Kola-Nut Ltd purchased 5240 batches of soda bottles which were placed into the warehouse, and which had a per-unit cost of $1000.

DR Inventory $5,240,000    CR Accounts Payable $5,240,000

There was an increase in the inventory (asset) account, and also an increase in the accounts payable (liability) account. 5240 batches of soda bottles x $1,000 = $5,240,000

525 Club Disco is an organization which specializes in providing their customers with dance venue rentals for large family gatherings. This month, Club Disco has estimated that 25% of the accounts receivable might not end up being collectable, based on past experience. The accounts receivable will need to be adjusted from its current balance of $81000.

DR Bad Debt expense $20,250    CR Allowance for Doubtful Accounts $20,250

The bad debts (expense) and the allowance for doubtful accounts (contra-asset) have both increased by: 25% x $81,000 = $20,250

526 Hogtown Records is a privately-held corporation which focuses on their niche of premium audio services for local musicians to record their music albums. This December, Hogtown Records has paid each of the company's 1800 owners an annual dividend in the amount of $13000.

DR Retained Earnings $23,400,000    CR Cash $23,400,000

The retained earnings (equity) and the cash accounts have both decreased by: 1800 owners x $13,000 = $23,400,000

527 Hogtown Records provides their customers with audio services for local musicians to record their music albums. This year, Hogtown Records has provided 1300 albums each of which earned revenues of $1750.

DR Accounts Receivable $2,275,000   CR Sales $2,275,000

The accounts receivable (asset) and the sales (revenue) accounts have both increased by: 13/1 /2lbums x $1,750 = $2,275,000

528 David & Johnson is a company which offers their customers a wide selection of legal services. Today David & Johnson signed up for a loan with a 5% interest rate, and so the bank immediately transferred cash to the company in the amount of $116000.

DR Cash $116,000   CR Loan Payable $116,000

The cash (asset) and the loan payable (liability) accounts have both increased by: $116,000. The interest rate does not affect this initial accounting entry, but it will be used for the calculation of interest expense when repayments are made in the future toward this loan.

529 NBG Media Corporation is a market leader that is well-known for their brand of broadcasting services for advertising agencies. Today, NBG Media Corporation bought equipment which has a 5 year useful life, and which had a cost of $9000.

DR Equipment $9,000   CR Accounts Payable $9,000

The equipment (asset) and the accounts payable (liability) accounts have both increased by: $9,000. The useful life does not affect this original accounting entry, but it will be used to calculate depreciation of the asset in the future.

530 David & Johnson is a market leader that is well-known for their brand of legal services. David & Johnson has just received a cash payment for the full amount that this customer owed to the company for all of their purchases to date. The outstanding balance which has now been paid was $16000.

DR Cash $16,000   CR Accounts Receivable $16,000

The cash (asset) account has increased, and the accounts receivable (asset) account has decreased by $16,000.

531 Pharma Drug Company Ltd. sells various medications. This month, Pharma Drug Company Ltd. paid for 1 month of rent for the warehouse room, which has a monthly cost of $1100.

DR Rent expense $1,100    CR Accounts Payable $1,100

The rent (expense) and the accounts payable (liability) accounts are both increased by one month's worth of rent, which is $1,100.

532 Kola-Nut Ltd is a corporation which sells soft drinks. This month, Kola-Nut Ltd paid for 1 month of rent for their company's office space. Each month, the rent owing was $17000.

DR Rent expense $17,000    CR Accounts Payable $17,000

The rent (expense) and the accounts payable (liability) accounts are both increased by one month's worth of rent, which is $17,000.

533 Kola-Nut Ltd is an organization which specializes in providing their customers with soft drinks. This month, Kola-Nut Ltd paid for 1 month of rent for the warehouse room, which has a monthly cost of $1200.

DR Rent expense $1,200    CR Accounts Payable $1,200

The rent (expense) and the accounts payable (liability) accounts are both increased by one month's worth of rent, which is $1,200.

534 Kola-Nut Ltd provides their customers with soft drinks. This week, Kola-Nut Ltd purchased 4470 batches of soda bottles which were placed into the warehouse, and which had a per-unit cost of $1800.

DR Inventory $8,046,000    CR Accounts Payable $8,046,000

There was an increase in the inventory (asset) account, and also an increase in the accounts payable (liability) account. 4470 batches of soda bottles x $1,800 = $8,046,000

535 Grand Convention Ltd offers their customers a wide range of banquet hall rentals for corporate meetings. This month, Grand Convention Ltd paid for 1 month of rent for their company's office space. Each month, the rent owing was $15000.

DR Rent expense $15,000    CR Accounts Payable $15,000

The rent (expense) and the accounts payable (liability) accounts are both increased by one month's worth of rent, which is $15,000.

536 Jameson & Jameson is a company which offers their customers a wide selection of soap products. Today Jameson & Jameson signed up for a loan with a 5% interest rate, and so the bank immediately transferred cash to the company in the amount of $112000.

DR Cash $112,000    CR Loan Payable $112,000

The cash (asset) and the loan payable (liability) accounts have both increased by: $112,000. The interest rate does not affect this initial accounting entry, but it will be used for the calculation of interest expense when repayments are made in the future toward this loan.

537 NY Fitness sells various gym memberships for professional sports teams. This December, NY Fitness recognized 1 year of depreciation on a building which had a total useful life of 25 years, and which had originally been bought for $974000.

DR Depreciation expense $38,960    CR Accumulated Depreciation $38,960

The depreciation (expense) account and the accumulated depreciation (contra-asset) accounts have both increased by: $974,000 divided by 25 years = $38,960 depreciation per year.

538 Pharma Drug Company Ltd. is an organization which specializes in providing their customers with medications. This January, Pharma Drug Company Ltd. has made an advance payment to cover the next 12 months of utility bills, which have a monthly cost of $2600.

DR Prepaid Expense $31,200    CR Cash $31,200

The prepaid expense (asset) account has increased, and the cash (asset) account has decreased by: 12 months x $2,600 per month = $31,200 for the year.

539 Pharma Drug Company Ltd. sells several different types of medications. Today Pharma Drug Company Ltd. signed up for a loan with a 5% interest rate, and so the bank immediately transferred cash to the company in the amount of $109000.

DR Cash $109,000    CR Loan Payable $109,000

The cash (asset) and the loan payable (liability) accounts have both increased by: $109,000. The interest rate does not affect this initial accounting entry, but it will be used for the calculation of interest expense when repayments are made in the future toward this loan.

540    AC&C Ltd. sells various cell phone plans. This January, AC&C Ltd. has made an advance payment to cover the next 12 months of utility bills, which have a monthly cost of $2200.

DR Prepaid Expense $26,400   CR Cash $26,400

The prepaid expense (asset) account has increased, and the cash (asset) account has decreased by: 12 months x $2,200 per month = $26,400 for the year.

541    David & Johnson is a corporation which sells legal services. David & Johnson has just provided 1900 large orders which had been paid for in advance last year. Each order was in the amount of $2300.

DR Unearned Revenue $4,370,000   CR Sales $4,370,000

The unearned revenue (liability) account has decreased and the and the sales (revenue) account has increased by: 19/1 /2arge orders x $2,300 = $4,370,000

542    Kola-Nut Ltd sells several different types of soft drinks. This week, Kola-Nut Ltd purchased 3370 batches of soda bottles which were placed into the warehouse, and which had a per-unit cost of $2700.

DR Inventory $9,099,000   CR Accounts Payable $9,099,000

There was an increase in the inventory (asset) account, and also an increase in the accounts payable (liability) account. 3370 batches of soda bottles x $2,700 = $9,099,000

543    Grand Convention Ltd is a company which offers their customers a wide selection of banquet hall rentals for corporate meetings. This month, Grand Convention Ltd paid for 1 month of rent for their company's office space. Each month, the rent owing was $16000.

DR Rent expense $16,000   CR Accounts Payable $16,000

The rent (expense) and the accounts payable (liability) accounts are both increased by one month's worth of rent, which is $16,000.

544    NBG Media Corporation is an organization which specializes in providing their
       customers with broadcasting services for advertising agencies.  Today NBG
       Media Corporation signed up for a loan with a 5% interest rate, and so the bank
       immediately transferred cash to the company in the amount of $73000.

       DR Cash $73,000    CR Loan Payable $73,000

       The cash (asset) and the loan payable (liability) accounts have both increased
       by: $73,000. The interest rate does not affect this initial accounting entry, but it
       will be used for the calculation of interest expense when repayments are made in
       the future toward this loan.

545    Mount Tessory Academy sells several different types of private school education.
       Mount Tessory Academy has just provided 1100 large orders which had been
       paid for in advance last year. Each order was in the amount of $1400.

       DR Unearned Revenue $1,540,000    CR Sales $1,540,000

       The unearned revenue (liability) account has decreased and the and the sales
       (revenue) account has increased by: 11/1 /2arge orders x $1,400 = $1,540,000

546    Fairway Malls is a privately-held corporation which focuses on their niche of
       premium retail spaces in their shopping centers.  This month, Fairway Malls paid
       1 monthly loan repayment towards their long-term note payable. The interest
       portion was 60% of the payment. The total amount paid in cash was $23000.

       DR Interest Expense $13,800    DR Loan Payable $9,200    CR Cash $23,000

       The interest (expense) account has increased by $23,000 x 0.6 = $13,800. The
       loan payable (liability) has decreased by $23,000 x 0.4 = $9,200. The cash
       (asset) account has decreased by the full amount of the payment, which is
       $23,000

547    Pharma Drug Company Ltd. is a market leader that is well-known for their brand
       of medications.  Today Pharma Drug Company Ltd. signed up for a loan with a
       5% interest rate, and so the bank immediately transferred cash to the company in
       the amount of $20000.

       DR Cash $20,000    CR Loan Payable $20,000

       The cash (asset) and the loan payable (liability) accounts have both increased
       by: $20,000. The interest rate does not affect this initial accounting entry, but it
       will be used for the calculation of interest expense when repayments are made in
       the future toward this loan.

548 Fairway Malls is a corporation which sells retail spaces in their shopping centers. Today, Fairway Malls received payment upfront for 1600 large orders which will not be provided until early next year. Each order was in the amount of $2500.

DR Cash $4,000,000   CR Unearned Revenue $4,000,000

The cash (asset) and the unearned revenue (liability) accounts have both increased by: 1600 large orders x $2,500 = $4,000,000

549 Sprike Inc is a market leader that is well-known for their brand of athletic apparel. This week, Sprike Inc purchased 4490 batches of athletic t-shirts which were placed into the warehouse, and which had a per-unit cost of $1100.

DR Inventory $4,939,000   CR Accounts Payable $4,939,000

There was an increase in the inventory (asset) account, and also an increase in the accounts payable (liability) account. 4490 batches of athletic t-shirts x $1,100 = $4,939,000

550 Jameson & Jameson is a corporation which sells soap products. This week, Jameson & Jameson purchased 3920 truckloads of bars of soap which were placed into the warehouse, and which had a per-unit cost of $2400.

DR Inventory $9,408,000   CR Accounts Payable $9,408,000

There was an increase in the inventory (asset) account, and also an increase in the accounts payable (liability) account. 3920 truckloads of bars of soap x $2,400 = $9,408,000

551 LA Met Theatre Company sells various live theatrical performances. This January, LA Met Theatre Company has made an advance payment to cover the next 12 months of utility bills, which have a monthly cost of $1600.

DR Prepaid Expense $19,200   CR Cash $19,200

The prepaid expense (asset) account has increased, and the cash (asset) account has decreased by: 12 months x $1,600 per month = $19,200 for the year.

552    McGerald's is a privately-held corporation which focuses on their niche of premium fast food meals. Today, McGerald's bought equipment which has a 5 year useful life, and which had a cost of $21000.

DR Equipment $21,000    CR Accounts Payable $21,000

The equipment (asset) and the accounts payable (liability) accounts have both increased by: $21,000. The useful life does not affect this original accounting entry, but it will be used to calculate depreciation of the asset in the future.

553    Jameson & Jameson sells various soap products. Today Jameson & Jameson signed up for a loan with a 5% interest rate, and so the bank immediately transferred cash to the company in the amount of $37000.

DR Cash $37,000    CR Loan Payable $37,000

The cash (asset) and the loan payable (liability) accounts have both increased by: $37,000. The interest rate does not affect this initial accounting entry, but it will be used for the calculation of interest expense when repayments are made in the future toward this loan.

554    Comedy 253 sells various live performances of stand-up comedy. Today, Comedy 253 received payment upfront for 1900 large orders which will not be provided until early next year. Each order was in the amount of $1500.

DR Cash $2,850,000    CR Unearned Revenue $2,850,000

The cash (asset) and the unearned revenue (liability) accounts have both increased by: 1900 large orders x $1,500 = $2,850,000

555    NY Fitness is a company which offers their customers a wide selection of gym memberships for professional sports teams. NY Fitness has just purchased a building using cash, which has an expected useful life of 30 years, and which had a total cost of $459000.

DR Building $459,000    CR Cash $459,000

The building (asset) account has increased, and the cash (asset) account has decreased by: $459,000. The useful life does not affect this original accounting entry, but it will be used to calculate depreciation of the asset in the future.

556    McGerald's offers their customers a wide range of fast food meals. This December, McGerald's recognized 1 year of depreciation on a building which had a total useful life of 25 years, and which had originally been bought for $280000.

DR Depreciation expense $11,200    CR Accumulated Depreciation $11,200

The depreciation (expense) account and the accumulated depreciation (contra-asset) accounts have both increased by: $280,000 divided by 25 years = $11,200 depreciation per year.

557    NY Fitness is a company which offers their customers a wide selection of gym memberships for professional sports teams. This December, NY Fitness recognized 1 year of depreciation on a building which had a total useful life of 25 years, and which had originally been bought for $618000.

DR Depreciation expense $24,720    CR Accumulated Depreciation $24,720

The depreciation (expense) account and the accumulated depreciation (contra-asset) accounts have both increased by: $618,000 divided by 25 years = $24,720 depreciation per year.

558    AC&C Ltd. sells several different types of cell phone plans. This month, AC&C Ltd. has estimated that 5% of the accounts receivable might not end up being collectable, based on past experience. The accounts receivable will need to be adjusted from its current balance of $38000.

DR Bad Debt expense $1,900    CR Allowance for Doubtful Accounts $1,900

The bad debts (expense) and the allowance for doubtful accounts (contra-asset) have both increased by: 5% x $38,000 = $1,900

559    A to Z Event Guru Ltd is a market leader that is well-known for their brand of start-to-finish event planning services for large gatherings. This month, A to Z Event Guru Ltd must amortize 1 month worth of utility bills which they had prepaid at the beginning of the year. The amount that they had paid upfront for the year was $12000.

DR Utilities expense $1,000    CR Prepaid Expense $1,000

The utilities (expense) account has increased and the prepaid expense (asset) account has decreased by: $12,000 for the year, divided by 12 months = $1,000

560 Grand Convention Ltd is a company which offers their customers a wide selection of banquet hall rentals for corporate meetings. This month, Grand Convention Ltd paid for 1 month of rent for their company's office space. Each month, the rent owing was $9000.

DR Rent expense $9,000   CR Accounts Payable $9,000

The rent (expense) and the accounts payable (liability) accounts are both increased by one month's worth of rent, which is $9,000.

561 David & Johnson is a market leader that is well-known for their brand of legal services. This December, David & Johnson recognized 1 year of depreciation on a building which had a total useful life of 25 years, and which had originally been bought for $74000.

DR Depreciation expense $2,960   CR Accumulated Depreciation $2,960

The depreciation (expense) account and the accumulated depreciation (contra-asset) accounts have both increased by: $74,000 divided by 25 years = $2,960 depreciation per year.

562 Comedy 253 sells several different types of live performances of stand-up comedy. Comedy 253 has just provided 1600 large orders which had been paid for in advance last year. Each order was in the amount of $1400.

DR Unearned Revenue $2,240,000   CR Sales $2,240,000

The unearned revenue (liability) account has decreased and the and the sales (revenue) account has increased by: 16/1 /2arge orders x $1,400 = $2,240,000

563 A to Z Event Guru Ltd sells several different types of start-to-finish event planning services for large gatherings. This week, A to Z Event Guru Ltd paid each of the 1000 staff members their bi-weekly wages, which per person had a cost of $2200.

DR Wage expense $2,200,000   CR Accounts Payable $2,200,000

The wage (expense) and the accounts payable (liability) accounts have both increased by: 1000 staff members x $2,200 = $2,200,000

564 Mount Tessory Academy sells several different types of private school education. Today, Mount Tessory Academy has paid cash to their supplier to fully pay off their account payable balance, which was $96000.

DR Accounts Payable $96,000    CR Cash $96,000

The accounts payable (liability) and cash (asset) accounts have both increased by $96,000.

565 LA Met Theatre Company is an organization which specializes in providing their customers with live theatrical performances. This December, LA Met Theatre Company recognized 1 year of depreciation on equipment which had a total useful life of 10 years, and which had originally cost $190000.

DR Depreciation expense $19,000    CR Accumulated Depreciation $19,000

The depreciation (expense) account and the accumulated depreciation (contra-asset) accounts have both increased by: $190,000 divided by 10 years = $19,000 depreciation per year.

566 A to Z Event Guru Ltd provides their customers with start-to-finish event planning services for large gatherings. This week, A to Z Event Guru Ltd paid each of the 2440 staff members their bi-weekly wages, which per person had a cost of $1500.

DR Wage expense $3,660,000    CR Accounts Payable $3,660,000

The wage (expense) and the accounts payable (liability) accounts have both increased by: 2440 staff members x $1,500 = $3,660,000

567 Fairway Malls is a corporation which sells retail spaces in their shopping centers. This week, Fairway Malls paid each of the 3650 staff members their bi-weekly wages, which per person had a cost of $1000.

DR Wage expense $3,650,000    CR Accounts Payable $3,650,000

The wage (expense) and the accounts payable (liability) accounts have both increased by: 3650 staff members x $1,000 = $3,650,000

568 Cirque du Lune offers their customers a wide range of circus performances. This month, Cirque du Lune paid for 1 month of rent for their company's office space. Each month, the rent owing was $17000.

DR Rent expense $17,000    CR Accounts Payable $17,000

The rent (expense) and the accounts payable (liability) accounts are both increased by one month's worth of rent, which is $17,000.

569     Comedy 253 sells several different types of live performances of stand-up
        comedy.  This December, Comedy 253 recognized 1 year of depreciation on a
        building which had a total useful life of 25 years, and which had originally been
        bought for $565000.

        DR Depreciation expense $22,600    CR Accumulated Depreciation $22,600

        The depreciation (expense) account and the accumulated depreciation (contra-
        asset) accounts have both increased by: $565,000 divided by 25 years = $22,600
        depreciation per year.

570     Payday Now is a company which offers their customers a wide selection of short-
        term loan arrangements.  This month, Payday Now must amortize 1 month worth
        of utility bills which they had prepaid at the beginning of the year. The amount
        that they had paid upfront for the year was $38400.

        DR Utilities expense $3,200    CR Prepaid Expense $3,200

        The utilities (expense) account has increased and the prepaid expense (asset)
        account has decreased by: $38,400 for the year, divided by 12 months = $3,200

571     Jameson & Jameson sells several different types of soap products.  This month,
        Jameson & Jameson paid for 1 month of rent for the warehouse room, which has
        a monthly cost of $2300.

        DR Rent expense $2,300    CR Accounts Payable $2,300

        The rent (expense) and the accounts payable (liability) accounts are both
        increased by one month's worth of rent, which is $2,300.

572     Grand Convention Ltd offers their customers a wide range of banquet hall rentals
        for corporate meetings.  This month, Grand Convention Ltd paid for 1 month of
        rent for their company's office space. Each month, the rent owing was $21000.

        DR Rent expense $21,000    CR Accounts Payable $21,000

        The rent (expense) and the accounts payable (liability) accounts are both
        increased by one month's worth of rent, which is $21,000.

573 Comedy 253 is a corporation which sells live performances of stand-up comedy. This January, Comedy 253 has made an advance payment to cover the next 12 months of utility bills, which have a monthly cost of $1700.

DR Prepaid Expense $20,400   CR Cash $20,400

The prepaid expense (asset) account has increased, and the cash (asset) account has decreased by: 12 months x $1,700 per month = $20,400 for the year.

574 Sprike Inc is a corporation which sells athletic apparel. Sprike Inc has just purchased a building using cash, which has an expected useful life of 30 years, and which had a total cost of $74000.

DR Building $74,000   CR Cash $74,000

The building (asset) account has increased, and the cash (asset) account has decreased by: $74,000. The useful life does not affect this original accounting entry, but it will be used to calculate depreciation of the asset in the future.

575 Kola-Nut Ltd is an organization which specializes in providing their customers with soft drinks. Today, Kola-Nut Ltd received an upfront payment for 1700 batches of soda bottles which will be provided to the customer 6 months from now. The payment for each was $2100.

DR Cash $3,570,000   CR Unearned Revenue $3,570,000

The cash (asset) and the unearned revenue (liability) accounts have both increased by: 1700 batches of soda bottles x $2,100 = $3,570,000

576 Paytech Ltd sells several different types of payroll transaction processing services. This January, Paytech Ltd has made an advance payment to cover the next 12 months of utility bills, which have a monthly cost of $1400.

DR Prepaid Expense $16,800   CR Cash $16,800

The prepaid expense (asset) account has increased, and the cash (asset) account has decreased by: 12 months x $1,400 per month = $16,800 for the year.

577    Grand Convention Ltd is a privately-held corporation which focuses on their niche of premium banquet hall rentals for corporate meetings.  This month, Grand Convention Ltd must amortize 1 month worth of utility bills which they had prepaid at the beginning of the year. The amount that they had paid upfront for the year was $21600.

DR Utilities expense $1,800    CR Prepaid Expense $1,800

The utilities (expense) account has increased and the prepaid expense (asset) account has decreased by: $21,600 for the year, divided by 12 months = $1,800

578    Pharma Drug Company Ltd. sells various medications.  Today Pharma Drug Company Ltd. sold 19100 batches of pills which had a 30% mark-up. They had originally been bought from their suppliers for a unit cost of $1950.

DR Accounts Receivable $48,418,500    DR Cost of Goods Sold $37,245,000
CR Sales $48,418,500    CR Inventory $37,245,000

This transaction increases the accounts receivable (asset) account, the sales (revenue) account, and the cost of goods sold (expense) account. The inventory (asset) account has decreased. 19100 batches of pills x $1,950 = $37,245,000. The 30% markup applies to the sales and accounts receivable amounts, i.e. $37,245,000 x 1.30 = $48,418,500

579    Mr. Mop is a corporation which sells household cleaners.  Today Mr. Mop sold 27600 tons of cleaning solution which had a 30% mark-up. They had originally been bought from their suppliers for a unit cost of $1150.

DR Accounts Receivable $41,262,000    DR Cost of Goods Sold $31,740,000
CR Sales $41,262,000    CR Inventory $31,740,000

This transaction increases the accounts receivable (asset) account, the sales (revenue) account, and the cost of goods sold (expense) account. The inventory (asset) account has decreased. 27600 tons of cleaning solution x $1,150 = $31,740,000.  The 30% markup applies to the sales and accounts receivable amounts, i.e. $31,740,000 x 1.30 = $41,262,000

580    Pharma Drug Company Ltd. sells various medications.  Pharma Drug Company Ltd. has just purchased a building using cash, which has an expected useful life of 30 years, and which had a total cost of $50000.

DR Building $50,000    CR Cash $50,000

The building (asset) account has increased, and the cash (asset) account has decreased by: $50,000. The useful life does not affect this original accounting entry, but it will be used to calculate depreciation of the asset in the future.

581 Mount Tessory Academy is a market leader that is well-known for their brand of private school education. This December, Mount Tessory Academy recognized 1 year of depreciation on equipment which had a total useful life of 10 years, and which had originally cost $230000.

DR Depreciation expense $23,000    CR Accumulated Depreciation $23,000

The depreciation (expense) account and the accumulated depreciation (contra-asset) accounts have both increased by: $230,000 divided by 10 years = $23,000 depreciation per year.

582 Toyonda is a corporation which sells cars. Today Toyonda signed up for a loan with a 5% interest rate, and so the bank immediately transferred cash to the company in the amount of $97000.

DR Cash $97,000    CR Loan Payable $97,000

The cash (asset) and the loan payable (liability) accounts have both increased by: $97,000. The interest rate does not affect this initial accounting entry, but it will be used for the calculation of interest expense when repayments are made in the future toward this loan.

583 Kola-Nut Ltd is a privately-held corporation which focuses on their niche of premium soft drinks. This month, Kola-Nut Ltd accepted 17800 batches of soda bottles which were returned by customers. These products had been marked up by 35% and they had originally been bought at a per-unit cost of $2700.

DR Sales Returns $64,881,000    DR Inventory $48,060,000    CR Accounts Receivable $64,881,000    CR Cost of Goods Sold $48,060,000

This transaction increases the sales returns (contra-revenue) account, and the inventory (asset) account. The accounts receivable (asset) account and the cost of goods sold (expense) account have both decreased. 17800 batches of soda bottles x $2,700 = $48,060,000. The 35% markup applies to the sales returns and accounts receivable amounts, i.e. $48,060,000 x 1.35 = $64,881,000

584 LA Met Theatre Company offers their customers a wide range of live theatrical performances. This year, LA Met Theatre Company has provided 2200 shows each of which earned revenues of $1160.

DR Accounts Receivable $2,552,000    CR Sales $2,552,000

The accounts receivable (asset) and the sales (revenue) accounts have both increased by: 22/1 /2hows x $1,160 = $2,552,000

246

585 Mr. Mop sells various household cleaners. Today Mr. Mop sold 44500 tons of cleaning solution which had a 30% mark-up. They had originally been bought from their suppliers for a unit cost of $2560.

DR Accounts Receivable $148,096,000   DR Cost of Goods Sold $113,920,000
CR Sales $148,096,000   CR Inventory $113,920,000

This transaction increases the accounts receivable (asset) account, the sales (revenue) account, and the cost of goods sold (expense) account. The inventory (asset) account has decreased. 44500 tons of cleaning solution x $2,560 = $113,920,000. The 30% markup applies to the sales and accounts receivable amounts, i.e. $113,920,000 x 1.30 = $148,096,000

586 Mr. Mop is a privately-held corporation which focuses on their niche of premium household cleaners. This month, Mr. Mop paid 1 monthly loan repayment towards their long-term note payable. The interest portion was 60% of the payment. The total amount paid in cash was $21000.

DR Interest Expense $12,600   DR Loan Payable $8,400   CR Cash $21,000

The interest (expense) account has increased by $21,000 x 0.6 = $12,600. The loan payable (liability) has decreased by $21,000 x 0.4 = $8,400. The cash (asset) account has decreased by the full amount of the payment, which is $21,000

587 Club Disco is a corporation which sells dance venue rentals for large family gatherings. This January, Club Disco has made an advance payment to cover the next 12 months of utility bills, which have a monthly cost of $1200.

DR Prepaid Expense $14,400   CR Cash $14,400

The prepaid expense (asset) account has increased, and the cash (asset) account has decreased by: 12 months x $1,200 per month = $14,400 for the year.

588 David & Johnson provides their customers with legal services. Today, David & Johnson has paid cash to their supplier to fully pay off their account payable balance, which was $9000.

DR Accounts Payable $9,000   CR Cash $9,000

The accounts payable (liability) and cash (asset) accounts have both increased by $9,000.

589 McGerald's sells various fast food meals. This December, McGerald's recognized 1 year of depreciation on equipment which had a total useful life of 10 years, and which had originally cost $120000.

DR Depreciation expense $12,000    CR Accumulated Depreciation $12,000

The depreciation (expense) account and the accumulated depreciation (contra-asset) accounts have both increased by: $120,000 divided by 10 years = $12,000 depreciation per year.

590 Comedy 253 is a market leader that is well-known for their brand of live performances of stand-up comedy. This year, Comedy 253 has provided 1000 shows each of which earned revenues of $1110.

DR Accounts Receivable $1,110,000    CR Sales $1,110,000

The accounts receivable (asset) and the sales (revenue) accounts have both increased by: 10/1 /2hows x $1,110 = $1,110,000

591 Paytech Ltd is a privately-held corporation which focuses on their niche of premium payroll transaction processing services. This January, Paytech Ltd has made an advance payment to cover the next 12 months of utility bills, which have a monthly cost of $1000.

DR Prepaid Expense $12,000    CR Cash $12,000

The prepaid expense (asset) account has increased, and the cash (asset) account has decreased by: 12 months x $1,000 per month = $12,000 for the year.

592 Jameson & Jameson is an organization which specializes in providing their customers with soap products. This week, Jameson & Jameson purchased 1390 truckloads of bars of soap which were placed into the warehouse, and which had a per-unit cost of $1700.

DR Inventory $2,363,000    CR Accounts Payable $2,363,000

There was an increase in the inventory (asset) account, and also an increase in the accounts payable (liability) account. 1390 truckloads of bars of soap x $1,700 = $2,363,000

593    Sprike Inc sells various athletic apparel.  This December, Sprike Inc recognized 1 year of depreciation on a building which had a total useful life of 25 years, and which had originally been bought for $297000.

DR Depreciation expense $11,880    CR Accumulated Depreciation $11,880

The depreciation (expense) account and the accumulated depreciation (contra-asset) accounts have both increased by: $297,000 divided by 25 years = $11,880 depreciation per year.

594    Club Disco provides their customers with dance venue rentals for large family gatherings.  This December, Club Disco has paid each of the company's 1100 owners an annual dividend in the amount of $26000.

DR Retained Earnings $28,600,000    CR Cash $28,600,000

The retained earnings (equity) and the cash accounts have both decreased by: 1100 owners x $26,000 = $28,600,000

595    Paytech Ltd is a corporation which sells payroll transaction processing services.  Today, Paytech Ltd bought equipment which has a 5 year useful life, and which had a cost of $22000.

DR Equipment $22,000    CR Accounts Payable $22,000

The equipment (asset) and the accounts payable (liability) accounts have both increased by: $22,000. The useful life does not affect this original accounting entry, but it will be used to calculate depreciation of the asset in the future.

596    LA Met Theatre Company is a company which offers their customers a wide selection of live theatrical performances.  This week, LA Met Theatre Company paid each of the 1630 staff members their bi-weekly wages, which per person had a cost of $1000.

DR Wage expense $1,630,000    CR Accounts Payable $1,630,000

The wage (expense) and the accounts payable (liability) accounts have both increased by: 1630 staff members x $1,000 = $1,630,000

597    Cirque du Lune sells several different types of circus performances. This month, Cirque du Lune paid 1 monthly loan repayment towards their long-term note payable. The interest portion was 60% of the payment. The total amount paid in cash was $11000.

DR Interest Expense $6,600    DR Loan Payable $4,400    CR Cash $11,000

The interest (expense) account has increased by $11,000 x 0.6 = $6,600. The loan payable (liability) has decreased by $11,000 x 0.4 = $4,400. The cash (asset) account has decreased by the full amount of the payment, which is $11,000

598    NBG Media Corporation is a privately-held corporation which focuses on their niche of premium broadcasting services for advertising agencies. This December, NBG Media Corporation recognized 1 year of depreciation on equipment which had a total useful life of 10 years, and which had originally cost $80000.

DR Depreciation expense $8,000    CR Accumulated Depreciation $8,000

The depreciation (expense) account and the accumulated depreciation (contra-asset) accounts have both increased by: $80,000 divided by 10 years = $8,000 depreciation per year.

599    A to Z Event Guru Ltd is a market leader that is well-known for their brand of start-to-finish event planning services for large gatherings. This month, A to Z Event Guru Ltd must amortize 1 month worth of utility bills which they had prepaid at the beginning of the year. The amount that they had paid upfront for the year was $12000.

DR Utilities expense $1,000    CR Prepaid Expense $1,000

The utilities (expense) account has increased and the prepaid expense (asset) account has decreased by: $12,000 for the year, divided by 12 months = $1,000

600    David & Johnson sells various legal services. This year, David & Johnson has provided 1700 billable hours each of which earned revenues of $2600.

DR Accounts Receivable $4,420,000    CR Sales $4,420,000

The accounts receivable (asset) and the sales (revenue) accounts have both increased by: 17/1 /2illable hours x $2,600 = $4,420,000

601 Comedy 253 sells various live performances of stand-up comedy. This month, Comedy 253 must amortize 1 month worth of utility bills which they had prepaid at the beginning of the year. The amount that they had paid upfront for the year was $12000.

DR Utilities expense $1,000    CR Prepaid Expense $1,000

The utilities (expense) account has increased and the prepaid expense (asset) account has decreased by: $12,000 for the year, divided by 12 months = $1,000

602 Cirque du Lune sells several different types of circus performances. Today, Cirque du Lune bought equipment which has a 5 year useful life, and which had a cost of $14000.

DR Equipment $14,000    CR Accounts Payable $14,000

The equipment (asset) and the accounts payable (liability) accounts have both increased by: $14,000. The useful life does not affect this original accounting entry, but it will be used to calculate depreciation of the asset in the future.

603 Jameson & Jameson is a market leader that is well-known for their brand of soap products. Today, Jameson & Jameson received an upfront payment for 5850 truckloads of bars of soap which will be provided to the customer 6 months from now. The payment for each was $2500.

DR Cash $14,625,000    CR Unearned Revenue $14,625,000

The cash (asset) and the unearned revenue (liability) accounts have both increased by: 5850 truckloads of bars of soap x $2,500 = $14,625,000

604 David & Johnson sells several different types of legal services. This January, David & Johnson has made an advance payment to cover the next 12 months of utility bills, which have a monthly cost of $1600.

DR Prepaid Expense $19,200    CR Cash $19,200

The prepaid expense (asset) account has increased, and the cash (asset) account has decreased by: 12 months x $1,600 per month = $19,200 for the year.

605    Jameson & Jameson is a corporation which sells soap products. This month, Jameson & Jameson has estimated that 20% of the accounts receivable might not end up being collectable, based on past experience. The accounts receivable will need to be adjusted from its current balance of $91000.

DR Bad Debt expense $18,200    CR Allowance for Doubtful Accounts $18,200

The bad debts (expense) and the allowance for doubtful accounts (contra-asset) have both increased by: 20% x $91,000 = $18,200

606    Payday Now is an organization which specializes in providing their customers with short-term loan arrangements. This January, Payday Now has made an advance payment to cover the next 12 months of utility bills, which have a monthly cost of $2700.

DR Prepaid Expense $32,400    CR Cash $32,400

The prepaid expense (asset) account has increased, and the cash (asset) account has decreased by: 12 months x $2,700 per month = $32,400 for the year.

607    Payday Now is a privately-held corporation which focuses on their niche of premium short-term loan arrangements. This week, Payday Now paid each of the 3940 staff members their bi-weekly wages, which per person had a cost of $1900.

DR Wage expense $7,486,000    CR Accounts Payable $7,486,000

The wage (expense) and the accounts payable (liability) accounts have both increased by: 3940 staff members x $1,900 = $7,486,000

608    Payday Now sells several different types of short-term loan arrangements. Payday Now has just provided 1600 large orders which had been paid for in advance last year. Each order was in the amount of $2700.

DR Unearned Revenue $4,320,000    CR Sales $4,320,000

The unearned revenue (liability) account has decreased and the and the sales (revenue) account has increased by: 16/1 /2arge orders x $2,700 = $4,320,000

609     A to Z Event Guru Ltd is a market leader that is well-known for their brand of start-to-finish event planning services for large gatherings. This January, A to Z Event Guru Ltd has made an advance payment to cover the next 12 months of utility bills, which have a monthly cost of $1800.

DR Prepaid Expense $21,600     CR Cash $21,600

The prepaid expense (asset) account has increased, and the cash (asset) account has decreased by: 12 months x $1,800 per month = $21,600 for the year.

610     Jameson & Jameson sells several different types of soap products. Today, Jameson & Jameson bought equipment which has a 5 year useful life, and which had a cost of $22000.

DR Equipment $22,000     CR Accounts Payable $22,000

The equipment (asset) and the accounts payable (liability) accounts have both increased by: $22,000. The useful life does not affect this original accounting entry, but it will be used to calculate depreciation of the asset in the future.

611     Kola-Nut Ltd is a corporation which sells soft drinks. This month, Kola-Nut Ltd has estimated that 30% of the accounts receivable might not end up being collectable, based on past experience. The accounts receivable will need to be adjusted from its current balance of $95000.

DR Bad Debt expense $28,500     CR Allowance for Doubtful Accounts $28,500

The bad debts (expense) and the allowance for doubtful accounts (contra-asset) have both increased by: 30% x $95,000 = $28,500

612     Comedy 253 provides their customers with live performances of stand-up comedy. This month, Comedy 253 paid for 1 month of rent for their company's office space. Each month, the rent owing was $21000.

DR Rent expense $21,000     CR Accounts Payable $21,000

The rent (expense) and the accounts payable (liability) accounts are both increased by one month's worth of rent, which is $21,000.

613     Mr. Mop is a company which offers their customers a wide selection of household cleaners. Today, Mr. Mop received an upfront payment for 5540 tons of cleaning solution which will be provided to the customer 6 months from now. The payment for each was $2600.

DR Cash $14,404,000    CR Unearned Revenue $14,404,000

The cash (asset) and the unearned revenue (liability) accounts have both increased by: 5540 tons of cleaning solution x $2,600 = $14,404,000

614     Air America is a market leader that is well-known for their brand of global flights. Air America has just received a cash payment for the full amount that this customer owed to the company for all of their purchases to date. The outstanding balance which has now been paid was $15000.

DR Cash $15,000    CR Accounts Receivable $15,000

The cash (asset) account has increased, and the accounts receivable (asset) account has decreased by $15,000.

615     Pharma Drug Company Ltd. sells several different types of medications. This month, Pharma Drug Company Ltd. paid for 1 month of rent for the warehouse room, which has a monthly cost of $2800.

DR Rent expense $2,800    CR Accounts Payable $2,800

The rent (expense) and the accounts payable (liability) accounts are both increased by one month's worth of rent, which is $2,800.

616     Sprike Inc is a corporation which sells athletic apparel. This week, Sprike Inc purchased 4660 batches of athletic t-shirts which were placed into the warehouse, and which had a per-unit cost of $1900.

DR Inventory $8,854,000    CR Accounts Payable $8,854,000

There was an increase in the inventory (asset) account, and also an increase in the accounts payable (liability) account. 4660 batches of athletic t-shirts x $1,900 = $8,854,000

617     Pharma Drug Company Ltd. is a company which offers their customers a wide selection of medications. This month, Pharma Drug Company Ltd. paid for 1 month of rent for the warehouse room, which has a monthly cost of $2400.

DR Rent expense $2,400    CR Accounts Payable $2,400

The rent (expense) and the accounts payable (liability) accounts are both increased by one month's worth of rent, which is $2,400.

618   Air America is a corporation which sells global flights. This month, Air America paid 1 monthly loan repayment towards their long-term note payable. The interest portion was 60% of the payment. The total amount paid in cash was $11000.

DR Interest Expense $6,600   DR Loan Payable $4,400   CR Cash $11,000

The interest (expense) account has increased by $11,000 x 0.6 = $6,600. The loan payable (liability) has decreased by $11,000 x 0.4 = $4,400. The cash (asset) account has decreased by the full amount of the payment, which is $11,000

619   Cirque du Lune is a company which offers their customers a wide selection of circus performances. Cirque du Lune has just received a cash payment for the full amount that this customer owed to the company for all of their purchases to date. The outstanding balance which has now been paid was $45000.

DR Cash $45,000   CR Accounts Receivable $45,000

The cash (asset) account has increased, and the accounts receivable (asset) account has decreased by $45,000.

620   Club Disco provides their customers with dance venue rentals for large family gatherings. This year, Club Disco has provided 1800 evening rentals each of which earned revenues of $2610.

DR Accounts Receivable $4,698,000   CR Sales $4,698,000

The accounts receivable (asset) and the sales (revenue) accounts have both increased by: 18/1 /2vening rentals x $2,610 = $4,698,000

621   Cirque du Lune is a privately-held corporation which focuses on their niche of premium circus performances. Cirque du Lune has just provided 1600 large orders which had been paid for in advance last year. Each order was in the amount of $1800.

DR Unearned Revenue $2,880,000   CR Sales $2,880,000

The unearned revenue (liability) account has decreased and the and the sales (revenue) account has increased by: 16/1 /2arge orders x $1,800 = $2,880,000

622    Jameson & Jameson is an organization which specializes in providing their customers with soap products. This December, Jameson & Jameson recognized 1 year of depreciation on equipment which had a total useful life of 10 years, and which had originally cost $150000.

DR Depreciation expense $15,000   CR Accumulated Depreciation $15,000

The depreciation (expense) account and the accumulated depreciation (contra-asset) accounts have both increased by: $150,000 divided by 10 years = $15,000 depreciation per year.

623    Mr. Mop sells several different types of household cleaners. This month, Mr. Mop paid for 1 month of rent for the warehouse room, which has a monthly cost of $1300.

DR Rent expense $1,300   CR Accounts Payable $1,300

The rent (expense) and the accounts payable (liability) accounts are both increased by one month's worth of rent, which is $1,300.

624    AC&C Ltd. is an organization which specializes in providing their customers with cell phone plans. Today AC&C Ltd. signed up for a loan with a 5% interest rate, and so the bank immediately transferred cash to the company in the amount of $34000.

DR Cash $34,000   CR Loan Payable $34,000

The cash (asset) and the loan payable (liability) accounts have both increased by: $34,000. The interest rate does not affect this initial accounting entry, but it will be used for the calculation of interest expense when repayments are made in the future toward this loan.

625    AC&C Ltd. is a market leader that is well-known for their brand of cell phone plans. This December, AC&C Ltd. has paid each of the company's 1500 owners an annual dividend in the amount of $8000.

DR Retained Earnings $12,000,000   CR Cash $12,000,000

The retained earnings (equity) and the cash accounts have both decreased by: 1500 owners x $8,000 = $12,000,000

626    Fairway Malls sells various retail spaces in their shopping centers. This
       December, Fairway Malls recognized 1 year of depreciation on equipment which
       had a total useful life of 10 years, and which had originally cost $130000.

       DR Depreciation expense $13,000    CR Accumulated Depreciation $13,000

       The depreciation (expense) account and the accumulated depreciation (contra-
       asset) accounts have both increased by: $130,000 divided by 10 years = $13,000
       depreciation per year.

627    NBG Media Corporation is a market leader that is well-known for their brand of
       broadcasting services for advertising agencies. Today, NBG Media Corporation
       has paid cash to their supplier to fully pay off their account payable balance,
       which was $31000.

       DR Accounts Payable $31,000    CR Cash $31,000

       The accounts payable (liability) and cash (asset) accounts have both increased
       by $31,000.

628    Toyonda is a corporation which sells cars. Today, Toyonda bought equipment
       which has a 5 year useful life, and which had a cost of $11000.

       DR Equipment $11,000    CR Accounts Payable $11,000

       The equipment (asset) and the accounts payable (liability) accounts have both
       increased by: $11,000. The useful life does not affect this original accounting
       entry, but it will be used to calculate depreciation of the asset in the future.

629    Mount Tessory Academy sells various private school education subscriptions.
       This December, Mount Tessory Academy recognized 1 year of depreciation on a
       building which had a total useful life of 25 years, and which had originally been
       bought for $178000.

       DR Depreciation expense $7,120    CR Accumulated Depreciation $7,120

       The depreciation (expense) account and the accumulated depreciation (contra-
       asset) accounts have both increased by: $178,000 divided by 25 years = $7,120
       depreciation per year.

630 Kola-Nut Ltd is a company which offers their customers a wide selection of soft drinks. Kola-Nut Ltd has just purchased a building using cash, which has an expected useful life of 30 years, and which had a total cost of $233000.

DR Building $233,000   CR Cash $233,000

The building (asset) account has increased, and the cash (asset) account has decreased by: $233,000. The useful life does not affect this original accounting entry, but it will be used to calculate depreciation of the asset in the future.

631 David & Johnson is a corporation which sells legal services. Today, David & Johnson received payment upfront for 2100 large orders which will not be provided until early next year. Each order was in the amount of $2700.

DR Cash $5,670,000   CR Unearned Revenue $5,670,000

The cash (asset) and the unearned revenue (liability) accounts have both increased by: 2100 large orders x $2,700 = $5,670,000

632 NY Fitness provides their customers with gym memberships for professional sports teams. NY Fitness has just provided 2400 large orders which had been paid for in advance last year. Each order was in the amount of $2100.

DR Unearned Revenue $5,040,000   CR Sales $5,040,000

The unearned revenue (liability) account has decreased and the and the sales (revenue) account has increased by: 24/1 /2arge orders x $2,100 = $5,040,000

633 Hogtown Records is a corporation which sells audio services for local musicians to record their music albums. This month, Hogtown Records paid for 1 month of rent for their company's office space. Each month, the rent owing was $20000.

DR Rent expense $20,000   CR Accounts Payable $20,000

The rent (expense) and the accounts payable (liability) accounts are both increased by one month's worth of rent, which is $20,000.

634 Jameson & Jameson sells several different types of soap products. This month, Jameson & Jameson paid 1 monthly loan repayment towards their long-term note payable. The interest portion was 60% of the payment. The total amount paid in cash was $17000.

DR Interest Expense $10,200   DR Loan Payable $6,800   CR Cash $17,000

The interest (expense) account has increased by $17,000 x 0.6 = $10,200. The loan payable (liability) has decreased by $17,000 x 0.4 = $6,800. The cash (asset) account has decreased by the full amount of the payment, which is $17,000

635 Comedy 253 provides their customers with live performances of stand-up comedy. This December, Comedy 253 recognized 1 year of depreciation on a building which had a total useful life of 25 years, and which had originally been bought for $805000.

DR Depreciation expense $32,200   CR Accumulated Depreciation $32,200

The depreciation (expense) account and the accumulated depreciation (contra-asset) accounts have both increased by: $805,000 divided by 25 years = $32,200 depreciation per year.

636 Fairway Malls is a privately-held corporation which focuses on their niche of premium retail spaces in their shopping centers. Today, Fairway Malls bought equipment which has a 5 year useful life, and which had a cost of $25000.

DR Equipment $25,000   CR Accounts Payable $25,000

The equipment (asset) and the accounts payable (liability) accounts have both increased by: $25,000. The useful life does not affect this original accounting entry, but it will be used to calculate depreciation of the asset in the future.

637 Payday Now sells various short-term loan arrangements. Payday Now has just provided 1200 large orders which had been paid for in advance last year. Each order was in the amount of $1500.

DR Unearned Revenue $1,800,000   CR Sales $1,800,000

The unearned revenue (liability) account has decreased and the and the sales (revenue) account has increased by: 12/1 /2arge orders x $1,500 = $1,800,000

638     Pharma Drug Company Ltd. sells various medications.  This week, Pharma Drug Company Ltd. purchased 2730 batches of pills which were placed into the warehouse, and which had a per-unit cost of $2000.

DR Inventory $5,460,000   CR Accounts Payable $5,460,000

There was an increase in the inventory (asset) account, and also an increase in the accounts payable (liability) account. 2730 batches of pills x $2,000 = $5,460,000

639     Mr. Mop is a company which offers their customers a wide selection of household cleaners.  This January, Mr. Mop has made an advance payment to cover the next 12 months of utility bills, which have a monthly cost of $1000.

DR Prepaid Expense $12,000   CR Cash $12,000

The prepaid expense (asset) account has increased, and the cash (asset) account has decreased by: 12 months x $1,000 per month = $12,000 for the year.

640     Hogtown Records is a privately-held corporation which focuses on their niche of premium audio services for local musicians to record their music albums.  Today, Hogtown Records received payment upfront for 2200 large orders which will not be provided until early next year. Each order was in the amount of $2700.

DR Cash $5,940,000   CR Unearned Revenue $5,940,000

The cash (asset) and the unearned revenue (liability) accounts have both increased by: 2200 large orders x $2,700 = $5,940,000

641     Payday Now sells several different types of short-term loan arrangements.  This January, Payday Now has made an advance payment to cover the next 12 months of utility bills, which have a monthly cost of $1100.

DR Prepaid Expense $13,200   CR Cash $13,200

The prepaid expense (asset) account has increased, and the cash (asset) account has decreased by: 12 months x $1,100 per month = $13,200 for the year.

642     Jameson & Jameson is a company which offers their customers a wide selection
        of soap products.  Today Jameson & Jameson sold 20300 truckloads of bars of
        soap which had a 30% mark-up. They had originally been bought from their
        suppliers for a unit cost of $1370.

        DR Accounts Receivable $36,154,300    DR Cost of Goods Sold $27,811,000
        CR Sales $36,154,300    CR Inventory $27,811,000

        This transaction increases the accounts receivable (asset) account, the sales
        (revenue) account, and the cost of goods sold (expense) account. The inventory
        (asset) account has decreased. 20300 truckloads of bars of soap x $1,370 =
        $27,811,000.  The 30% markup applies to the sales and accounts receivable
        amounts, i.e. $27,811,000 x 1.30 = $36,154,300

643     Fairway Malls offers their customers a wide range of retail spaces in their
        shopping centers.  This month, Fairway Malls paid for 1 month of rent for their
        company's office space. Each month, the rent owing was $11000.

        DR Rent expense $11,000    CR Accounts Payable $11,000

        The rent (expense) and the accounts payable (liability) accounts are both
        increased by one month's worth of rent, which is $11,000.

644     Comedy 253 sells various live performances of stand-up comedy.  Today,
        Comedy 253 bought equipment which has a 5 year useful life, and which had a
        cost of $15000.

        DR Equipment $15,000    CR Accounts Payable $15,000

        The equipment (asset) and the accounts payable (liability) accounts have both
        increased by: $15,000. The useful life does not affect this original accounting
        entry, but it will be used to calculate depreciation of the asset in the future.

645     Mount Tessory Academy sells several different types of private school education.
        Today, Mount Tessory Academy received payment upfront for 1100 large orders
        which will not be provided until early next year. Each order was in the amount of
        $1800.

        DR Cash $1,980,000    CR Unearned Revenue $1,980,000

        The cash (asset) and the unearned revenue (liability) accounts have both
        increased by: 1100 large orders x $1,800 = $1,980,000

646    Sprike Inc provides their customers with athletic apparel. This month, Sprike Inc paid for 1 month of rent for the warehouse room, which has a monthly cost of $1500.

DR Rent expense $1,500    CR Accounts Payable $1,500

The rent (expense) and the accounts payable (liability) accounts are both increased by one month's worth of rent, which is $1,500.

647    Pharma Drug Company Ltd. sells several different types of medications. Today, Pharma Drug Company Ltd. received an upfront payment for 4810 batches of pills which will be provided to the customer 6 months from now. The payment for each was $1900.

DR Cash $9,139,000    CR Unearned Revenue $9,139,000

The cash (asset) and the unearned revenue (liability) accounts have both increased by: 4810 batches of pills x $1,900 = $9,139,000

648    LA Met Theatre Company is an organization which specializes in providing their customers with live theatrical performances. LA Met Theatre Company has just purchased a building using cash, which has an expected useful life of 30 years, and which had a total cost of $772000.

DR Building $772,000    CR Cash $772,000

The building (asset) account has increased, and the cash (asset) account has decreased by: $772,000. The useful life does not affect this original accounting entry, but it will be used to calculate depreciation of the asset in the future.

649    Mr. Mop is a company which offers their customers a wide selection of household cleaners. Today Mr. Mop sold 38100 tons of cleaning solution which had a 30% mark-up. They had originally been bought from their suppliers for a unit cost of $1780.

DR Accounts Receivable $88,163,400    DR Cost of Goods Sold $67,818,000
CR Sales $88,163,400    CR Inventory $67,818,000

This transaction increases the accounts receivable (asset) account, the sales (revenue) account, and the cost of goods sold (expense) account. The inventory (asset) account has decreased. 38100 tons of cleaning solution x $1,780 = $67,818,000. The 30% markup applies to the sales and accounts receivable amounts, i.e. $67,818,000 x 1.30 = $88,163,400

650    Fairway Malls sells several different types of retail spaces in their shopping centers. This month, Fairway Malls must amortize 1 month worth of utility bills which they had prepaid at the beginning of the year. The amount that they had paid upfront for the year was $13200.

DR Utilities expense $1,100    CR Prepaid Expense $1,100

The utilities (expense) account has increased and the prepaid expense (asset) account has decreased by: $13,200 for the year, divided by 12 months = $1,100

651    David & Johnson sells various legal services. This year, David & Johnson has provided 1600 billable hours each of which earned revenues of $1810.

DR Accounts Receivable $2,896,000    CR Sales $2,896,000

The accounts receivable (asset) and the sales (revenue) accounts have both increased by: 16/1 /2illable hours x $1,810 = $2,896,000

652    AC&C Ltd. sells various cell phone plans. This month, AC&C Ltd. has estimated that 25% of the accounts receivable might not end up being collectable, based on past experience. The accounts receivable will need to be adjusted from its current balance of $93000.

DR Bad Debt expense $23,250    CR Allowance for Doubtful Accounts $23,250

The bad debts (expense) and the allowance for doubtful accounts (contra-asset) have both increased by: 25% x $93,000 = $23,250

653    Mr. Mop provides their customers with household cleaners. This month, Mr. Mop paid for 1 month of rent for the warehouse room, which has a monthly cost of $1800.

DR Rent expense $1,800    CR Accounts Payable $1,800

The rent (expense) and the accounts payable (liability) accounts are both increased by one month's worth of rent, which is $1,800.

654    Fairway Malls is a corporation which sells retail spaces in their shopping centers. This year, Fairway Malls has provided 1400 monthly retail space rentals each of which earned revenues of $1440.

DR Accounts Receivable $2,016,000    CR Sales $2,016,000

The accounts receivable (asset) and the sales (revenue) accounts have both increased by: 14/1 /2onthly retail space rentals x $1,440 = $2,016,000

655    Sprike Inc provides their customers with athletic apparel. Today, Sprike Inc received an upfront payment for 5760 batches of athletic t-shirts which will be provided to the customer 6 months from now. The payment for each was $2100.

DR Cash $12,096,000    CR Unearned Revenue $12,096,000

The cash (asset) and the unearned revenue (liability) accounts have both increased by: 5760 batches of athletic t-shirts x $2,100 = $12,096,000

656    Hogtown Records offers their customers a wide range of audio services for local musicians to record their music albums. Today, Hogtown Records bought equipment which has a 5 year useful life, and which had a cost of $26000.

DR Equipment $26,000    CR Accounts Payable $26,000

The equipment (asset) and the accounts payable (liability) accounts have both increased by: $26,000. The useful life does not affect this original accounting entry, but it will be used to calculate depreciation of the asset in the future.

657    Mr. Mop sells several different types of household cleaners. Mr. Mop has just purchased a building using cash, which has an expected useful life of 30 years, and which had a total cost of $808000.

DR Building $808,000    CR Cash $808,000

The building (asset) account has increased, and the cash (asset) account has decreased by: $808,000. The useful life does not affect this original accounting entry, but it will be used to calculate depreciation of the asset in the future.

658    Fairway Malls provides their customers with retail spaces in their shopping centers. This week, Fairway Malls paid each of the 2690 staff members their bi-weekly wages, which per person had a cost of $1700.

DR Wage expense $4,573,000    CR Accounts Payable $4,573,000

The wage (expense) and the accounts payable (liability) accounts have both increased by: 2690 staff members x $1,700 = $4,573,000

659    Cirque du Lune sells various circus performances. Cirque du Lune has just purchased a building using cash, which has an expected useful life of 30 years, and which had a total cost of $362000.

DR Building $362,000    CR Cash $362,000

The building (asset) account has increased, and the cash (asset) account has decreased by: $362,000. The useful life does not affect this original accounting entry, but it will be used to calculate depreciation of the asset in the future.

660 Kola-Nut Ltd provides their customers with soft drinks. This month, Kola-Nut Ltd must amortize 1 month worth of utility bills which they had prepaid at the beginning of the year. The amount that they had paid upfront for the year was $28800.

DR Utilities expense $2,400   CR Prepaid Expense $2,400

The utilities (expense) account has increased and the prepaid expense (asset) account has decreased by: $28,800 for the year, divided by 12 months = $2,400

661 LA Met Theatre Company is a privately-held corporation which focuses on their niche of premium live theatrical performances. This December, LA Met Theatre Company has paid each of the company's 1000 owners an annual dividend in the amount of $24000.

DR Retained Earnings $24,000,000   CR Cash $24,000,000

The retained earnings (equity) and the cash accounts have both decreased by: 1000 owners x $24,000 = $24,000,000

662 Cirque du Lune is a privately-held corporation which focuses on their niche of premium circus performances. Today Cirque du Lune signed up for a loan with a 5% interest rate, and so the bank immediately transferred cash to the company in the amount of $49000.

DR Cash $49,000   CR Loan Payable $49,000

The cash (asset) and the loan payable (liability) accounts have both increased by: $49,000. The interest rate does not affect this initial accounting entry, but it will be used for the calculation of interest expense when repayments are made in the future toward this loan.

663 Mr. Mop is a company which offers their customers a wide selection of household cleaners. This month, Mr. Mop accepted 11000 tons of cleaning solution which were returned by customers. These products had been marked up by 35% and they had originally been bought at a per-unit cost of $1000.

DR Sales Returns $14,850,000   DR Inventory $11,000,000   CR Accounts Receivable $14,850,000   CR Cost of Goods Sold $11,000,000

This transaction increases the sales returns (contra-revenue) account, and the inventory (asset) account. The accounts receivable (asset) account and the cost of goods sold (expense) account have both decreased. 11000 tons of cleaning solution x $1,000 = $11,000,000. The 35% markup applies to the sales returns and accounts receivable amounts, i.e. $11,000,000 x 1.35 = $14,850,000

664  Toyonda is an organization which specializes in providing their customers with cars. Today, Toyonda has paid cash to their supplier to fully pay off their account payable balance, which was $63000.

DR Accounts Payable $63,000    CR Cash $63,000

The accounts payable (liability) and cash (asset) accounts have both increased by $63,000.

665  LA Met Theatre Company is an organization which specializes in providing their customers with live theatrical performances.  This January, LA Met Theatre Company has made an advance payment to cover the next 12 months of utility bills, which have a monthly cost of $1400.

DR Prepaid Expense $16,800    CR Cash $16,800

The prepaid expense (asset) account has increased, and the cash (asset) account has decreased by: 12 months x $1,400 per month = $16,800 for the year.

666  Sprike Inc provides their customers with athletic apparel.  Today Sprike Inc sold 8700 batches of athletic t-shirts which had a 30% mark-up. They had originally been bought from their suppliers for a unit cost of $1490.

DR Accounts Receivable $16,851,900    DR Cost of Goods Sold $12,963,000
CR Sales $16,851,900    CR Inventory $12,963,000

This transaction increases the accounts receivable (asset) account, the sales (revenue) account, and the cost of goods sold (expense) account. The inventory (asset) account has decreased. 8700 batches of athletic t-shirts x $1,490 = $12,963,000.  The 30% markup applies to the sales and accounts receivable amounts, i.e. $12,963,000 x 1.30 = $16,851,900

667  NY Fitness offers their customers a wide range of gym memberships for professional sports teams.  NY Fitness has just provided 1500 large orders which had been paid for in advance last year. Each order was in the amount of $2600.

DR Unearned Revenue $3,900,000    CR Sales $3,900,000

The unearned revenue (liability) account has decreased and the and the sales (revenue) account has increased by: 15/1 /2arge orders x $2,600 = $3,900,000

668    Grand Convention Ltd is a market leader that is well-known for their brand of banquet hall rentals for corporate meetings. This month, Grand Convention Ltd has estimated that 5% of the accounts receivable might not end up being collectable, based on past experience. The accounts receivable will need to be adjusted from its current balance of $54000.

DR Bad Debt expense $2,700    CR Allowance for Doubtful Accounts $2,700

The bad debts (expense) and the allowance for doubtful accounts (contra-asset) have both increased by: 5% x $54,000 = $2,700

669    NY Fitness is a company which offers their customers a wide selection of gym memberships for professional sports teams. This year, NY Fitness has provided 1000 team memberships each of which earned revenues of $2890.

DR Accounts Receivable $2,890,000    CR Sales $2,890,000

The accounts receivable (asset) and the sales (revenue) accounts have both increased by: 10/1 /2eam memberships x $2,890 = $2,890,000

670    Fairway Malls is a privately-held corporation which focuses on their niche of premium retail spaces in their shopping centers. This week, Fairway Malls paid each of the 3280 staff members their bi-weekly wages, which per person had a cost of $1100.

DR Wage expense $3,608,000    CR Accounts Payable $3,608,000

The wage (expense) and the accounts payable (liability) accounts have both increased by: 3280 staff members x $1,100 = $3,608,000

671    Club Disco sells various dance venue rentals for large family gatherings. This January, Club Disco has made an advance payment to cover the next 12 months of utility bills, which have a monthly cost of $2300.

DR Prepaid Expense $27,600    CR Cash $27,600

The prepaid expense (asset) account has increased, and the cash (asset) account has decreased by: 12 months x $2,300 per month = $27,600 for the year.

672    Kola-Nut Ltd is a corporation which sells soft drinks.  This month, Kola-Nut Ltd paid for 1 month of rent for the warehouse room, which has a monthly cost of $2500.

DR Rent expense $2,500    CR Accounts Payable $2,500

The rent (expense) and the accounts payable (liability) accounts are both increased by one month's worth of rent, which is $2,500.

673    Pharma Drug Company Ltd. is a market leader that is well-known for their brand of medications.  This month, Pharma Drug Company Ltd. paid for 1 month of rent for the warehouse room, which has a monthly cost of $1500.

DR Rent expense $1,500    CR Accounts Payable $1,500

The rent (expense) and the accounts payable (liability) accounts are both increased by one month's worth of rent, which is $1,500.

674    Fairway Malls is a company which offers their customers a wide selection of retail spaces in their shopping centers.  This year, Fairway Malls has provided 1200 monthly retail space rentals each of which earned revenues of $1410.

DR Accounts Receivable $1,692,000    CR Sales $1,692,000

The accounts receivable (asset) and the sales (revenue) accounts have both increased by: 12/1 /2onthly retail space rentals x $1,410 = $1,692,000

675    Pharma Drug Company Ltd. is a market leader that is well-known for their brand of medications.  This month, Pharma Drug Company Ltd. accepted 21600 batches of pills which were returned by customers. These products had been marked up by 35% and they had originally been bought at a per-unit cost of $2800.

DR Sales Returns $81,648,000    DR Inventory $60,480,000    CR Accounts Receivable $81,648,000    CR Cost of Goods Sold $60,480,000

This transaction increases the sales returns (contra-revenue) account, and the inventory (asset) account. The accounts receivable (asset) account and the cost of goods sold (expense) account have both decreased. 21600 batches of pills x $2,800 = $60,480,000. The 35% markup applies to the sales returns and accounts receivable amounts, i.e. $60,480,000 x 1.35 = $81,648,000

676    LA Met Theatre Company is a privately-held corporation which focuses on their niche of premium live theatrical performances. Today LA Met Theatre Company signed up for a loan with a 5% interest rate, and so the bank immediately transferred cash to the company in the amount of $84000.

DR Cash $84,000    CR Loan Payable $84,000

The cash (asset) and the loan payable (liability) accounts have both increased by: $84,000. The interest rate does not affect this initial accounting entry, but it will be used for the calculation of interest expense when repayments are made in the future toward this loan.

677    Pharma Drug Company Ltd. is a market leader that is well-known for their brand of medications. Today Pharma Drug Company Ltd. sold 51800 batches of pills which had a 30% mark-up. They had originally been bought from their suppliers for a unit cost of $2000.

DR Accounts Receivable $134,680,000    DR Cost of Goods Sold $103,600,000
CR Sales $134,680,000    CR Inventory $103,600,000

This transaction increases the accounts receivable (asset) account, the sales (revenue) account, and the cost of goods sold (expense) account. The inventory (asset) account has decreased. 51800 batches of pills x $2,000 = $103,600,000. The 30% markup applies to the sales and accounts receivable amounts, i.e. $103,600,000 x 1.30 = $134,680,000

678    Club Disco is a corporation which sells dance venue rentals for large family gatherings. This December, Club Disco recognized 1 year of depreciation on a building which had a total useful life of 25 years, and which had originally been bought for $960000.

DR Depreciation expense $38,400    CR Accumulated Depreciation $38,400

The depreciation (expense) account and the accumulated depreciation (contra-asset) accounts have both increased by: $960,000 divided by 25 years = $38,400 depreciation per year.

679    Jameson & Jameson is a corporation which sells soap products. This month, Jameson & Jameson paid for 1 month of rent for their company's office space. Each month, the rent owing was $15000.

DR Rent expense $15,000    CR Accounts Payable $15,000

The rent (expense) and the accounts payable (liability) accounts are both increased by one month's worth of rent, which is $15,000.

680 Kola-Nut Ltd is an organization which specializes in providing their customers with soft drinks. This week, Kola-Nut Ltd purchased 5470 batches of soda bottles which were placed into the warehouse, and which had a per-unit cost of $2700.

DR Inventory $14,769,000    CR Accounts Payable $14,769,000

There was an increase in the inventory (asset) account, and also an increase in the accounts payable (liability) account. 5470 batches of soda bottles x $2,700 = $14,769,000

681 Paytech Ltd is a privately-held corporation which focuses on their niche of premium payroll transaction processing services. This month, Paytech Ltd has estimated that 10% of the accounts receivable might not end up being collectable, based on past experience. The accounts receivable will need to be adjusted from its current balance of $89000.

DR Bad Debt expense $8,900    CR Allowance for Doubtful Accounts $8,900

The bad debts (expense) and the allowance for doubtful accounts (contra-asset) have both increased by: 10% x $89,000 = $8,900

682 LA Met Theatre Company is a corporation which sells live theatrical performances. LA Met Theatre Company has just received a cash payment for the full amount that this customer owed to the company for all of their purchases to date. The outstanding balance which has now been paid was $86000.

DR Cash $86,000    CR Accounts Receivable $86,000

The cash (asset) account has increased, and the accounts receivable (asset) account has decreased by $86,000.

683 Comedy 253 sells various live performances of stand-up comedy. This January, Comedy 253 has made an advance payment to cover the next 12 months of utility bills, which have a monthly cost of $2500.

DR Prepaid Expense $30,000    CR Cash $30,000

The prepaid expense (asset) account has increased, and the cash (asset) account has decreased by: 12 months x $2,500 per month = $30,000 for the year.

270

684     Grand Convention Ltd is a market leader that is well-known for their brand of banquet hall rentals for corporate meetings. This December, Grand Convention Ltd recognized 1 year of depreciation on equipment which had a total useful life of 10 years, and which had originally cost $220000.

DR Depreciation expense $22,000    CR Accumulated Depreciation $22,000

The depreciation (expense) account and the accumulated depreciation (contra-asset) accounts have both increased by: $220,000 divided by 10 years = $22,000 depreciation per year.

685     Paytech Ltd is an organization which specializes in providing their customers with payroll transaction processing services. This December, Paytech Ltd has paid each of the company's 1700 owners an annual dividend in the amount of $13000.

DR Retained Earnings $22,100,000    CR Cash $22,100,000

The retained earnings (equity) and the cash accounts have both decreased by: 1700 owners x $13,000 = $22,100,000

686     Fairway Malls is a corporation which sells retail spaces in their shopping centers. This year, Fairway Malls has provided 2400 monthly retail space rentals each of which earned revenues of $1250.

DR Accounts Receivable $3,000,000    CR Sales $3,000,000

The accounts receivable (asset) and the sales (revenue) accounts have both increased by: 24/1 /2onthly retail space rentals x $1,250 = $3,000,000

687     Jameson & Jameson is a corporation which sells soap products. This month, Jameson & Jameson accepted 28200 truckloads of bars of soap which were returned by customers. These products had been marked up by 35% and they had originally been bought at a per-unit cost of $1400.

DR Sales Returns $53,298,000    DR Inventory $39,480,000    CR Accounts Receivable $53,298,000    CR Cost of Goods Sold $39,480,000

This transaction increases the sales returns (contra-revenue) account, and the inventory (asset) account. The accounts receivable (asset) account and the cost of goods sold (expense) account have both decreased. 28200 truckloads of bars of soap x $1,400 = $39,480,000. The 35% markup applies to the sales returns and accounts receivable amounts, i.e. $39,480,000 x 1.35 = $53,298,000

688    Kola-Nut Ltd is a company which offers their customers a wide selection of soft drinks. Today, Kola-Nut Ltd received an upfront payment for 3930 batches of soda bottles which will be provided to the customer 6 months from now. The payment for each was $1100.

DR Cash $4,323,000    CR Unearned Revenue $4,323,000

The cash (asset) and the unearned revenue (liability) accounts have both increased by: 3930 batches of soda bottles x $1,100 = $4,323,000

689    Mr. Mop is a privately-held corporation which focuses on their niche of premium household cleaners. Today, Mr. Mop received an upfront payment for 1150 tons of cleaning solution which will be provided to the customer 6 months from now. The payment for each was $2000.

DR Cash $2,300,000    CR Unearned Revenue $2,300,000

The cash (asset) and the unearned revenue (liability) accounts have both increased by: 1150 tons of cleaning solution x $2,000 = $2,300,000

690    NBG Media Corporation is a market leader that is well-known for their brand of broadcasting services for advertising agencies. This month, NBG Media Corporation must amortize 1 month worth of utility bills which they had prepaid at the beginning of the year. The amount that they had paid upfront for the year was $36000.

DR Utilities expense $3,000    CR Prepaid Expense $3,000

The utilities (expense) account has increased and the prepaid expense (asset) account has decreased by: $36,000 for the year, divided by 12 months = $3,000

691    NY Fitness sells several different types of gym memberships for professional sports teams. Today, NY Fitness received payment upfront for 2400 large orders which will not be provided until early next year. Each order was in the amount of $2800.

DR Cash $6,720,000    CR Unearned Revenue $6,720,000

The cash (asset) and the unearned revenue (liability) accounts have both increased by: 2400 large orders x $2,800 = $6,720,000

692   Jameson & Jameson is a corporation which sells soap products. This December, Jameson & Jameson has paid each of the company's 1200 owners an annual dividend in the amount of $17000.

DR Retained Earnings $20,400,000   CR Cash $20,400,000

The retained earnings (equity) and the cash accounts have both decreased by: 1200 owners x $17,000 = $20,400,000

693   Sprike Inc is a company which offers their customers a wide selection of athletic apparel.  Today, Sprike Inc received an upfront payment for 5170 batches of athletic t-shirts which will be provided to the customer 6 months from now. The payment for each was $2700.

DR Cash $13,959,000   CR Unearned Revenue $13,959,000

The cash (asset) and the unearned revenue (liability) accounts have both increased by: 5170 batches of athletic t-shirts x $2,700 = $13,959,000

694   Payday Now is a privately-held corporation which focuses on their niche of premium short-term loan arrangements.  This month, Payday Now has estimated that 30% of the accounts receivable might not end up being collectable, based on past experience. The accounts receivable will need to be adjusted from its current balance of $28000.

DR Bad Debt expense $8,400   CR Allowance for Doubtful Accounts $8,400

The bad debts (expense) and the allowance for doubtful accounts (contra-asset) have both increased by: 30% x $28,000 = $8,400

695   Comedy 253 is a corporation which sells live performances of stand-up comedy. Today, Comedy 253 has paid cash to their supplier to fully pay off their account payable balance, which was $47000.

DR Accounts Payable $47,000   CR Cash $47,000

The accounts payable (liability) and cash (asset) accounts have both increased by $47,000.

696   Payday Now is an organization which specializes in providing their customers with short-term loan arrangements.  This year, Payday Now has provided 1900 payday loans each of which earned revenues of $1500.

DR Accounts Receivable $2,850,000   CR Sales $2,850,000

The accounts receivable (asset) and the sales (revenue) accounts have both increased by: 19/1 /2ayday loans x $1,500 = $2,850,000

697     Pharma Drug Company Ltd. is an organization which specializes in providing their customers with medications.  This month, Pharma Drug Company Ltd. paid for 1 month of rent for the warehouse room, which has a monthly cost of $1100.

DR Rent expense $1,100    CR Accounts Payable $1,100

The rent (expense) and the accounts payable (liability) accounts are both increased by one month's worth of rent, which is $1,100.

698     NY Fitness sells several different types of gym memberships for professional sports teams.  Today, NY Fitness received payment upfront for 2300 large orders which will not be provided until early next year. Each order was in the amount of $2400.

DR Cash $5,520,000    CR Unearned Revenue $5,520,000

The cash (asset) and the unearned revenue (liability) accounts have both increased by: 2300 large orders x $2,400 = $5,520,000

699     Air America is an organization which specializes in providing their customers with global flights.  Today, Air America received payment upfront for 2000 large orders which will not be provided until early next year. Each order was in the amount of $1700.

DR Cash $3,400,000    CR Unearned Revenue $3,400,000

The cash (asset) and the unearned revenue (liability) accounts have both increased by: 2000 large orders x $1,700 = $3,400,000

700     A to Z Event Guru Ltd is a corporation which sells start-to-finish event planning services for large gatherings.  This month, A to Z Event Guru Ltd paid for 1 month of rent for their company's office space. Each month, the rent owing was $17000.

DR Rent expense $17,000    CR Accounts Payable $17,000

The rent (expense) and the accounts payable (liability) accounts are both increased by one month's worth of rent, which is $17,000.

701 Pharma Drug Company Ltd. is a market leader that is well-known for their brand of medications. This month, Pharma Drug Company Ltd. accepted 4000 batches of pills which were returned by customers. These products had been marked up by 35% and they had originally been bought at a per-unit cost of $1600.

DR Sales Returns $8,640,000   DR Inventory $6,400,000   CR Accounts Receivable $8,640,000   CR Cost of Goods Sold $6,400,000

This transaction increases the sales returns (contra-revenue) account, and the inventory (asset) account. The accounts receivable (asset) account and the cost of goods sold (expense) account have both decreased. 4000 batches of pills x $1,600 = $6,400,000. The 35% markup applies to the sales returns and accounts receivable amounts, i.e. $6,400,000 x 1.35 = $8,640,000

702 Sprike Inc is a company which offers their customers a wide selection of athletic apparel. This month, Sprike Inc must amortize 1 month worth of utility bills which they had prepaid at the beginning of the year. The amount that they had paid upfront for the year was $20400.

DR Utilities expense $1,700   CR Prepaid Expense $1,700

The utilities (expense) account has increased and the prepaid expense (asset) account has decreased by: $20,400 for the year, divided by 12 months = $1,700

703 Jameson & Jameson is a privately-held corporation which focuses on their niche of premium soap products. Today Jameson & Jameson sold 45900 truckloads of bars of soap which had a 30% mark-up. They had originally been bought from their suppliers for a unit cost of $1960.

DR Accounts Receivable $116,953,200   DR Cost of Goods Sold $89,964,000 CR Sales $116,953,200   CR Inventory $89,964,000

This transaction increases the accounts receivable (asset) account, the sales (revenue) account, and the cost of goods sold (expense) account. The inventory (asset) account has decreased. 45900 truckloads of bars of soap x $1,960 = $89,964,000. The 30% markup applies to the sales and accounts receivable amounts, i.e. $89,964,000 x 1.30 = $116,953,200

704     Grand Convention Ltd is a privately-held corporation which focuses on their niche of premium banquet hall rentals for corporate meetings. Grand Convention Ltd has just received a cash payment for the full amount that this customer owed to the company for all of their purchases to date. The outstanding balance which has now been paid was $37000.

DR Cash $37,000     CR Accounts Receivable $37,000

The cash (asset) account has increased, and the accounts receivable (asset) account has decreased by $37,000.

705     Kola-Nut Ltd sells various soft drinks. This month, Kola-Nut Ltd paid for 1 month of rent for the warehouse room, which has a monthly cost of $1900.

DR Rent expense $1,900     CR Accounts Payable $1,900

The rent (expense) and the accounts payable (liability) accounts are both increased by one month's worth of rent, which is $1,900.

706     Mr. Mop sells various household cleaners. This week, Mr. Mop purchased 1960 tons of cleaning solution which were placed into the warehouse, and which had a per-unit cost of $1300.

DR Inventory $2,548,000     CR Accounts Payable $2,548,000

There was an increase in the inventory (asset) account, and also an increase in the accounts payable (liability) account. 1960 tons of cleaning solution x $1,300 = $2,548,000

707     Payday Now sells various short-term loan arrangements. This month, Payday Now must amortize 1 month worth of utility bills which they had prepaid at the beginning of the year. The amount that they had paid upfront for the year was $30000.

DR Utilities expense $2,500     CR Prepaid Expense $2,500

The utilities (expense) account has increased and the prepaid expense (asset) account has decreased by: $30,000 for the year, divided by 12 months = $2,500

708 Pharma Drug Company Ltd. offers their customers a wide range of medications. This week, Pharma Drug Company Ltd. purchased 3080 batches of pills which were placed into the warehouse, and which had a per-unit cost of $1500.

DR Inventory $4,620,000 CR Accounts Payable $4,620,000

There was an increase in the inventory (asset) account, and also an increase in the accounts payable (liability) account. 3080 batches of pills x $1,500 = $4,620,000

709 Sprike Inc offers their customers a wide range of athletic apparel. This month, Sprike Inc accepted 3300 batches of athletic t-shirts which were returned by customers. These products had been marked up by 35% and they had originally been bought at a per-unit cost of $2000.

DR Sales Returns $8,910,000 DR Inventory $6,600,000 CR Accounts Receivable $8,910,000 CR Cost of Goods Sold $6,600,000

This transaction increases the sales returns (contra-revenue) account, and the inventory (asset) account. The accounts receivable (asset) account and the cost of goods sold (expense) account have both decreased. 3300 batches of athletic t-shirts x $2,000 = $6,600,000. The 35% markup applies to the sales returns and accounts receivable amounts, i.e. $6,600,000 x 1.35 = $8,910,000

710 Jameson & Jameson sells various soap products. This week, Jameson & Jameson paid each of the 3750 staff members their bi-weekly wages, which per person had a cost of $1500.

DR Wage expense $5,625,000 CR Accounts Payable $5,625,000

The wage (expense) and the accounts payable (liability) accounts have both increased by: 3750 staff members x $1,500 = $5,625,000

711 David & Johnson is a market leader that is well-known for their brand of legal services. Today David & Johnson signed up for a loan with a 5% interest rate, and so the bank immediately transferred cash to the company in the amount of $113000.

DR Cash $113,000 CR Loan Payable $113,000

The cash (asset) and the loan payable (liability) accounts have both increased by: $113,000. The interest rate does not affect this initial accounting entry, but it will be used for the calculation of interest expense when repayments are made in the future toward this loan.

712    NBG Media Corporation is a company which offers their customers a wide selection of broadcasting services for advertising agencies. This December, NBG Media Corporation recognized 1 year of depreciation on a building which had a total useful life of 25 years, and which had originally been bought for $688000.

DR Depreciation expense $27,520    CR Accumulated Depreciation $27,520

The depreciation (expense) account and the accumulated depreciation (contra-asset) accounts have both increased by: $688,000 divided by 25 years = $27,520 depreciation per year.

713    Kola-Nut Ltd is a corporation which sells soft drinks. This December, Kola-Nut Ltd has paid each of the company's 1500 owners an annual dividend in the amount of $23000.

DR Retained Earnings $34,500,000    CR Cash $34,500,000

The retained earnings (equity) and the cash accounts have both decreased by: 1500 owners x $23,000 = $34,500,000

714    Kola-Nut Ltd sells several different types of soft drinks. Kola-Nut Ltd has just received a cash payment for the full amount that this customer owed to the company for all of their purchases to date. The outstanding balance which has now been paid was $46000.

DR Cash $46,000    CR Accounts Receivable $46,000

The cash (asset) account has increased, and the accounts receivable (asset) account has decreased by $46,000.

715    Mount Tessory Academy is a privately-held corporation which focuses on their niche of premium private school education. This December, Mount Tessory Academy recognized 1 year of depreciation on equipment which had a total useful life of 10 years, and which had originally cost $100000.

DR Depreciation expense $10,000    CR Accumulated Depreciation $10,000

The depreciation (expense) account and the accumulated depreciation (contra-asset) accounts have both increased by: $100,000 divided by 10 years = $10,000 depreciation per year.

716    Hogtown Records sells several different types of audio services for local musicians to record their music albums.  Today, Hogtown Records bought equipment which has a 5 year useful life, and which had a cost of $19000.

DR Equipment $19,000    CR Accounts Payable $19,000

The equipment (asset) and the accounts payable (liability) accounts have both increased by: $19,000. The useful life does not affect this original accounting entry, but it will be used to calculate depreciation of the asset in the future.

717    Comedy 253 is a corporation which sells live performances of stand-up comedy. Comedy 253 has just received a cash payment for the full amount that this customer owed to the company for all of their purchases to date. The outstanding balance which has now been paid was $8000.

DR Cash $8,000    CR Accounts Receivable $8,000

The cash (asset) account has increased, and the accounts receivable (asset) account has decreased by $8,000.

718    LA Met Theatre Company is a company which offers their customers a wide selection of live theatrical performances.  LA Met Theatre Company has just purchased a building using cash, which has an expected useful life of 30 years, and which had a total cost of $218000.

DR Building $218,000    CR Cash $218,000

The building (asset) account has increased, and the cash (asset) account has decreased by: $218,000. The useful life does not affect this original accounting entry, but it will be used to calculate depreciation of the asset in the future.

719    Kola-Nut Ltd sells various soft drinks.  Today Kola-Nut Ltd sold 19300 batches of soda bottles which had a 30% mark-up. They had originally been bought from their suppliers for a unit cost of $1070.

DR Accounts Receivable $26,846,300    DR Cost of Goods Sold $20,651,000
CR Sales $26,846,300    CR Inventory $20,651,000

This transaction increases the accounts receivable (asset) account, the sales (revenue) account, and the cost of goods sold (expense) account. The inventory (asset) account has decreased. 19300 batches of soda bottles x $1,070 = $20,651,000.  The 30% markup applies to the sales and accounts receivable amounts, i.e. $20,651,000 x 1.30 = $26,846,300

279

720 Pharma Drug Company Ltd. sells several different types of medications. This month, Pharma Drug Company Ltd. paid 1 monthly loan repayment towards their long-term note payable. The interest portion was 60% of the payment. The total amount paid in cash was $25000.

DR Interest Expense $15,000    DR Loan Payable $10,000    CR Cash $25,000

The interest (expense) account has increased by $25,000 x 0.6 = $15,000. The loan payable (liability) has decreased by $25,000 x 0.4 = $10,000. The cash (asset) account has decreased by the full amount of the payment, which is $25,000

721 Hogtown Records provides their customers with audio services for local musicians to record their music albums. Today, Hogtown Records received payment upfront for 1600 large orders which will not be provided until early next year. Each order was in the amount of $1300.

DR Cash $2,080,000    CR Unearned Revenue $2,080,000

The cash (asset) and the unearned revenue (liability) accounts have both increased by: 1600 large orders x $1,300 = $2,080,000

722 Pharma Drug Company Ltd. provides their customers with medications. Today Pharma Drug Company Ltd. sold 47800 batches of pills which had a 30% mark-up. They had originally been bought from their suppliers for a unit cost of $2100.

DR Accounts Receivable $130,494,000    DR Cost of Goods Sold $100,380,000
CR Sales $130,494,000    CR Inventory $100,380,000

This transaction increases the accounts receivable (asset) account, the sales (revenue) account, and the cost of goods sold (expense) account. The inventory (asset) account has decreased. 47800 batches of pills x $2,100 = $100,380,000. The 30% markup applies to the sales and accounts receivable amounts, i.e. $100,380,000 x 1.30 = $130,494,000

723 Sprike Inc sells several different types of athletic apparel. This January, Sprike Inc has made an advance payment to cover the next 12 months of utility bills, which have a monthly cost of $2100.

DR Prepaid Expense $25,200    CR Cash $25,200

The prepaid expense (asset) account has increased, and the cash (asset) account has decreased by: 12 months x $2,100 per month = $25,200 for the year.

724 Pharma Drug Company Ltd. provides their customers with medications. This month, Pharma Drug Company Ltd. accepted 29200 batches of pills which were returned by customers. These products had been marked up by 35% and they had originally been bought at a per-unit cost of $1900.

DR Sales Returns $74,898,000   DR Inventory $55,480,000   CR Accounts Receivable $74,898,000   CR Cost of Goods Sold $55,480,000

This transaction increases the sales returns (contra-revenue) account, and the inventory (asset) account. The accounts receivable (asset) account and the cost of goods sold (expense) account have both decreased. 29200 batches of pills x $1,900 = $55,480,000. The 35% markup applies to the sales returns and accounts receivable amounts, i.e. $55,480,000 x 1.35 = $74,898,000

725 Sprike Inc is an organization which specializes in providing their customers with athletic apparel. This month, Sprike Inc paid for 1 month of rent for the warehouse room, which has a monthly cost of $2100.

DR Rent expense $2,100   CR Accounts Payable $2,100

The rent (expense) and the accounts payable (liability) accounts are both increased by one month's worth of rent, which is $2,100.

726 Kola-Nut Ltd offers their customers a wide range of soft drinks. This month, Kola-Nut Ltd paid for 1 month of rent for the warehouse room, which has a monthly cost of $1600.

DR Rent expense $1,600   CR Accounts Payable $1,600

The rent (expense) and the accounts payable (liability) accounts are both increased by one month's worth of rent, which is $1,600.

727 Jameson & Jameson is a market leader that is well-known for their brand of soap products. This December, Jameson & Jameson recognized 1 year of depreciation on equipment which had a total useful life of 10 years, and which had originally cost $180000.

DR Depreciation expense $18,000   CR Accumulated Depreciation $18,000

The depreciation (expense) account and the accumulated depreciation (contra-asset) accounts have both increased by: $180,000 divided by 10 years = $18,000 depreciation per year.

728     Cirque du Lune provides their customers with circus performances. This December, Cirque du Lune has paid each of the company's 1500 owners an annual dividend in the amount of $12000.

DR Retained Earnings $18,000,000    CR Cash $18,000,000

The retained earnings (equity) and the cash accounts have both decreased by: 1500 owners x $12,000 = $18,000,000

729     David & Johnson is a corporation which sells legal services. Today, David & Johnson received payment upfront for 1100 large orders which will not be provided until early next year. Each order was in the amount of $2300.

DR Cash $2,530,000    CR Unearned Revenue $2,530,000

The cash (asset) and the unearned revenue (liability) accounts have both increased by: 1100 large orders x $2,300 = $2,530,000

730     Payday Now provides their customers with short-term loan arrangements. This month, Payday Now paid for 1 month of rent for their company's office space. Each month, the rent owing was $10000.

DR Rent expense $10,000    CR Accounts Payable $10,000

The rent (expense) and the accounts payable (liability) accounts are both increased by one month's worth of rent, which is $10,000.

731     Paytech Ltd sells several different types of payroll transaction processing services. This month, Paytech Ltd has estimated that 25% of the accounts receivable might not end up being collectable, based on past experience. The accounts receivable will need to be adjusted from its current balance of $64000.

DR Bad Debt expense $16,000    CR Allowance for Doubtful Accounts $16,000

The bad debts (expense) and the allowance for doubtful accounts (contra-asset) have both increased by: 25% x $64,000 = $16,000

732     Club Disco is a market leader that is well-known for their brand of dance venue rentals for large family gatherings. Today, Club Disco bought equipment which has a 5 year useful life, and which had a cost of $10000.

DR Equipment $10,000    CR Accounts Payable $10,000

The equipment (asset) and the accounts payable (liability) accounts have both increased by: $10,000. The useful life does not affect this original accounting entry, but it will be used to calculate depreciation of the asset in the future.

733    Club Disco is a corporation which sells dance venue rentals for large family gatherings. Club Disco has just received a cash payment for the full amount that this customer owed to the company for all of their purchases to date. The outstanding balance which has now been paid was $65000.

DR Cash $65,000    CR Accounts Receivable $65,000

The cash (asset) account has increased, and the accounts receivable (asset) account has decreased by $65,000.

734    Mr. Mop is a privately-held corporation which focuses on their niche of premium household cleaners. Today, Mr. Mop received an upfront payment for 4870 tons of cleaning solution which will be provided to the customer 6 months from now. The payment for each was $1100.

DR Cash $5,357,000    CR Unearned Revenue $5,357,000

The cash (asset) and the unearned revenue (liability) accounts have both increased by: 4870 tons of cleaning solution x $1,100 = $5,357,000

735    Jameson & Jameson sells various soap products. This month, Jameson & Jameson paid for 1 month of rent for the warehouse room, which has a monthly cost of $1700.

DR Rent expense $1,700    CR Accounts Payable $1,700

The rent (expense) and the accounts payable (liability) accounts are both increased by one month's worth of rent, which is $1,700.

736    Fairway Malls is a company which offers their customers a wide selection of retail spaces in their shopping centers. This December, Fairway Malls recognized 1 year of depreciation on equipment which had a total useful life of 10 years, and which had originally cost $200000.

DR Depreciation expense $20,000    CR Accumulated Depreciation $20,000

The depreciation (expense) account and the accumulated depreciation (contra-asset) accounts have both increased by: $200,000 divided by 10 years = $20,000 depreciation per year.

737 Fairway Malls is a market leader that is well-known for their brand of retail spaces in their shopping centers. Fairway Malls has just received a cash payment for the full amount that this customer owed to the company for all of their purchases to date. The outstanding balance which has now been paid was $13000.

DR Cash $13,000    CR Accounts Receivable $13,000

The cash (asset) account has increased, and the accounts receivable (asset) account has decreased by $13,000.

738 Comedy 253 provides their customers with live performances of stand-up comedy. This year, Comedy 253 has provided 1600 shows each of which earned revenues of $1900.

DR Accounts Receivable $3,040,000    CR Sales $3,040,000

The accounts receivable (asset) and the sales (revenue) accounts have both increased by: 16/1 /2hows x $1,900 = $3,040,000

739 Sprike Inc sells various athletic apparel. This month, Sprike Inc paid for 1 month of rent for the warehouse room, which has a monthly cost of $1100.

DR Rent expense $1,100    CR Accounts Payable $1,100

The rent (expense) and the accounts payable (liability) accounts are both increased by one month's worth of rent, which is $1,100.

740 LA Met Theatre Company is a market leader that is well-known for their brand of live theatrical performances. This week, LA Met Theatre Company paid each of the 1540 staff members their bi-weekly wages, which per person had a cost of $1600.

DR Wage expense $2,464,000    CR Accounts Payable $2,464,000

The wage (expense) and the accounts payable (liability) accounts have both increased by: 1540 staff members x $1,600 = $2,464,000

741 Toyonda is a corporation which sells cars. This month, Toyonda must amortize 1 month worth of utility bills which they had prepaid at the beginning of the year. The amount that they had paid upfront for the year was $28800.

DR Utilities expense $2,400    CR Prepaid Expense $2,400

The utilities (expense) account has increased and the prepaid expense (asset) account has decreased by: $28,800 for the year, divided by 12 months = $2,400

742    Mr. Mop sells several different types of household cleaners. Today, Mr. Mop received an upfront payment for 3610 tons of cleaning solution which will be provided to the customer 6 months from now. The payment for each was $2700.

DR Cash $9,747,000    CR Unearned Revenue $9,747,000

The cash (asset) and the unearned revenue (liability) accounts have both increased by: 3610 tons of cleaning solution x $2,700 = $9,747,000

743    Paytech Ltd is a company which offers their customers a wide selection of payroll transaction processing services. This December, Paytech Ltd recognized 1 year of depreciation on a building which had a total useful life of 25 years, and which had originally been bought for $72000.

DR Depreciation expense $2,880    CR Accumulated Depreciation $2,880

The depreciation (expense) account and the accumulated depreciation (contra-asset) accounts have both increased by: $72,000 divided by 25 years = $2,880 depreciation per year.

744    Jameson & Jameson is an organization which specializes in providing their customers with soap products. This week, Jameson & Jameson purchased 5620 truckloads of bars of soap which were placed into the warehouse, and which had a per-unit cost of $2600.

DR Inventory $14,612,000    CR Accounts Payable $14,612,000

There was an increase in the inventory (asset) account, and also an increase in the accounts payable (liability) account. 5620 truckloads of bars of soap x $2,600 = $14,612,000

745    Paytech Ltd sells various payroll transaction processing services. Today, Paytech Ltd received payment upfront for 2100 large orders which will not be provided until early next year. Each order was in the amount of $2000.

DR Cash $4,200,000    CR Unearned Revenue $4,200,000

The cash (asset) and the unearned revenue (liability) accounts have both increased by: 2100 large orders x $2,000 = $4,200,000

746 Payday Now is a company which offers their customers a wide selection of short-term loan arrangements. Today, Payday Now has paid cash to their supplier to fully pay off their account payable balance, which was $21000.

DR Accounts Payable $21,000   CR Cash $21,000

The accounts payable (liability) and cash (asset) accounts have both increased by $21,000.

747 Jameson & Jameson is a company which offers their customers a wide selection of soap products. Today, Jameson & Jameson has paid cash to their supplier to fully pay off their account payable balance, which was $32000.

DR Accounts Payable $32,000   CR Cash $32,000

The accounts payable (liability) and cash (asset) accounts have both increased by $32,000.

748 Mr. Mop offers their customers a wide range of household cleaners. Today, Mr. Mop received an upfront payment for 2410 tons of cleaning solution which will be provided to the customer 6 months from now. The payment for each was $1500.

DR Cash $3,615,000   CR Unearned Revenue $3,615,000

The cash (asset) and the unearned revenue (liability) accounts have both increased by: 2410 tons of cleaning solution x $1,500 = $3,615,000

749 Pharma Drug Company Ltd. provides their customers with medications. This month, Pharma Drug Company Ltd. accepted 7600 batches of pills which were returned by customers. These products had been marked up by 35% and they had originally been bought at a per-unit cost of $2400.

DR Sales Returns $24,624,000   DR Inventory $18,240,000   CR Accounts Receivable $24,624,000   CR Cost of Goods Sold $18,240,000

This transaction increases the sales returns (contra-revenue) account, and the inventory (asset) account. The accounts receivable (asset) account and the cost of goods sold (expense) account have both decreased. 7600 batches of pills x $2,400 = $18,240,000. The 35% markup applies to the sales returns and accounts receivable amounts, i.e. $18,240,000 x 1.35 = $24,624,000

750    LA Met Theatre Company is a company which offers their customers a wide selection of live theatrical performances. LA Met Theatre Company has just received a cash payment for the full amount that this customer owed to the company for all of their purchases to date. The outstanding balance which has now been paid was $65000.

DR Cash $65,000    CR Accounts Receivable $65,000

The cash (asset) account has increased, and the accounts receivable (asset) account has decreased by $65,000.

751    Sprike Inc offers their customers a wide range of athletic apparel. This week, Sprike Inc purchased 3460 batches of athletic t-shirts which were placed into the warehouse, and which had a per-unit cost of $1000.

DR Inventory $3,460,000    CR Accounts Payable $3,460,000

There was an increase in the inventory (asset) account, and also an increase in the accounts payable (liability) account. 3460 batches of athletic t-shirts x $1,000 = $3,460,000

752    McGerald's offers their customers a wide range of fast food meals. Today, McGerald's has paid cash to their supplier to fully pay off their account payable balance, which was $65000.

DR Accounts Payable $65,000    CR Cash $65,000

The accounts payable (liability) and cash (asset) accounts have both increased by $65,000.

753    Pharma Drug Company Ltd. offers their customers a wide range of medications. This month, Pharma Drug Company Ltd. accepted 16900 batches of pills which were returned by customers. These products had been marked up by 35% and they had originally been bought at a per-unit cost of $2500.

DR Sales Returns $57,037,500   DR Inventory $42,250,000   CR Accounts Receivable $57,037,500   CR Cost of Goods Sold $42,250,000

This transaction increases the sales returns (contra-revenue) account, and the inventory (asset) account. The accounts receivable (asset) account and the cost of goods sold (expense) account have both decreased. 16900 batches of pills x $2,500 = $42,250,000. The 35% markup applies to the sales returns and accounts receivable amounts, i.e. $42,250,000 x 1.35 = $57,037,500

754 Sprike Inc is a privately-held corporation which focuses on their niche of premium athletic apparel. This week, Sprike Inc purchased 2760 batches of athletic t-shirts which were placed into the warehouse, and which had a per-unit cost of $1600.

DR Inventory $4,416,000    CR Accounts Payable $4,416,000

There was an increase in the inventory (asset) account, and also an increase in the accounts payable (liability) account. 2760 batches of athletic t-shirts x $1,600 = $4,416,000

755 Comedy 253 is a corporation which sells live performances of stand-up comedy. Today, Comedy 253 received payment upfront for 1800 large orders which will not be provided until early next year. Each order was in the amount of $2400.

DR Cash $4,320,000    CR Unearned Revenue $4,320,000

The cash (asset) and the unearned revenue (liability) accounts have both increased by: 1800 large orders x $2,400 = $4,320,000

756 Paytech Ltd is a privately-held corporation which focuses on their niche of premium payroll transaction processing services. This year, Paytech Ltd has provided 1800 batches of transactions for the current period each of which earned revenues of $2350.

DR Accounts Receivable $4,230,000    CR Sales $4,230,000

The accounts receivable (asset) and the sales (revenue) accounts have both increased by: 18/1 /2atches of transactions for the current period x $2,350 = $4,230,000

757 Kola-Nut Ltd sells various soft drinks. Today Kola-Nut Ltd sold 37000 batches of soda bottles which had a 30% mark-up. They had originally been bought from their suppliers for a unit cost of $1740.

DR Accounts Receivable $83,694,000    DR Cost of Goods Sold $64,380,000
CR Sales $83,694,000    CR Inventory $64,380,000

This transaction increases the accounts receivable (asset) account, the sales (revenue) account, and the cost of goods sold (expense) account. The inventory (asset) account has decreased. 37000 batches of soda bottles x $1,740 = $64,380,000. The 30% markup applies to the sales and accounts receivable amounts, i.e. $64,380,000 x 1.30 = $83,694,000

758    Jameson & Jameson is an organization which specializes in providing their customers with soap products. This month, Jameson & Jameson paid for 1 month of rent for the warehouse room, which has a monthly cost of $1000.

DR Rent expense $1,000    CR Accounts Payable $1,000

The rent (expense) and the accounts payable (liability) accounts are both increased by one month's worth of rent, which is $1,000.

759    Club Disco provides their customers with dance venue rentals for large family gatherings. Club Disco has just provided 1400 large orders which had been paid for in advance last year. Each order was in the amount of $2400.

DR Unearned Revenue $3,360,000    CR Sales $3,360,000

The unearned revenue (liability) account has decreased and the and the sales (revenue) account has increased by: 14/1 /2arge orders x $2,400 = $3,360,000

760    Mr. Mop provides their customers with household cleaners. This month, Mr. Mop has estimated that 30% of the accounts receivable might not end up being collectable, based on past experience. The accounts receivable will need to be adjusted from its current balance of $57000.

DR Bad Debt expense $17,100    CR Allowance for Doubtful Accounts $17,100

The bad debts (expense) and the allowance for doubtful accounts (contra-asset) have both increased by: 30% x $57,000 = $17,100

761    Mr. Mop is a market leader that is well-known for their brand of household cleaners. This December, Mr. Mop has paid each of the company's 2100 owners an annual dividend in the amount of $26000.

DR Retained Earnings $54,600,000    CR Cash $54,600,000

The retained earnings (equity) and the cash accounts have both decreased by: 2100 owners x $26,000 = $54,600,000

762     LA Met Theatre Company is a corporation which sells live theatrical performances. This month, LA Met Theatre Company paid 1 monthly loan repayment towards their long-term note payable. The interest portion was 60% of the payment. The total amount paid in cash was $18000.

DR Interest Expense $10,800    DR Loan Payable $7,200    CR Cash $18,000

The interest (expense) account has increased by $18,000 x 0.6 = $10,800. The loan payable (liability) has decreased by $18,000 x 0.4 = $7,200. The cash (asset) account has decreased by the full amount of the payment, which is $18,000

763     Fairway Malls sells various retail spaces in their shopping centers. Today, Fairway Malls has paid cash to their supplier to fully pay off their account payable balance, which was $88000.

DR Accounts Payable $88,000    CR Cash $88,000

The accounts payable (liability) and cash (asset) accounts have both increased by $88,000.

764     Mr. Mop is a company which offers their customers a wide selection of household cleaners. This month, Mr. Mop paid 1 monthly loan repayment towards their long-term note payable. The interest portion was 60% of the payment. The total amount paid in cash was $20000.

DR Interest Expense $12,000    DR Loan Payable $8,000    CR Cash $20,000

The interest (expense) account has increased by $20,000 x 0.6 = $12,000. The loan payable (liability) has decreased by $20,000 x 0.4 = $8,000. The cash (asset) account has decreased by the full amount of the payment, which is $20,000

765     Fairway Malls is a market leader that is well-known for their brand of retail spaces in their shopping centers. Today Fairway Malls signed up for a loan with a 5% interest rate, and so the bank immediately transferred cash to the company in the amount of $72000.

DR Cash $72,000    CR Loan Payable $72,000

The cash (asset) and the loan payable (liability) accounts have both increased by: $72,000. The interest rate does not affect this initial accounting entry, but it will be used for the calculation of interest expense when repayments are made in the future toward this loan.

766    David & Johnson is a privately-held corporation which focuses on their niche of premium legal services. David & Johnson has just received a cash payment for the full amount that this customer owed to the company for all of their purchases to date. The outstanding balance which has now been paid was $24000.

DR Cash $24,000    CR Accounts Receivable $24,000

The cash (asset) account has increased, and the accounts receivable (asset) account has decreased by $24,000.

767    Cirque du Lune offers their customers a wide range of circus performances. Today, Cirque du Lune received payment upfront for 1600 large orders which will not be provided until early next year. Each order was in the amount of $2200.

DR Cash $3,520,000    CR Unearned Revenue $3,520,000

The cash (asset) and the unearned revenue (liability) accounts have both increased by: 1600 large orders x $2,200 = $3,520,000

768    Kola-Nut Ltd offers their customers a wide range of soft drinks. This month, Kola-Nut Ltd accepted 26000 batches of soda bottles which were returned by customers. These products had been marked up by 35% and they had originally been bought at a per-unit cost of $1200.

DR Sales Returns $42,120,000    DR Inventory $31,200,000    CR Accounts Receivable $42,120,000    CR Cost of Goods Sold $31,200,000

This transaction increases the sales returns (contra-revenue) account, and the inventory (asset) account. The accounts receivable (asset) account and the cost of goods sold (expense) account have both decreased. 26000 batches of soda bottles x $1,200 = $31,200,000. The 35% markup applies to the sales returns and accounts receivable amounts, i.e. $31,200,000 x 1.35 = $42,120,000

769    A to Z Event Guru Ltd is a company which offers their customers a wide selection of start-to-finish event planning services for large gatherings. This week, A to Z Event Guru Ltd paid each of the 3400 staff members their bi-weekly wages, which per person had a cost of $2800.

DR Wage expense $9,520,000    CR Accounts Payable $9,520,000

The wage (expense) and the accounts payable (liability) accounts have both increased by: 3400 staff members x $2,800 = $9,520,000

770    Kola-Nut Ltd sells various soft drinks.  This December, Kola-Nut Ltd recognized 1 year of depreciation on equipment which had a total useful life of 10 years, and which had originally cost $160000.

DR Depreciation expense $16,000    CR Accumulated Depreciation $16,000

The depreciation (expense) account and the accumulated depreciation (contra-asset) accounts have both increased by: $160,000 divided by 10 years = $16,000 depreciation per year.

771    Jameson & Jameson is an organization which specializes in providing their customers with soap products.  This December, Jameson & Jameson recognized 1 year of depreciation on a building which had a total useful life of 25 years, and which had originally been bought for $752000.

DR Depreciation expense $30,080    CR Accumulated Depreciation $30,080

The depreciation (expense) account and the accumulated depreciation (contra-asset) accounts have both increased by: $752,000 divided by 25 years = $30,080 depreciation per year.

772    Kola-Nut Ltd is a corporation which sells soft drinks.  Today Kola-Nut Ltd sold 46700 batches of soda bottles which had a 30% mark-up. They had originally been bought from their suppliers for a unit cost of $1200.

DR Accounts Receivable $72,852,000    DR Cost of Goods Sold $56,040,000
CR Sales $72,852,000    CR Inventory $56,040,000

This transaction increases the accounts receivable (asset) account, the sales (revenue) account, and the cost of goods sold (expense) account. The inventory (asset) account has decreased. 46700 batches of soda bottles x $1,200 = $56,040,000.  The 30% markup applies to the sales and accounts receivable amounts, i.e. $56,040,000 x 1.30 = $72,852,000

773    Kola-Nut Ltd sells several different types of soft drinks.  This December, Kola-Nut Ltd recognized 1 year of depreciation on equipment which had a total useful life of 10 years, and which had originally cost $220000.

DR Depreciation expense $22,000    CR Accumulated Depreciation $22,000

The depreciation (expense) account and the accumulated depreciation (contra-asset) accounts have both increased by: $220,000 divided by 10 years = $22,000 depreciation per year.

774    Air America sells various global flights. Air America has just provided 2200 large orders which had been paid for in advance last year. Each order was in the amount of $2200.

DR Unearned Revenue $4,840,000    CR Sales $4,840,000

The unearned revenue (liability) account has decreased and the and the sales (revenue) account has increased by: 22/1 /2arge orders x $2,200 = $4,840,000

775    Paytech Ltd provides their customers with payroll transaction processing services. This month, Paytech Ltd must amortize 1 month worth of utility bills which they had prepaid at the beginning of the year. The amount that they had paid upfront for the year was $34800.

DR Utilities expense $2,900    CR Prepaid Expense $2,900

The utilities (expense) account has increased and the prepaid expense (asset) account has decreased by: $34,800 for the year, divided by 12 months = $2,900

776    Mr. Mop is a privately-held corporation which focuses on their niche of premium household cleaners. This December, Mr. Mop recognized 1 year of depreciation on a building which had a total useful life of 25 years, and which had originally been bought for $576000.

DR Depreciation expense $23,040    CR Accumulated Depreciation $23,040

The depreciation (expense) account and the accumulated depreciation (contra-asset) accounts have both increased by: $576,000 divided by 25 years = $23,040 depreciation per year.

777    Kola-Nut Ltd is a privately-held corporation which focuses on their niche of premium soft drinks. This month, Kola-Nut Ltd has estimated that 15% of the accounts receivable might not end up being collectable, based on past experience. The accounts receivable will need to be adjusted from its current balance of $30000.

DR Bad Debt expense $4,500    CR Allowance for Doubtful Accounts $4,500

The bad debts (expense) and the allowance for doubtful accounts (contra-asset) have both increased by: 15% x $30,000 = $4,500

778 Mr. Mop is an organization which specializes in providing their customers with household cleaners. This month, Mr. Mop paid for 1 month of rent for their company's office space. Each month, the rent owing was $12000.

DR Rent expense $12,000    CR Accounts Payable $12,000

The rent (expense) and the accounts payable (liability) accounts are both increased by one month's worth of rent, which is $12,000.

779 Sprike Inc sells several different types of athletic apparel. Sprike Inc has just received a cash payment for the full amount that this customer owed to the company for all of their purchases to date. The outstanding balance which has now been paid was $90000.

DR Cash $90,000    CR Accounts Receivable $90,000

The cash (asset) account has increased, and the accounts receivable (asset) account has decreased by $90,000.

780 Pharma Drug Company Ltd. is an organization which specializes in providing their customers with medications. Today Pharma Drug Company Ltd. sold 36700 batches of pills which had a 30% mark-up. They had originally been bought from their suppliers for a unit cost of $2920.

DR Accounts Receivable $139,313,200    DR Cost of Goods Sold $107,164,000
CR Sales $139,313,200    CR Inventory $107,164,000

This transaction increases the accounts receivable (asset) account, the sales (revenue) account, and the cost of goods sold (expense) account. The inventory (asset) account has decreased. 36700 batches of pills x $2,920 = $107,164,000. The 30% markup applies to the sales and accounts receivable amounts, i.e. $107,164,000 x 1.30 = $139,313,200

781 NBG Media Corporation is a market leader that is well-known for their brand of broadcasting services for advertising agencies. Today, NBG Media Corporation has paid cash to their supplier to fully pay off their account payable balance, which was $89000.

DR Accounts Payable $89,000    CR Cash $89,000

The accounts payable (liability) and cash (asset) accounts have both increased by $89,000.

782    NY Fitness is an organization which specializes in providing their customers with gym memberships for professional sports teams. This month, NY Fitness paid for 1 month of rent for their company's office space. Each month, the rent owing was $12000.

DR Rent expense $12,000    CR Accounts Payable $12,000

The rent (expense) and the accounts payable (liability) accounts are both increased by one month's worth of rent, which is $12,000.

783    Kola-Nut Ltd is a company which offers their customers a wide selection of soft drinks. Today, Kola-Nut Ltd received an upfront payment for 5270 batches of soda bottles which will be provided to the customer 6 months from now. The payment for each was $1300.

DR Cash $6,851,000    CR Unearned Revenue $6,851,000

The cash (asset) and the unearned revenue (liability) accounts have both increased by: 5270 batches of soda bottles x $1,300 = $6,851,000

784    Payday Now provides their customers with short-term loan arrangements. This month, Payday Now has estimated that 20% of the accounts receivable might not end up being collectable, based on past experience. The accounts receivable will need to be adjusted from its current balance of $26000.

DR Bad Debt expense $5,200    CR Allowance for Doubtful Accounts $5,200

The bad debts (expense) and the allowance for doubtful accounts (contra-asset) have both increased by: 20% x $26,000 = $5,200

785    Mr. Mop is a market leader that is well-known for their brand of household cleaners. This December, Mr. Mop has paid each of the company's 1100 owners an annual dividend in the amount of $9000.

DR Retained Earnings $9,900,000    CR Cash $9,900,000

The retained earnings (equity) and the cash accounts have both decreased by: 1100 owners x $9,000 = $9,900,000

786 A to Z Event Guru Ltd is a market leader that is well-known for their brand of start-to-finish event planning services for large gatherings. This month, A to Z Event Guru Ltd paid for 1 month of rent for their company's office space. Each month, the rent owing was $19000.

DR Rent expense $19,000    CR Accounts Payable $19,000

The rent (expense) and the accounts payable (liability) accounts are both increased by one month's worth of rent, which is $19,000.

787 Paytech Ltd sells various payroll transaction processing services. Paytech Ltd has just purchased a building using cash, which has an expected useful life of 30 years, and which had a total cost of $292000.

DR Building $292,000    CR Cash $292,000

The building (asset) account has increased, and the cash (asset) account has decreased by: $292,000. The useful life does not affect this original accounting entry, but it will be used to calculate depreciation of the asset in the future.

788 Air America offers their customers a wide range of global flights. Air America has just provided 1000 large orders which had been paid for in advance last year. Each order was in the amount of $2400.

DR Unearned Revenue $2,400,000    CR Sales $2,400,000

The unearned revenue (liability) account has decreased and the and the sales (revenue) account has increased by: 10/1 /2arge orders x $2,400 = $2,400,000

789 Pharma Drug Company Ltd. sells several different types of medications. Pharma Drug Company Ltd. has just purchased a building using cash, which has an expected useful life of 30 years, and which had a total cost of $709000.

DR Building $709,000    CR Cash $709,000

The building (asset) account has increased, and the cash (asset) account has decreased by: $709,000. The useful life does not affect this original accounting entry, but it will be used to calculate depreciation of the asset in the future.

790 Comedy 253 is a company which offers their customers a wide selection of live performances of stand-up comedy. This year, Comedy 253 has provided 2100 shows each of which earned revenues of $2680.

DR Accounts Receivable $5,628,000    CR Sales $5,628,000

The accounts receivable (asset) and the sales (revenue) accounts have both increased by: 21/1 /2hows x $2,680 = $5,628,000

791     David & Johnson sells several different types of legal services.  David & Johnson has just provided 1300 large orders which had been paid for in advance last year. Each order was in the amount of $2400.

DR Unearned Revenue $3,120,000    CR Sales $3,120,000

The unearned revenue (liability) account has decreased and the and the sales (revenue) account has increased by: 13/1 /2arge orders x $2,400 = $3,120,000

792     Kola-Nut Ltd is a corporation which sells soft drinks.  Today Kola-Nut Ltd sold 19300 batches of soda bottles which had a 30% mark-up. They had originally been bought from their suppliers for a unit cost of $2920.

DR Accounts Receivable $73,262,800    DR Cost of Goods Sold $56,356,000
CR Sales $73,262,800    CR Inventory $56,356,000

This transaction increases the accounts receivable (asset) account, the sales (revenue) account, and the cost of goods sold (expense) account. The inventory (asset) account has decreased. 19300 batches of soda bottles x $2,920 = $56,356,000.  The 30% markup applies to the sales and accounts receivable amounts, i.e. $56,356,000 x 1.30 = $73,262,800

793     Pharma Drug Company Ltd. is a corporation which sells medications.  This week, Pharma Drug Company Ltd. purchased 3900 batches of pills which were placed into the warehouse, and which had a per-unit cost of $2500.

DR Inventory $9,750,000    CR Accounts Payable $9,750,000

There was an increase in the inventory (asset) account, and also an increase in the accounts payable (liability) account. 3900 batches of pills x $2,500 = $9,750,000

794     Club Disco is an organization which specializes in providing their customers with dance venue rentals for large family gatherings.  This year, Club Disco has provided 2300 evening rentals each of which earned revenues of $1300.

DR Accounts Receivable $2,990,000    CR Sales $2,990,000

The accounts receivable (asset) and the sales (revenue) accounts have both increased by: 23/1 /2vening rentals x $1,300 = $2,990,000

795    Comedy 253 is a privately-held corporation which focuses on their niche of premium live performances of stand-up comedy. This month, Comedy 253 paid for 1 month of rent for their company's office space. Each month, the rent owing was $26000.

DR Rent expense $26,000    CR Accounts Payable $26,000

The rent (expense) and the accounts payable (liability) accounts are both increased by one month's worth of rent, which is $26,000.

796    Kola-Nut Ltd is an organization which specializes in providing their customers with soft drinks. Today Kola-Nut Ltd sold 26600 batches of soda bottles which had a 30% mark-up. They had originally been bought from their suppliers for a unit cost of $2310.

DR Accounts Receivable $79,879,800    DR Cost of Goods Sold $61,446,000
CR Sales $79,879,800    CR Inventory $61,446,000

This transaction increases the accounts receivable (asset) account, the sales (revenue) account, and the cost of goods sold (expense) account. The inventory (asset) account has decreased. 26600 batches of soda bottles x $2,310 = $61,446,000.  The 30% markup applies to the sales and accounts receivable amounts, i.e. $61,446,000 x 1.30 = $79,879,800

797    Pharma Drug Company Ltd. is a privately-held corporation which focuses on their niche of premium medications.  This month, Pharma Drug Company Ltd. accepted 7800 batches of pills which were returned by customers. These products had been marked up by 35% and they had originally been bought at a per-unit cost of $1700.

DR Sales Returns $17,901,000    DR Inventory $13,260,000    CR Accounts Receivable $17,901,000    CR Cost of Goods Sold $13,260,000

This transaction increases the sales returns (contra-revenue) account, and the inventory (asset) account. The accounts receivable (asset) account and the cost of goods sold (expense) account have both decreased. 7800 batches of pills x $1,700 = $13,260,000. The 35% markup applies to the sales returns and accounts receivable amounts, i.e. $13,260,000 x 1.35 = $17,901,000

798 Hogtown Records is a company which offers their customers a wide selection of audio services for local musicians to record their music albums. This year, Hogtown Records has provided 2300 albums each of which earned revenues of $1010.

DR Accounts Receivable $2,323,000    CR Sales $2,323,000

The accounts receivable (asset) and the sales (revenue) accounts have both increased by: 23/1 /2lbums x $1,010 = $2,323,000

799 AC&C Ltd. sells several different types of cell phone plans. This December, AC&C Ltd. recognized 1 year of depreciation on a building which had a total useful life of 25 years, and which had originally been bought for $891000.

DR Depreciation expense $35,640    CR Accumulated Depreciation $35,640

The depreciation (expense) account and the accumulated depreciation (contra-asset) accounts have both increased by: $891,000 divided by 25 years = $35,640 depreciation per year.

800 Pharma Drug Company Ltd. sells various medications. Today, Pharma Drug Company Ltd. received an upfront payment for 2700 batches of pills which will be provided to the customer 6 months from now. The payment for each was $2000.

DR Cash $5,400,000    CR Unearned Revenue $5,400,000

The cash (asset) and the unearned revenue (liability) accounts have both increased by: 2700 batches of pills x $2,000 = $5,400,000

801 AC&C Ltd. is a corporation which sells cell phone plans. AC&C Ltd. has just received a cash payment for the full amount that this customer owed to the company for all of their purchases to date. The outstanding balance which has now been paid was $77000.

DR Cash $77,000    CR Accounts Receivable $77,000

The cash (asset) account has increased, and the accounts receivable (asset) account has decreased by $77,000.

802 Sprike Inc provides their customers with athletic apparel. This month, Sprike Inc paid for 1 month of rent for their company's office space. Each month, the rent owing was $10000.

DR Rent expense $10,000    CR Accounts Payable $10,000

The rent (expense) and the accounts payable (liability) accounts are both increased by one month's worth of rent, which is $10,000.

803     McGerald's is an organization which specializes in providing their customers with fast food meals. This December, McGerald's recognized 1 year of depreciation on a building which had a total useful life of 25 years, and which had originally been bought for $46000.

DR Depreciation expense $1,840    CR Accumulated Depreciation $1,840

The depreciation (expense) account and the accumulated depreciation (contra-asset) accounts have both increased by: $46,000 divided by 25 years = $1,840 depreciation per year.

804     McGerald's is a market leader that is well-known for their brand of fast food meals. Today, McGerald's has paid cash to their supplier to fully pay off their account payable balance, which was $80000.

DR Accounts Payable $80,000    CR Cash $80,000

The accounts payable (liability) and cash (asset) accounts have both increased by $80,000.

805     LA Met Theatre Company is an organization which specializes in providing their customers with live theatrical performances. This month, LA Met Theatre Company paid for 1 month of rent for their company's office space. Each month, the rent owing was $12000.

DR Rent expense $12,000    CR Accounts Payable $12,000

The rent (expense) and the accounts payable (liability) accounts are both increased by one month's worth of rent, which is $12,000.

806     Pharma Drug Company Ltd. is a privately-held corporation which focuses on their niche of premium medications. Today Pharma Drug Company Ltd. sold 12100 batches of pills which had a 30% mark-up. They had originally been bought from their suppliers for a unit cost of $1630.

DR Accounts Receivable $25,639,900    DR Cost of Goods Sold $19,723,000
CR Sales $25,639,900    CR Inventory $19,723,000

This transaction increases the accounts receivable (asset) account, the sales (revenue) account, and the cost of goods sold (expense) account. The inventory (asset) account has decreased. 12100 batches of pills x $1,630 = $19,723,000. The 30% markup applies to the sales and accounts receivable amounts, i.e. $19,723,000 x 1.30 = $25,639,900

807 Air America is a market leader that is well-known for their brand of global flights. This December, Air America recognized 1 year of depreciation on equipment which had a total useful life of 10 years, and which had originally cost $170000.

DR Depreciation expense $17,000   CR Accumulated Depreciation $17,000

The depreciation (expense) account and the accumulated depreciation (contra-asset) accounts have both increased by: $170,000 divided by 10 years = $17,000 depreciation per year.

808 NY Fitness sells several different types of gym memberships for professional sports teams. This month, NY Fitness paid for 1 month of rent for their company's office space. Each month, the rent owing was $26000.

DR Rent expense $26,000   CR Accounts Payable $26,000

The rent (expense) and the accounts payable (liability) accounts are both increased by one month's worth of rent, which is $26,000.

809 NBG Media Corporation offers their customers a wide range of broadcasting services for advertising agencies. This month, NBG Media Corporation must amortize 1 month worth of utility bills which they had prepaid at the beginning of the year. The amount that they had paid upfront for the year was $45600.

DR Utilities expense $3,800   CR Prepaid Expense $3,800

The utilities (expense) account has increased and the prepaid expense (asset) account has decreased by: $45,600 for the year, divided by 12 months = $3,800

810 Pharma Drug Company Ltd. offers their customers a wide range of medications. This month, Pharma Drug Company Ltd. accepted 14300 batches of pills which were returned by customers. These products had been marked up by 35% and they had originally been bought at a per-unit cost of $1600.

DR Sales Returns $30,888,000   DR Inventory $22,880,000   CR Accounts Receivable $30,888,000   CR Cost of Goods Sold $22,880,000

This transaction increases the sales returns (contra-revenue) account, and the inventory (asset) account. The accounts receivable (asset) account and the cost of goods sold (expense) account have both decreased. 14300 batches of pills x $1,600 = $22,880,000. The 35% markup applies to the sales returns and accounts receivable amounts, i.e. $22,880,000 x 1.35 = $30,888,000

811   Mr. Mop offers their customers a wide range of household cleaners. This month, Mr. Mop paid for 1 month of rent for their company's office space. Each month, the rent owing was $16000.

DR Rent expense $16,000    CR Accounts Payable $16,000

The rent (expense) and the accounts payable (liability) accounts are both increased by one month's worth of rent, which is $16,000.

812   Grand Convention Ltd is a corporation which sells banquet hall rentals for corporate meetings. This year, Grand Convention Ltd has provided 2100 corporate events each of which earned revenues of $2240.

DR Accounts Receivable $4,704,000    CR Sales $4,704,000

The accounts receivable (asset) and the sales (revenue) accounts have both increased by: 21/1 /2orporate events x $2,240 = $4,704,000

813   Club Disco is a privately-held corporation which focuses on their niche of premium dance venue rentals for large family gatherings. This December, Club Disco recognized 1 year of depreciation on equipment which had a total useful life of 10 years, and which had originally cost $180000.

DR Depreciation expense $18,000    CR Accumulated Depreciation $18,000

The depreciation (expense) account and the accumulated depreciation (contra-asset) accounts have both increased by: $180,000 divided by 10 years = $18,000 depreciation per year.

814   Club Disco is a corporation which sells dance venue rentals for large family gatherings. Today, Club Disco received payment upfront for 1000 large orders which will not be provided until early next year. Each order was in the amount of $1400.

DR Cash $1,400,000    CR Unearned Revenue $1,400,000

The cash (asset) and the unearned revenue (liability) accounts have both increased by: 1000 large orders x $1,400 = $1,400,000

815     Kola-Nut Ltd is a corporation which sells soft drinks. This week, Kola-Nut Ltd purchased 1400 batches of soda bottles which were placed into the warehouse, and which had a per-unit cost of $2800.

DR Inventory $3,920,000    CR Accounts Payable $3,920,000

There was an increase in the inventory (asset) account, and also an increase in the accounts payable (liability) account. 1400 batches of soda bottles x $2,800 = $3,920,000

816     Jameson & Jameson provides their customers with soap products. This January, Jameson & Jameson has made an advance payment to cover the next 12 months of utility bills, which have a monthly cost of $1300.

DR Prepaid Expense $15,600    CR Cash $15,600

The prepaid expense (asset) account has increased, and the cash (asset) account has decreased by: 12 months x $1,300 per month = $15,600 for the year.

817     Mr. Mop offers their customers a wide range of household cleaners. This month, Mr. Mop must amortize 1 month worth of utility bills which they had prepaid at the beginning of the year. The amount that they had paid upfront for the year was $19200.

DR Utilities expense $1,600    CR Prepaid Expense $1,600

The utilities (expense) account has increased and the prepaid expense (asset) account has decreased by: $19,200 for the year, divided by 12 months = $1,600

818     David & Johnson offers their customers a wide range of legal services. Today, David & Johnson received payment upfront for 1600 large orders which will not be provided until early next year. Each order was in the amount of $1500.

DR Cash $2,400,000    CR Unearned Revenue $2,400,000

The cash (asset) and the unearned revenue (liability) accounts have both increased by: 1600 large orders x $1,500 = $2,400,000

819    Kola-Nut Ltd provides their customers with soft drinks.  This December, Kola-Nut Ltd recognized 1 year of depreciation on a building which had a total useful life of 25 years, and which had originally been bought for $215000.

DR Depreciation expense $8,600    CR Accumulated Depreciation $8,600

The depreciation (expense) account and the accumulated depreciation (contra-asset) accounts have both increased by: $215,000 divided by 25 years = $8,600 depreciation per year.

820    David & Johnson provides their customers with legal services.  This month, David & Johnson paid for 1 month of rent for their company's office space. Each month, the rent owing was $25000.

DR Rent expense $25,000    CR Accounts Payable $25,000

The rent (expense) and the accounts payable (liability) accounts are both increased by one month's worth of rent, which is $25,000.

821    A to Z Event Guru Ltd sells several different types of start-to-finish event planning services for large gatherings.  This December, A to Z Event Guru Ltd recognized 1 year of depreciation on a building which had a total useful life of 25 years, and which had originally been bought for $314000.

DR Depreciation expense $12,560    CR Accumulated Depreciation $12,560

The depreciation (expense) account and the accumulated depreciation (contra-asset) accounts have both increased by: $314,000 divided by 25 years = $12,560 depreciation per year.

822    Pharma Drug Company Ltd. is a company which offers their customers a wide selection of medications.  This month, Pharma Drug Company Ltd. has estimated that 20% of the accounts receivable might not end up being collectable, based on past experience. The accounts receivable will need to be adjusted from its current balance of $102000.

DR Bad Debt expense $20,400    CR Allowance for Doubtful Accounts $20,400

The bad debts (expense) and the allowance for doubtful accounts (contra-asset) have both increased by: 20% x $102,000 = $20,400

823    Mount Tessory Academy is a company which offers their customers a wide selection of private school education. This December, Mount Tessory Academy recognized 1 year of depreciation on a building which had a total useful life of 25 years, and which had originally been bought for $219000.

DR Depreciation expense $8,760    CR Accumulated Depreciation $8,760

The depreciation (expense) account and the accumulated depreciation (contra-asset) accounts have both increased by: $219,000 divided by 25 years = $8,760 depreciation per year.

824    Fairway Malls is an organization which specializes in providing their customers with retail spaces in their shopping centers. This month, Fairway Malls paid 1 monthly loan repayment towards their long-term note payable. The interest portion was 60% of the payment. The total amount paid in cash was $26000.

DR Interest Expense $15,600    DR Loan Payable $10,400    CR Cash $26,000

The interest (expense) account has increased by $26,000 x 0.6 = $15,600. The loan payable (liability) has decreased by $26,000 x 0.4 = $10,400. The cash (asset) account has decreased by the full amount of the payment, which is $26,000

825    Air America offers their customers a wide range of global flights. This December, Air America has paid each of the company's 1900 owners an annual dividend in the amount of $12000.

DR Retained Earnings $22,800,000    CR Cash $22,800,000

The retained earnings (equity) and the cash accounts have both decreased by: 1900 owners x $12,000 = $22,800,000

826    Toyonda sells several different types of cars. This December, Toyonda recognized 1 year of depreciation on a building which had a total useful life of 25 years, and which had originally been bought for $385000.

DR Depreciation expense $15,400    CR Accumulated Depreciation $15,400

The depreciation (expense) account and the accumulated depreciation (contra-asset) accounts have both increased by: $385,000 divided by 25 years = $15,400 depreciation per year.

827    Mr. Mop sells various household cleaners.  Today, Mr. Mop bought equipment which has a 5 year useful life, and which had a cost of $22000.

DR Equipment $22,000    CR Accounts Payable $22,000

The equipment (asset) and the accounts payable (liability) accounts have both increased by: $22,000. The useful life does not affect this original accounting entry, but it will be used to calculate depreciation of the asset in the future.

828    Kola-Nut Ltd is an organization which specializes in providing their customers with soft drinks.  Today Kola-Nut Ltd signed up for a loan with a 5% interest rate, and so the bank immediately transferred cash to the company in the amount of $32000.

DR Cash $32,000    CR Loan Payable $32,000

The cash (asset) and the loan payable (liability) accounts have both increased by: $32,000. The interest rate does not affect this initial accounting entry, but it will be used for the calculation of interest expense when repayments are made in the future toward this loan.

829    A to Z Event Guru Ltd is a corporation which sells start-to-finish event planning services for large gatherings.  Today A to Z Event Guru Ltd signed up for a loan with a 5% interest rate, and so the bank immediately transferred cash to the company in the amount of $77000.

DR Cash $77,000    CR Loan Payable $77,000

The cash (asset) and the loan payable (liability) accounts have both increased by: $77,000. The interest rate does not affect this initial accounting entry, but it will be used for the calculation of interest expense when repayments are made in the future toward this loan.

830    Kola-Nut Ltd is a corporation which sells soft drinks.  This week, Kola-Nut Ltd purchased 4630 batches of soda bottles which were placed into the warehouse, and which had a per-unit cost of $2700.

DR Inventory $12,501,000    CR Accounts Payable $12,501,000

There was an increase in the inventory (asset) account, and also an increase in the accounts payable (liability) account. 4630 batches of soda bottles x $2,700 = $12,501,000

831    Fairway Malls provides their customers with retail spaces in their shopping centers. This month, Fairway Malls must amortize 1 month worth of utility bills which they had prepaid at the beginning of the year. The amount that they had paid upfront for the year was $13200.

DR Utilities expense $1,100    CR Prepaid Expense $1,100

The utilities (expense) account has increased and the prepaid expense (asset) account has decreased by: $13,200 for the year, divided by 12 months = $1,100

832    NBG Media Corporation provides their customers with broadcasting services for advertising agencies. Today, NBG Media Corporation bought equipment which has a 5 year useful life, and which had a cost of $15000.

DR Equipment $15,000    CR Accounts Payable $15,000

The equipment (asset) and the accounts payable (liability) accounts have both increased by: $15,000. The useful life does not affect this original accounting entry, but it will be used to calculate depreciation of the asset in the future.

833    Pharma Drug Company Ltd. is a company which offers their customers a wide selection of medications. Today, Pharma Drug Company Ltd. received an upfront payment for 3360 batches of pills which will be provided to the customer 6 months from now. The payment for each was $2800.

DR Cash $9,408,000    CR Unearned Revenue $9,408,000

The cash (asset) and the unearned revenue (liability) accounts have both increased by: 3360 batches of pills x $2,800 = $9,408,000

834    NBG Media Corporation is a privately-held corporation which focuses on their niche of premium broadcasting services for advertising agencies. This December, NBG Media Corporation recognized 1 year of depreciation on a building which had a total useful life of 25 years, and which had originally been bought for $845000.

DR Depreciation expense $33,800    CR Accumulated Depreciation $33,800

The depreciation (expense) account and the accumulated depreciation (contra-asset) accounts have both increased by: $845,000 divided by 25 years = $33,800 depreciation per year.

835    Mr. Mop offers their customers a wide range of household cleaners.  This month, Mr. Mop paid for 1 month of rent for their company's office space. Each month, the rent owing was $8000.

DR Rent expense $8,000    CR Accounts Payable $8,000

The rent (expense) and the accounts payable (liability) accounts are both increased by one month's worth of rent, which is $8,000.

836    Sprike Inc is a privately-held corporation which focuses on their niche of premium athletic apparel.  This month, Sprike Inc paid for 1 month of rent for the warehouse room, which has a monthly cost of $2300.

DR Rent expense $2,300    CR Accounts Payable $2,300

The rent (expense) and the accounts payable (liability) accounts are both increased by one month's worth of rent, which is $2,300.

837    NY Fitness offers their customers a wide range of gym memberships for professional sports teams.  This December, NY Fitness recognized 1 year of depreciation on a building which had a total useful life of 25 years, and which had originally been bought for $158000.

DR Depreciation expense $6,320    CR Accumulated Depreciation $6,320

The depreciation (expense) account and the accumulated depreciation (contra-asset) accounts have both increased by: $158,000 divided by 25 years = $6,320 depreciation per year.

838    Cirque du Lune sells several different types of circus performances.  This year, Cirque du Lune has provided 2000 shows each of which earned revenues of $1360.

DR Accounts Receivable $2,720,000    CR Sales $2,720,000

The accounts receivable (asset) and the sales (revenue) accounts have both increased by: 20/1 /2hows x $1,360 = $2,720,000

839    Mr. Mop provides their customers with household cleaners.  This month, Mr. Mop paid for 1 month of rent for their company's office space. Each month, the rent owing was $8000.

DR Rent expense $8,000    CR Accounts Payable $8,000

The rent (expense) and the accounts payable (liability) accounts are both increased by one month's worth of rent, which is $8,000.

840  Jameson & Jameson offers their customers a wide range of soap products. Today Jameson & Jameson sold 41900 truckloads of bars of soap which had a 30% mark-up. They had originally been bought from their suppliers for a unit cost of $1670.

DR Accounts Receivable $90,964,900    DR Cost of Goods Sold $69,973,000
CR Sales $90,964,900    CR Inventory $69,973,000

This transaction increases the accounts receivable (asset) account, the sales (revenue) account, and the cost of goods sold (expense) account. The inventory (asset) account has decreased. 41900 truckloads of bars of soap x $1,670 = $69,973,000. The 30% markup applies to the sales and accounts receivable amounts, i.e. $69,973,000 x 1.30 = $90,964,900

841  Cirque du Lune is a privately-held corporation which focuses on their niche of premium circus performances. This year, Cirque du Lune has provided 1000 shows each of which earned revenues of $2910.

DR Accounts Receivable $2,910,000    CR Sales $2,910,000

The accounts receivable (asset) and the sales (revenue) accounts have both increased by: 10/1 /2hows x $2,910 = $2,910,000

842  Fairway Malls provides their customers with retail spaces in their shopping centers. Today Fairway Malls signed up for a loan with a 5% interest rate, and so the bank immediately transferred cash to the company in the amount of $102000.

DR Cash $102,000    CR Loan Payable $102,000

The cash (asset) and the loan payable (liability) accounts have both increased by: $102,000. The interest rate does not affect this initial accounting entry, but it will be used for the calculation of interest expense when repayments are made in the future toward this loan.

843  Pharma Drug Company Ltd. is a company which offers their customers a wide selection of medications. This week, Pharma Drug Company Ltd. purchased 4260 batches of pills which were placed into the warehouse, and which had a per-unit cost of $2200.

DR Inventory $9,372,000    CR Accounts Payable $9,372,000

There was an increase in the inventory (asset) account, and also an increase in the accounts payable (liability) account. 4260 batches of pills x $2,200 = $9,372,000

844     AC&C Ltd. sells various cell phone plans. AC&C Ltd. has just provided 1900 large orders which had been paid for in advance last year. Each order was in the amount of $1000.

DR Unearned Revenue $1,900,000    CR Sales $1,900,000

The unearned revenue (liability) account has decreased and the and the sales (revenue) account has increased by: 19/1 /2arge orders x $1,000 = $1,900,000

845     Mr. Mop sells various household cleaners. Today, Mr. Mop received an upfront payment for 1120 tons of cleaning solution which will be provided to the customer 6 months from now. The payment for each was $1000.

DR Cash $1,120,000    CR Unearned Revenue $1,120,000

The cash (asset) and the unearned revenue (liability) accounts have both increased by: 1120 tons of cleaning solution x $1,000 = $1,120,000

846     Grand Convention Ltd sells several different types of banquet hall rentals for corporate meetings. Grand Convention Ltd has just purchased a building using cash, which has an expected useful life of 30 years, and which had a total cost of $424000.

DR Building $424,000    CR Cash $424,000

The building (asset) account has increased, and the cash (asset) account has decreased by: $424,000. The useful life does not affect this original accounting entry, but it will be used to calculate depreciation of the asset in the future.

847     Jameson & Jameson is a corporation which sells soap products. This week, Jameson & Jameson purchased 1470 truckloads of bars of soap which were placed into the warehouse, and which had a per-unit cost of $1400.

DR Inventory $2,058,000    CR Accounts Payable $2,058,000

There was an increase in the inventory (asset) account, and also an increase in the accounts payable (liability) account. 1470 truckloads of bars of soap x $1,400 = $2,058,000

848     NY Fitness is an organization which specializes in providing their customers with gym memberships for professional sports teams. This year, NY Fitness has provided 2300 team memberships each of which earned revenues of $1690.

DR Accounts Receivable $3,887,000    CR Sales $3,887,000

The accounts receivable (asset) and the sales (revenue) accounts have both increased by: 23/1 /2eam memberships x $1,690 = $3,887,000

849     Pharma Drug Company Ltd. is a privately-held corporation which focuses on their niche of premium medications. Today, Pharma Drug Company Ltd. received an upfront payment for 2260 batches of pills which will be provided to the customer 6 months from now. The payment for each was $2600.

DR Cash $5,876,000    CR Unearned Revenue $5,876,000

The cash (asset) and the unearned revenue (liability) accounts have both increased by: 2260 batches of pills x $2,600 = $5,876,000

850     David & Johnson is a privately-held corporation which focuses on their niche of premium legal services. Today, David & Johnson received payment upfront for 2300 large orders which will not be provided until early next year. Each order was in the amount of $1700.

DR Cash $3,910,000    CR Unearned Revenue $3,910,000

The cash (asset) and the unearned revenue (liability) accounts have both increased by: 2300 large orders x $1,700 = $3,910,000

851     AC&C Ltd. provides their customers with cell phone plans. This year, AC&C Ltd. has provided 1600 monthly cell phone service each of which earned revenues of $2800.

DR Accounts Receivable $4,480,000    CR Sales $4,480,000

The accounts receivable (asset) and the sales (revenue) accounts have both increased by: 16/1 /2onthly cell phone service x $2,800 = $4,480,000

852     NY Fitness is a market leader that is well-known for their brand of gym memberships for professional sports teams. Today, NY Fitness received payment upfront for 2300 large orders which will not be provided until early next year. Each order was in the amount of $2100.

DR Cash $4,830,000    CR Unearned Revenue $4,830,000

The cash (asset) and the unearned revenue (liability) accounts have both increased by: 2300 large orders x $2,100 = $4,830,000

853 AC&C Ltd. is a market leader that is well-known for their brand of cell phone plans. Today, AC&C Ltd. has paid cash to their supplier to fully pay off their account payable balance, which was $18000.

DR Accounts Payable $18,000   CR Cash $18,000

The accounts payable (liability) and cash (asset) accounts have both increased by $18,000.

854 Toyonda sells various cars. This January, Toyonda has made an advance payment to cover the next 12 months of utility bills, which have a monthly cost of $2200.

DR Prepaid Expense $26,400   CR Cash $26,400

The prepaid expense (asset) account has increased, and the cash (asset) account has decreased by: 12 months x $2,200 per month = $26,400 for the year.

855 Pharma Drug Company Ltd. is a corporation which sells medications. This week, Pharma Drug Company Ltd. purchased 4580 batches of pills which were placed into the warehouse, and which had a per-unit cost of $1100.

DR Inventory $5,038,000   CR Accounts Payable $5,038,000

There was an increase in the inventory (asset) account, and also an increase in the accounts payable (liability) account. 4580 batches of pills x $1,100 = $5,038,000

856 Comedy 253 offers their customers a wide range of live performances of stand-up comedy. Today, Comedy 253 bought equipment which has a 5 year useful life, and which had a cost of $18000.

DR Equipment $18,000   CR Accounts Payable $18,000

The equipment (asset) and the accounts payable (liability) accounts have both increased by: $18,000. The useful life does not affect this original accounting entry, but it will be used to calculate depreciation of the asset in the future.

857    Grand Convention Ltd is a market leader that is well-known for their brand of banquet hall rentals for corporate meetings. This month, Grand Convention Ltd has estimated that 15% of the accounts receivable might not end up being collectable, based on past experience. The accounts receivable will need to be adjusted from its current balance of $85000.

DR Bad Debt expense $12,750    CR Allowance for Doubtful Accounts $12,750

The bad debts (expense) and the allowance for doubtful accounts (contra-asset) have both increased by: 15% x $85,000 = $12,750

858    Grand Convention Ltd provides their customers with banquet hall rentals for corporate meetings. This month, Grand Convention Ltd must amortize 1 month worth of utility bills which they had prepaid at the beginning of the year. The amount that they had paid upfront for the year was $37200.

DR Utilities expense $3,100    CR Prepaid Expense $3,100

The utilities (expense) account has increased and the prepaid expense (asset) account has decreased by: $37,200 for the year, divided by 12 months = $3,100

859    Kola-Nut Ltd sells several different types of soft drinks. This month, Kola-Nut Ltd accepted 18400 batches of soda bottles which were returned by customers. These products had been marked up by 35% and they had originally been bought at a per-unit cost of $1300.

DR Sales Returns $32,292,000    DR Inventory $23,920,000    CR Accounts Receivable $32,292,000    CR Cost of Goods Sold $23,920,000

This transaction increases the sales returns (contra-revenue) account, and the inventory (asset) account. The accounts receivable (asset) account and the cost of goods sold (expense) account have both decreased. 18400 batches of soda bottles x $1,300 = $23,920,000. The 35% markup applies to the sales returns and accounts receivable amounts, i.e. $23,920,000 x 1.35 = $32,292,000

860    Cirque du Lune offers their customers a wide range of circus performances. This month, Cirque du Lune has estimated that 25% of the accounts receivable might not end up being collectable, based on past experience. The accounts receivable will need to be adjusted from its current balance of $48000.

DR Bad Debt expense $12,000    CR Allowance for Doubtful Accounts $12,000

The bad debts (expense) and the allowance for doubtful accounts (contra-asset) have both increased by: 25% x $48,000 = $12,000

861 Club Disco is a privately-held corporation which focuses on their niche of premium dance venue rentals for large family gatherings. This December, Club Disco recognized 1 year of depreciation on equipment which had a total useful life of 10 years, and which had originally cost $180000.

DR Depreciation expense $18,000    CR Accumulated Depreciation $18,000

The depreciation (expense) account and the accumulated depreciation (contra-asset) accounts have both increased by: $180,000 divided by 10 years = $18,000 depreciation per year.

862 Pharma Drug Company Ltd. provides their customers with medications. This month, Pharma Drug Company Ltd. has estimated that 25% of the accounts receivable might not end up being collectable, based on past experience. The accounts receivable will need to be adjusted from its current balance of $89000.

DR Bad Debt expense $22,250    CR Allowance for Doubtful Accounts $22,250

The bad debts (expense) and the allowance for doubtful accounts (contra-asset) have both increased by: 25% x $89,000 = $22,250

863 Hogtown Records sells several different types of audio services for local musicians to record their music albums. This January, Hogtown Records has made an advance payment to cover the next 12 months of utility bills, which have a monthly cost of $1000.

DR Prepaid Expense $12,000    CR Cash $12,000

The prepaid expense (asset) account has increased, and the cash (asset) account has decreased by: 12 months x $1,000 per month = $12,000 for the year.

864 Comedy 253 is a privately-held corporation which focuses on their niche of premium live performances of stand-up comedy. Comedy 253 has just received a cash payment for the full amount that this customer owed to the company for all of their purchases to date. The outstanding balance which has now been paid was $91000.

DR Cash $91,000    CR Accounts Receivable $91,000

The cash (asset) account has increased, and the accounts receivable (asset) account has decreased by $91,000.

865 Kola-Nut Ltd is a corporation which sells soft drinks. Today Kola-Nut Ltd sold 4600 batches of soda bottles which had a 30% mark-up. They had originally been bought from their suppliers for a unit cost of $2520.

DR Accounts Receivable $15,069,600    DR Cost of Goods Sold $11,592,000
CR Sales $15,069,600    CR Inventory $11,592,000

This transaction increases the accounts receivable (asset) account, the sales (revenue) account, and the cost of goods sold (expense) account. The inventory (asset) account has decreased. 4600 batches of soda bottles x $2,520 = $11,592,000. The 30% markup applies to the sales and accounts receivable amounts, i.e. $11,592,000 x 1.30 = $15,069,600

866 Payday Now is a privately-held corporation which focuses on their niche of premium short-term loan arrangements. Today, Payday Now received payment upfront for 1800 large orders which will not be provided until early next year. Each order was in the amount of $2700.

DR Cash $4,860,000    CR Unearned Revenue $4,860,000

The cash (asset) and the unearned revenue (liability) accounts have both increased by: 1800 large orders x $2,700 = $4,860,000

867 AC&C Ltd. is a privately-held corporation which focuses on their niche of premium cell phone plans. This month, AC&C Ltd. must amortize 1 month worth of utility bills which they had prepaid at the beginning of the year. The amount that they had paid upfront for the year was $19200.

DR Utilities expense $1,600    CR Prepaid Expense $1,600

The utilities (expense) account has increased and the prepaid expense (asset) account has decreased by: $19,200 for the year, divided by 12 months = $1,600

868 Payday Now is a privately-held corporation which focuses on their niche of premium short-term loan arrangements. This January, Payday Now has made an advance payment to cover the next 12 months of utility bills, which have a monthly cost of $1000.

DR Prepaid Expense $12,000    CR Cash $12,000

The prepaid expense (asset) account has increased, and the cash (asset) account has decreased by: 12 months x $1,000 per month = $12,000 for the year.

869 NBG Media Corporation sells several different types of broadcasting services for advertising agencies. NBG Media Corporation has just received a cash payment for the full amount that this customer owed to the company for all of their purchases to date. The outstanding balance which has now been paid was $35000.

DR Cash $35,000    CR Accounts Receivable $35,000

The cash (asset) account has increased, and the accounts receivable (asset) account has decreased by $35,000.

870 Kola-Nut Ltd sells several different types of soft drinks. This month, Kola-Nut Ltd paid 1 monthly loan repayment towards their long-term note payable. The interest portion was 60% of the payment. The total amount paid in cash was $19000.

DR Interest Expense $11,400    DR Loan Payable $7,600    CR Cash $19,000

The interest (expense) account has increased by $19,000 x 0.6 = $11,400. The loan payable (liability) has decreased by $19,000 x 0.4 = $7,600. The cash (asset) account has decreased by the full amount of the payment, which is $19,000

871 Hogtown Records provides their customers with audio services for local musicians to record their music albums. This month, Hogtown Records paid for 1 month of rent for their company's office space. Each month, the rent owing was $21000.

DR Rent expense $21,000    CR Accounts Payable $21,000

The rent (expense) and the accounts payable (liability) accounts are both increased by one month's worth of rent, which is $21,000.

872 Toyonda provides their customers with cars. Today, Toyonda bought equipment which has a 5 year useful life, and which had a cost of $20000.

DR Equipment $20,000    CR Accounts Payable $20,000

The equipment (asset) and the accounts payable (liability) accounts have both increased by: $20,000. The useful life does not affect this original accounting entry, but it will be used to calculate depreciation of the asset in the future.

873 Payday Now is a corporation which sells short-term loan arrangements. This January, Payday Now has made an advance payment to cover the next 12 months of utility bills, which have a monthly cost of $1200.

DR Prepaid Expense $14,400    CR Cash $14,400

The prepaid expense (asset) account has increased, and the cash (asset) account has decreased by: 12 months x $1,200 per month = $14,400 for the year.

874 Hogtown Records is a corporation which sells audio services for local musicians to record their music albums. Hogtown Records has just purchased a building using cash, which has an expected useful life of 30 years, and which had a total cost of $469000.

DR Building $469,000    CR Cash $469,000

The building (asset) account has increased, and the cash (asset) account has decreased by: $469,000. The useful life does not affect this original accounting entry, but it will be used to calculate depreciation of the asset in the future.

875 Air America is a privately-held corporation which focuses on their niche of premium global flights. This January, Air America has made an advance payment to cover the next 12 months of utility bills, which have a monthly cost of $2700.

DR Prepaid Expense $32,400    CR Cash $32,400

The prepaid expense (asset) account has increased, and the cash (asset) account has decreased by: 12 months x $2,700 per month = $32,400 for the year.

876 Air America sells various global flights. This month, Air America has estimated that 10% of the accounts receivable might not end up being collectable, based on past experience. The accounts receivable will need to be adjusted from its current balance of $28000.

DR Bad Debt expense $2,800    CR Allowance for Doubtful Accounts $2,800

The bad debts (expense) and the allowance for doubtful accounts (contra-asset) have both increased by: 10% x $28,000 = $2,800

877    Pharma Drug Company Ltd. is a market leader that is well-known for their brand of medications. This January, Pharma Drug Company Ltd. has made an advance payment to cover the next 12 months of utility bills, which have a monthly cost of $1100.

DR Prepaid Expense $13,200    CR Cash $13,200

The prepaid expense (asset) account has increased, and the cash (asset) account has decreased by: 12 months x $1,100 per month = $13,200 for the year.

878    Mr. Mop sells various household cleaners. This month, Mr. Mop accepted 3000 tons of cleaning solution which were returned by customers. These products had been marked up by 35% and they had originally been bought at a per-unit cost of $2100.

DR Sales Returns $8,505,000    DR Inventory $6,300,000    CR Accounts Receivable $8,505,000    CR Cost of Goods Sold $6,300,000

This transaction increases the sales returns (contra-revenue) account, and the inventory (asset) account. The accounts receivable (asset) account and the cost of goods sold (expense) account have both decreased. 3000 tons of cleaning solution x $2,100 = $6,300,000. The 35% markup applies to the sales returns and accounts receivable amounts, i.e. $6,300,000 x 1.35 = $8,505,000

879    Sprike Inc is an organization which specializes in providing their customers with athletic apparel. This month, Sprike Inc paid for 1 month of rent for the warehouse room, which has a monthly cost of $1500.

DR Rent expense $1,500    CR Accounts Payable $1,500

The rent (expense) and the accounts payable (liability) accounts are both increased by one month's worth of rent, which is $1,500.

880    Pharma Drug Company Ltd. is a corporation which sells medications. Today, Pharma Drug Company Ltd. received an upfront payment for 1590 batches of pills which will be provided to the customer 6 months from now. The payment for each was $2100.

DR Cash $3,339,000    CR Unearned Revenue $3,339,000

The cash (asset) and the unearned revenue (liability) accounts have both increased by: 1590 batches of pills x $2,100 = $3,339,000

881   Grand Convention Ltd sells several different types of banquet hall rentals for corporate meetings.  This month, Grand Convention Ltd paid 1 monthly loan repayment towards their long-term note payable. The interest portion was 60% of the payment. The total amount paid in cash was $18000.

DR Interest Expense $10,800    DR Loan Payable $7,200    CR Cash $18,000

The interest (expense) account has increased by $18,000 x 0.6 = $10,800. The loan payable (liability) has decreased by $18,000 x 0.4 = $7,200. The cash (asset) account has decreased by the full amount of the payment, which is $18,000

882   Jameson & Jameson is a company which offers their customers a wide selection of soap products.  This month, Jameson & Jameson paid for 1 month of rent for the warehouse room, which has a monthly cost of $1900.

DR Rent expense $1,900    CR Accounts Payable $1,900

The rent (expense) and the accounts payable (liability) accounts are both increased by one month's worth of rent, which is $1,900.

883   Payday Now is a company which offers their customers a wide selection of short-term loan arrangements.  This month, Payday Now has estimated that 10% of the accounts receivable might not end up being collectable, based on past experience. The accounts receivable will need to be adjusted from its current balance of $100000.

DR Bad Debt expense $10,000    CR Allowance for Doubtful Accounts $10,000

The bad debts (expense) and the allowance for doubtful accounts (contra-asset) have both increased by: 10% x $100,000 = $10,000

884   Mr. Mop is an organization which specializes in providing their customers with household cleaners.  This month, Mr. Mop paid for 1 month of rent for the warehouse room, which has a monthly cost of $2500.

DR Rent expense $2,500    CR Accounts Payable $2,500

The rent (expense) and the accounts payable (liability) accounts are both increased by one month's worth of rent, which is $2,500.

885 Air America is an organization which specializes in providing their customers with global flights. Air America has just received a cash payment for the full amount that this customer owed to the company for all of their purchases to date. The outstanding balance which has now been paid was $39000.

DR Cash $39,000    CR Accounts Receivable $39,000

The cash (asset) account has increased, and the accounts receivable (asset) account has decreased by $39,000.

886 Comedy 253 offers their customers a wide range of live performances of stand-up comedy. Today, Comedy 253 has paid cash to their supplier to fully pay off their account payable balance, which was $65000.

DR Accounts Payable $65,000    CR Cash $65,000

The accounts payable (liability) and cash (asset) accounts have both increased by $65,000.

887 AC&C Ltd. offers their customers a wide range of cell phone plans. AC&C Ltd. has just received a cash payment for the full amount that this customer owed to the company for all of their purchases to date. The outstanding balance which has now been paid was $35000.

DR Cash $35,000    CR Accounts Receivable $35,000

The cash (asset) account has increased, and the accounts receivable (asset) account has decreased by $35,000.

888 A to Z Event Guru Ltd offers their customers a wide range of start-to-finish event planning services for large gatherings. This December, A to Z Event Guru Ltd recognized 1 year of depreciation on equipment which had a total useful life of 10 years, and which had originally cost $110000.

DR Depreciation expense $11,000    CR Accumulated Depreciation $11,000

The depreciation (expense) account and the accumulated depreciation (contra-asset) accounts have both increased by: $110,000 divided by 10 years = $11,000 depreciation per year.

889 Grand Convention Ltd is a company which offers their customers a wide selection of banquet hall rentals for corporate meetings. Today Grand Convention Ltd signed up for a loan with a 5% interest rate, and so the bank immediately transferred cash to the company in the amount of $70000.

DR Cash $70,000    CR Loan Payable $70,000

The cash (asset) and the loan payable (liability) accounts have both increased by: $70,000. The interest rate does not affect this initial accounting entry, but it will be used for the calculation of interest expense when repayments are made in the future toward this loan.

890 Hogtown Records sells several different types of audio services for local musicians to record their music albums. This December, Hogtown Records has paid each of the company's 2400 owners an annual dividend in the amount of $8000.

DR Retained Earnings $19,200,000    CR Cash $19,200,000

The retained earnings (equity) and the cash accounts have both decreased by: 2400 owners x $8,000 = $19,200,000

891 Fairway Malls offers their customers a wide range of retail spaces in their shopping centers. This January, Fairway Malls has made an advance payment to cover the next 12 months of utility bills, which have a monthly cost of $1000.

DR Prepaid Expense $12,000    CR Cash $12,000

The prepaid expense (asset) account has increased, and the cash (asset) account has decreased by: 12 months x $1,000 per month = $12,000 for the year.

892 Fairway Malls sells various retail spaces in their shopping centers. This December, Fairway Malls recognized 1 year of depreciation on a building which had a total useful life of 25 years, and which had originally been bought for $636000.

DR Depreciation expense $25,440    CR Accumulated Depreciation $25,440

The depreciation (expense) account and the accumulated depreciation (contra-asset) accounts have both increased by: $636,000 divided by 25 years = $25,440 depreciation per year.

893    Club Disco provides their customers with dance venue rentals for large family gatherings. This month, Club Disco must amortize 1 month worth of utility bills which they had prepaid at the beginning of the year. The amount that they had paid upfront for the year was $14400.

DR Utilities expense $1,200    CR Prepaid Expense $1,200

The utilities (expense) account has increased and the prepaid expense (asset) account has decreased by: $14,400 for the year, divided by 12 months = $1,200

894    NBG Media Corporation is a corporation which sells broadcasting services for advertising agencies. This month, NBG Media Corporation paid for 1 month of rent for their company's office space. Each month, the rent owing was $11000.

DR Rent expense $11,000    CR Accounts Payable $11,000

The rent (expense) and the accounts payable (liability) accounts are both increased by one month's worth of rent, which is $11,000.

895    NY Fitness is an organization which specializes in providing their customers with gym memberships for professional sports teams. This December, NY Fitness recognized 1 year of depreciation on a building which had a total useful life of 25 years, and which had originally been bought for $587000.

DR Depreciation expense $23,480    CR Accumulated Depreciation $23,480

The depreciation (expense) account and the accumulated depreciation (contra-asset) accounts have both increased by: $587,000 divided by 25 years = $23,480 depreciation per year.

896    Comedy 253 is an organization which specializes in providing their customers with live performances of stand-up comedy. This month, Comedy 253 paid 1 monthly loan repayment towards their long-term note payable. The interest portion was 60% of the payment. The total amount paid in cash was $17000.

DR Interest Expense $10,200    DR Loan Payable $6,800    CR Cash $17,000

The interest (expense) account has increased by $17,000 x 0.6 = $10,200. The loan payable (liability) has decreased by $17,000 x 0.4 = $6,800. The cash (asset) account has decreased by the full amount of the payment, which is $17,000

897 Kola-Nut Ltd is an organization which specializes in providing their customers with soft drinks. Today, Kola-Nut Ltd received an upfront payment for 2610 batches of soda bottles which will be provided to the customer 6 months from now. The payment for each was $1100.

DR Cash $2,871,000    CR Unearned Revenue $2,871,000

The cash (asset) and the unearned revenue (liability) accounts have both increased by: 2610 batches of soda bottles x $1,100 = $2,871,000

898 David & Johnson is a company which offers their customers a wide selection of legal services. David & Johnson has just purchased a building using cash, which has an expected useful life of 30 years, and which had a total cost of $908000.

DR Building $908,000    CR Cash $908,000

The building (asset) account has increased, and the cash (asset) account has decreased by: $908,000. The useful life does not affect this original accounting entry, but it will be used to calculate depreciation of the asset in the future.

899 Mount Tessory Academy provides their customers with private school education. This year, Mount Tessory Academy has provided 2000 annual tuition memberships each of which earned revenues of $2030.

DR Accounts Receivable $4,060,000    CR Sales $4,060,000

The accounts receivable (asset) and the sales (revenue) accounts have both increased by: 20/1 /2nnual tuition memberships x $2,030 = $4,060,000

900 Paytech Ltd is a market leader that is well-known for their brand of payroll transaction processing services. This December, Paytech Ltd recognized 1 year of depreciation on equipment which had a total useful life of 10 years, and which had originally cost $110000.

DR Depreciation expense $11,000    CR Accumulated Depreciation $11,000

The depreciation (expense) account and the accumulated depreciation (contra-asset) accounts have both increased by: $110,000 divided by 10 years = $11,000 depreciation per year.

901     Mount Tessory Academy is a corporation which sells private school education. This December, Mount Tessory Academy has paid each of the company's 1100 owners an annual dividend in the amount of $9000.

DR Retained Earnings $9,900,000    CR Cash $9,900,000

The retained earnings (equity) and the cash accounts have both decreased by: 1100 owners x $9,000 = $9,900,000

902     Pharma Drug Company Ltd. is a company which offers their customers a wide selection of medications. Today, Pharma Drug Company Ltd. received an upfront payment for 3650 batches of pills which will be provided to the customer 6 months from now. The payment for each was $1400.

DR Cash $5,110,000    CR Unearned Revenue $5,110,000

The cash (asset) and the unearned revenue (liability) accounts have both increased by: 3650 batches of pills x $1,400 = $5,110,000

903     Sprike Inc is a corporation which sells athletic apparel. Today, Sprike Inc received an upfront payment for 1790 batches of athletic t-shirts which will be provided to the customer 6 months from now. The payment for each was $2500.

DR Cash $4,475,000    CR Unearned Revenue $4,475,000

The cash (asset) and the unearned revenue (liability) accounts have both increased by: 1790 batches of athletic t-shirts x $2,500 = $4,475,000

904     Sprike Inc sells various athletic apparel. This January, Sprike Inc has made an advance payment to cover the next 12 months of utility bills, which have a monthly cost of $1500.

DR Prepaid Expense $18,000    CR Cash $18,000

The prepaid expense (asset) account has increased, and the cash (asset) account has decreased by: 12 months x $1,500 per month = $18,000 for the year.

905     Mount Tessory Academy offers their customers a wide range of private school education. Today, Mount Tessory Academy has paid cash to their supplier to fully pay off their account payable balance, which was $96000.

DR Accounts Payable $96,000    CR Cash $96,000

The accounts payable (liability) and cash (asset) accounts have both increased by $96,000.

906    Pharma Drug Company Ltd. is a privately-held corporation which focuses on their niche of premium medications. This month, Pharma Drug Company Ltd. accepted 5900 batches of pills which were returned by customers. These products had been marked up by 35% and they had originally been bought at a per-unit cost of $1400.

DR Sales Returns $11,151,000   DR Inventory $8,260,000   CR Accounts Receivable $11,151,000   CR Cost of Goods Sold $8,260,000

This transaction increases the sales returns (contra-revenue) account, and the inventory (asset) account. The accounts receivable (asset) account and the cost of goods sold (expense) account have both decreased. 5900 batches of pills x $1,400 = $8,260,000. The 35% markup applies to the sales returns and accounts receivable amounts, i.e. $8,260,000 x 1.35 = $11,151,000

907    LA Met Theatre Company is a privately-held corporation which focuses on their niche of premium live theatrical performances. Today LA Met Theatre Company signed up for a loan with a 5% interest rate, and so the bank immediately transferred cash to the company in the amount of $104000.

DR Cash $104,000   CR Loan Payable $104,000

The cash (asset) and the loan payable (liability) accounts have both increased by: $104,000. The interest rate does not affect this initial accounting entry, but it will be used for the calculation of interest expense when repayments are made in the future toward this loan.

908    Fairway Malls sells various retail spaces in their shopping centers. This December, Fairway Malls recognized 1 year of depreciation on equipment which had a total useful life of 10 years, and which had originally cost $210000.

DR Depreciation expense $21,000   CR Accumulated Depreciation $21,000

The depreciation (expense) account and the accumulated depreciation (contra-asset) accounts have both increased by: $210,000 divided by 10 years = $21,000 depreciation per year.

909    Mr. Mop is a privately-held corporation which focuses on their niche of premium household cleaners. This month, Mr. Mop paid for 1 month of rent for the warehouse room, which has a monthly cost of $1700.

DR Rent expense $1,700   CR Accounts Payable $1,700

The rent (expense) and the accounts payable (liability) accounts are both increased by one month's worth of rent, which is $1,700.

910     A to Z Event Guru Ltd offers their customers a wide range of start-to-finish event planning services for large gatherings. Today, A to Z Event Guru Ltd has paid cash to their supplier to fully pay off their account payable balance, which was $72000.

DR Accounts Payable $72,000    CR Cash $72,000

The accounts payable (liability) and cash (asset) accounts have both increased by $72,000.

911     Mr. Mop is a privately-held corporation which focuses on their niche of premium household cleaners. Today Mr. Mop sold 41300 tons of cleaning solution which had a 30% mark-up. They had originally been bought from their suppliers for a unit cost of $2960.

DR Accounts Receivable $158,922,400    DR Cost of Goods Sold $122,248,000
CR Sales $158,922,400    CR Inventory $122,248,000

This transaction increases the accounts receivable (asset) account, the sales (revenue) account, and the cost of goods sold (expense) account. The inventory (asset) account has decreased. 41300 tons of cleaning solution x $2,960 = $122,248,000. The 30% markup applies to the sales and accounts receivable amounts, i.e. $122,248,000 x 1.30 = $158,922,400

912     Kola-Nut Ltd is a privately-held corporation which focuses on their niche of premium soft drinks. Today, Kola-Nut Ltd received an upfront payment for 3040 batches of soda bottles which will be provided to the customer 6 months from now. The payment for each was $1200.

DR Cash $3,648,000    CR Unearned Revenue $3,648,000

The cash (asset) and the unearned revenue (liability) accounts have both increased by: 3040 batches of soda bottles x $1,200 = $3,648,000

913     NY Fitness is an organization which specializes in providing their customers with gym memberships for professional sports teams. NY Fitness has just received a cash payment for the full amount that this customer owed to the company for all of their purchases to date. The outstanding balance which has now been paid was $71000.

DR Cash $71,000    CR Accounts Receivable $71,000

The cash (asset) account has increased, and the accounts receivable (asset) account has decreased by $71,000.

914     Fairway Malls offers their customers a wide range of retail spaces in their shopping centers. Fairway Malls has just purchased a building using cash, which has an expected useful life of 30 years, and which had a total cost of $831000.

DR Building $831,000    CR Cash $831,000

The building (asset) account has increased, and the cash (asset) account has decreased by: $831,000. The useful life does not affect this original accounting entry, but it will be used to calculate depreciation of the asset in the future.

915     McGerald's sells several different types of fast food meals. Today McGerald's signed up for a loan with a 5% interest rate, and so the bank immediately transferred cash to the company in the amount of $34000.

DR Cash $34,000    CR Loan Payable $34,000

The cash (asset) and the loan payable (liability) accounts have both increased by: $34,000. The interest rate does not affect this initial accounting entry, but it will be used for the calculation of interest expense when repayments are made in the future toward this loan.

916     Sprike Inc offers their customers a wide range of athletic apparel. Today, Sprike Inc bought equipment which has a 5 year useful life, and which had a cost of $15000.

DR Equipment $15,000    CR Accounts Payable $15,000

The equipment (asset) and the accounts payable (liability) accounts have both increased by: $15,000. The useful life does not affect this original accounting entry, but it will be used to calculate depreciation of the asset in the future.

917     Jameson & Jameson sells several different types of soap products. Jameson & Jameson has just purchased a building using cash, which has an expected useful life of 30 years, and which had a total cost of $912000.

DR Building $912,000    CR Cash $912,000

The building (asset) account has increased, and the cash (asset) account has decreased by: $912,000. The useful life does not affect this original accounting entry, but it will be used to calculate depreciation of the asset in the future.

918    Jameson & Jameson is a company which offers their customers a wide selection of soap products. This week, Jameson & Jameson purchased 4460 truckloads of bars of soap which were placed into the warehouse, and which had a per-unit cost of $2300.

DR Inventory $10,258,000    CR Accounts Payable $10,258,000

There was an increase in the inventory (asset) account, and also an increase in the accounts payable (liability) account. 4460 truckloads of bars of soap x $2,300 = $10,258,000

919    Club Disco offers their customers a wide range of dance venue rentals for large family gatherings. This year, Club Disco has provided 1800 evening rentals each of which earned revenues of $2520.

DR Accounts Receivable $4,536,000    CR Sales $4,536,000

The accounts receivable (asset) and the sales (revenue) accounts have both increased by: 18/1 /2vening rentals x $2,520 = $4,536,000

920    Pharma Drug Company Ltd. is an organization which specializes in providing their customers with medications. This month, Pharma Drug Company Ltd. has estimated that 5% of the accounts receivable might not end up being collectable, based on past experience. The accounts receivable will need to be adjusted from its current balance of $77000.

DR Bad Debt expense $3,850    CR Allowance for Doubtful Accounts $3,850

The bad debts (expense) and the allowance for doubtful accounts (contra-asset) have both increased by: 5% x $77,000 = $3,850

921    Mr. Mop is a corporation which sells household cleaners. This week, Mr. Mop purchased 3430 tons of cleaning solution which were placed into the warehouse, and which had a per-unit cost of $1900.

DR Inventory $6,517,000    CR Accounts Payable $6,517,000

There was an increase in the inventory (asset) account, and also an increase in the accounts payable (liability) account. 3430 tons of cleaning solution x $1,900 = $6,517,000

922    Hogtown Records sells several different types of audio services for local musicians to record their music albums.  This month, Hogtown Records must amortize 1 month worth of utility bills which they had prepaid at the beginning of the year. The amount that they had paid upfront for the year was $44400.

DR Utilities expense $3,700    CR Prepaid Expense $3,700

The utilities (expense) account has increased and the prepaid expense (asset) account has decreased by: $44,400 for the year, divided by 12 months = $3,700

923    Kola-Nut Ltd is a corporation which sells soft drinks.  Today, Kola-Nut Ltd has paid cash to their supplier to fully pay off their account payable balance, which was $64000.

DR Accounts Payable $64,000    CR Cash $64,000

The accounts payable (liability) and cash (asset) accounts have both increased by $64,000.

924    Jameson & Jameson provides their customers with soap products.  This month, Jameson & Jameson accepted 17700 truckloads of bars of soap which were returned by customers. These products had been marked up by 35% and they had originally been bought at a per-unit cost of $1300.

DR Sales Returns $31,063,500    DR Inventory $23,010,000    CR Accounts Receivable $31,063,500    CR Cost of Goods Sold $23,010,000

This transaction increases the sales returns (contra-revenue) account, and the inventory (asset) account. The accounts receivable (asset) account and the cost of goods sold (expense) account have both decreased. 17700 truckloads of bars of soap x $1,300 = $23,010,000. The 35% markup applies to the sales returns and accounts receivable amounts, i.e. $23,010,000 x 1.35 = $31,063,500

925    Mr. Mop offers their customers a wide range of household cleaners.  This month, Mr. Mop must amortize 1 month worth of utility bills which they had prepaid at the beginning of the year. The amount that they had paid upfront for the year was $13200.

DR Utilities expense $1,100    CR Prepaid Expense $1,100

The utilities (expense) account has increased and the prepaid expense (asset) account has decreased by: $13,200 for the year, divided by 12 months = $1,100

926    Fairway Malls sells several different types of retail spaces in their shopping centers. This month, Fairway Malls has estimated that 5% of the accounts receivable might not end up being collectable, based on past experience. The accounts receivable will need to be adjusted from its current balance of $74000.

DR Bad Debt expense $3,700    CR Allowance for Doubtful Accounts $3,700

The bad debts (expense) and the allowance for doubtful accounts (contra-asset) have both increased by: 5% x $74,000 = $3,700

927    AC&C Ltd. is a company which offers their customers a wide selection of cell phone plans. This month, AC&C Ltd. paid for 1 month of rent for their company's office space. Each month, the rent owing was $18000.

DR Rent expense $18,000    CR Accounts Payable $18,000

The rent (expense) and the accounts payable (liability) accounts are both increased by one month's worth of rent, which is $18,000.

928    NBG Media Corporation offers their customers a wide range of broadcasting services for advertising agencies. This month, NBG Media Corporation paid 1 monthly loan repayment towards their long-term note payable. The interest portion was 60% of the payment. The total amount paid in cash was $26000.

DR Interest Expense $15,600    DR Loan Payable $10,400    CR Cash $26,000

The interest (expense) account has increased by $26,000 x 0.6 = $15,600. The loan payable (liability) has decreased by $26,000 x 0.4 = $10,400. The cash (asset) account has decreased by the full amount of the payment, which is $26,000

929    David & Johnson sells several different types of legal services. Today, David & Johnson received payment upfront for 2300 large orders which will not be provided until early next year. Each order was in the amount of $2100.

DR Cash $4,830,000    CR Unearned Revenue $4,830,000

The cash (asset) and the unearned revenue (liability) accounts have both increased by: 2300 large orders x $2,100 = $4,830,000

930 Club Disco sells various dance venue rentals for large family gatherings. Club Disco has just provided 1400 large orders which had been paid for in advance last year. Each order was in the amount of $2400.

DR Unearned Revenue $3,360,000    CR Sales $3,360,000

The unearned revenue (liability) account has decreased and the and the sales (revenue) account has increased by: 14/1 /2arge orders x $2,400 = $3,360,000

931 Kola-Nut Ltd sells various soft drinks. This month, Kola-Nut Ltd paid for 1 month of rent for the warehouse room, which has a monthly cost of $1200.

DR Rent expense $1,200    CR Accounts Payable $1,200

The rent (expense) and the accounts payable (liability) accounts are both increased by one month's worth of rent, which is $1,200.

932 McGerald's sells various fast food meals. This month, McGerald's has estimated that 10% of the accounts receivable might not end up being collectable, based on past experience. The accounts receivable will need to be adjusted from its current balance of $82000.

DR Bad Debt expense $8,200    CR Allowance for Doubtful Accounts $8,200

The bad debts (expense) and the allowance for doubtful accounts (contra-asset) have both increased by: 10% x $82,000 = $8,200

933 Pharma Drug Company Ltd. offers their customers a wide range of medications. This month, Pharma Drug Company Ltd. paid 1 monthly loan repayment towards their long-term note payable. The interest portion was 60% of the payment. The total amount paid in cash was $17000.

DR Interest Expense $10,200    DR Loan Payable $6,800    CR Cash $17,000

The interest (expense) account has increased by $17,000 x 0.6 = $10,200. The loan payable (liability) has decreased by $17,000 x 0.4 = $6,800. The cash (asset) account has decreased by the full amount of the payment, which is $17,000

934 McGerald's sells various fast food meals.  Today McGerald's signed up for a loan with a 5% interest rate, and so the bank immediately transferred cash to the company in the amount of $27000.

DR Cash $27,000    CR Loan Payable $27,000

The cash (asset) and the loan payable (liability) accounts have both increased by: $27,000. The interest rate does not affect this initial accounting entry, but it will be used for the calculation of interest expense when repayments are made in the future toward this loan.

935 Mount Tessory Academy is a market leader that is well-known for their brand of private school education.  This month, Mount Tessory Academy must amortize 1 month worth of utility bills which they had prepaid at the beginning of the year. The amount that they had paid upfront for the year was $18000.

DR Utilities expense $1,500    CR Prepaid Expense $1,500

The utilities (expense) account has increased and the prepaid expense (asset) account has decreased by: $18,000 for the year, divided by 12 months = $1,500

936 Comedy 253 is a privately-held corporation which focuses on their niche of premium live performances of stand-up comedy.  Comedy 253 has just provided 1600 large orders which had been paid for in advance last year. Each order was in the amount of $2700.

DR Unearned Revenue $4,320,000    CR Sales $4,320,000

The unearned revenue (liability) account has decreased and the and the sales (revenue) account has increased by: 16/1 /2arge orders x $2,700 = $4,320,000

937 Air America is a privately-held corporation which focuses on their niche of premium global flights.  This December, Air America has paid each of the company's 1500 owners an annual dividend in the amount of $16000.

DR Retained Earnings $24,000,000    CR Cash $24,000,000

The retained earnings (equity) and the cash accounts have both decreased by: 1500 owners x $16,000 = $24,000,000

938    Grand Convention Ltd is a privately-held corporation which focuses on their niche of premium banquet hall rentals for corporate meetings. This December, Grand Convention Ltd has paid each of the company's 1200 owners an annual dividend in the amount of $22000.

DR Retained Earnings $26,400,000    CR Cash $26,400,000

The retained earnings (equity) and the cash accounts have both decreased by: 1200 owners x $22,000 = $26,400,000

939    NY Fitness is a market leader that is well-known for their brand of gym memberships for professional sports teams. This month, NY Fitness must amortize 1 month worth of utility bills which they had prepaid at the beginning of the year. The amount that they had paid upfront for the year was $40800.

DR Utilities expense $3,400    CR Prepaid Expense $3,400

The utilities (expense) account has increased and the prepaid expense (asset) account has decreased by: $40,800 for the year, divided by 12 months = $3,400

940    Payday Now offers their customers a wide range of short-term loan arrangements. This month, Payday Now must amortize 1 month worth of utility bills which they had prepaid at the beginning of the year. The amount that they had paid upfront for the year was $13200.

DR Utilities expense $1,100    CR Prepaid Expense $1,100

The utilities (expense) account has increased and the prepaid expense (asset) account has decreased by: $13,200 for the year, divided by 12 months = $1,100

941    Jameson & Jameson sells various soap products. This month, Jameson & Jameson must amortize 1 month worth of utility bills which they had prepaid at the beginning of the year. The amount that they had paid upfront for the year was $39600.

DR Utilities expense $3,300    CR Prepaid Expense $3,300

The utilities (expense) account has increased and the prepaid expense (asset) account has decreased by: $39,600 for the year, divided by 12 months = $3,300

942     Mount Tessory Academy sells various private school education subscriptions. Today Mount Tessory Academy signed up for a loan with a 5% interest rate, and so the bank immediately transferred cash to the company in the amount of $57000.

DR Cash $57,000    CR Loan Payable $57,000

The cash (asset) and the loan payable (liability) accounts have both increased by: $57,000. The interest rate does not affect this initial accounting entry, but it will be used for the calculation of interest expense when repayments are made in the future toward this loan.

943     LA Met Theatre Company is an organization which specializes in providing their customers with live theatrical performances.  Today LA Met Theatre Company signed up for a loan with a 5% interest rate, and so the bank immediately transferred cash to the company in the amount of $37000.

DR Cash $37,000    CR Loan Payable $37,000

The cash (asset) and the loan payable (liability) accounts have both increased by: $37,000. The interest rate does not affect this initial accounting entry, but it will be used for the calculation of interest expense when repayments are made in the future toward this loan.

944     NY Fitness offers their customers a wide range of gym memberships for professional sports teams.  This January, NY Fitness has made an advance payment to cover the next 12 months of utility bills, which have a monthly cost of $2700.

DR Prepaid Expense $32,400    CR Cash $32,400

The prepaid expense (asset) account has increased, and the cash (asset) account has decreased by: 12 months x $2,700 per month = $32,400 for the year.

945     LA Met Theatre Company is a market leader that is well-known for their brand of live theatrical performances.  Today, LA Met Theatre Company bought equipment which has a 5 year useful life, and which had a cost of $12000.

DR Equipment $12,000    CR Accounts Payable $12,000

The equipment (asset) and the accounts payable (liability) accounts have both increased by: $12,000. The useful life does not affect this original accounting entry, but it will be used to calculate depreciation of the asset in the future.

946     NBG Media Corporation offers their customers a wide range of broadcasting services for advertising agencies. Today, NBG Media Corporation has paid cash to their supplier to fully pay off their account payable balance, which was $45000.

DR Accounts Payable $45,000    CR Cash $45,000

The accounts payable (liability) and cash (asset) accounts have both increased by $45,000.

947     Fairway Malls is a corporation which sells retail spaces in their shopping centers. Today, Fairway Malls received payment upfront for 1900 large orders which will not be provided until early next year. Each order was in the amount of $2800.

DR Cash $5,320,000    CR Unearned Revenue $5,320,000

The cash (asset) and the unearned revenue (liability) accounts have both increased by: 1900 large orders x $2,800 = $5,320,000

948     NY Fitness is a market leader that is well-known for their brand of gym memberships for professional sports teams. This January, NY Fitness has made an advance payment to cover the next 12 months of utility bills, which have a monthly cost of $1300.

DR Prepaid Expense $15,600    CR Cash $15,600

The prepaid expense (asset) account has increased, and the cash (asset) account has decreased by: 12 months x $1,300 per month = $15,600 for the year.

949     LA Met Theatre Company is a corporation which sells live theatrical performances. This December, LA Met Theatre Company recognized 1 year of depreciation on equipment which had a total useful life of 10 years, and which had originally cost $220000.

DR Depreciation expense $22,000    CR Accumulated Depreciation $22,000

The depreciation (expense) account and the accumulated depreciation (contra-asset) accounts have both increased by: $220,000 divided by 10 years = $22,000 depreciation per year.

950 Club Disco offers their customers a wide range of dance venue rentals for large family gatherings. This December, Club Disco recognized 1 year of depreciation on a building which had a total useful life of 25 years, and which had originally been bought for $437000.

DR Depreciation expense $17,480   CR Accumulated Depreciation $17,480

The depreciation (expense) account and the accumulated depreciation (contra-asset) accounts have both increased by: $437,000 divided by 25 years = $17,480 depreciation per year.

951 NY Fitness sells various gym memberships for professional sports teams. Today, NY Fitness received payment upfront for 1500 large orders which will not be provided until early next year. Each order was in the amount of $2300.

DR Cash $3,450,000   CR Unearned Revenue $3,450,000

The cash (asset) and the unearned revenue (liability) accounts have both increased by: 1500 large orders x $2,300 = $3,450,000

952 Grand Convention Ltd is a market leader that is well-known for their brand of banquet hall rentals for corporate meetings. This week, Grand Convention Ltd paid each of the 3810 staff members their bi-weekly wages, which per person had a cost of $2600.

DR Wage expense $9,906,000   CR Accounts Payable $9,906,000

The wage (expense) and the accounts payable (liability) accounts have both increased by: 3810 staff members x $2,600 = $9,906,000

953 Jameson & Jameson is a corporation which sells soap products. This month, Jameson & Jameson accepted 17000 truckloads of bars of soap which were returned by customers. These products had been marked up by 35% and they had originally been bought at a per-unit cost of $1400.

DR Sales Returns $32,130,000   DR Inventory $23,800,000   CR Accounts Receivable $32,130,000   CR Cost of Goods Sold $23,800,000

This transaction increases the sales returns (contra-revenue) account, and the inventory (asset) account. The accounts receivable (asset) account and the cost of goods sold (expense) account have both decreased. 17000 truckloads of bars of soap x $1,400 = $23,800,000. The 35% markup applies to the sales returns and accounts receivable amounts, i.e. $23,800,000 x 1.35 = $32,130,000

954     Jameson & Jameson offers their customers a wide range of soap products. This December, Jameson & Jameson has paid each of the company's 1700 owners an annual dividend in the amount of $18000.

DR Retained Earnings $30,600,000    CR Cash $30,600,000

The retained earnings (equity) and the cash accounts have both decreased by: 1700 owners x $18,000 = $30,600,000

955     AC&C Ltd. sells several different types of cell phone plans. Today AC&C Ltd. signed up for a loan with a 5% interest rate, and so the bank immediately transferred cash to the company in the amount of $75000.

DR Cash $75,000    CR Loan Payable $75,000

The cash (asset) and the loan payable (liability) accounts have both increased by: $75,000. The interest rate does not affect this initial accounting entry, but it will be used for the calculation of interest expense when repayments are made in the future toward this loan.

956     Kola-Nut Ltd offers their customers a wide range of soft drinks. This month, Kola-Nut Ltd paid for 1 month of rent for the warehouse room, which has a monthly cost of $1800.

DR Rent expense $1,800    CR Accounts Payable $1,800

The rent (expense) and the accounts payable (liability) accounts are both increased by one month's worth of rent, which is $1,800.

957     A to Z Event Guru Ltd is a corporation which sells start-to-finish event planning services for large gatherings. This week, A to Z Event Guru Ltd paid each of the 3350 staff members their bi-weekly wages, which per person had a cost of $1300.

DR Wage expense $4,355,000    CR Accounts Payable $4,355,000

The wage (expense) and the accounts payable (liability) accounts have both increased by: 3350 staff members x $1,300 = $4,355,000

958     Comedy 253 provides their customers with live performances of stand-up comedy.  Comedy 253 has just received a cash payment for the full amount that this customer owed to the company for all of their purchases to date. The outstanding balance which has now been paid was $15000.

DR Cash $15,000    CR Accounts Receivable $15,000

The cash (asset) account has increased, and the accounts receivable (asset) account has decreased by $15,000.

959     NY Fitness is an organization which specializes in providing their customers with gym memberships for professional sports teams.  This month, NY Fitness paid for 1 month of rent for their company's office space. Each month, the rent owing was $12000.

DR Rent expense $12,000    CR Accounts Payable $12,000

The rent (expense) and the accounts payable (liability) accounts are both increased by one month's worth of rent, which is $12,000.

960     Mr. Mop is a corporation which sells household cleaners.  This month, Mr. Mop accepted 20700 tons of cleaning solution which were returned by customers. These products had been marked up by 35% and they had originally been bought at a per-unit cost of $2700.

DR Sales Returns $75,451,500    DR Inventory $55,890,000    CR Accounts Receivable $75,451,500    CR Cost of Goods Sold $55,890,000

This transaction increases the sales returns (contra-revenue) account, and the inventory (asset) account. The accounts receivable (asset) account and the cost of goods sold (expense) account have both decreased. 20700 tons of cleaning solution x $2,700 = $55,890,000. The 35% markup applies to the sales returns and accounts receivable amounts, i.e. $55,890,000 x 1.35 = $75,451,500

961     Jameson & Jameson is an organization which specializes in providing their customers with soap products.  This month, Jameson & Jameson paid for 1 month of rent for the warehouse room, which has a monthly cost of $1200.

DR Rent expense $1,200    CR Accounts Payable $1,200

The rent (expense) and the accounts payable (liability) accounts are both increased by one month's worth of rent, which is $1,200.

962     LA Met Theatre Company provides their customers with live theatrical performances.  This week, LA Met Theatre Company paid each of the 2150 staff members their bi-weekly wages, which per person had a cost of $2200.

DR Wage expense $4,730,000    CR Accounts Payable $4,730,000

The wage (expense) and the accounts payable (liability) accounts have both increased by: 2150 staff members x $2,200 = $4,730,000

963     Kola-Nut Ltd offers their customers a wide range of soft drinks.  This month, Kola-Nut Ltd accepted 24900 batches of soda bottles which were returned by customers. These products had been marked up by 35% and they had originally been bought at a per-unit cost of $2100.

DR Sales Returns $70,591,500    DR Inventory $52,290,000    CR Accounts Receivable $70,591,500    CR Cost of Goods Sold $52,290,000

This transaction increases the sales returns (contra-revenue) account, and the inventory (asset) account. The accounts receivable (asset) account and the cost of goods sold (expense) account have both decreased. 24900 batches of soda bottles x $2,100 = $52,290,000. The 35% markup applies to the sales returns and accounts receivable amounts, i.e. $52,290,000 x 1.35 = $70,591,500

964     Comedy 253 is a company which offers their customers a wide selection of live performances of stand-up comedy.  Comedy 253 has just purchased a building using cash, which has an expected useful life of 30 years, and which had a total cost of $644000.

DR Building $644,000    CR Cash $644,000

The building (asset) account has increased, and the cash (asset) account has decreased by: $644,000. The useful life does not affect this original accounting entry, but it will be used to calculate depreciation of the asset in the future.

965     Payday Now offers their customers a wide range of short-term loan arrangements.  Payday Now has just provided 1000 large orders which had been paid for in advance last year. Each order was in the amount of $2000.

DR Unearned Revenue $2,000,000    CR Sales $2,000,000

The unearned revenue (liability) account has decreased and the and the sales (revenue) account has increased by: 10/1 /2arge orders x $2,000 = $2,000,000

966  Jameson & Jameson is a market leader that is well-known for their brand of soap products. This December, Jameson & Jameson recognized 1 year of depreciation on equipment which had a total useful life of 10 years, and which had originally cost $190000.

DR Depreciation expense $19,000    CR Accumulated Depreciation $19,000

The depreciation (expense) account and the accumulated depreciation (contra-asset) accounts have both increased by: $190,000 divided by 10 years = $19,000 depreciation per year.

967  Sprike Inc is a corporation which sells athletic apparel. Today, Sprike Inc received an upfront payment for 3540 batches of athletic t-shirts which will be provided to the customer 6 months from now. The payment for each was $2600.

DR Cash $9,204,000    CR Unearned Revenue $9,204,000

The cash (asset) and the unearned revenue (liability) accounts have both increased by: 3540 batches of athletic t-shirts x $2,600 = $9,204,000

968  Air America is an organization which specializes in providing their customers with global flights. This month, Air America paid 1 monthly loan repayment towards their long-term note payable. The interest portion was 60% of the payment. The total amount paid in cash was $22000.

DR Interest Expense $13,200    DR Loan Payable $8,800    CR Cash $22,000

The interest (expense) account has increased by $22,000 x 0.6 = $13,200. The loan payable (liability) has decreased by $22,000 x 0.4 = $8,800. The cash (asset) account has decreased by the full amount of the payment, which is $22,000

969  Toyonda sells several different types of cars. This month, Toyonda paid 1 monthly loan repayment towards their long-term note payable. The interest portion was 60% of the payment. The total amount paid in cash was $16000.

DR Interest Expense $9,600    DR Loan Payable $6,400    CR Cash $16,000

The interest (expense) account has increased by $16,000 x 0.6 = $9,600. The loan payable (liability) has decreased by $16,000 x 0.4 = $6,400. The cash (asset) account has decreased by the full amount of the payment, which is $16,000

970     Mr. Mop offers their customers a wide range of household cleaners. This month, Mr. Mop accepted 2800 tons of cleaning solution which were returned by customers. These products had been marked up by 35% and they had originally been bought at a per-unit cost of $1300.

DR Sales Returns $4,914,000    DR Inventory $3,640,000    CR Accounts Receivable $4,914,000    CR Cost of Goods Sold $3,640,000

This transaction increases the sales returns (contra-revenue) account, and the inventory (asset) account. The accounts receivable (asset) account and the cost of goods sold (expense) account have both decreased. 2800 tons of cleaning solution x $1,300 = $3,640,000. The 35% markup applies to the sales returns and accounts receivable amounts, i.e. $3,640,000 x 1.35 = $4,914,000

971     David & Johnson is a market leader that is well-known for their brand of legal services. This month, David & Johnson paid 1 monthly loan repayment towards their long-term note payable. The interest portion was 60% of the payment. The total amount paid in cash was $13000.

DR Interest Expense $7,800    DR Loan Payable $5,200    CR Cash $13,000

The interest (expense) account has increased by $13,000 x 0.6 = $7,800. The loan payable (liability) has decreased by $13,000 x 0.4 = $5,200. The cash (asset) account has decreased by the full amount of the payment, which is $13,000

972     Air America is a market leader that is well-known for their brand of global flights. This January, Air America has made an advance payment to cover the next 12 months of utility bills, which have a monthly cost of $1600.

DR Prepaid Expense $19,200    CR Cash $19,200

The prepaid expense (asset) account has increased, and the cash (asset) account has decreased by: 12 months x $1,600 per month = $19,200 for the year.

973     McGerald's is a market leader that is well-known for their brand of fast food meals. McGerald's has just provided 1900 large orders which had been paid for in advance last year. Each order was in the amount of $2800.

DR Unearned Revenue $5,320,000    CR Sales $5,320,000

The unearned revenue (liability) account has decreased and the and the sales (revenue) account has increased by: 19/1 /2arge orders x $2,800 = $5,320,000

974    Comedy 253 is an organization which specializes in providing their customers with live performances of stand-up comedy. This month, Comedy 253 must amortize 1 month worth of utility bills which they had prepaid at the beginning of the year. The amount that they had paid upfront for the year was $32400.

DR Utilities expense $2,700    CR Prepaid Expense $2,700

The utilities (expense) account has increased and the prepaid expense (asset) account has decreased by: $32,400 for the year, divided by 12 months = $2,700

975    Mount Tessory Academy offers their customers a wide range of private school education. Today, Mount Tessory Academy has paid cash to their supplier to fully pay off their account payable balance, which was $80000.

DR Accounts Payable $80,000    CR Cash $80,000

The accounts payable (liability) and cash (asset) accounts have both increased by $80,000.

976    Pharma Drug Company Ltd. sells various medications. This month, Pharma Drug Company Ltd. paid for 1 month of rent for the warehouse room, which has a monthly cost of $2100.

DR Rent expense $2,100    CR Accounts Payable $2,100

The rent (expense) and the accounts payable (liability) accounts are both increased by one month's worth of rent, which is $2,100.

977    Cirque du Lune is an organization which specializes in providing their customers with circus performances. This December, Cirque du Lune recognized 1 year of depreciation on a building which had a total useful life of 25 years, and which had originally been bought for $770000.

DR Depreciation expense $30,800    CR Accumulated Depreciation $30,800

The depreciation (expense) account and the accumulated depreciation (contra-asset) accounts have both increased by: $770,000 divided by 25 years = $30,800 depreciation per year.

978    Mr. Mop is a privately-held corporation which focuses on their niche of premium household cleaners. Mr. Mop has just received a cash payment for the full amount that this customer owed to the company for all of their purchases to date. The outstanding balance which has now been paid was $82000.

DR Cash $82,000    CR Accounts Receivable $82,000

The cash (asset) account has increased, and the accounts receivable (asset) account has decreased by $82,000.

979    Kola-Nut Ltd is an organization which specializes in providing their customers with soft drinks. Today, Kola-Nut Ltd received an upfront payment for 1090 batches of soda bottles which will be provided to the customer 6 months from now. The payment for each was $1900.

DR Cash $2,071,000    CR Unearned Revenue $2,071,000

The cash (asset) and the unearned revenue (liability) accounts have both increased by: 1090 batches of soda bottles x $1,900 = $2,071,000

980    Pharma Drug Company Ltd. offers their customers a wide range of medications. This month, Pharma Drug Company Ltd. must amortize 1 month worth of utility bills which they had prepaid at the beginning of the year. The amount that they had paid upfront for the year was $22800.

DR Utilities expense $1,900    CR Prepaid Expense $1,900

The utilities (expense) account has increased and the prepaid expense (asset) account has decreased by: $22,800 for the year, divided by 12 months = $1,900

981    Jameson & Jameson is a privately-held corporation which focuses on their niche of premium soap products. This week, Jameson & Jameson purchased 3670 truckloads of bars of soap which were placed into the warehouse, and which had a per-unit cost of $1500.

DR Inventory $5,505,000    CR Accounts Payable $5,505,000

There was an increase in the inventory (asset) account, and also an increase in the accounts payable (liability) account. 3670 truckloads of bars of soap x $1,500 = $5,505,000

982    NY Fitness is a corporation which sells gym memberships for professional sports teams.  Today NY Fitness signed up for a loan with a 5% interest rate, and so the bank immediately transferred cash to the company in the amount of $42000.

DR Cash $42,000    CR Loan Payable $42,000

The cash (asset) and the loan payable (liability) accounts have both increased by: $42,000. The interest rate does not affect this initial accounting entry, but it will be used for the calculation of interest expense when repayments are made in the future toward this loan.

983    Kola-Nut Ltd is a company which offers their customers a wide selection of soft drinks.  Today Kola-Nut Ltd signed up for a loan with a 5% interest rate, and so the bank immediately transferred cash to the company in the amount of $111000.

DR Cash $111,000    CR Loan Payable $111,000

The cash (asset) and the loan payable (liability) accounts have both increased by: $111,000. The interest rate does not affect this initial accounting entry, but it will be used for the calculation of interest expense when repayments are made in the future toward this loan.

984    Pharma Drug Company Ltd. provides their customers with medications.  Today Pharma Drug Company Ltd. signed up for a loan with a 5% interest rate, and so the bank immediately transferred cash to the company in the amount of $111000.

DR Cash $111,000    CR Loan Payable $111,000

The cash (asset) and the loan payable (liability) accounts have both increased by: $111,000. The interest rate does not affect this initial accounting entry, but it will be used for the calculation of interest expense when repayments are made in the future toward this loan.

985    Grand Convention Ltd is a market leader that is well-known for their brand of banquet hall rentals for corporate meetings.  This December, Grand Convention Ltd recognized 1 year of depreciation on equipment which had a total useful life of 10 years, and which had originally cost $110000.

DR Depreciation expense $11,000    CR Accumulated Depreciation $11,000

The depreciation (expense) account and the accumulated depreciation (contra-asset) accounts have both increased by: $110,000 divided by 10 years = $11,000 depreciation per year.

986 Fairway Malls sells various retail spaces in their shopping centers. Today, Fairway Malls received payment upfront for 2000 large orders which will not be provided until early next year. Each order was in the amount of $2200.

DR Cash $4,400,000    CR Unearned Revenue $4,400,000

The cash (asset) and the unearned revenue (liability) accounts have both increased by: 2000 large orders x $2,200 = $4,400,000

987 Sprike Inc provides their customers with athletic apparel. Today Sprike Inc sold 29900 batches of athletic t-shirts which had a 30% mark-up. They had originally been bought from their suppliers for a unit cost of $1190.

DR Accounts Receivable $46,255,300    DR Cost of Goods Sold $35,581,000
CR Sales $46,255,300    CR Inventory $35,581,000

This transaction increases the accounts receivable (asset) account, the sales (revenue) account, and the cost of goods sold (expense) account. The inventory (asset) account has decreased. 29900 batches of athletic t-shirts x $1,190 = $35,581,000. The 30% markup applies to the sales and accounts receivable amounts, i.e. $35,581,000 x 1.30 = $46,255,300

988 Jameson & Jameson offers their customers a wide range of soap products. This month, Jameson & Jameson paid for 1 month of rent for the warehouse room, which has a monthly cost of $2100.

DR Rent expense $2,100    CR Accounts Payable $2,100

The rent (expense) and the accounts payable (liability) accounts are both increased by one month's worth of rent, which is $2,100.

989 Kola-Nut Ltd is a privately-held corporation which focuses on their niche of premium soft drinks. This month, Kola-Nut Ltd paid for 1 month of rent for the warehouse room, which has a monthly cost of $1900.

DR Rent expense $1,900    CR Accounts Payable $1,900

The rent (expense) and the accounts payable (liability) accounts are both increased by one month's worth of rent, which is $1,900.

990 Toyonda offers their customers a wide range of cars. This January, Toyonda has made an advance payment to cover the next 12 months of utility bills, which have a monthly cost of $2200.

DR Prepaid Expense $26,400   CR Cash $26,400

The prepaid expense (asset) account has increased, and the cash (asset) account has decreased by: 12 months x $2,200 per month = $26,400 for the year.

991 Mr. Mop provides their customers with household cleaners. This week, Mr. Mop purchased 2010 tons of cleaning solution which were placed into the warehouse, and which had a per-unit cost of $1200.

DR Inventory $2,412,000   CR Accounts Payable $2,412,000

There was an increase in the inventory (asset) account, and also an increase in the accounts payable (liability) account. 2010 tons of cleaning solution x $1,200 = $2,412,000

992 Toyonda is a market leader that is well-known for their brand of cars. Today, Toyonda bought equipment which has a 5 year useful life, and which had a cost of $20000.

DR Equipment $20,000   CR Accounts Payable $20,000

The equipment (asset) and the accounts payable (liability) accounts have both increased by: $20,000. The useful life does not affect this original accounting entry, but it will be used to calculate depreciation of the asset in the future.

993 Fairway Malls sells several different types of retail spaces in their shopping centers. This month, Fairway Malls has estimated that 20% of the accounts receivable might not end up being collectable, based on past experience. The accounts receivable will need to be adjusted from its current balance of $73000.

DR Bad Debt expense $14,600   CR Allowance for Doubtful Accounts $14,600

The bad debts (expense) and the allowance for doubtful accounts (contra-asset) have both increased by: 20% x $73,000 = $14,600

994    AC&C Ltd. sells various cell phone plans.  This January, AC&C Ltd. has made an advance payment to cover the next 12 months of utility bills, which have a monthly cost of $1500.

DR Prepaid Expense $18,000    CR Cash $18,000

The prepaid expense (asset) account has increased, and the cash (asset) account has decreased by: 12 months x $1,500 per month = $18,000 for the year.

995    Kola-Nut Ltd is a corporation which sells soft drinks.  Today, Kola-Nut Ltd has paid cash to their supplier to fully pay off their account payable balance, which was $57000.

DR Accounts Payable $57,000    CR Cash $57,000

The accounts payable (liability) and cash (asset) accounts have both increased by $57,000.

996    A to Z Event Guru Ltd is a corporation which sells start-to-finish event planning services for large gatherings.  This month, A to Z Event Guru Ltd paid 1 monthly loan repayment towards their long-term note payable. The interest portion was 60% of the payment. The total amount paid in cash was $19000.

DR Interest Expense $11,400    DR Loan Payable $7,600    CR Cash $19,000

The interest (expense) account has increased by $19,000 x 0.6 = $11,400. The loan payable (liability) has decreased by $19,000 x 0.4 = $7,600. The cash (asset) account has decreased by the full amount of the payment, which is $19,000

997    Club Disco is an organization which specializes in providing their customers with dance venue rentals for large family gatherings.  This December, Club Disco has paid each of the company's 1300 owners an annual dividend in the amount of $8000.

DR Retained Earnings $10,400,000    CR Cash $10,400,000

The retained earnings (equity) and the cash accounts have both decreased by: 1300 owners x $8,000 = $10,400,000

998    Cirque du Lune is a market leader that is well-known for their brand of circus performances. Today, Cirque du Lune received payment upfront for 1100 large orders which will not be provided until early next year. Each order was in the amount of $1300.

DR Cash $1,430,000    CR Unearned Revenue $1,430,000

The cash (asset) and the unearned revenue (liability) accounts have both increased by: 1100 large orders x $1,300 = $1,430,000

999    McGerald's sells several different types of fast food meals. Today, McGerald's received payment upfront for 1900 large orders which will not be provided until early next year. Each order was in the amount of $2400.

DR Cash $4,560,000    CR Unearned Revenue $4,560,000

The cash (asset) and the unearned revenue (liability) accounts have both increased by: 1900 large orders x $2,400 = $4,560,000

1000    Air America sells various global flights. Today, Air America has paid cash to their supplier to fully pay off their account payable balance, which was $9000.

DR Accounts Payable $9,000    CR Cash $9,000

The accounts payable (liability) and cash (asset) accounts have both increased by $9,000.

Take a look at these comprehensive books on Amazon!
Paperback and ebook formats are both available
**Introductory Accounting Double Entry Exercises (Expanded Edition):**
**40 Full Cycle Accounting Cases with Complete Solutions**
**Introductory Accounting Double Entry Exercises:**
**20 Full Cycle Accounting Cases with Complete Solutions**

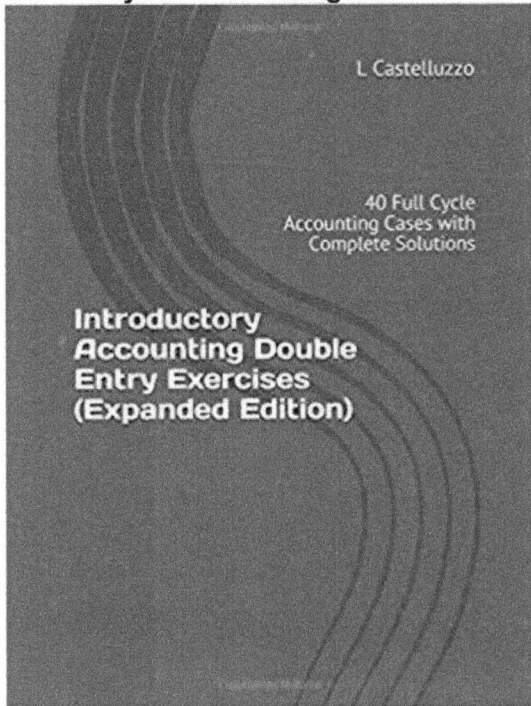

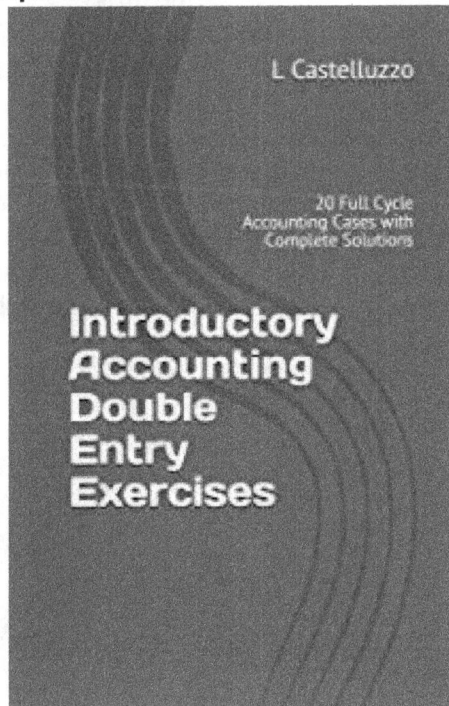

L Castelluzzo

40 Full Cycle
Accounting Cases with
Complete Solutions

Introductory
Accounting Double
Entry Exercises
(Expanded Edition)

L Castelluzzo

20 Full Cycle
Accounting Cases with
Complete Solutions

Introductory
Accounting
Double
Entry
Exercises

Financial accounting and managerial accounting exercises are also available, as well as audit, and case writing.

Introductory Accounting Exercise Workbook Combo Edition:
755 Practice Questions and Business Cases Pertaining to Financial Accounting, Management Accounting and Financial Audit
Financial Audit Exercise Workbook:
156 Multiple Choice Practice Questions with Solutions
Introductory Double Entry Accounting Practice Workbook:
1000 Questions with Solutions
Introductory Double Entry Accounting Workbook:
800 Multiple Choice Questions with Solutions and Explanations
Introductory Quantitative Analysis Workbook: Management Decision Making:
1000 Mini Business Cases with Questions and Full Solutions
Introduction to Case Writing for Accountants:
23 Business Cases Pertaining to Financial Accounting, Key Performance Indicators and Audit